THE CHINESE ECONOMIC TRANSFORMATION

VIEWS FROM YOUNG ECONOMISTS

Other titles in the China Update Book Series include:

The titles are available online at press.anu.edu.au/publications/series/china-update

THE CHINESE ECONOMIC TRANSFORMATION

VIEWS FROM YOUNG ECONOMISTS

EDITED BY
LIGANG SONG, YIXIAO ZHOU
AND LUKE HURST

Australian
National
University

PRESS

社会科学文献出版社
SOCIAL SCIENCES ACADEMIC PRESS (CHINA)

ANU PRESS

Published by ANU Press
The Australian National University
Acton ACT 2601, Australia
Email: anupress@anu.edu.au

Available to download for free at press.anu.edu.au

ISBN (print): 9781760463120
ISBN (online): 9781760463137

WorldCat (print): 1128893516
WorldCat (online): 1103671205

DOI: 10.22459/CET.2019

Cover design and layout by ANU Press

Contents

Figures

Tables

Contributors

Chen Chen, BHP

Moyu Chen, Peking University

Zhixiao Dong, Central University of Finance and Economics

Huiqing Gao, State Information Center of China

Jane Golley, The Australian National University

Qin Gou, Central University of Finance and Economics

Xiao He, Chinese Academy of Social Sciences

Yiping Huang, Peking University

Luke Hurst, Asialink Business

Sherry Tao Kong, Peking University

Ran Li, World Bank

Zhikuo Liu, Shanghai University of Finance and Economics

Zhongyu Ma, State Information Center of China

Yu Sheng, Peking University

Ligang Song, The Australian National University

Deborah H.Y. Tan, BHP

Bijun Wang, Chinese Academy of Social Sciences

Jiao Wang, University of Melbourne

Meiyan Wang, Chinese Academy of Social Sciences

Yongjie Wang, Chinese Academy of Social Sciences

Zhichao Wen, State Information Center of China

Guiying Laura Wu, Nanyang Technological University

Mi Xie, Tongji University

Weihua Yin, State Information Center of China

Liqing Zhang, Central University of Finance and Economics

Yan Zhang, Central University of Finance and Economics

Yuhan Zhao, Peking University

Ninghua Zhong, Tongji University

Yixiao Zhou, The Australian National University

Acknowledgements

The China Economy Program (CEP) at the Crawford School of Public Policy in The Australian National University (ANU) acknowledges the financial support provided by BHP Billiton for China Update 2019. We thank the program support provided by CEP Project Manager Timothy Cronin, Crawford School of Public Policy, our colleagues from the East Asia Forum (EAF) at ANU and Asialink Business. This year's book is the 19th volume in the update book series. China Update 2019 provides a platform for young economists to discuss various issues relating to the Chinese economic transformation. We sincerely thank our contributors for their valuable contributions to this year's book. Thanks also go to ANU Press, notably Emily Hazlewood, Lorena Kanellopoulos and Jan Borrie, for their expeditious publication of the book series every year. We thank the Social Sciences Academic Press (China) of the Chinese Academy of Social Sciences in Beijing for translating and publishing the Chinese version of the book each year—making this valuable research available to a wider readership.

Abbreviations

ATT	average treatment effect on treated
BRICS	Brazil, Russia, India, China and South Africa
CBRC	China Banking Regulatory Commission
CCAP	China Centre for Agricultural Policy
CDB	China Development Bank
CFIUS	Committee on Foreign Investment in the United States
China Exim Bank	China Export–Import Bank
CNOOC	China National Offshore Oil Corporation
CPI	consumer price index
CSMAR	China Stock Market & Accounting Research Database
CSRC	China Securities Regulatory Commission
CULS	China Urban Labour Survey
DID	difference-in-differences
DSGE	dynamic stochastic general equilibrium
ECB	European Central Bank
EU	European Union
FDI	foreign direct investment
FDIR index	FDI regulatory restrictiveness index
FIRB	Foreign Investment Review Board
GDP	gross domestic product
GFC	Global Financial Crisis
GMM	generalised method of moments
GMV	gross merchandise volume
hukou	household registration status
ICT	information and communication technology
ILO	International Labour Organization
IMF	International Monetary Fund
IOR	relative inequality of opportunity
LIBOR	London Interbank Offered Rate
LPM	linear probability model
LTC	long-term contract

M2	money supply
MOFCOM	Ministry of Commerce
MRPC	marginal revenue product of capital
Mt/a	million tonnes per annum
NBS	National Bureau of Statistics of China
NSE	nonstandard employment
ODI	outward direct investment
OECD	Organisation for Economic Co-operation and Development
OLS	ordinary least squares
OPEC	Organization of the Petroleum Exporting Countries
P&O	Peninsular and Oriental Steam Navigation Company
PBC	People's Bank of China
PPP	purchasing power parity
QFII	qualified foreign institutional investors
R&D	research and development
RMB	renminbi
ROA	return on assets
SASAC	State-owned Assets Supervision and Administration Commission
SME	small and medium-sized enterprise
SOB	state-owned bank
SOE	state-owned enterprise
SWF	sovereign wealth fund
TFP	total factor productivity
TFPR	total factor productivity revenue
TPP	Trans-Pacific Partnership
TTIP	Transatlantic Trade and Investment Partnership
WIPO	World Intellectual Property Organization
WTO	World Trade Organization

1. Deepening reform and opening-up for China to grow into a high-income country

Ligang Song, Yixiao Zhou and Luke Hurst

Searching for new engines of growth

In the past four decades, the Chinese economy has experienced three growth surges. The first took place following the period of 'reform and opening-up' from the late 1970s; the second occurred following the implementation of taxation reforms in 1994; and the third happened after China's accession to the World Trade Organization (WTO) in 2001 (Figure 1.1). Over the entire period of reform (1978–2018), the annual growth rate of the economy was more than 9 per cent and China's per capita income reached US$9,600 in 2018. Rapid growth in China has led to its economy making up a greater share of both the Asian and the global economies. In 1980, China contributed about 2 per cent of the global economy; in 2018, this was nearly 16 per cent (Figure 1.2). Furthermore, the importance of the Chinese economy is seen not only in its scale, but also in its contribution to global economic growth. In 2018, China was the largest contributor to global economic growth, at 32 per cent; emerging and developing economies excluding China contributed 44 per cent and the advanced economies contributed 24 per cent (Figure 1.3).

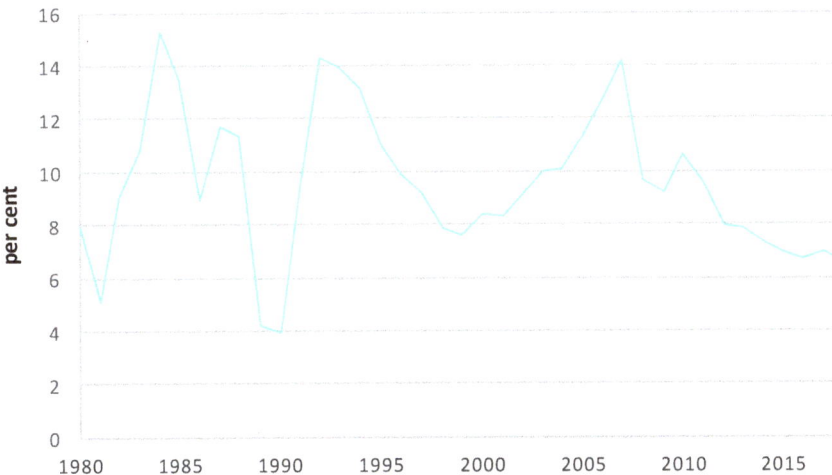

Figure 1.1 Official real GDP growth in China, annual percentage change, 1980–2018

Sources: IMF (various years).

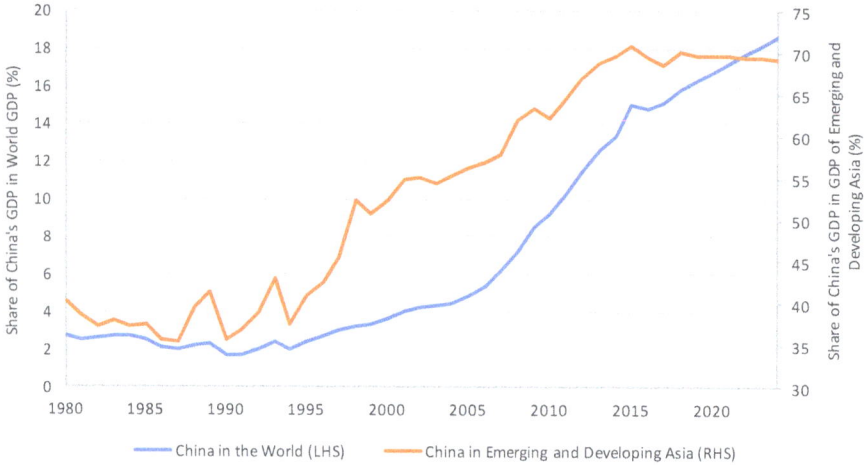

Figure 1.2 China's share of global GDP and of emerging and developing Asia GDP, 1980–2024 (per cent)

Note: Post-2017 data are estimated values.

Source: Authors' calculations based on data for GDP (in current US dollar prices) from IMF (2019).

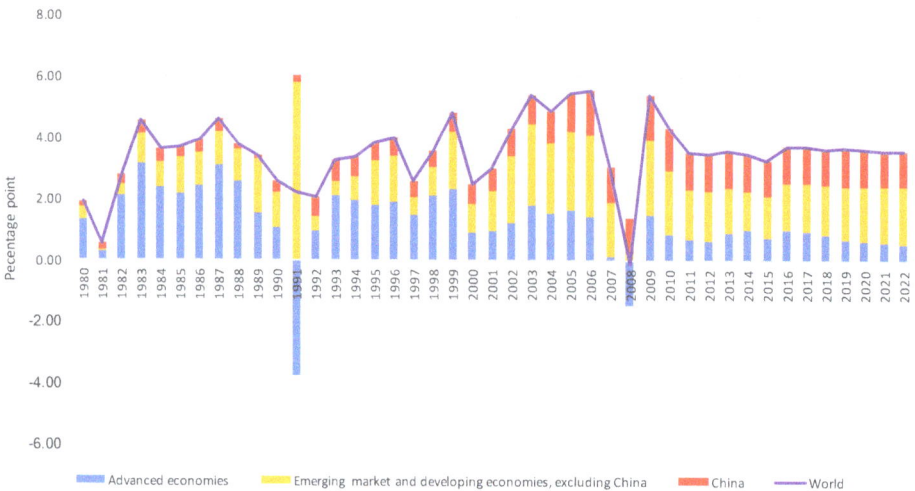

Figure 1.3 Contributions to global growth (yearly average)

Source: Authors' calculations from data on GDP based on the purchasing power parity (PPP) share of the global total and the growth rate of global GDP at constant prices (IMF various years).

While growth in China is still robust, it has been slowing since 2010, as a result of headwinds (Figure 1.1). A question one may ask is whether those headwinds will derail that economic growth and prevent China from reaching high-income status or whether there are ways by which China can overcome these headwinds and continue to grow, albeit at a slower trajectory, in the next phase of its development. In this chapter, we aim to understand some of the causes of the growth slowdown and identify new sources of long-term growth through the lens of growth theories.

The 'East Asian' growth model allowed several emerging countries and economies to become industrialised and to catch up with the living standards of the advanced economies. This model—featuring openness to trade and investment—has also benefited China since its reform and opening-up policies were introduced, and the Chinese economy has become increasingly integrated with the global economy. During this phase, the main drivers of growth were structural changes in the economy away from the agricultural sector towards the manufacturing and service sectors, which were propelled by fundamental reforms in both rural and urban areas (Figure 1.4). As workers move from rural to urban areas, the increase in labour combines with capital and imported technology to yield rapid productivity growth (Song et al. 2011).

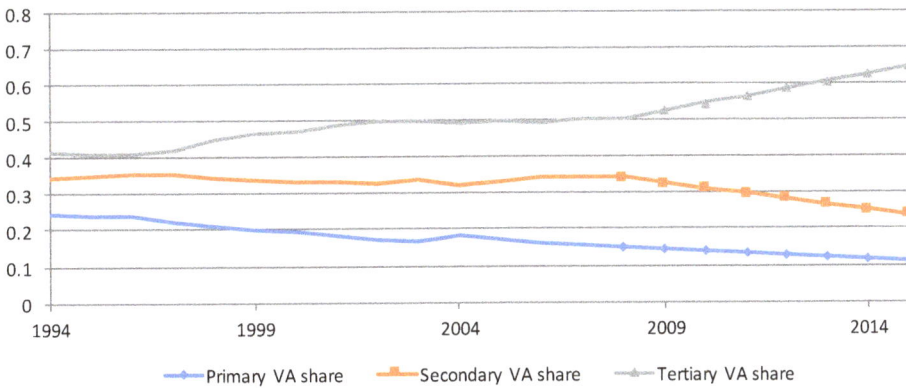

Figure 1.4 Value-added shares by sector in China, 1994–2016
Source: Authors' calculations based on data from WIOD (n.d.).

As China continues to catch up with the technology frontier and move up the global value chains, innovation has become increasingly necessary to sustain productivity growth. As innovation activities pick up, the research and development (R&D) intensity of the Chinese economy has been rising (Figure 1.5). However, innovation activities are intrinsically risky and the outcomes are often uncertain. Therefore, productivity growth naturally becomes harder to achieve, and this is one of the fundamental causes of the growth slowdown as observed in the continuous drop in China's total factor productivity (TFP) in recent years.

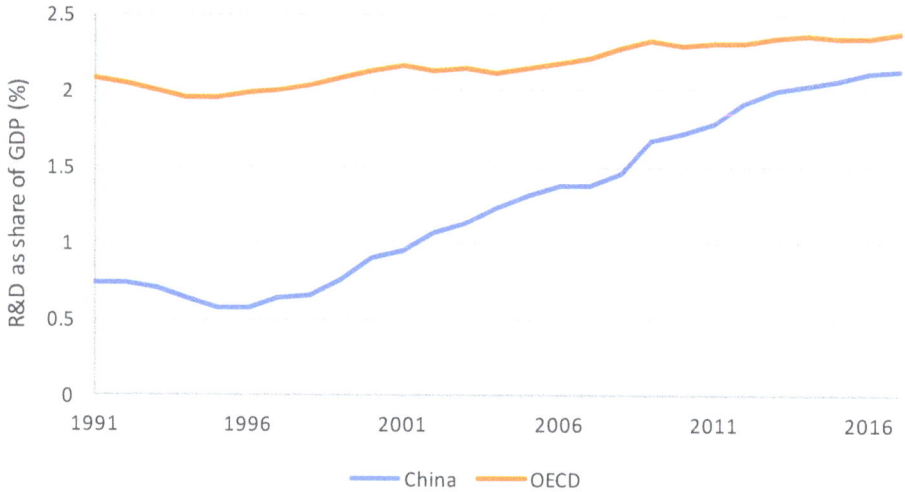

Figure 1.5 Research and development as a share of GDP (per cent)
Source: OECD (n.d.).

The second cause of the growth slowdown is China's ageing population, which causes a decline in the share of the working-age population in the total population. The share of those aged 15–64 in the total population reached a peak of 78 per cent in 2010 and has been declining since, to 72 per cent in 2017 (Figure 1.6). This demographic change reduces the labour supply. In the earlier model of growth, focusing on labour-intensive manufacturing production and trade, China relied on a large labour supply. Therefore, transitioning to new engines of sustainable growth and maintaining that growth over the long term will mean relying more on innovation and less on the supply of labour or factor inputs. Furthermore, the ageing population will bring about a lower savings rate, as was observed in Japan (Golley et al. 2018). Although China's previous rapid growth, combined with lagging social institutions and industrial reform, induced a very high savings rate among households and state-owned enterprises (SOEs) (Bayoumi et al. 2012), the savings rate has been falling in the past few years. The national savings rate peaked at 51.5 per cent of GDP in 2010 and fell to 46.4 per cent of GDP in 2017. The decline in the savings rate exerts downward pressure on domestic investment and the current account surplus, as shown in Figure 1.7.

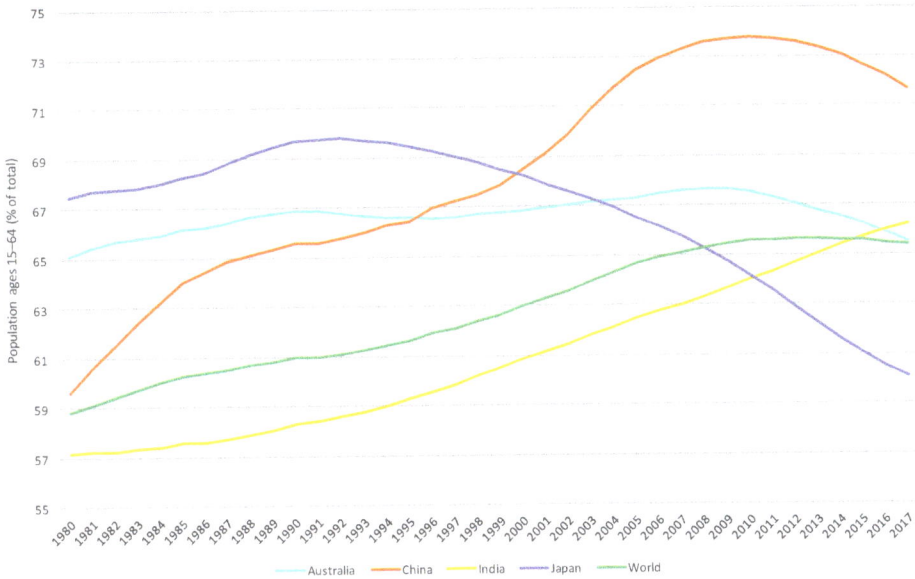

Figure 1.6 Share of population aged 15–64 (percentage of total)

Source: World Bank (2019b).

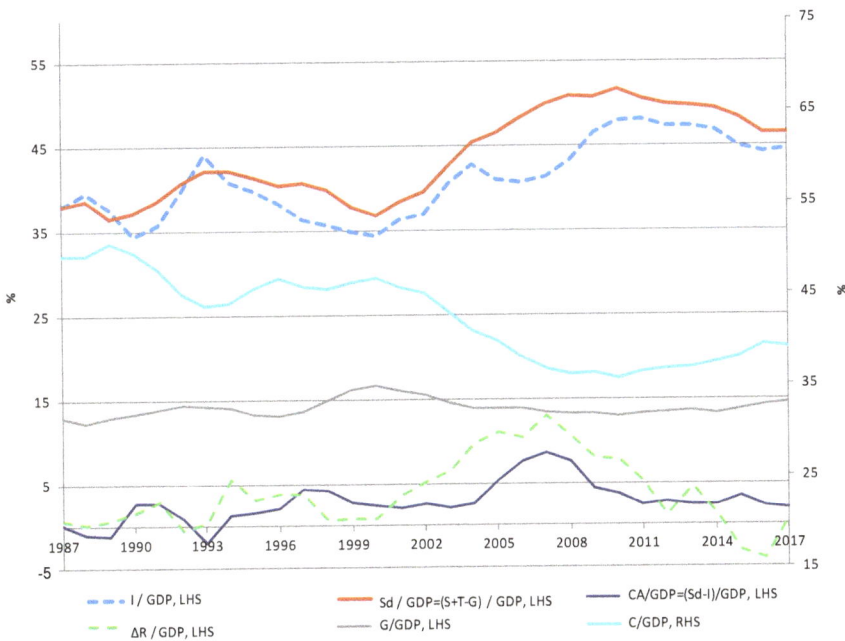

Figure 1.7 Savings, investment and external balance in the Chinese economy, 1987–2017

Note: I, C, CA, G, ΔR, S_d refer to investment, consumption, current account, government purchase, change in reserve, and domestic savings.

Sources: Authors' calculations based on data for the current account and change in official reserves from SAFE (n.d.) and other data from the CEIC Database.

The above analysis originates from supply-side factors, including technical, institutional and demographic changes. In the short run, demand-side factors also play important roles in determining the growth rate. More subdued investment and net export growth tend to slow GDP growth from the demand side of the growth equation.

Although we see in Figure 1.7 that consumption and government purchases have both grown as shares of GDP since 2010, the more recent data suggest that consumption growth has slowed since the second quarter of 2018 and government purchase is expansionary but cautious (Song and Zhou 2019). Investment growth is slowed both by lower savings growth, as discussed earlier, and by relatively weak business confidence. The contribution of investment growth to GDP growth fell from 2.1 percentage points in the third quarter of 2018 to 0.8 percentage points in the first quarter of 2019. Similarly, net exports weakened due to lower savings growth and the rise in trade tensions between China and the United States. Net export growth was in negative territory in the first three quarters of 2018 and returned to positive values in the fourth quarter of 2018 and the first quarter of 2019 (Figure 1.8).

At this juncture, the key questions are what the new drivers of economic growth will be and how to bring them about. The answer we propose is that there is still great room and scope for further reform to unleash a new round of relatively rapid and high-quality growth, which will allow China to become a high-income economy. We argue that new growth engines are to be found in the following areas. First, deepening institutional reform and improved institutional design and quality will allow the Chinse economy to be integrated more closely into global markets. This will require China, together with its trading partners, to uphold multilateral principles and the international rules-based trading system, and to explore ways in which that system can be reformed to accommodate new patterns of trade and investment flows. This task is especially important given the current trend of deglobalisation with rising protectionism. Second, further opening-up of goods, capital and labour markets and lowering of market barriers are required to expand global collaboration on research, innovation and business activities. Third, further improvements in education and skill levels and reduction in poverty are needed to enhance equality of opportunity and alleviate rising income inequality. There is still a significant gap between China and the advanced economies in terms of education levels and technical capability. Therefore, there will be significant room for Chinese talent to contribute more to the global technology pool.

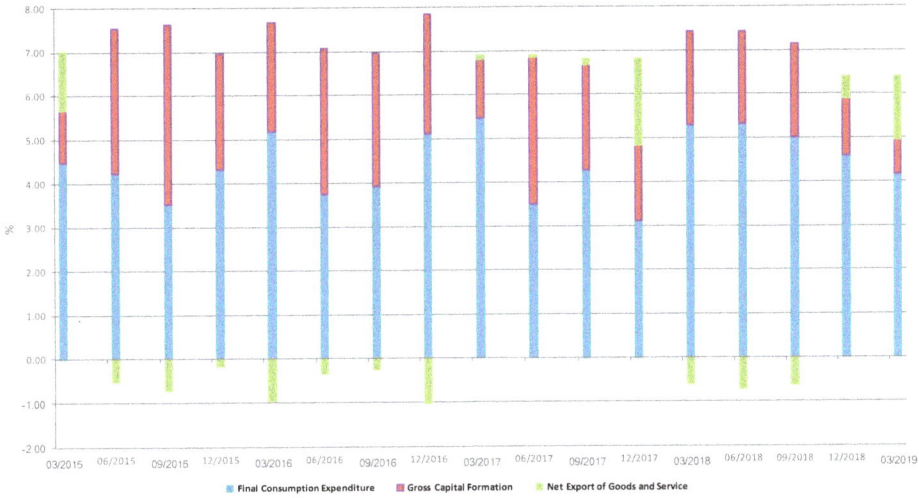

Figure 1.8 Contributors to GDP growth in China, 2015Q3– 2019Q1
Source: CEIC Database.

From the perspective of growth theories, it is worth noting that these reforms will help deliver endogenous technological and institutional innovations that will lead to higher productivity growth in the long run. It is well understood that the ultimate long-run driver of a country's growth performance is productivity growth (Solow 1956; OECD 2012). Also, importantly, contributions to the global technology pool can benefit all countries' technological progress and economic growth under market mechanisms (Jones and Romer 2010).

The first piece of evidence of the significant room for China to improve its business and institutional environments comes from the 'Doing Business' statistics reported by the World Bank (2019a). In 2019, the statistics for China are based on surveys conducted in Shanghai, one of the most mature commercial and international metropolitan cities in mainland China. The results show that China ranked 46 out of 190 countries and regions on the overall Ease of Doing Business Score. In comparison, the Hong Kong Special Administrative Region ranks fourth among all countries and regions. The more detailed rankings for various aspects of doing business provide a further sense of where the most stringent bottlenecks are and where future institutional and policy reforms can be focused (Figure 1.9).

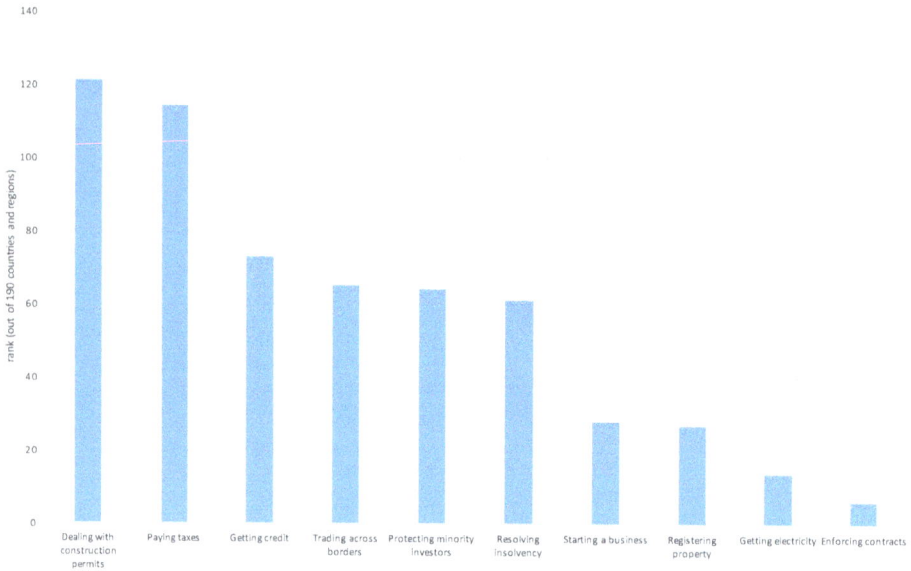

Figure 1.9 Ease of doing business rankings for China, 2019
Source: World Bank (2019a).

A positive development in enhancing the institutional environment is that a set of new policies has recently been introduced. One example of these is the introduction of the principle of 'competitive neutrality' in the 'Guiding Opinions on Promoting the Healthy Development of Small and Medium-Sized Enterprises' recently issued by the General Office of the Communist Party of China Central Committee and the General Office of the State Council (The State Council 2019). The guidelines require the implementation of policies that help small and medium-sized enterprises (SMEs) compete fairly in markets. Specifically, the guidelines emphasise policies that include lowering barriers to market entry, creating fair competition, providing easier access to credit, lowering the tax and regulatory burden, enhancing innovation, encouraging private entrepreneurship and reducing the influence of political connections.

The essence of the principle of competitive neutrality is that all actions taken by the government should have a neutral impact on market competition between SOEs and other enterprises—that is, government actions do not favour any actual or potential market participation. In particular, SOEs should not have an improper competitive advantage resulting from government policies or regulations. The principle of competitive neutrality was originally proposed by Australia in 1996 (Commonwealth of Australia 1996). At the time, it was stated that government commercial enterprises should not enjoy a net competitive advantage over their private sector competitors simply because they were owned by the government. This concept was later also explored in policy research conducted by the Organisation for Economic Co-operation and Development (OECD). Broadly summarised, there are four aspects of the concept: 1) in the case of SOEs providing public services or undertaking public policy functions, they should be given fair and transparent compensation for their costs; 2) there should be equal treatment of SOEs and other enterprises in regulation and government procurement; 3) in debt financing, SOEs should not benefit from explicit or implicit state guarantees; and 4) in equity financing, the state as a shareholder requires SOEs to provide market return on investment (Capobianco and Christiansen 2011). China has now adopted the concept of competitive neutrality in reforming its SOEs and nurturing the private sector. The United States has already applied the concept to the binding rules of its bilateral trade negotiations such as its free-trade agreement with Singapore, the new North American Free-Trade Agreement, the Trans-Pacific Partnership and the ongoing negotiations with Japan and the European Union, and between China and the European Union in terms of bilateral investment treaty negotiations.

Another encouraging development is the introduction of policies to further open markets to foreign investment. In financial markets, these measures include removing limits on the foreign ownership of local banks, scrapping size limits for foreign firms and allowing foreign insurance groups to set up in China. Under the new plans for financial liberalisation, the upper shareholding limits in a Chinese commercial bank for a single Chinese-funded bank or a single foreign-funded bank will be abolished simultaneously (Yu 2019). The National People's Congress adopted the new Foreign Investment Law in March 2019. Under this law, the principle of non-discrimination will be added to administrative approval procedures, along with increased financial penalties imposed on those who infringe trademark rights. In the meantime, the procedures and time it takes to receive construction permits will be sharply reduced (Hu 2019).

The above policies are aimed at helping attract overseas investment and helping China remain one of the world's leading destinations for foreign direct investment (FDI). After China's WTO accession, an unprecedented accumulation of foreign investment, combined with new access to markets in the advanced economies, delivered another growth surge in the country. However, there is still scope for foreign investment to contribute further to China's economic growth. And there is great potential in financial integration and opening-up to help enhance China's growth. Figure 1.10 shows that, although FDI in China has experienced very strong growth, its share in total investment in China has declined since 1994. As savings rates fall in China, more foreign investment will help generate investment and growth activities.

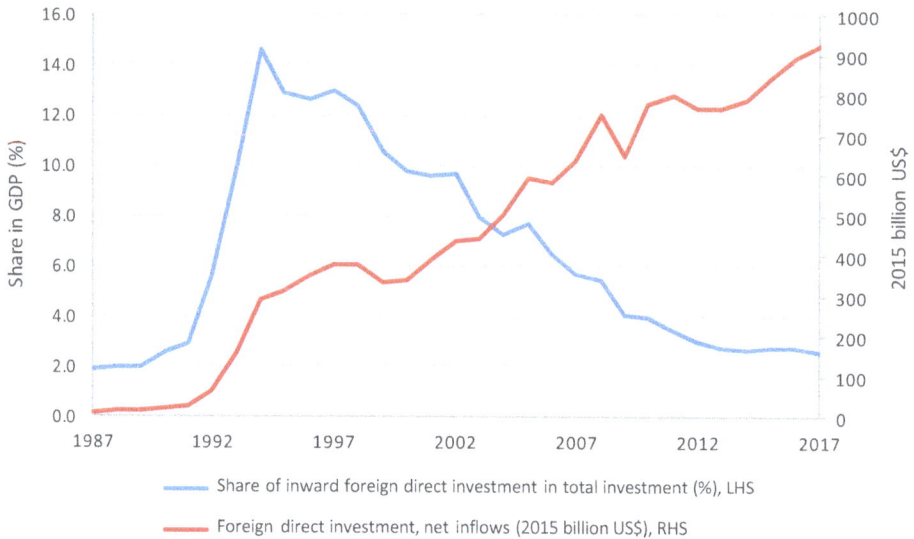

Figure 1.10 FDI inflows and its share of total domestic investment in China (per cent)

Notes: We obtain data for inward FDI as share of GDP in China. We calculate total domestic investment as a share of GDP in China. We then calculate the share of FDI inflows in total domestic investment by dividing the former by the latter. For the red series, real GDP is calculated in constant 2015 US dollars. This is then multiplied by the share of inward FDI in GDP to obtain inward FDI in constant 2015 US dollars.

Sources: Authors' calculations based on data from CEIC Database; IMF (various years); UNCTAD (n.d.).

Using new policy levers to move towards a more open, transparent and fair market environment for all firms and to link and integrate domestic and international rules for commerce will help the Chinese economy integrate more deeply and smoothly into the global market. It is well understood that trade helps firms stay competitive by exerting constant pressure to innovate and improve the quality of products and services in the international market (Bernard et al. 2007; Zhou and Song 2016). Furthermore, competing with foreign firms in the domestic market has similar effects. Although the contribution of net exports to GDP growth may wind down as a result of economic rebalancing towards more consumption-driven growth, the importance of openness extends beyond raising GDP and rests more on driving productivity growth.

Besides improvements in the institutional environment, another source of future growth is boosting the education and skill levels of individuals (Khor et al. 2016). Despite China's significant achievements in enhancing education, the Chinese economy still suffers a shortage of human capital compared with many other developing and advanced economies. Comparing the share of the labour force that has attained at least some upper secondary schooling (upper secondary attainment) in China with that in other countries (for example, high-income/OECD countries and a subset of G20 middle-income/Brazil, Russia, India, China and South Africa), Khor et al. (2016) find that, in 2010, only 24 per cent of China's entire labour force (individuals aged 25–64 years) had ever attended upper secondary school, and this rate was less than one-third of the average in OECD countries. China's overall upper secondary attainment rate and the attainment rate of its youngest workers (aged 25–34) are also the lowest of the BRICS countries (Brazil, Russia, India, China and South Africa), with the exception of India, for which data were not available. As human capital is critical for innovation and knowledge-based growth, continued investment in education and skills should be a policy priority.

This book consists of contributions from young economists who have closely researched the latest developments in the Chinese economy. Their new analytical perspectives and findings help us better understand and identify future directions for the Chinese economy, as seen through the eyes of the young.

Structure of the book

The book begins with a chapter by Guiying Laura Wu that details the challenges of capital allocation China is facing after 40 years of reform. To frame the discussion, Wu provides a comprehensive survey of the existing literature to construct a general framework with which to investigate the interaction of financial frictions and policy distortions with TFP loss. The chapter discusses the quantitative implications of aggregate efficiency loss within such a framework. Wu concludes that the structural reforms that are particularly relevant to capital misallocation are mainly those in the enterprise sector and the financial system. These findings provide a guide for future reforms to improve capital allocation.

Chapter 3 uses an impressive set of data, including 4 million Chinese manufacturing company samples from 1998 to 2013, to understand debt and credit misallocation in Chinese corporations. The authors—Ninghua Zhong, Mi Xie and Zhikuo Liu— find that, during the 16-year period analysed, most firms were deleveraging, with 'the simple average and median of debt ratio decreased from 65 per cent in 1998 to 51 per cent in 2013'. Of the companies that increased their leverage, most were large-scale, listed SOEs. Interestingly, the authors find that the characteristics of private firms change with the changes to leverage, but those of SOEs do not. The authors conclude that the huge amount of credit being allocated to the state sector is the reason for the declining credit efficiency in China.

The authors suggest that the 'main battlefield for deleveraging is the state-owned sector, especially inefficient and large enterprises, which usually have severe overcapacity', and the government should therefore promote market-oriented reforms of SOEs. But these SOE reforms need to be complemented by increased leverage in efficient areas with market-oriented reforms of commercial banks and other financial intermediaries so that valuable credit resources can be allocated to productive enterprises.

There is rising concern about the economic slowdown occurring in China. In Chapter 4, Jiao Wang and Ran Li develop an extension of the standard New Keynesian dynamic stochastic general equilibrium model to understand China's monetary policy, along with the main causes of fluctuations in the country's business cycle, providing a novel way of examining the rules governing China's monetary policy. Using a hybrid form of monetary policy rule, the authors find that the People's Bank of China adjusts the policy rate in response to inflation, output growth and real money growth. Neutral technology shocks are the main drivers of the fluctuations in output and consumption, while investment-specific technology shocks are the primary source of variations in investment. Wang and Li conclude that, after more than 30 years of driving high-speed economic development, a structural break in the development of neutral technology may have caused China's GDP growth to slow since 2010. This conclusion points to the need for the Chinese Government to encourage technological innovation and industrial upgrading.

In Chapter 5, Yuhan Zhao, Moyu Chen and Yu Sheng use extensive farm household survey data to investigate the evolution of the household registration (*hukou*) system at the provincial level between 1981 and 2013, and to understand its impact on off-farm employment in rural China. The authors also make a significant contribution by compiling a comprehensive indicator to capture the transtemporal and cross-regional changes in the household registration system during the post-reform period. The analysis finds that off-farm employment of rural labour increased with the relaxation of household registration policies during the post-reform period; this is particularly the case for full-time off-farm employment. The analysis implies that barriers related to the *hukou* system still prevent the integration of rural and urban labour markets.

Following on from the previous chapter's analysis of the impact of *hukou* reforms on off-farm employment, Chapter 6 investigates the growth, scale and characteristics of nonstandard employment (NSE) in China. Analysis of the 2016 China Urban Labour Survey (CULS), undertaken by Yongjie Wang, contributes three important findings: first, the proportion of NSE in urban China in 2016 was 34.95 per cent, indicating that NSE has become an important feature of China's labour market. Second, those working in NSE in China have comparably low levels of job satisfaction, low wages, high overtime rates, low social insurance coverage and inadequate wage rights protection. Third, labourers with lower levels of educational attainment, age disadvantages and those who are unmarried and have rural *hukou* are more likely than others to engage in NSE. Wang argues that targeted policies need to broaden the employment choices for those who are more likely to engage in NSE and measures need to be taken to strengthen the collective bargaining power of NSE workers by, for example, absorbing nonstandard workers into labour unions.

The development of rural e-commerce in China could unlock significant economic benefits, including more inclusive growth, poverty alleviation and inequality reduction. In Chapter 7, Sherry Tao Kong explores the ways in which the Chinese Government has 'not only allowed space for digital companies to experiment, but also introduced a wide range of policies and projects to improve the country's internet infrastructure to promote the development of e-commerce'. Through her analysis of the growth of Taobao villages across China, the author finds that the promise of e-commerce for rural development in China is not guaranteed: 'Reliable internet access, trustworthy digital transaction methods and convenient parcel delivery and logistics services are necessary but insufficient conditions to realise the promise of e-commerce in less-developed areas.' It also requires organic grassroots growth and supportive top-down policies.

Since the end of 2012, the Chinese Government has implemented a number of policies aimed at helping the country become a global leader in innovation. In Chapter 8, Zhongyu Ma, Huiqing Gao, Weihua Yin and Zhichao Wen use local survey data to understand the impact of these policies and the potential for improvement. The authors find that policies to promote innovation are working well. China is, however, in the early stages of innovation development and, consistent with theory, it is experiencing interruptions that slow progress. Two such interruptions include inconsistencies in the issuing of intellectual property policy and incomplete policy implementation. While China's innovation is currently in its initial phase—characterised by high investment—the authors suggest that these upfront costs will produce high yields in coming years.

In Chapter 9, Liqing Zhang, Yan Zhang and Zhixiao Dong investigate the effects of China's financial services liberalisation on the financial constraints of China's listed firms. The authors set up an exogenous policy measure of China's financial service liberalisation based on a thorough policy review. Using the latest panel data (for the period 2010–15), the analysis shows that China's financial liberalisation has diminished the financial constraints on the country's listed firms; notably, China's formal external financing channels through banks and other financial institutions have been enhanced by trade credit, especially for larger firms. The analysis also supports the idea that financial liberalisation eliminates ownership discrimination.

The development of China's SMEs is vital to the country's future economic growth, job creation and innovation. In Chapter 10, Qin Gou and Yiping Huang analyse whether the SME financial support scheme has effectively promoted banks' credit allocation to SMEs. The authors use a unique bank branch survey dataset to analyse the impact of the policy. The analysis suggests there have been mixed outcomes, with increased lending to SMEs that fell short of the initial loan requirements, while other SMEs that exceeded the initial loan requirements received smaller loans.

On the costs of the scheme, Gou and Huang note that it increases the credit risk of small banks and decreases their profits. The authors suggest the business, financial and innovation environments need to be fundamentally improved.

One of the biggest threats to the global economy is the escalating trade war between the United States and China. In Chapter 11, Deborah H.Y. Tan and Chen Chen use the G-cubed multi-country model to understand the potential costs of the China–US trade war and suggest ways to mitigate them. The findings suggest that a bilateral trade war will impose larger costs on China in the short term, while the United States will suffer a similar adverse impact on growth in the medium term. The authors note that, while the current policy approach of the Chinese Government of matching tariffs is the 'sensible and conservative option that cushions the economy adequately in the near to medium terms, while reducing the chances of international repercussions', the government has more severe options available, such as redeploying US holdings, if it is 'pushed into a very tight corner'.

In Chapter 12, Jane Golley, Yixiao Zhou and Meiyan Wang investigate the level of equal opportunity in the annual labour income of Chinese individuals, with a focus on the role of gender. In their analysis of data from the 2010 Survey of Chinese Women's Social Status, the authors show that 'gender is the number one determinant of unequal opportunities, ahead of socioeconomic, regional and urban–rural divides'. The analysis goes on to assess the underlying causes of gender earnings inequality; this micro-analysis indicates that gender (via returns on education) and marriage are the most significant determinants of the gender income gap. Based on the findings, Golley, Zhou and Wang offer a number of important policy recommendations, including targeting education policies at girls from poor rural families, assisting young women to exit the agricultural sector and find off-farm employment and ongoing reform to the *hukou* system.

As Chinese companies invest overseas in larger numbers and on larger projects, they are encountering a number of political obstacles in host countries. In Chapter 13, Bijun Wang and Xiao He provide one of the first empirical investigations into Chinese outward direct investment (ODI) projects that have been blocked. Using a unique dataset, the authors find that several factors increase the likelihood of an investment being blocked, including large scale, technological intensity and a poor bilateral relationship with the host country. Given these characteristics are commonly associated with blocked investments, Wang and Xiao recommend several strategies to reduce the probability of Chinese projects encountering obstacles, including breaking large-scale investments into multiple smaller investments, focusing on industries that receive less public and government scrutiny and increasing intellectual property protections and R&D spending in host countries.

The final chapter by Luke Hurst follows on from Chapter 13 by providing a detailed case study of Chinese investment during the iron ore boom. The chapter considers two important questions: Does access to state capital reduce the ability of others to compete in the market? And is the Chinese state using capital to lock up strategic resources?

Using a unique dataset of 50 iron ore procurement arrangements, the findings suggest that state-owned financing institutions were involved in the majority of investments and most investments were undertaken by central and provincial-level SOEs in concert with non-Chinese partners. However, Chinese iron ore investors were most often operating outside their core competency and lacked long-run ownership advantages. The lack of iron ore development and operating competence meant they generally paired with a non-Chinese specialised fringe iron ore producer. The preference for quasi-integration through joint ventures with non-Chinese fringe iron ore producers means that Chinese state support effectively lowered barriers to market entry for non-Chinese fringe iron ore miners. On the second question, the application of a scorecard approach to the procurement data found that, instead of tying up resources, China's aggregate iron ore procurement arrangements have led to a broadening of the competitive global supply base and increased access to iron ore for other buyers in the Asian market, as did the Japanese procurement arrangements in the 1970s and 1980s. This finding is consistent with research on Chinese oil procurement.

References

Bayoumi, T., Tong, H. and Wei, S.J. (2012), *The Chinese corporate savings puzzle: A firm-level cross-country perspective*, Working Paper No. 202012, Hong Kong: Hong Kong Institute for Monetary Research, available from: EconPapers.repec.org/RePEc:hkm:wpaper:202012.

Bernard, A.B., Jensen, J.B., Redding, S.J. and Schott, P.K. (2007), Firms in international trade, *Journal of Economic Perspectives* 21(3): 105–30. doi.org/10.1257/jep.21.3.105.

Capobianco, A. and Christiansen, H. (2011), *Competitive neutrality and state-owned enterprises: Challenges and policy options*, OECD Corporate Governance Working Paper No. 1, Paris: Organisation for Economic Co-operation and Development, available from: www.oecd-ilibrary.org/docserver/5kg9xfgjdhg6-en.pdf?expires=1559644294&id=id& accname=guest&checksum=784BBA6AF1A94075A5BBCB546658F3E2.

Commonwealth of Australia (1996), *Commonwealth Competitive Neutrality Policy Statement*, June, Canberra: Department of Treasury, available from: archive.treasury.gov.au/documents/275/PDF/cnps.pdf.

Golley, J., Tyers, R. and Zhou, Y. (2018), Fertility and savings contractions in China: Long-run global implications, *The World Economy* 41(11): 3194–220. doi.org/10.1111/twec.12602.

Hu, Y. (2019), Foreign businesses get assurance as new trade rules ensure equality, *Policy Watch*, 9 April, Beijing: The State Council of the People's Republic of China, available from: english.gov.cn/policies/policy_watch/2019/04/09/content_281476600762343.htm.

International Monetary Fund (IMF) (various years), *World Economic Outlook*, Washington, DC: IMF.

International Monetary Fund (IMF) (2019), *World Economic Outlook Database*, April, Washington, DC: IMF, available from: www.imf.org/external/pubs/ft/weo/2019/01/weodata/index.aspx.

Jones, C.I. and Romer, P.M. (2010), The new Kaldor facts: Ideas, institutions, population, and human capital, *American Economic Journal: Macroeconomics* 2(1): 224–45. doi.org/10.1257/mac.2.1.224.

Khor, N., Pang, L., Liu, C., Chang, F., Mo, D., Lovalka, P. and Rozelle, S. (2016), China's looming human capital crisis: Upper secondary educational attainment rates and the middle-income trap, *The China Quarterly* 228: 905–26. doi.org/10.1017/S0305741016001119.

Organisation for Economic Co-operation and Development (OECD) (n.d.), *OECD Database*, Paris: OECD Publishing, available from: data.oecd.org/.

Organisation for Economic Co-operation and Development (OECD) (2012), *Looking to 2060: A global vision of long-term growth*, OECD Economics Department Policy Notes No. 15, Paris: OECD Publishing.

Solow, R. (1956), A contribution to the theory of economic growth, *The Quarterly Journal of Economics* 70(1): 65–94. doi.org/10.2307/1884513.

Song, L. and Zhou, Y. (2019), A balanced macroeconomic approach could be China's panacea, *East Asia Forum*, 6 March, available from: www.eastasiaforum.org/2019/03/06/a-balanced-macroeconomic-approach-could-be-chinas-panacea/.

Song, Z., Storesletten, K. and Zilibotti, F. (2011), Growing like China, *American Economic Review* 101: 202–41. doi.org/10.1257/aer.101.1.196.

State Administration of Foreign Exchange (SAFE) (n.d.), *Data and Statistics*, Beijing: SAFE, available from: www.safe.gov.cn/en/.

The State Council of the People's Republic of China (2019), *Guiding Opinions on Promoting the Healthy Development of Small and Medium-Sized Enterprises*, Beijing, available from: www.gov.cn/zhengce/2019-04-07/content_5380299.htm.

United Nations Conference on Trade and Development (UNCTAD) (n.d.), Statistics database, Geneva: UNCTAD, available from: unctad.org/en/Pages/statistics.aspx.

World Bank (2019a), *Doing Business: Measuring business regulations*, Washington, DC: The World Bank Group, available from: www.doingbusiness.org/en/rankings.

World Bank (2019b), *World Bank Open Data*, Washington, DC: The World Bank Group, available from: data.worldbank.org/.

World Input Output Database (WIOD) (n.d.), available from: www.wiod.org/home.

Yu, C. (2019), Opening-up to boost finance sector, *Policy Watch*, 4 May, Beijing: The State Council of the People's Republic of China, available from: english.gov.cn/policies/policy _watch/2019/05/04/content_281476643005930.htm.

Zhou, Y. and Song, L. (2016), International trade and R&D investment: Evidence from Chinese manufacturing firms, *China and World Economy* 24(1): 63–84. doi.org/10.1111/ cwe.12144.

2. China's economic development: A perspective on capital misallocation

Guiying Laura Wu

Among the abundant and growing literature aiming to understand the miracle of China's economic development, the contribution of capital reallocation to aggregate total factor productivity (TFP) gain has offered an important perspective. This chapter first describes the general framework that links resource misallocation with TFP loss. It then surveys the empirical evidence of capital misallocation in China and discusses the quantitative implications for aggregate efficiency loss within such a framework. Two potentially interesting sources of capital misallocation are investigated: financial frictions and policy distortions. These sources highlight the remaining challenges in capital allocation that China faces after 40 years of reform.

Framework: Capital misallocation and TFP loss

Why was real gross domestic product (GDP) per capita in China only one-fortieth of that in the United States 40 years ago? And more generally, why are some countries so rich while others are so poor? An important finding economists have reached in the past two decades is that the differences in aggregate TFP are the dominant source of differences in GDP per capita. According to a growth accounting framework in Zhu (2012), growth in aggregate TFP has contributed more than 70 per cent to per capita GDP growth in China. What, then, has caused the substantial improvement in the aggregate TFP in China in the past four decades?

A new and growing literature, as surveyed in Restuccia and Rogerson (2013), argues that resource misallocation across heterogeneous firms in an economy lowers its aggregate TFP. For example, McKinsey Global Institute country and sector studies found large differences across firms within the same sector in many less-developed countries (South Korea, Brazil, Turkey and India). In fact, in many of these cases, the most productive firms within most sectors have productivity levels comparable with those in Western Europe and the United States, but there is a long tail of very low-productivity firms. If resources could be reallocated from the low-productivity firms to high-productivity firms within a country, the aggregate output would increase even with the same amount of production factors, which would lead to an increase in the measured aggregate TFP. This means the efficiency of resource allocation offers a new perspective with which to understand cross-country income differences: the aggregate TFP loss in poor countries relative to the first-best aggregate TFP they could achieve may arise from the resource misallocation in those countries. Although full liberalisation is a thought experiment, since there are many frictions that impede perfect reallocation in reality, one way to interpret this framework is to gauge the potential gain in aggregate TFP if such friction could be removed under a first-best situation.

Among various production factors, capital misallocation has been documented as a prevailing empirical phenomenon, both in less-developed economies in general (for example, Banerjee and Moll 2010) and in China in particular. In fact, the reallocation of capital within the manufacturing sector is a focal point in explaining the miracle of China's economic development in Song et al. (2011).

Evidence of capital misallocation

Evidence of capital misallocation in China takes many forms. There are two ways to summarise this evidence: first, a direct approach to studying the cost of capital or return on investment and, second, an indirect approach to infer the misallocation from the dispersion of marginal product of capital.

We start to present the evidence using the first approach. Although the aggregate marginal product of capital in China is about 20 per cent, as in Bai et al. (2006)— a relatively high but still reasonable value by international standards for developing economies—there is a very different picture when we look at the evidence for the cost of capital or return on investment at more disaggregated levels.

In a cross-country comparative study, Allen et al. (2005) find that China's corporate governance, accounting standards and investor protection systems are poor at best, measured by existing standards in the literature, while its banking system is not well developed and is to a large degree inefficient. The Shanghai Stock Exchange and Shenzhen Stock Exchange have been growing rapidly since their inception in 1992, but their scale and importance are still not comparable with other channels of financing—in particular, the banking sector—for the entire economy. In this environment, Chinese firms must rely heavily on retained earnings to finance investment and operational costs. However, financial repression is far from uniform: Chinese banks, which are mostly state-owned, tend to offer easier credit to state-owned enterprises (SOEs), with less screening, higher lines of credit, lower interest rates and fewer collateral requirements. The Chinese stock market is disproportionately dominated by the SOEs and large semiprivatised SOEs. Not surprisingly, firms in the informal sector are subject to strong discrimination in credit markets. Many successful non-SOEs do not use any channel of formal financing during development (Allen et al. 2005: Figs 3-A and 3-B).

Consistent with this institutional background and based on a survey covering a stratified random sample of 12,400 firms in 120 cities in China with firm-level accounting information for the period 2002–04, Dollar and Wei (2007) examine the presence of systematic distortions in capital allocation that result in uneven marginal returns to capital across firm ownership type, region and sector. They provide a systematic comparison of investment efficiency among wholly and partially state-owned, wholly and partially foreign-owned and domestic privately owned firms, conditioned on their sector, location and size characteristics. They find that, even after a quarter of a century of reforms, SOEs still have significantly lower returns to capital, on average, than domestic private or foreign-owned firms. Similarly, certain regions and sectors have consistently lower returns to capital than other regions and sectors. The findings in this pioneering work have been confirmed by many subsequent studies, as surveyed below.

A second source of evidence involves fitting a production function to firm-level data and directly estimating the distribution of marginal products. A key paper in advancing this structural approach is Hsieh and Klenow (2009). They assume that there are firm-specific wedges affecting total production and capital—essentially modelled as 'taxes'. As a result of these wedges, firms produce amounts different to what would be dictated by their productivity and also may have different capital–labour ratios. If there are no firm-specific distortions and all firms within a sector have the same markup, the TFP revenue (TFPR) will be equalised across firms within a sector. In general, variation of TFPR within a sector will be a measure of misallocation.

Hsieh and Klenow (2009) quantify the potential extent of misallocation using microdata on plants in the manufacturing sector in China, India and the United States. First, they find that there is greater dispersion of TFPR in India and China than in the United States. For example, for TFPR, the 90–10 ratio is 1.59 in China, 1.60 in India and 1.19 in the United States. Second, they estimate that this could account for lower aggregate productivity. In particular, their estimates suggest that this type of misallocation could increase TFP in China by 30 to 50 per cent and in India by 40 to 60 per cent. Finally, they also find evidence for more rapid reallocation towards firms with higher TFPR in China than even in the United States, possibly reflecting rapid reallocation as less-efficient SOEs are being weeded out there. But reallocation away from less-efficient firms seems slower in India.

As pointed out by Restuccia and Rogerson (2013), the finding in Hsieh and Klenow (2009) remains the single strongest piece of evidence to support the idea that misallocation is an important component of cross-country differences in TFP. However, the highly parametric assumptions on preferences and production technology in this approach also face methodological challenges. The validity of the inference in Hsieh and Klenow (2009) hinges on two conditions: 1) average and marginal revenue products have the same dispersion; and 2) the dispersion of marginal revenue products—a mirror image of price heterogeneity—reflects the magnitude of misallocation. Both conditions are strict. Condition (1) applies only to environments with homogeneous output and demand elasticities. Condition (2) will not necessarily hold in a dynamic environment with frictions such as adjustment costs. When it comes to the data, this approach needs another condition—that measurement errors do not add to the dispersions. Violation of any of the conditions would lead to biased estimations.

To address these concerns, Song and Wu (2015) develop a new method of identifying capital misallocation in a more general environment, where none of the conditions has to hold. The new method has a distinctive feature of matching a set of first and second moments of both the revenue–capital ratio and the profit–revenue ratio. The profit–revenue ratio, which has not yet been explored in the misallocation literature, plays an important role in identification. Specifically, Song and Wu (2015) match the variance of the revenue–capital and profit–revenue ratios and the cross correlation between the two ratios. The three empirical moments allow them to back out the three parameters governing the magnitude of the misallocation and unobserved heterogeneities in output and demand elasticities. In addition, while the original approach uses cross-sectional data, the new method explores intergroup variations in panel data, which can effectively mitigate the bias caused by capital adjustment costs and measurement errors.

Song and Wu (2015) then apply the structural estimation to firm-level panel data from the industrial survey conducted by China's National Bureau of Statistics (NBS), using the generalised approach. They find that a full correction of capital misallocation would increase China's manufacturing output by 20 per cent. In contrast, the original Hsieh and Klenow (2009) approach implies a much larger efficiency gain, of 35 per cent. This suggests that, first, it is indeed important to control for the unobserved heterogeneities in output and demand elasticities, investment frictions and measurement errors, to infer the correct magnitude of TFP loss from dispersion in marginal products. Second, even after controlling all these factors, one still identifies substantial TFP loss from capital misallocation in China, which confirms the main finding in Hsieh and Klenow (2009) and the misallocation literature at large.

The seminal framework of Hsieh and Klenow (2009) has inspired many important studies. For example, Brandt et al. (2013) focus on factor misallocation at a more aggregate level, between provinces and between the state and nonstate sectors in China's non-agricultural economy, which includes both manufacturing and services, and covering a longer period, from 1985 to 2007. They also decompose the overall TFP loss into the losses due to interprovincial and intraprovincial intersectoral distortions. They find, first, on average, the misallocation of factors across provinces and sectors resulted in a reduction of non-agricultural TFP of at least 20 per cent, with the intraprovincial distortions accounting for more than half of the total loss.

Second, TFP losses from interprovincial distortions were relatively constant over the entire period. Third, despite significant interprovincial labour flows, the TFP loss from interprovincial labour market distortions remains high due to an increase in the cross-province dispersion in TFP. Fourth, the measure of intraprovincial distortions declined sharply between 1985 and 1997, contributing to 0.52 per cent of non-agricultural TFP growth per year, but then increased significantly in the past 10 years, reducing the non-agricultural TFP growth rate by 0.5 per cent a year. Finally, almost all of the intraprovincial distortions were due to the misallocation of capital between the state and nonstate sectors, which increased sharply in recent years.

Sources of capital misallocation

The qualitative significance and quantitative importance of capital misallocation in China raise one pertinent research question: what are the underlying factors that cause the misallocation? Two natural candidates have attracted increasing interest in recent literature: capital market imperfections due to financial frictions and nonmarket distortions induced by government policies.

It is obviously difficult to make a clear distinction between financial frictions and policy distortions. They are not necessarily very different in conceptual terms, and they may also overlap with a number of other frictions and distortions that are very similar. Therefore, in this chapter, we narrow the definition of financial friction strictly to those factors that are due to imperfect information or imperfect enforcement in the capital market that would cause capital misallocation even in developed economies. We ask to what extent such factors contribute to the observed capital misallocation. This implies that all those nontypical financial frictions are labelled as policy distortions in a very broad sense.

Financial frictions

Quantifying how much of the observed capital misallocation can be attributed to financial frictions is the central theme of some recent literature—for example, Moll (2014) and Midrigan and Xu (2014), among many others. While modelling details and estimated magnitudes differ, these studies share a common methodology: they develop theoretical models and gauge the size of TFP loss by calibrating model parameters to match the distribution and dynamics of output across production units. Despite the financial underdevelopment and substantial capital misallocation in China, there have been relatively few studies that directly link financial frictions with capital misallocation and TFP loss in China. Ek and Wu (2018) and Wu (2018) are two attempts in this direction. Both papers offer novel identification strategies that differ from the existing literature and apply such strategies to detailed firm-level panel data from China's *Annual Survey of Industrial Enterprises*, covering the period 1998 to 2007.

Ek and Wu (2018) directly estimate the effect of financial frictions on capital misallocation using an inference from investment–cash flow sensitivity. Although investment–cash flow sensitivity is frequently used as an indicator of financing constraint, and financing constraint is a consequence of financial frictions, there has not been any research that connects capital misallocation directly to investment–cash flow sensitivity. This chapter fills this gap by providing a simple yet consequential theoretical model, which links the heterogeneity in investment–cash flow sensitivity—a common indicator of financing constraint—to the dispersion of the marginal revenue product of capital (MRPC), which is a direct measure of allocative inefficiency.

The validity of this new approach, of course, depends crucially on the answers to two methodological questions. First, is investment–cash flow sensitivity a reliable indicator of financing constraint? Even in perfect capital markets, cash flow sensitivity may result from measurement errors in Tobin's q, from imperfect competition and/or decreasing returns to scale, from the presence of capital adjustment costs or from a combination of measurement errors in Q and identification problems. Furthermore, a firm's cash flow position is endogenous to its productivity shocks and may contain information about its investment opportunities.

To address these concerns, Ek and Wu (2018) present a structural model of costly external finance. Firms in this model are allowed to face imperfect competition and/or use decreasing returns to scale technology. In the absence of any friction, their model generates the same optimal condition as those models in the recent literature: optimal capital stock is only a function of current output, Jorgensonian user cost of capital and production technology. This allows them to develop an empirical specification for investment that does not rely on Tobin's q. They then consider an autoregressive–distributed lag structure to accommodate the possibility of capital adjustment costs, which yields an error correction specification, as in Bond et al. (2003). Under the null hypothesis of no financial friction, cash flow should not affect investment under this specification. Ek and Wu (2018) allow for the potential endogeneity of cash flow in their estimation using generalised method of moments techniques. They test whether the cash flow terms show significantly different predictive powers across those samples that produce significantly different investment–cash flow sensitivities.

The second concern about investment–cash flow sensitivity and financing constraint is the well-known Kaplan and Zingales critique. Kaplan and Zingales (1997) argue that investment–cash flow sensitivities do not always monotonically increase as firms become more financially constrained. Thus, one cannot in general use estimates of investment–cash flow sensitivities to proxy the severity of financial frictions. The theoretical model in Ek and Wu (2018) shows that the relationship between investment–cash flow sensitivities and the severity of financial frictions indeed depends on the curvature of the profit function and the cost function of external finance. However, even though more financially constrained firms do not necessarily exhibit higher sensitivity, it remains the case that unconstrained firms should display no investment–cash flow sensitivity. Therefore, finding that one group of firms has positively significant sensitivity while the other group shows no sensitivity is a sufficient, though not necessary, condition of capital misallocation, which is indeed the general pattern of the empirical findings. Given that Ek and Wu's identification strategy only relies on investment–cash flow sensitivities and not excess investment–cash flow sensitivities, it is not subject to the Kaplan and Zingales critique.

When they apply the error correction investment model to a 10-year balanced panel of US Compustat database firms, Ek and Wu (2018) do not detect any investment–cash flow sensitivity. In contrast, there are significant sensitivities for a 10-year balanced panel of Chinese firms. Within Chinese firms, when splitting the sample using any criterion based on age, size, ownership or political connection, and for both the balanced and the unbalanced panels, they obtain significant cash flow effects for firms that are young, small, non-SOEs and without political connections. The resulting aggregate TFP loss implied by these investment–cash flow sensitivities is 4 to 5.2 per cent for the balanced panel and 10 to 15.2 per cent for the unbalanced panel.

While Ek and Wu (2018) take a structural approach, the identification strategy in Wu (2018) is more of a reduced-form approach. In particular, it uses a program evaluation perspective to quantify the effects on capital misallocation of both financial frictions and policy distortions.

Financial frictions versus policy distortions

As mentioned earlier in this chapter, a stylised fact of the Chinese economy is that the cost of capital, the return to investment or the proxies for the MRPC differs significantly across firms with different ownership types. This distinct phenomenon has often been taken as direct evidence of policy distortions in capital allocation. After all, ownership should not matter for MRPC in a world without policy distortions, were ownership orthogonal of other firm characteristics that may affect MRPC. However, as a less-developed economy, China also has a less-developed capital market with a lagged legal, auditing and contracting environment. If firms with different ownership types systematically differ in other characteristics, such as age and size, and if such characteristics do affect MRPC because of financial frictions, even in the absence of policy distortions, these firms could still have different MRPC under an imperfect capital market.

The unique institutional feature on firm ownership type and MRPC dispersion in China inspires us to design the following identification strategy. Imagine an investment-promoting program that offers favourable treatment to some firms. The treatment status of a firm depends on its ownership type. The exact treatment may take various forms—for example, an investment tax credit or a special bank loan with a low interest rate. The effect of the treatment is to lower the generalised user cost of capital, or the mirror image of the MRPC of those treated firms. Firms differ not only in their treatment status, but also in a set of firm characteristics, known as covariates in an evaluation problem, through which financial frictions operate to affect their MRPC. The average treatment effect of the program on MRPC dispersion can then be decomposed into the average treatment effect on treated (ATT) and the selection bias. The ATT is the difference between the actual MRPC of those treated and the counterfactual MRPC of those treated had they not received the treatment, which identifies the effect of policy distortions on the average MRPC dispersion across ownership type. The selection bias is the MRPC difference between the treated and the untreated in the absence of treatment, which captures the effect of financial frictions on the average MRPC dispersion across ownership.

In applying this identification strategy, Wu (2018) considers a structural model with both policy distortions and financial frictions. To nest those microfoundations that have been the most common building blocks in the recent literature on financial frictions and aggregate TFP, Wu allows for two types of highly synthesised reduced-form financial constraints. The aggregate TFP loss in the model economy depends on the dispersion of the firm-specific MRPC, which is determined by some joint distribution of a set of parameters. These parameters govern the magnitude of firm-specific policy distortions and financial frictions and characterise the state of firm productivity and internal funds. Wu then conducts propensity score matching based on a set of covariates that are suggested by the model through which financial frictions may affect MRPC, even in the absence of policy distortions. These covariates are exactly the same as those that appear in the vast theoretical and empirical literature on financial frictions. However, by matching firms that have different treatment status but are otherwise similar in terms of these covariates, one does not have to take a stand on the functional relations among these observed covariates and MRPC; nor does one need to specify the exact causal direction between the treatment status and the observed covariates.

The detailed firm-level panel data from China's *Annual Survey of Industrial Enterprises* is employed to obtain point effect estimates on the ATT and the selection bias across different firm ownership types. For example, not surprisingly, an SOE, on average, has an MRPC 42 per cent lower than that of a domestic privately owned firm, where policy distortions and financial frictions lower its MRPC by 22 and 20 per cent, respectively. More interestingly, the average MRPC of a foreign-owned firm is 2 per cent lower than that of a domestic privately owned firm. But without policy distortions, its MRPC would be 20 per cent higher than that of a domestic privately owned firm due to financial frictions. This suggests that foreign-owned firms in fact receive similar levels of favourable policy distortions to state-owned firms.

Although such estimates are interesting in their own right, what truly helps us answer our research questions is a byproduct of the matching procedure—a counterfactual MRPC of those treated firms had they not received the treatment. Using this information, Wu (2018) calculates the aggregate TFP losses in a hypothetical economy without policy distortions, which turn out to vary from 7.3 to 9.4 per cent over the period 2000–07. Thus, her estimates of the effect of financial frictions on aggregate TFP loss are in line with Ek and Wu's (2018), based on the same dataset but using a completely different approach. The annual average aggregate TFP loss in the actual economy reaches 27.5 per cent. This implies that 70 per cent of the aggregate TFP loss can be attributed to policy distortions. It also finds that the policy distortions have reduced the average MRPC in China by 15.5 per cent, which provides one possible explanation for China's unusually high investment rate.

Policy distortions

Although a large literature has identified the policy distortions as an underlying source of capital misallocation and aggregate TFP loss in China, the policy distortions used in most papers are modelled in only an abstract and generic way. To offer specific policy implications, it is important to identify specific institutional factors that have distorted capital allocation.

Using matched samples of firms with balanced covariates, Wu (2018) evaluates several popular hypotheses on why the Chinese Government has introduced various rules, regulations and institutions that favour certain firms. From the public finance perspective, the first possible reason for a government to favour a firm is that the firm contributes significant tax revenue.

Second, a government may also distort capital allocation to pursue specific industrial policies. For example, China is well known for having adopted an export-led growth strategy since the beginning of its 'reform and opening-up' policy (Lin 2012). More recently, it has been suggested that China practices a form of state capitalism in a vertical industrial structure: SOEs are explicitly or implicitly allowed to monopolise key upstream industries, while the downstream industries are largely open to private competition (Li et al. 2015). Under these two hypotheses, firms in upstream industries that are exporting can expect to receive favourable policy distortions.

Third, the well-known trade-off between growth and stability facing the Chinese Government has often been taken as an argument to justify policy distortions. To minimise social unease and reduce resistance to reform, the government may have a strong political motivation to maintain employment stability. For example, to avoid laying off workers or shutting factories during an economic downturn, the government usually asks the state-owned banks to bail out loss-making SOEs, which creates a problem known as the 'soft-budget constraint' (Qian and Roland 1998; Brandt and Zhu 2001). Under this rationale, we may regard the government as a risk-averse social planner that optimally allocates capital according to the capital asset pricing model. If so, firms that are countercyclical have a smaller beta and only need to offer a lower required rate of return on capital.

Finally, differing from all the above hypotheses, which assume a benevolent government, an alternative hypothesis is that the government prefers firms with political connections. For example, Communist Party membership has been found to help private entrepreneurs obtain loans from banks or other state institutions (Li et al. 2008; Guo et al. 2014). Firms with government-appointed or government-connected chief executive officers are found to face much less severe financial constraints (Fan et al. 2007; Cull et al. 2015). Since there is no information regarding a firm's entrepreneur or chief executive officer in our dataset, whether the firm has a labour union is adopted as an alternative measure of political connection. Unlike labour unions in most Western countries, which help workers collectively bargain with employers for higher wages and better working conditions, Chinese labour unions pass on the ideology of the Communist Party to the workers and monitor whether the firm is 'politically correct' or at least is operating consistently with Communist Party policy.

To test these interesting hypotheses, Wu (2018) implements a regression using the restricted sample of matched firms. The dependent variable is the difference between the actual MRPC of a firm in a year and its counterfactual MRPC had the firm not received the favourable treatment in that year. The independent variables include the six factors inferred from the popular hypotheses. This produces a set of interesting findings. First, the actual MRPC of those firms that contribute high tax revenue is in fact higher than their counterfactual MRPC. This denies the first hypothesis that firms receive favourable policy distortions in capital because they contribute more tax revenue. Instead, it suggests that those firms that have received favourable policy distortions in capital also receive favourable tax treatment, such as tax breaks or direct subsidies. Second, averaging across the years, and all else being equal, a firm that is an exporter, belongs to an upstream industry and has a labour union has an MRPC 14 per cent, 2.6 per cent and 14.9 per cent, respectively, lower than otherwise. Finally, beta is the only variable whose estimates change the signs from significantly positive to insignificantly negative over our sample period. A positive coefficient on beta is consistent with the capital asset pricing model, thus verifying the motivation of policy distortions as a trade-off between risk and return. The fact that beta becomes irrelevant after 2005 seems to indicate that employment stability was no longer a major concern for the government in more recent years. The same pattern is highlighted in Hsieh and Song (2015) using different evidence.

Three conclusions therefore can be draw from the empirical exercises. First, favourable policy distortions in capital go hand-in-hand with favourable tax treatment. Second, pursuing an export-led growth strategy and practising state capitalism are two important factors that drive policy distortions. Political connection with the Communist Party is another reason for firms to receive favourable treatment. Finally, concern about the trade-off between return and risk also leads to policy distortions but is relevant only in the early years of the study period.

Conclusions and policy implications

In recognising that both financial frictions and policy distortions have caused capital misallocation and aggregate TFP losses in China, this chapter uses an important perspective to understand China's economic development in the past four decades, thanks to both the development of the financial environment and the economic reforms correcting overall policy distortions. To the extent that large and persistent capital misallocation still exists after 40 years of reform, the factors identified in this chapter can be interpreted as directions for further reform. The structural reforms that are particularly relevant to capital misallocation are mainly in the enterprise sector and the financial system—for example, those reforms proposed by the World Bank and the Development Research Centre of the State Council (2013).

References

Allen, F., Qian, J. and Qian, M. (2005), Law, finance, and economic growth in China, *Journal of Financial Economics* 77(1): 57–116. doi.org/10.1016/j.jfineco.2004.06.010.

Bai, C., Hsieh, C. and Qian, Y. (2006), The return to capital in China, *Brookings Papers on Economic Activity* 2: 61–88. doi.org/10.1353/eca.2007.0000.

Banerjee, A.V. and Moll, B. (2010), Why does misallocation persist?, *American Economic Journal: Macroeconomics* 2(1): 189–206. doi.org/10.1257/mac.2.1.189.

Bond, S., Elston, J.A., Mairesse, J. and Mulkay, B. (2003), Financial factors and investment in Belgium, France, Germany, and the United Kingdom: A comparison using company panel data, *Review of Economics and Statistics* 85(1): 153–65. doi.org/10.1162/003465303762687776.

Brandt, L., Tombe, T. and Zhu, X. (2013), Factor market distortions across time, space, and sectors in China, *Review of Economic Dynamics* 16(1): 39–58. doi.org/10.1016/j.red.2012.10.002.

Brandt, L. and Zhu, X. (2001), Soft budget constraint and inflation cycles: A positive model of the macro-dynamics in China during transition, *Journal of Development Economics* 64(2): 437–57. doi.org/10.1016/S0304-3878(00)00145-0.

Cull, R., Li, W., Sun, B. and Xu, L. (2015), Government connections and financial constraints: Evidence from a large representative sample of Chinese firms, *Journal of Corporate Finance* 32: 271–94. doi.org/10.1016/j.jcorpfin.2014.10.012.

Dollar, D. and Wei, S. (2007), *Das (wasted) kapital: Firm ownership and investment efficiency in China*, NBER Working Paper No. 13103, Cambridge, MA: National Bureau of Economic Research. doi.org/10.3386/w13103.

Ek, C. and Wu, G. (2018), Investment–cash flow sensitivities and capital misallocation, *Journal of Development Economics* 133: 220–30. doi.org/10.1016/j.jdeveco.2018.02.003.

Fan, J., Wong, T.J. and Zhang, T. (2007), Politically connected CEOs, corporate governance, and post-IPO performance of China's newly partially privatized firms, *Journal of Financial Economics* 84(2): 330–57. doi.org/10.1016/j.jfineco.2006.03.008.

Guo, D., Jiang, K., Kim, B. and Xu, C. (2014), Political economy of private firms in China, *Journal of Comparative Economics* 42(2): 286–303. doi.org/10.1016/j.jce.2014.03.006.

Hsieh, C. and Klenow, P. (2009), Misallocation and manufacturing TFP in China and India, *Quarterly Journal of Economics* 124(4): 1403–48. doi.org/10.1162/qjec.2009.124.4.1403.

Hsieh, C. and Song, Z. (2015), Grasp the large, let go of the small: The transformation of the state sector in China, *Brookings Papers on Economic Activity* (Spring): 295–346. doi.org/10.3386/w21006.

Kaplan, S.N. and Zingales, L. (1997), Do investment–cash flow sensitivities provide useful measures of financing constraints?, *Quarterly Journal of Economics* 112(1): 196–215. doi.org/10.1162/003355397555163.

Li, H., Meng, L., Wang, Q. and Zhou, L. (2008), Political connections, financing and firm performance: Evidence from Chinese private firms, *Journal of Development Economics* 87(2): 283–99. doi.org/10.1016/j.jdeveco.2007.03.001.

Li, X., Liu, X. and Wang, Y. (2015), A model of China's state capitalism, August. doi.org/10.2139/ssrn.2061521.

Lin, J.Y. (2012), *Demystifying the Chinese*, Cambridge: Cambridge University Press.

Midrigan, V. and Xu, D.Y. (2014), Finance and misallocation: Evidence from plant-level data, *American Economic Review* 104(2): 422–58. doi.org/10.1257/aer.104.2.422.

Moll, B. (2014), Productivity losses from financial frictions: Can self-financing undo capital misallocation?, *American Economic Review* 104(10): 3186–221. doi.org/10.1257/aer.104.10.3186.

Qian, Y. and Roland, G. (1998), Federalism and the soft budget constraint, *American Economic Review* 88(5): 1143–62.

Restuccia, D. and Rogerson, R. (2013), Misallocation and productivity, *Review of Economic Dynamics* 16(1): 1–10. doi.org/10.1016/j.red.2012.11.003.

Song, Z., Storesletten, K. and Zilibotti, F. (2011), Growing like China, *American Economic Review* 101(1): 196–233. doi.org/10.1257/aer.101.1.196.

Song, Z. and Wu, G. (2015), *Identifying capital misallocation*, Working Paper, available from: www.lingnan.sysu.edu.cn/UploadFiles/xsbg/2015/6/201506230815012648.pdf.

World Bank and the Development Research Centre of the State Council (2013), *China 2030: Building a modern, harmonious, and creative society*, Washington, DC: The World Bank.

Wu, G. (2018), Capital misallocation in China: Financial frictions or policy distortions?, *Journal of Development Economics* 130: 203–23. doi.org/10.1016/j.jdeveco.2017.10.014.

Zhu, X. (2012), Understanding China's growth: Past, present, and future, *Journal of Economics Perspectives* 26(4): 103–24. doi.org/10.1257/jep.26.4.103.

3. Chinese corporate debt and credit misallocation

Ninghua Zhong, Mi Xie and Zhikuo Liu[1]

Introduction

After the 2008–09 Global Financial Crisis (GFC), the efficiency of credit allocation in China's financial system dropped significantly. According to Figure 3.1, it took about RMB1 (US$0.14) of new credit to create a unit of gross domestic product (GDP) by 2008, but this credit intensity has since risen sharply and recently reached more than RMB3 (US$0.48).

Meanwhile, China's broad measure of money supply (M2) surged after 2008, from RMB47 trillion (US$6.8 trillion) in 2008 to RMB155 trillion (US$23.3 trillion) in 2016 (Figure 3.2). That is, in eight years, M2 increased by more than RMB100 trillion (US$16.6 trillion). Recently, China's M2 has exceeded US$20 trillion, surpassing the largest economies in the world, including the United States, in absolute terms. In addition, the ratio of M2 to GDP in China has reached more than 200 per cent.

Combined, these data indicate that although the total amount of credit and financial resources is skyrocketing, the efficiency of their allocation is significantly deteriorating. In other words, large amounts of money have been allocated to inefficient areas or even wasted, resulting in a phenomenon called 'finance does not support entities', which is heatedly debated in mainland China.

With the declining efficiency of credit allocation, the overall rate of leveraging in China is on the rise. According to estimations by the Chinese Academy of Social Sciences and various other organisations,[2] China's total debt had reached RMB168 trillion (US$27 trillion) and the ratio of total debt to GDP was up to 249 per cent by the end of 2015. This level was in line with that of some developed countries, including the United States, the United Kingdom and the euro area, but was much

1   We thank Wing Thye Woo and other seminar participants at the Asian Economic Panel for valuable comments and suggestions. Ninghua Zhong acknowledges financial support from the National High-Level Talents Special Support Program (Young Top-Notch Talent Program), the Fok Ying-Tong Education Foundation of China (Grant No. 161081), the National Social Science Foundation of China (Grant No. 13&ZD015) and the Start-Up Research Grant of Tongji University (Grant No. 180144). Zhikuo Liu acknowledges financial support from the National Natural Science Foundation of China (Grant No. 71503159) and the Program for Innovative Research Team of Shanghai University of Finance and Economics.
2   See the briefing meeting held by the Information Department of the State Council: www.toutiao.com/i6296377658741621249/; and the report in the *Financial Times*: www.ftchinese.com/story/001067266?full=y.

higher than that of developing countries such as Brazil (146 per cent) and India (128 per cent). It is estimated that this ratio is still currently above 250 per cent—that is, total debt exceeds RMB200 trillion (US$30 trillion) (Sohu Finance and Economics 2017).

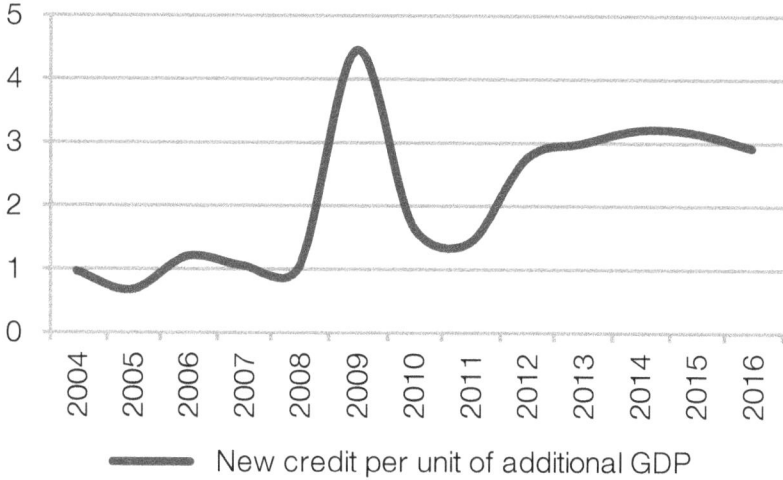

Figure 3.1 Credit intensity (new credit/additional GDP) rising further
Sources: CEIC Global Economic Database and NBS.

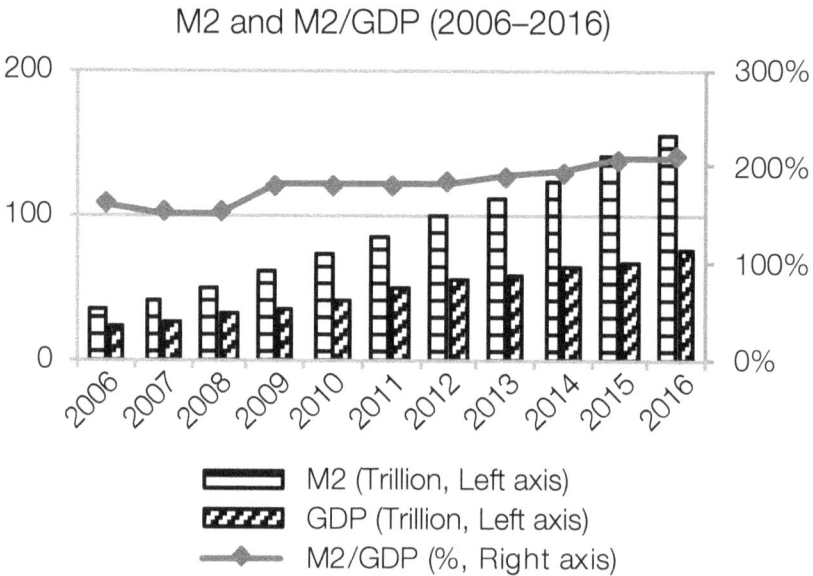

Figure 3.2 Funding supply surges: increasing M2 and M2/GDP
Sources: CEIC Global Economic Database and NBS.

Intriguingly, against the soaring trend of China's corporate debt, many Chinese small and medium-sized enterprises (SMEs), as well as private firms, have found it increasingly difficult to obtain loans from the formal financial sector. On the other hand, the overall economy urgently needs to transform towards being innovation-driven. Thus, more financial support is needed, and it is therefore argued that China should continue to use leverage.

Considering these factors, it is difficult to conclude whether China should continue leveraging. In fact, for a complicated economy such as China's, any general conclusion could be biased and any unified policies and measurements may be inefficient. Perhaps, rather than discussing the overall 'optimal debt ratio' for the Chinese economy, we should first pin down some basic facts, such as: where is the leverage across different sectors, industries, regions, ownership types and periods? This is the first question we want to answer in this chapter.

Several recent reports have pointed out that nonfinancial enterprises have the highest debt across different sectors in China (for example, enterprise, residential and government), and that debt has risen rapidly since 2008. During the period 2004–08, such debt accounted for less than 100 per cent of China's GDP (Sina Finance 2017), whereas it reached 105.4 per cent of GDP in 2010, surpassing that of all other major countries (China News 2012). It continued to soar in the following years and reached 163 per cent in June 2015 (Caixin 2016). Moreover, according to estimates by Standard & Poor's (2014), by the end of 2013, the total debt of nonfinancial enterprises in China was US$14.2 trillion, exceeding that in the United States (US$13.1 trillion). They further predicted that, by the end of 2018, China's corporate debt would account for more than one-third of total corporate debt worldwide.

This chapter also examines the changes in corporate leveraging in China, mainly using data from China's industrial enterprises that were above designated scale during the period 1998–2013,[3] which come from the *Annual Survey of Industrial Enterprises* conducted by the National Bureau of Statistics of China (NBS various years). We first analyse the debt ratio (that is, total liabilities/total assets) of nearly 4 million observations in this dataset. As can be seen from Figure 3.3, the simple average and median of debt ratio decreased from 65 per cent in 1998 to 51 per cent in 2013, representing a decline of 14 percentage points in 15 years and an average decline of nearly 1 percentage point annually.

---

3   During the period 1998–2006, those enterprises designated as being above scale were the entire state-owned industrial sector and the non–state-owned enterprises with an annual operating income of RMB5 million (US$0.68 million) or more. From the beginning of 2007, it excluded those whose annual operating income was less than RMB5 million even if they were SOEs. Furthermore, the standard has been raised from an annual operating income of RMB5 million to RMB20 million (US$3.17 million) since 2011.

Furthermore, breaking down total debt into short-term debt (matured within one year) and long-term debt, we find that the ratio of average short-term debt to total assets decreased from 55 per cent in 1998 to 47 per cent in 2013 (see Figure 3.4), and the ratio of average long-term debt decreased from 11 per cent in 1998 to 6 per cent in 2013 (see Figure 3.5). That is, the short-term debt ratio declined by 8 percentage points during the sample period, while the long-term debt ratio only declined by 5 percentage points, so the short-term debt ratio contributes more to the decline in total debt ratio. However, given the very low initial level of long-term liabilities, it takes a much larger decrease indeed. It is worth noting that the median long-term debt ratio was zero for most years, indicating that more than half of the sampled enterprises were unable to obtain any long-term debt.

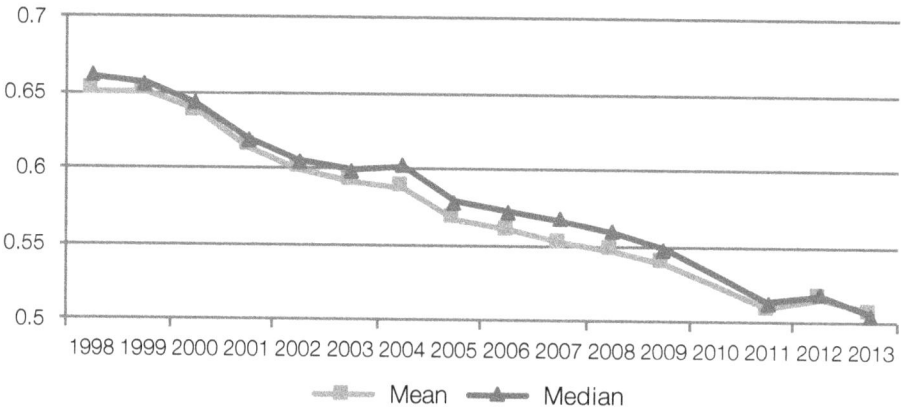

Figure 3.3 Average debt ratio of China's unlisted industrial enterprises
Source: NBS (various years).

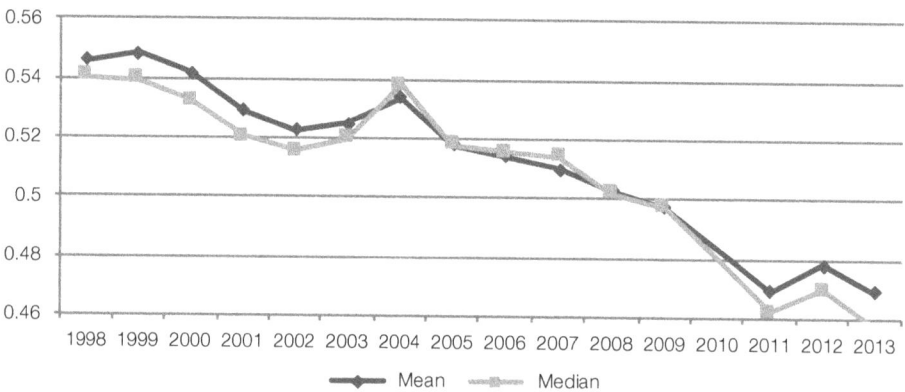

Figure 3.4 Short-term debt ratio of China's unlisted industrial enterprises
Source: NBS (various years).

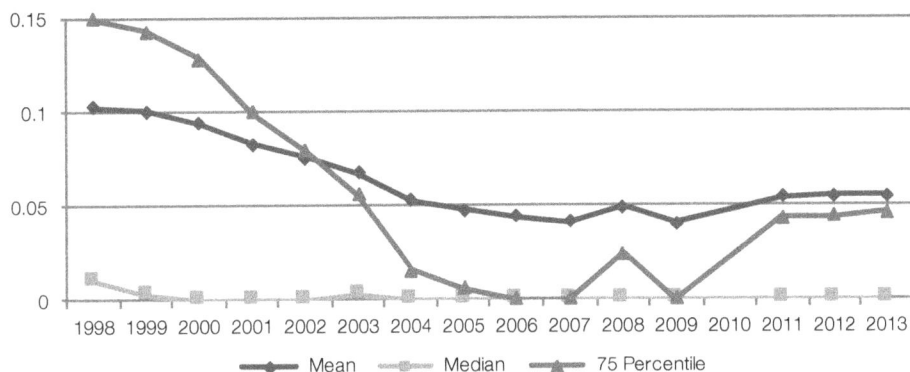

Figure 3.5 Long-term debt ratio of China's unlisted industrial enterprises
Source: NBS (various years).

This declining trend is inconsistent with the rising corporate debt ratio that we have observed in the aggregate data. We thus deduce that it is a small sample of firms that have raised their leverage significantly. We thus divide the whole sample according to different standards and provide detailed statistical descriptions in section two. After elaborative examination, we summarise the following six facts.

- **Fact 1:** The longer a firm remains in the sample, the smaller is the decline in its debt ratio.

- **Fact 2:** The debt ratio of large enterprises decreased slightly, whereas that of SMEs dropped significantly.

- **Fact 3:** The decreasing range of the debt ratio of heavy industrial enterprises was generally much smaller than that of light industrial enterprises; and the average debt ratio of public utility enterprises was on the rise.

- **Fact 4:** The average debt ratio of enterprises in north-eastern and central China decreased the most—by more than 20 per cent—whereas the ratios of those enterprises in the developed eastern regions were quite stable.

- **Fact 5:** The average debt ratio of state-owned enterprises (SOEs) was always higher than that of private enterprises, which was, in turn, higher than that of foreign-funded enterprises. Among all types of enterprises, the average debt ratio of SOEs dropped the most. It is worth noting that the average debt ratio of longstanding SOEs was stable and rose after 2009.

- **Fact 6:** The average debt ratio of manufacturing enterprises listed on the Main Board was on the rise and surpassed that of unlisted companies after 2009.

Although these facts are simple statistical descriptions, they may provide an important basis for discussing the debt ratio in China and correct some existing mainstream views. First, in recent years, many media and institutional reports have focused on the record high debt ratios in China after the GFC, creating an idea that the debt ratio of Chinese enterprises is generally on the rise. In fact, our six facts show that the increase in debt ratios is sharply concentrated in thousands of enterprises, most of which are large, state-owned and listed companies.

The following statistics best emphasise the sharp concentration of Chinese corporate debt. The data for Chinese industrial enterprises include about 345,000 enterprises for 2013; those enterprises had debts totalling RMB49.1 trillion (US$7.4 trillion). Nearly half of the total debt was held by the top 2,000 enterprises (RMB13.5 trillion; US$2 trillion) and more than one-quarter was held by the top 500 enterprises (RMB23.5 trillion; US$3.5 trillion). We also analysed the second dataset—that of Chinese listed firms—and obtained similar findings. According to our estimation, in 2015, the top 300 heavily indebted listed enterprises owed 82 per cent of all debt, amounting to RMB16 trillion (US$2.4 trillion), and the top 50 enterprises owed 54 per cent of all debt, amounting to RMB11 trillion (US$1.7 trillion).

Among them, PetroChina—China's largest oil and gas producer—was the most indebted listed company, owing RMB1 trillion (US$150 billion) in 2015. It was followed by China State Construction Engineering Corporation, China Petroleum and Chemical Corporation, China Railway Construction Corporation, China Railway Group Limited and China Communications Construction Corporation (which was listed in 2012 and did not release data before 2011). In 2015, those five companies held total debts of more than RMB3 trillion (US$450 billion). In addition, according to the *21st Century Business Herald*, by the end of 2015, the total debt of the seven major coal enterprises in Shanxi exceeded RMB1.1 trillion (US$180 billion).[4]

Thus, China's corporate debt issue is highly 'structural'. Most debts are held by a small fraction of companies, whereas the debt ratio in most companies is declining.

After establishing the basic facts, sections three and four of this chapter attempt to further explore the question of whether the changing debt ratio is supported by economic fundamentals using both firm-level (that is, microlevel) and aggregate-level (that is, macrolevel) data. China is not an exception to the rule that the rapid growth of developing countries is usually accompanied by an increase in the debt of the enterprise sector. Therefore, we need more precise analysis to answer the question of whether the rising leverage of nonfinancial enterprises is supported by their fundamentals—because, in the past few decades, with the rapid marketisation process in China, some of the main characteristics of Chinese enterprises have changed significantly. For example, their profitability has improved significantly (see Figure 3.6). It is reasonable for an enterprise to borrow more money from outside based on its rising profitability, because its expected cash flows will allow it

---

4   See 'Shanxi's seven major coal enterprises' debts reach Y1.1 trillion, and rely on government's subsidies to pay wages', *China mining*, www.chinamining.org.cn/index.php?m=content&c=index&a=show&catid=8&id=17540.

to repay more debt.[5] Similarly, some enterprises in China—mainly large SOEs—have experienced rapid capital deepening. In other words, they have more fixed assets. It is also reasonable for these enterprises to borrow more because they have more collateral; if they cannot repay, they can sell off fixed assets. Such increases in leveraging are backed by economic fundamentals.

On the other hand, there are some increases in leverage that are not supported by the economic fundamentals and are thus deeply concerning. For example, many recent discussions have referred to state-owned 'zombie' enterprises. According to Tan et al. (2016), in 2007, 12.1 per cent of Chinese industrial enterprises were zombie firms, and their proportions of assets and liabilities were 10.7 per cent and 13.4 per cent, respectively.[6] It is estimated that these proportions rose significantly after the GFC. The profitability of these enterprises is extremely low or even negative; nevertheless, even with high debt, they could survive if given substantial loans through the banking system. Meanwhile, many more profitable private enterprises are unable to borrow from banks. Such a contrast leads to reasonable conjectures about increasing credit misallocation.

To explore this issue, in section three, we start by referring to the literature on Western capital structure and examining the changes in six important corporate characteristics that determine credit financing. We find that the average size of Chinese enterprises during the period 1998–2013 increased and their operational risk rose; the proportion of tangible assets (mainly fixed assets and inventories) has been declining and profitability has been continuously increasing. These changes are a result at the firm (micro) level of the transformation of China's economy towards being market-oriented. As competition in domestic and foreign product markets is becoming more intense, operational risks are increasing, while the profitability and scale of the surviving enterprises are becoming stronger and larger. In addition, market competition also forces enterprises to adopt a more competitive approach to production. Therefore, Chinese enterprises are constantly transforming to labour-intensive and light capitalisation, which is shown in the declining share of tangible assets.

These changing firm characteristics have varying influence on leveraging, therefore, we further refer to the standard regression models in the literature on Western capital structure to examine the relationships between these variables and the debt ratio. We find that, in the sample of private enterprises, the regression results are highly consistent with the Western literature; also, the changes in firm characteristics are consistent with changes in the debt ratio. For example: 1) the operating risk is negatively related to the debt ratio, so the rise in business risk may result in a decrease

---

5   On the other hand, enterprises with high profitability tend to rely less on external capital because they can generate enough cash flow.

6   The methodology for identifying zombie enterprises refers to the CHK approach presented in Caballero et al. (2008).

of the debt ratio; 2) the tangible asset is the collateral of debt financing and is positively related to the debt ratio, the decline of which may lead to a decline in the debt ratio; and 3) the average profit margin of an enterprise is negatively related to the debt ratio—that is, the relationship between internal cash and external financing is an alternative. Therefore, the increase in profitability may also be the reason for the declining debt ratio. We hence draw a preliminary conclusion that the financing decisions of private enterprises are in line with the principles of marketisation.

In the sample of SOEs, however, except for the profit margin, other important firm characteristics are insignificant or even have an unexpected sign; we can hardly explain the change in the debt ratio of SOEs by the changes in firm characteristics. Apart from these analyses, we have also examined Chinese listed enterprises and found there were about 160 listed SOEs whose profits (earnings) before interest and tax were not enough to pay off interest. These enterprises could only keep borrowing to repay old debts; as a result, the debt 'snowballs'. This also indicates that the liabilities of some SOEs are too high, which eventually results in an excessive interest burden.

In section four, we use the aggregate-level (macro-level) data to provide further evidence of SOEs' overleveraging. We find that state-owned industrial enterprises as a whole have been increasing their leveraging since 2008 and their overall debt ratio rose from 58 per cent in 2008 to 62 per cent in 2016, whereas the private sector has been underaccelerating its deleveraging, with the overall average debt ratio falling from 58 per cent to 52 per cent. In other words, the private sector has been deleveraging for more than a decade. Moreover, recently, private industrial enterprises as a whole contributed nearly 40 per cent of the total profit of all industrial enterprises, while their liabilities accounted for only 20 per cent of the total. In contrast, state-owned industrial enterprises as a whole contributed less than 20 per cent of total profit, while their liabilities accounted for more than 40 per cent of the total. According to the Ministry of Finance, the total debt of the Chinese SOE sector has reached RMB100 trillion (US$15.1 trillion), whereas the return on total assets is only 1.91 per cent. Therefore, we draw a preliminary conclusion that the leveraging of SOEs is not supported by the economic fundamentals, and there are some nonmarket factors that are driving up their leverage.

It is noteworthy that this conclusion is also consistent with another important phenomenon that emerged after the GFC: SOEs are heavily involved in shadow banking activities such as entrusted lending or loans (China Business Journal 2011). This suggests these enterprises do not have good investment opportunities themselves but are able to borrow large amounts of money from the financial system at a lower cost and then lend to others (for example, to the private sector) to obtain the interest spread, which also proves that the debt ratio of these SOEs is too high.

This chapter differs significantly from the existing research on the capital structure of Chinese enterprises. Much of the research has been made by applying standard empirical tests from Western literature directly to Chinese enterprises and examining the power of the mainstream capital structure theories such as the 'pecking order theory' and 'trade-off theory' to impact Chinese corporate debt. For example, Chen (2004) finds that the capital structure of listed companies in China is not in line with the classic pecking order theory; rather, the order of their financing is retained earnings, equity financing and debt financing. Chen and Strange (2005) find that, unlike the expectation of the trade-off theory, Chinese listed companies do not show a stable optimal debt ratio. Newman et al. (2012) examined 1,539 privately owned SMEs in Zhejiang Province and found that firm size was positively correlated with the debt ratio, and there was a significant negative correlation between profitability and the debt ratio, which was consistent with the expectation of the pecking order theory. However, the relationship between the proportion of fixed assets and the debt ratio is not significant.

Other literature focuses on whether the main determinants of a firm's capital structure in a developed country can explain the capital structure of Chinese listed companies. For example, Huang and Song (2006) find that the correlations between the debt ratio of listed companies in China and firm size—and between the debt ratio and the proportion of fixed assets, profitability, nondebt tax shields and growth—are basically consistent with the empirical findings from developed countries; the main difference is that the share of long-term debt in Chinese companies is very low. Bhabra et al. (2008) examine the long-term debt ratio of listed companies in China and find that it is positively related to firm size and the proportion of tangible assets, but negatively correlated with profitability and growth.

In contrast to this research, Li et al. (2009) consider unique institutional factors in China, and their work is the most like our chapter. They study the capital structure of Chinese industrial firms during the period 2000–03. They find that state-owned and private enterprises have higher debt ratios than foreign-funded firms. In addition, in areas where the legal environment and the banking system are more developed, enterprises have lower total debt ratios.

The existing literature has focused on cross-sectional differences, whereas our chapter examines the changes in the time series—that is, trying to understand the significant changes in the debt ratio of Chinese enterprises in the context of China's overall economic transformation. As we will show later, during the relatively short sample period of 1998–2013, the debt ratio and key characteristics of Chinese enterprises have changed dramatically. Such dramatic changes only happen in rapidly transforming countries such as China. In mature economies such as the United States, both the financing and the main features of enterprises are much more stable; therefore, studies of the capital structure of Western enterprises naturally focus more on the cross-sectional differences.

More importantly, the main purpose of this chapter is not to test or develop the Western capital structure theories, but to provide valuable analysis of and suggestions for whether and how to deleverage in China. For these complicated issues, our research is still relatively preliminary. Our results indicate that a complete answer should include at least two parts. First, the financing decisions of some enterprises—mainly private enterprises—are generally in line with the principle of marketisation. For these enterprises, adequate capital supply should be guaranteed so that the enterprises with fundamental support can borrow enough money. Second, there are many 'nonmarket-oriented' factors in the determinants of SOE debt. Thus, we should cease the transfusion of funds to inefficient firms as soon as possible and allocate new loans to the most efficient areas. Meanwhile, we suggest selling SOEs' stock assets to repay the stock liabilities. Considering the already very high total leverage ratio in China, the efficiency of the allocation of incremental funds would determine the potential for China's medium and long-term future economic growth.

Where is the leverage?

The data

The first firm-level dataset we examine comes from the *Annual Survey of Industrial Enterprises* conducted by the NBS from 1998 to 2013 (the data for 2010 is missing because of very poor quality), and the total original number of observations is 3,911,364. We first examine the major accounting identities,[7] requiring that the absolute value of [total liabilities + owner's equity − total assets] be less than 1 per cent of total assets, resulting in 82,783 observations being deleted. Second, we check the identity of the total debt, requiring that the absolute value of [total debt − short-term debt − long-term debt] be less than 1 per cent of total assets, and delete 203,920 observations. Third, we delete 4,774 observations with current liabilities larger than total liabilities, 3,314 observations with long-term liabilities larger than total liabilities, and 30 observations with a negative main operating income. Thus, the new total number of observations is 3,616,543.

In addition, some of the analyses in this chapter use the data for listed firms during the period 1998–2013 from the China Stock Market & Accounting Research (CSMAR) Database. We delete the observations for nonindustrial enterprises, and exclude firms listed on the Small and Medium-Sized Enterprises Board and on the Growth Enterprise Market, which results in a total of 20,306 observations. We also do 1 per cent and 99 per cent Winsorization for each firm-level variable.

---

7   There is a large amount of missing data for 2008 and 2011–13 for short-term and long-term liabilities, so only non-missing samples are considered for the proofreading of debt identities.

Descriptive statistics on subsamples: Six facts

In this section, we present six facts about changes in the debt ratio of Chinese enterprises in the subsamples sorted by various standards. These facts are fundamental to further exploring China's leveraging issues.

Fact 1: The longer a firm remains in the sample, the smaller is the decline in its debt ratio

Fact 1 is the conclusion drawn by grouping the whole sample according to the number of consecutive years in which the enterprises exist in the database. We divide the enterprises into four groups, with the years of existence of the sample firms being 3, 7, 11 and 15 years. Figure 3.6 depicts the changes in the average debt ratio of these subsamples; the average debt ratio of the enterprises with continuous existence of more than three years was 67 per cent in 1998 and dropped to 48 per cent in 2008—a decrease of 19 percentage points. However, the average debt ratio of those firms that have existed for more than 15 years declined from 58 per cent to 54 per cent during this period—a decline of only 4 percentage points.

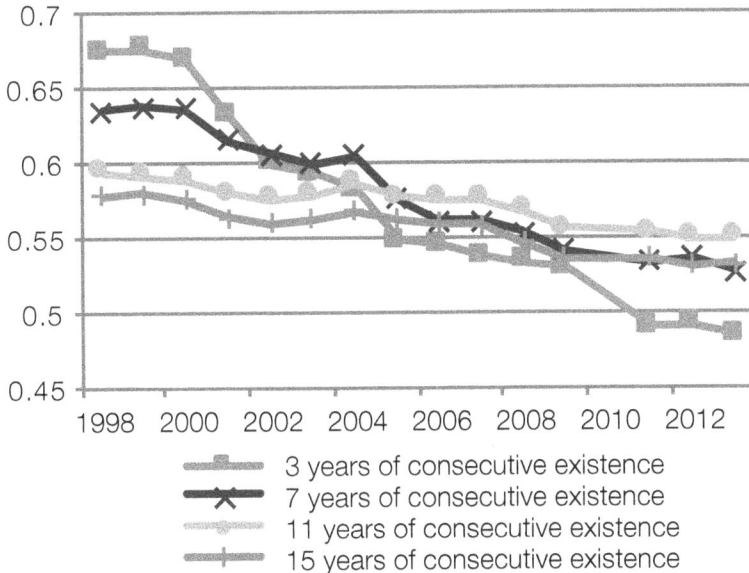

Figure 3.6 Debt ratio: Classified by years of existence

Source: NBS (various years).

Fact 2: The debt ratio of large enterprises decreased slightly, whereas that of SMEs dropped significantly

We then classify the whole sample according to the size of the enterprises and conclude Fact 2. The division of large and medium-sized enterprises is based on the principle of the 'Interim Provisions on Standards for Small and Medium-sized Enterprises' formulated by the State Economic and Trade Commission, the State Development Planning Commission, the Ministry of Finance and the NBS in 2003. Accordingly, companies with fewer than 2,000 employees, annual revenue of less than RMB300 million (US$45 million) or total assets of less than RMB400 million (US$60 million) are defined as SMEs, while the remainder are defined as large enterprises. Figure 3.7 shows that the debt ratio of large enterprises decreased slightly, to 57 per cent, in 2013 from 61 per cent in 1998, whereas that of SMEs saw decreased sharply to 51 per cent in 2013 from 65 per cent in 1998. That is, the debt ratio of SMEs decreased significantly.

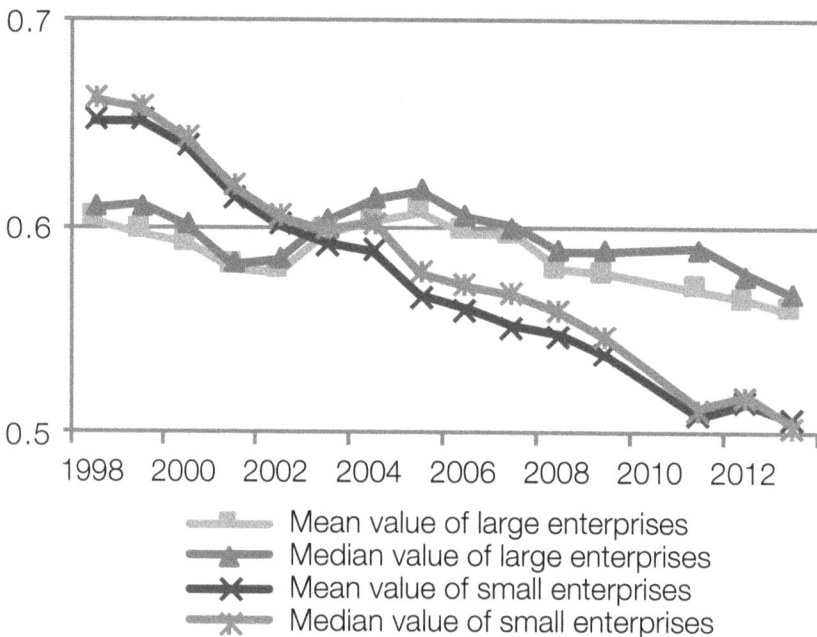

Legend:
- Mean value of large enterprises
- Median value of large enterprises
- Mean value of small enterprises
- Median value of small enterprises

Figure 3.7 Debt ratio: Classified by enterprise scale
Source: NBS (various years).

Fact 3: The decreasing range of the debt ratio in heavy industrial enterprises was generally much smaller than that of light industrial ones; and the average debt ratio of public utility enterprises was on the rise

Fact 3 is the conclusion drawn by grouping the whole sample according to the industry of the enterprise. We divide the sample companies into 39 groups according to the two-digit industry classification number in the national economy. Because of the large number of industry groups, we do not report the results individually. In general, the debt ratio of heavy industrial enterprises saw a much smaller decline than that of light industrial enterprises. Figure 3.8 reports the debt ratio of several typical industries. For example, the debt ratio in the coal mining and washing industries fell to 58 per cent in 2013 from 61 per cent in 1998, and farm and sideline food-processing industries saw their debt ratio drop to 44 per cent in 2013 from 72 per cent in 1998. The average debt ratio of public utility enterprises, however, was on the rise. For example, the average debt ratio of water production and supply enterprises rose to 55 per cent in 2013 from 40 per cent in 1998.

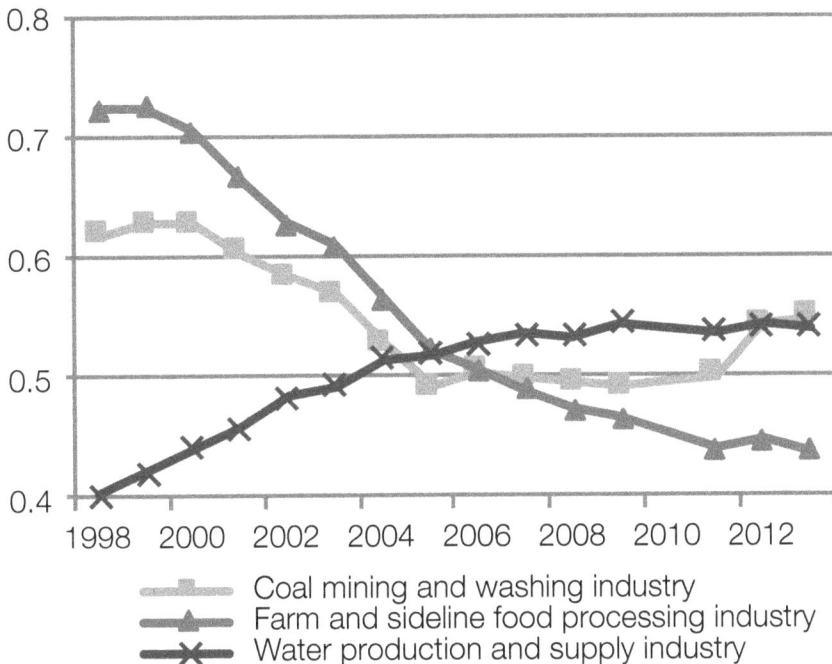

Figure 3.8 Debt ratio: Three typical industries

Source: NBS (various years).

Fact 4: The average debt ratio of enterprises in north-eastern and central China decreased the most, by more than 20 percentage points, whereas that of enterprises in the developed eastern regions was stable

We conclude Fact 4 by dividing the whole sample according to the province in which the enterprise is located. The average debt ratios of enterprises in north-eastern and central areas decreased by 20 percentage points, marking the maximum decline among different regions. Average debt ratios in the north-east, central and western regions were all about 69 per cent in 1998. The ratios declined to 45 per cent in the north-eastern and central regions by 2013 and to 55 per cent in the western region. The average debt ratio in the eastern region dropped by the smallest amount, to 55 per cent from 63 per cent in 1998 (see Figure 3.9). We have also examined the average debt ratio for each province and find six provinces stand out from the others. The average debt ratio in Beijing maintained a relatively stable trend; the ratio in Shanghai and Tianjin declined slightly while the average debt ratios in coastal districts such as Guangdong and Zhejiang increased slightly. Tibet was the only province with a significant increase (see Figure 3.10).

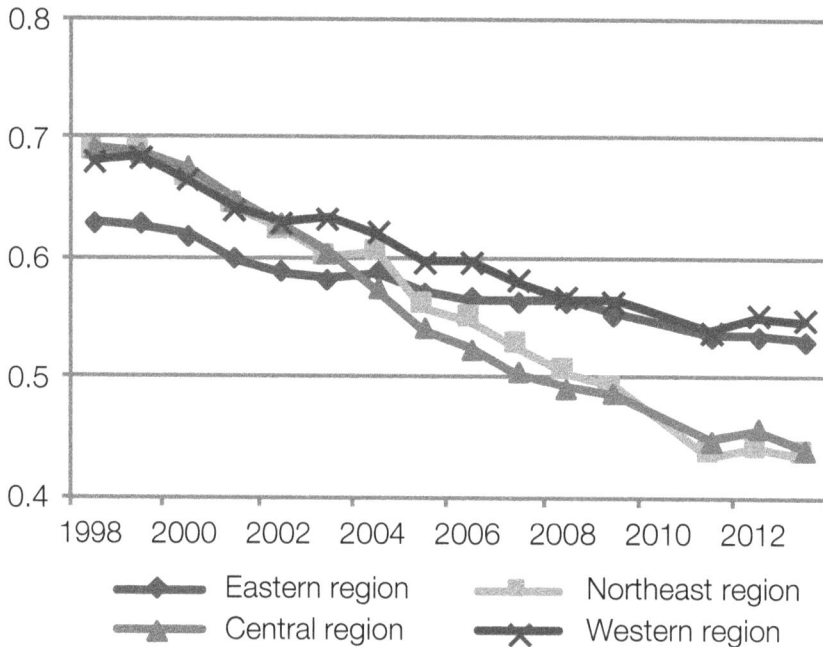

Figure 3.9 Debt ratio: Classified by enterprise region
Source: NBS (various years).

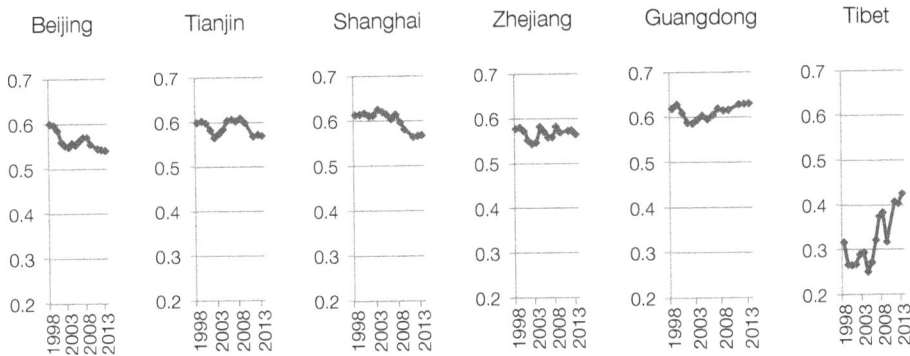

Figure 3.10 Debt ratio: Several special provinces

Source: NBS (various years).

Fact 5: The average debt ratio of SOEs was always higher than that of private enterprises, which was, in turn, higher than that of foreign-funded enterprises. Among all types of enterprises, the average debt ratio of SOEs dropped the most. It is worth noting that the average debt ratio of SOEs in the sample that have existed for a long time was stable and rose after 2009

Fact 5 is the conclusion drawn by grouping the whole sample according to the registration type of enterprises and then examining their average debt ratio.[8] During the period 1998–2013, the average debt ratio of SOEs dropped from 73 per cent to 62 per cent, compared with the decline from 58 per cent to 50 per cent for private enterprises and from 55 per cent to 50 per cent for foreign-funded enterprises (see Figure 3.11). The average debt ratio of SOEs has always been significantly higher than that in the private sector, while that in the private sector is generally higher than for foreign-funded enterprises.[9] In addition, it is worth noting that it is becoming increasingly difficult for private enterprises to borrow money, and this trend seems to have begun earlier, in 2004, not after the GFC.[10]

---

8   The state-owned group includes SOEs, state-owned joint enterprises, state and collectively owned enterprises and wholly SOEs. The private sector includes privately owned enterprises, private partnership enterprises, private-limited enterprises and enterprises limited by shares. The foreign-funded sector includes joint ventures, cooperative enterprises, Hong Kong–owned, Macau-owned and Taiwan-owned enterprises and Hong Kong, Macau and Taiwan Investment Co. Ltd (if the investors from Hong Kong, Macau and Taiwan gain an investment ratio of more than 25 per cent), and Sino–foreign cooperative ventures, Sino–foreign joint ventures, wholly foreign-owned enterprises and foreign investment companies (if the proportion of foreign investment exceeds 25 per cent). The mixed sector includes collective enterprises, joint stock limited enterprises (domestic capital) and other enterprises.

9   Regarding this result, Li et al. (2009) provide a careful discussion based on the dataset from the 2000–03 industrial census.

10 Of course, the GFC significantly affected the private sector's exports and reduced its profitability, thereby enhancing the demand for external funds. This makes the issue of private financing constraints more prominent.

Figure 3.11 also suggests that the decline in the debt ratio of SOEs was the largest during the period 1998–2013. However, a more interesting result about the correlation between ownership and firm capital structure is shown in Figure 3.12. By narrowing the sample to stable enterprises that existed in the database between 1998 and 2013 (that is, in existence over 15 years), we find the debt ratio of stable SOEs rose to 62 per cent in 2013 from 59 per cent in 1998, whereas the debt ratios of stable firms with other types of ownership were all declining.

Also noteworthy is the division within the state-owned sector in terms of access to loans. The average debt ratio of SOEs as a whole has decreased significantly, whereas only a small number among them has increased sharply. Based on this result, the reform of SOEs that was implemented in the past few decades seems to have broken the soft budgetary constraints of small and medium-sized SOEs. However, large SOEs still have easier access to capital, which could be the result of a policy—namely, 'managing the big, liberating the small'—taken by the Chinese central government since the late 1990s.

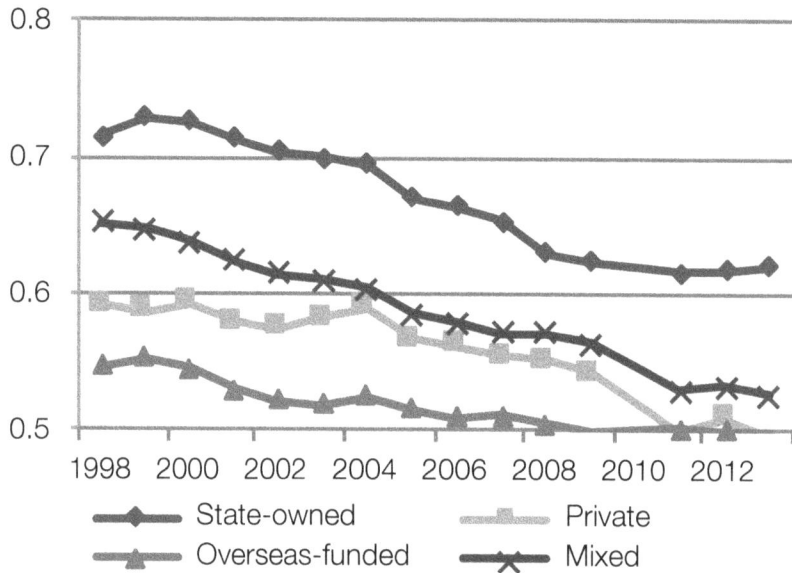

Figure 3.11 Debt ratio: Classified by ownership
Source: NBS (various years).

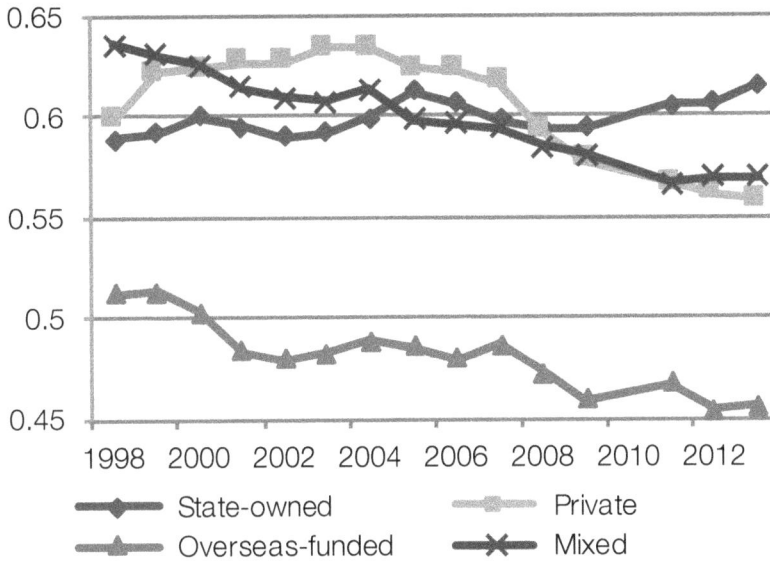

Figure 3.12 Debt ratio: Stable and persistent enterprises grouped according to ownership

Source: NBS (various years).

Fact 6: The average debt ratio of listed manufacturing enterprises was on the rise and surpassed that of unlisted companies after 2009

Finally, we put the debt ratios of listed and unlisted firms into one figure to conclude Fact 6. We use listed manufacturing companies that are traded on the main board of China's stock market, which is the only board that existed before 2004. The contrast is obvious for both the level and the trend of debt (see Figure 3.13). In 1998, the average debt ratio of listed manufacturing companies was 39 per cent. This amount is not unusual, because listed firms raise money through equity financing, and thus their proportion of debt financing is usually lower than that of unlisted firms.[11] However, a more important finding is that whereas the average debt ratio of unlisted manufacturing companies is declining, that of listed manufacturing companies has continued to rise and has reached 55 per cent, exceeding that of unlisted manufacturing enterprises since 2009.[12]

---

11 Huang and Song (2006) compare the debt ratio of listed companies in China with that of other countries. They find that the total debt ratio and long-term debt ratio of listed companies in China are significantly lower, while the proportion of equity financing is significantly higher. They suggest one of the reasons for this is the high valuation of listed companies in China. Some related literature (such as Chen 2004) proposes that one of the characteristics of the financing in Chinese listed companies is that equity financing has priority over bond financing.

12 The rise of the debt ratio in Chinese listed companies during this period is mentioned in some of the literature, such as Huang and Song (2006). The explanation they give is the development of the bond market. Nevertheless, they (along with other researchers) do not dig deeply into the analysis of this phenomenon.

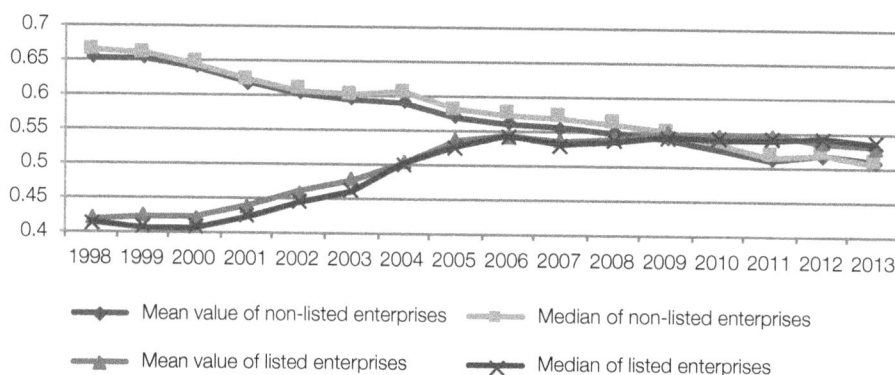

Figure 3.13 The opposing tendencies of debt ratios in listed and unlisted firms
Source: NBS (various years).

Is leveraging supported by economic fundamentals? Evidence from microlevel data

Changes in important firm characteristics

After describing the heterogeneous changes in the corporate debt ratio in China, we examine whether these changes are consistent with the changes in the characteristics of the enterprises. Hence, we focus on four key features of enterprises that are commonly tested in the literature on Western capital structure (see Rajan and Zingales 1995; Frank and Goyal 2003), including operational risk (volatility of profit), proportion of tangible assets, profitability and firm scale. Referring to previous research on the capital structure of Chinese enterprises (for example, Wu and Yue 2009), we also examine tax rates and nondebt tax shields. The changes in these six aspects over the period 1998–2013 are reported in Figures 3.14 to 3.19. As these six factors are the major dependent variables in the regressions reported later, we do not report their summary statistics, which have been provided in the figures.

What needs to be explained is as follows.

Our intention in this section is to explore whether changes in debt ratios are consistent with the changes of firm characteristics rather than to set up causal relationships. To demonstrate the causal relationships between various enterprise factors and the debt ratio probably requires exogenous shocks and well-designed identifications. The evidence provided in this chapter is mainly the correlation and therefore is relatively preliminary. Furthermore, our conclusion relies more on the results of the fixed-effects regression in the 'Regression analysis' subsection rather than the descriptive analysis in this subsection.

The two mainstream capital structure theories—pecking order theory and trade-off theory—offer different predictions for the relationships between these variables and the debt ratio. We do not elaborate here due to space limitations.

Given a positive or negative relationship between a factor and the debt ratio, different interpretations can be presented based on different theories. In this section, we provide only one explanation, which we consider to be the most intuitive, avoiding more detailed discussions intended to distinguish between different theories, which would take much more space.

Analysing changes in these characteristics is, in itself, important for understanding the overall economic transformation that has taken place in China during this period. However, the focus of this chapter is on discussing whether these changes in time-series are consistent with the change in debt ratios. As for the reasons behind the changes, we offer only speculation that should not be regarded as rigorous analyses or conclusions.

Operational risk

We first examine the changes in operational risk, measured by the company's standard deviation of the return on assets (ROA) over the past three years. This risk continued to rise after the late 1990s, soaring further in 2008, and then declining slightly (see Figure 3.14). The overall increase in this risk is due in part to the intense competition in China's domestic product market and also because Chinese enterprises are becoming more involved in international market competition. Fierce competition makes it increasingly difficult for an individual enterprise to control the market and maintain a stable profit margin. Fluctuations in profits thereby enhance the uncertainty of future cash flows, which in turn reduce the probability of enterprises being able to obtain external funds. Therefore, the increase in operational risk may be one reason for the overall decline in the debt ratio.

Furthermore, Figure 3.14 also suggests that the less time a company has existed, the greater is the increase in operational risk. For example, the operational risk of enterprises that existed continuously for more than three years rose from 4.9 per cent in 2000 to more than 10 per cent in 2011; however, the risk for firms existing for more than 11 years changed by a much smaller margin. The reason may be that the less time an enterprise exists, the greater is the probability it will be withdrawn from the sample, indicating that the enterprise has a greater risk of bankruptcy and greater probability of default, which also reduces the probability of obtaining external financing. Therefore, Figure 3.14 is consistent with Fact 1, which we observed in Figure 3.6—that is, the less time a firm exists in the sample, the greater is the decline in its debt ratio.

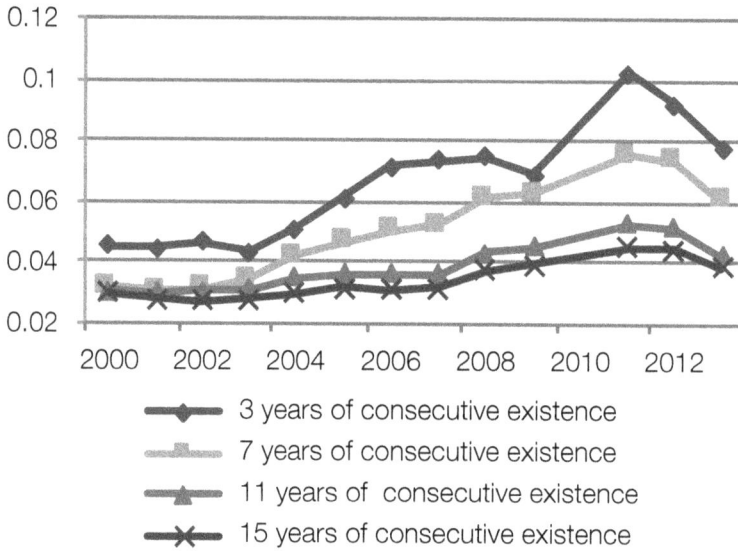

Figure 3.14 Operational risk: Classified by years of consecutive existence
Source: NBS (various years).

Proportion of tangible assets

The proportion of tangible assets—that is, the sum of net fixed assets and net inventories—in the total assets of Chinese enterprises declined from 63 per cent in 1998 to about 48 per cent in 2013, representing a decrease of 15 percentage points in total (see Figure 3.15). The ratio of fixed assets to total assets and the proportion of inventories fell by about 9 and 6 percentage points, respectively.

The decline in the proportion of fixed assets in enterprises is an important manifestation of China's economic transformation, indicating that the mode of firms' production is changing towards greater consistency with their comparative advantages. More specifically, they moved away from a capital-intensive mode during the planned economy period, which violated comparative advantages, to a labour-intensive mode (see Lin et al. 1998). The reasons for the decline in inventories are more complicated, possibly due to improvements in logistics or the decline of expected future demand.

Both fixed assets and inventories can be used as collateral for debt financing, so the scale of tangible assets is an important factor in determining the financing ability of an enterprise. The higher the proportion of tangible assets, the lower is the degree of information asymmetry between the enterprises and the banks—thereby, the stronger the borrowing ability a firm has, the easier it will be to obtain debt financing. So, the significant decrease in the proportion of tangible assets in Chinese enterprises in the period 1998–2013 is also likely to be an important reason for the overall decline in the debt ratio.[13]

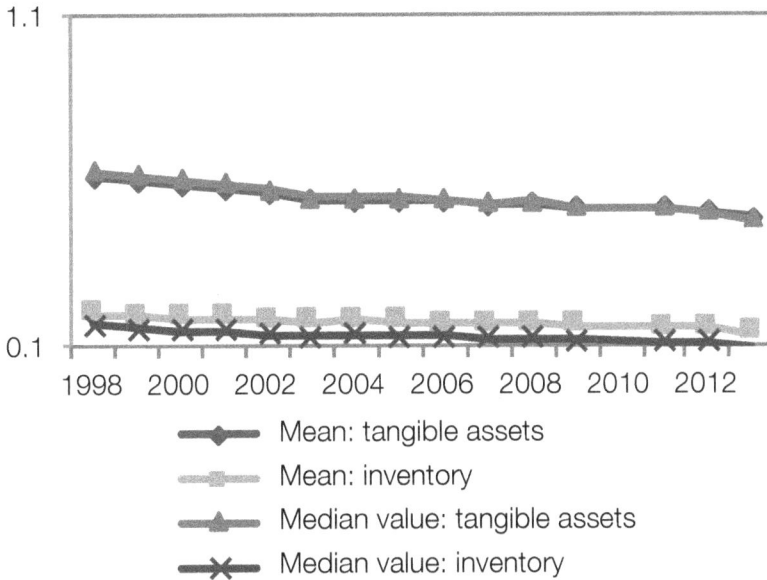

Figure 3.15 The proportion of tangible assets in Chinese enterprises
Source: NBS (various years).

Profitability

Figure 3.16 depicts the sales profit margin—that is, total profit/main business revenue—in four groups of enterprises classified by ownership. The profit margin of all types of enterprises in China continued to rise as a whole and reached a peak by 2011, after which it began to decline slightly. In terms of ownership, the average profit margin of SOEs rose from –1 per cent in 1998 to more than 3 per cent in 2011, whereas that of private enterprises was always the highest among the four categories; it started at less than 3 per cent in 1998 and rose to more than 6 per cent in 2011.

---

13 The changes in tangible assets can also explain Fact 3—that the debt ratio of typical heavy industrial enterprises is lower than that of typical light industrial enterprises in Figure 3.6. This may be due to the fact that the proportion of fixed assets of heavy industrial enterprises has declined by a relatively small margin. In addition, Figure 3.3 shows that the decline in the long-term debt ratio is even greater. Compared with short-term liabilities, long-term liabilities require a higher level of collateral. Bhabra et al. (2008) examine the capital structure of Chinese listed companies in different industries and find that capital-intensive firms such as those in manufacturing and utilities have more long-term debt. Therefore, the decline in tangible assets may also be an important reason.

An increase in the level of profitability means more internal funds, which reduces the need for external financing. Therefore, the continuous rising average profit margin in Chinese enterprises may also be one of the reasons for the overall decline in the debt ratio. Furthermore, the increase in the profit margin of SOEs is most significant among the four groups, which is consistent with the largest drop in their debt ratio, observed in Figure 3.11.

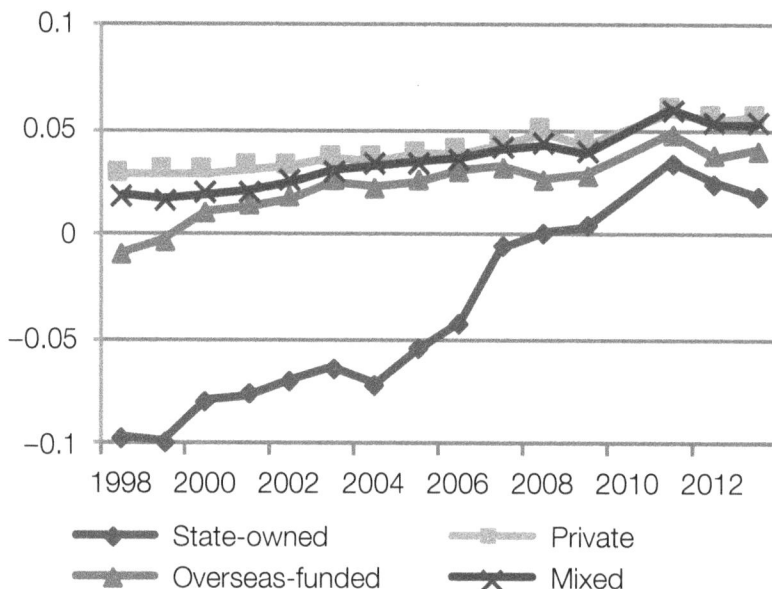

Figure 3.16 Sales profit margin: Enterprises grouped according to ownership
Source: NBS (various years).

Size

Figure 3.17 shows the size of four groups of enterprises, which is measured by the natural logarithm of total assets. The scale of Chinese enterprises as a whole was increasing—in particular, SOEs increased their average size by nearly 20 times from 1998 to 2013. Generally, the larger a company is, the lower is its probability of bankruptcy and the higher is its debt ratio. Therefore, the change in scale does not seem to explain the decline in the overall debt ratio of Chinese enterprises.

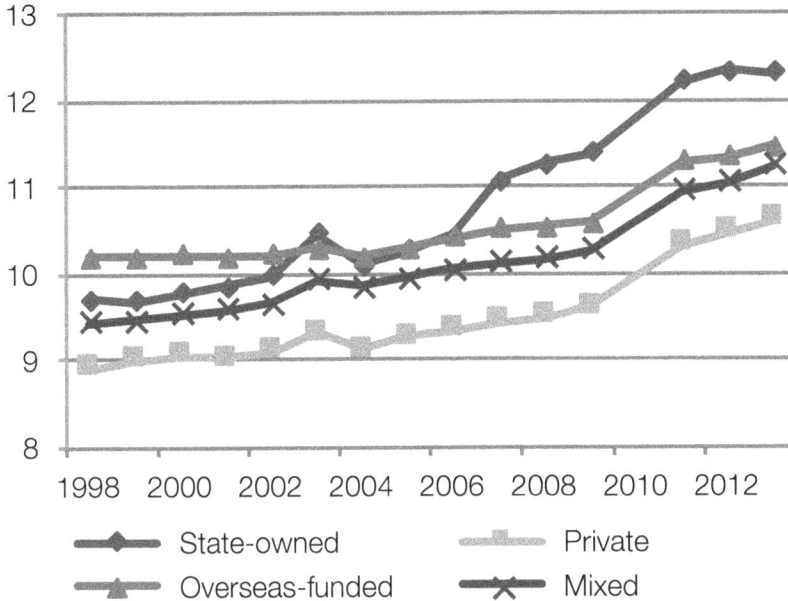

Figure 3.17 Size: Enterprises grouped according to ownership
Source: NBS (various years).

Tax rate

According to Western literature, the tax rate is an important factor in determining the capital structure of enterprises. Wu and Yue (2009) examine Chinese listed companies and find that change in taxation can lead to a change in the debt ratio. Enterprises should pay interest on debt financing and these expenses reduce their pre-tax profits, thereby reducing income tax. Thus, debt financing can offset part of the tax, which acts as a tax shield, and is the main benefit of debt described by the trade-off theory.

Figure 3.18 displays the income tax rate (income tax payable/total profit) of sample enterprises.[14] It shows that the average income tax rate of the whole sample rose during the period 1998–2013. At the same time, we also notice that a certain proportion of the sample enterprises have a negative rate. To eliminate the influence of these enterprises, we then calculate the tax rate for those enterprises with a positive level of income tax payable (see Figure 3.18). This shows that the average tax rate for this group of companies stabilised at 27 per cent before 2006, and then decreased sharply in 2007 and 2008, after which it stabilised again, at about 22 per cent.

---

14 Strictly speaking, the actual income tax rate (income tax expenses/total profit) should be used here. However, this index is not available in the dataset for Chinese industrial firms, so we could only approximate it with the total income tax payable. In addition, income tax expenses include current income tax payable and deferred income tax.

In short, it shows that there was no significant decrease in the level of tax that could be shielded by debt, so the change in taxation does not appear to be the main reason for the declining debt ratio.

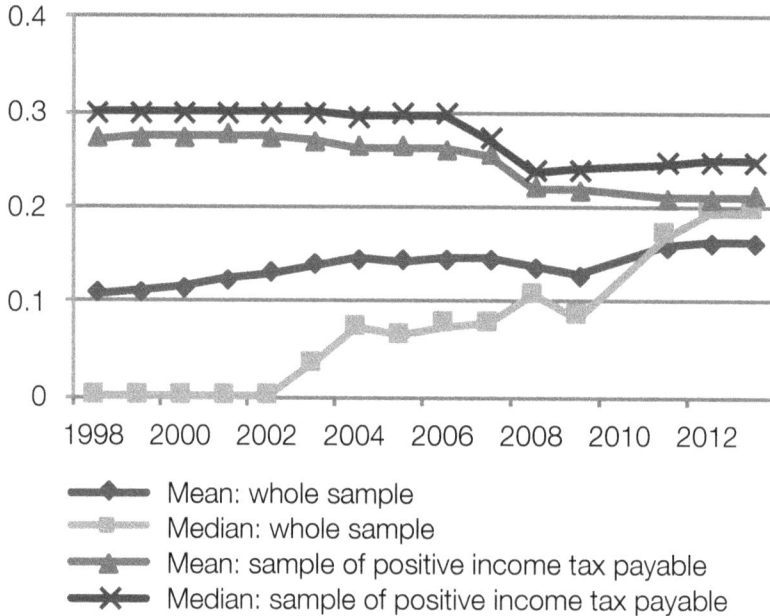

Figure 3.18 Income tax rate of Chinese enterprises
Source: NBS (various years).

Nondebt tax shield

Like tax shields, depreciation can also reduce the pre-tax profits of an enterprise, thereby reducing the tax payable; hence, it is called a nondebt tax shield, which has a substitute relationship with the debt tax shield and is measured by (depreciation/main operating revenue). It shows that the nondebt tax shields of the sample enterprises have dropped significantly as a whole (see Figure 3.19), which is consistent with the continuous decline in the proportion of fixed assets that we reported earlier and which should increase the incentive for companies to use debt shields to avoid taxation. According to Figures 3.18 and 3.19, the motivation for Chinese enterprises to use debt to avoid tax expenses has not been reduced, so tax considerations are not the main reason for the sharp decline in the debt ratio of Chinese enterprises.

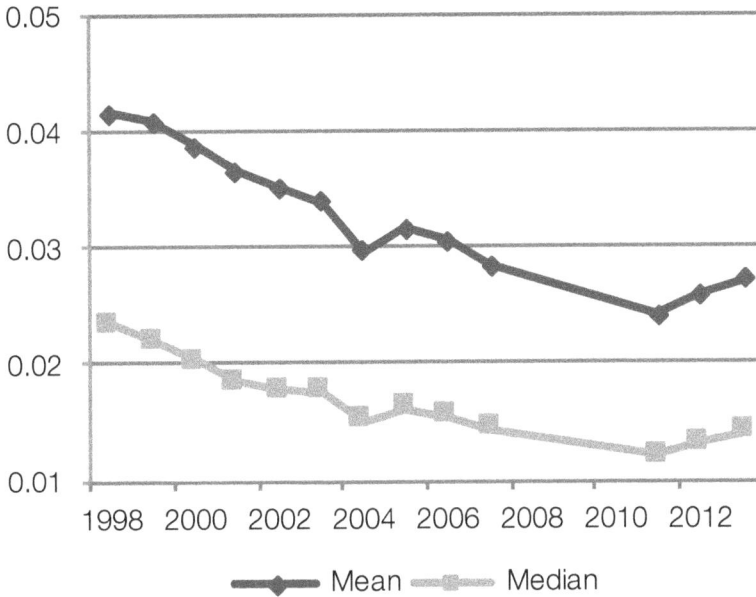

Figure 3.19 Nondebt tax shields of Chinese enterprises
Source: NBS (various years).

Regression analysis: Enterprise characteristics and debt ratio

Our analyses indicate that the overall decline in Chinese companies' debt ratio may be due in part to the significant changes in the main characteristics of these enterprises, especially their operational risk, profitability and proportion of tangible assets. We use regression analysis to examine more rigorously the relationship between these characteristic variables and the debt ratio.

The explained variable *TotLev* in Table 3.1 is the debt ratio of each enterprise in the current year. We further control the debt ratio in the previous year (L. *TotLev*), based on the existence of the 'optimal debt ratio' ($Levt_t^*$), which is indicated by the trade-off theory. It means that if the previous year's debt ratio ($Levt_{t-1}$) deviates from the optimal one, enterprises will adjust the actual debt ratio (Lev_t) to the optimal level in the current period, which is described by Equation 3.1.

Equation 3.1

$$Lev_t - Lev_{t-1} = \lambda(Lev_t^* - Lev_{t-1}) + \varepsilon_t$$

Table 3.1 Debt ratios of various enterprises in China: Benchmark regression

Variables	(1) All	(2) State	(3) Private	(4) Foreign
L.TotLev	0.269***	0.365***	0.194***	0.314***
	(0.002)	(0.006)	(0.003)	(0.004)
L.STDROA	−0.028***	0.017	−0.046***	0.025**
	(0.005)	(0.021)	(0.006)	(0.010)
L.Size	0.003***	−0.004*	0.005***	0.010***
	(0.001)	(0.002)	(0.001)	(0.001)
L.Tng	0.010***	0.003	0.004**	0.027***
	(0.001)	(0.005)	(0.002)	(0.003)
L.Npr	−0.158***	−0.088***	−0.184***	−0.168***
	(0.003)	(0.005)	(0.006)	(0.006)
L.tax	−0.020***	−0.028***	−0.015***	−0.029***
	(0.001)	(0.003)	(0.002)	(0.003)
Nonpositive*L.tax	0.056***	0.043***	0.065***	0.043***
	(0.004)	(0.008)	(0.006)	(0.010)
Observations	1,203,426	159,188	675,955	288,118
R-squared	0.825	0.879	0.821	0.818
Number of firm FE	328,727	47,290	212,433	70,412
Year dummies	YES	YES	YES	YES
Province*Year dummies	YES	YES	YES	YES
Industry*Year dummies	YES	YES	YES	YES

*** Statistically significant at the 1 per cent level
** Statistically significant at the 5 per cent level
* Statistically significant at the 10 per cent level
Note: Standard errors are in parentheses.

Here, λ is used to measure the speed of adjustment to the optimal level, depending on the characteristics of the enterprises and the macro situation (see Cook and Tang 2010). A more detailed explanation of this formula can be found in Flannery and Rangan (2006). The econometric model we use is the fixed-effect regression model. Because the debt ratio of the previous period is controlled, there may be a problem of first-order autocorrelation. However, Flannery and Rangan (2006) carefully examine various econometric models and conclude that sequence-related problems are not serious (see p. 479), whereas it is necessary to control the firm fixed effects and the annual dummy variables. Therefore, we refer to their study as well as follow-up ones (including Cook and Tang 2010) and use the ordinary fixed-effect regression model. The number of firm fixed effects controlled by each regression is reported in Table 3.1—for example, 328,727 different enterprises are included in the full-sample regression. It is worth noting that because we control the variable *STDROA*, the sample firms that are included in the regression should have existed for at least three consecutive years.

We also control a set of dummy variables, including the annual ones (15 in total), (province × year) (465 in total) and (industry × year) (570 in total). Using these dummy variables and the firm fixed effects, we control not only the effects of certain fixed characteristics of the enterprises (such as the ownership type or political connections) on the debt ratio, but also the regional factors that affect the adjustment of the corporate debt ratio in each province every year (for example, the overall credit situation of each province in that year), as well as industrial factors (for example, the prosperity of each industry in that year). In addition, the set of (industry × year) being controlled in the regressions equals the average annual debt ratio of each industry being controlled. Frank and Goyal (2009) find that the average debt ratio of an industry has a reliable and stable explanatory power over the corporate debt ratio. By controlling these groups of dummy variables, we try to minimise various endogenous issues between enterprise characteristics and the debt ratio. Firm characteristics are lagged by one period to reduce the reverse causalities between these variables and the debt ratio. Because of the control of these firm characteristics and many dummy variables, the R^2 of the regressions are all above 80 per cent.

The results using the full sample are reported in Column (1), while Columns (2), (3) and (4) report the results using the subsample of state-owned, private and foreign-funded enterprises, respectively.[15] Our findings are as follows: 1) the coefficient of L.*TotLev* is $(1 - \lambda)$, which means that the adjustment speed of private enterprises $(1 - 0.194)$ is higher than that of SOEs $(1 - 0.365)$; 2) the variable of *STDROA* is the standard deviation of ROA over the past three years, which is significantly negative in both the full sample and private enterprises, whereas it is not significant in the sample of SOEs; 3) *Size* is measured by the logarithm of total assets and is significantly positive in the full sample and for private enterprises, while being negative in the sample of SOEs (significance at the 10 per cent level); 4) as for the proportion of tangible assets to the total assets, *Tng* is significantly positive in the full sample and for private enterprises, but not significant in the sample of SOEs; 5) *Npr* represents the sales profit margin and is negative in all sets of samples, while its magnitude in the private enterprises sample is more than twice the effect for SOEs.

In sum, in the private sector, the relationships between these four variables and the debt ratio are consistent with the findings in the Western literature. The results in Columns (1) – (4) indicate that the financing decisions in Chinese private enterprises

---

15 There is also a type of enterprise with mixed ownership; because of the unclear ownership and space limitations, we do not report the relative results.

are more in line with those made by Western companies—in other words, they are more market-oriented. Nevertheless, only the result for the sales profit margin coincides with the Western empirical findings in the sample of Chinese SOEs.

In addition to these four factors, we divide the sample into two groups according to whether the enterprise's income tax payable is positive in the previous period. Thus, one group includes those enterprises with a positive tax rate (nonpositive = 0) and the other includes those with a negative rate (nonpositive = 1). In the group with a positive tax rate, the variable of L.*Tax* that represents the tax rate in the previous period is negatively correlated with the debt ratio, and the negative effect in the sample of SOEs is even greater. In the other group, because the tax rate itself is nonpositive and the estimated value of L.*Tax* is positive, the actual effect is also negative. Briefly stated, for Chinese enterprises, the higher the income tax rate in the previous period, the lower is the debt ratio in the later period. This seems to indicate that Chinese industrial enterprises do not deliberately add liabilities to reduce taxation, which is contrary to the conclusions obtained from the existing literature examining China's listed companies, including Huang and Song (2006) and Wu and Yue (2009). This issue is worth studying more carefully.

Through this analysis, we draw a preliminary conclusion that the financing decisions of some enterprises—most of which are private enterprises—are in accordance with the principle of marketisation. Meanwhile, the financing decisions of other enterprises—most of which are SOEs—contain many nonmarket factors. The financing behaviours of these enterprises lack support from the economic fundamentals. In other words, these firms have borrowed too much, which is not ideal because they must carry a high interest burden.

We have also examined Chinese listed companies to provide further evidence supporting our conclusions. According to our calculations, in 2015, there were more than 160 listed SOEs that did not have enough profits to cover their interest expenses (see Figure 3.20). What is worse, these enterprises had to borrow more money to repay the capital and interest; as a result, more and more debt is accumulated. We found that, from 2010 to 2015, the total liabilities of these 160 enterprises rose from RMB980 billion (US$145 billion) to RMB1.68 trillion (US$270 billion). In other words, the 160 enterprises in deficit borrowed RMB700 billion (US$130 billion) in additional debt during this period. This also means the debt ratio of these enterprises is so high that it leads to heavy interest burdens. It is worth noting that our estimates are consistent with the estimates made in 2016 by Wang and Zhong (2016)—that the proportion of nonfinancial companies listed on the main stock market board that had lower earnings before interest and tax than interest expenses was 11.7 per cent in the first half of 2015. This means that 160 to 200 large Chinese listed firms, most of which are state-owned, did not have enough profit to pay their interest.

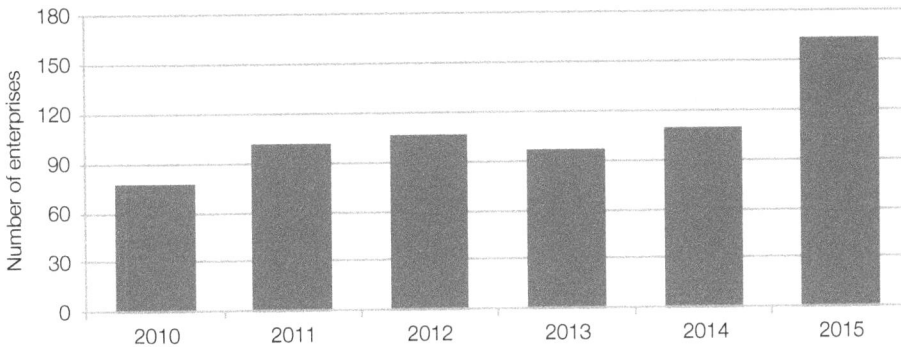

Figure 3.20 SOEs with heavy interest burdens

Source: CSMAR and authors' calculation.

Is leveraging supported by economic fundamentals? Evidence from aggregate-level data

In this section, we provide more evidence regarding who should be deleveraging and who should be leveraging. As shown in Figure 3.21, the state-owned sector as a whole continuously increased its leverage after 2008, as its average debt ratio rose from 59 per cent in 2008 to 62 per cent by 2016. Moreover, the total debt of the state-owned sector continues to rise. According to data released by the Ministry of Finance, by November 2017, the total liabilities of the Chinese state-owned sector reached RMB100 trillion (US$15.1 trillion). Among them, the total liabilities of the central SOEs were RMB51.5 trillion (US$7.8 trillion)—soaring by nearly 9.6 per cent compared with a year earlier—while those of local SOEs were RMB48.5 trillion (US$7.3 trillion), contributing to 12.3 per cent of year-on-year growth. The private sector has been deleveraging sharply, with the average debt ratio of private industrial enterprises falling from 56 per cent in 2008 to 50.7 per cent in 2016 (see Figure 3.21). In other words, the private sector has been deleveraging for more than a decade.

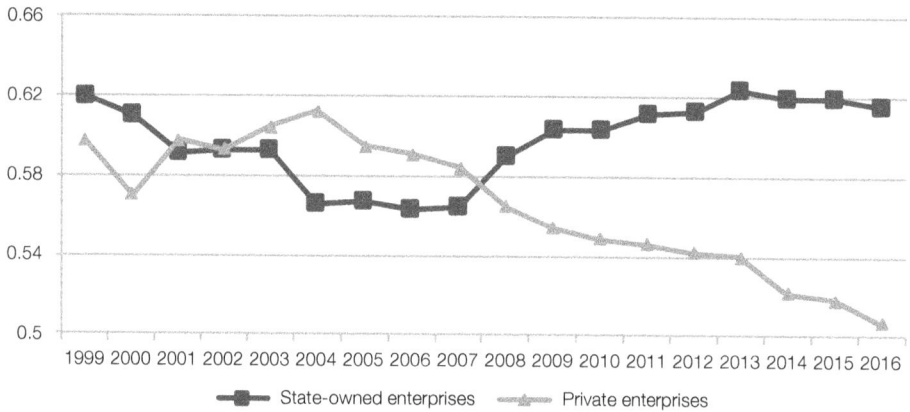

Figure 3.21 The average debt ratio: State-owned versus private enterprises
Source: NBS.

On the other hand, until recently, private industrial enterprises contributed nearly 40 per cent of the total profit of all industrial enterprises, whereas their liabilities accounted for only 20 per cent of the total (see Figure 3.22). This means that the financial resources used by the private sector are far below their economic contribution. In contrast, SOEs contributed less than 20 per cent of the total profit of all industrial enterprises, while their liabilities accounted for more than 40 per cent of the total.

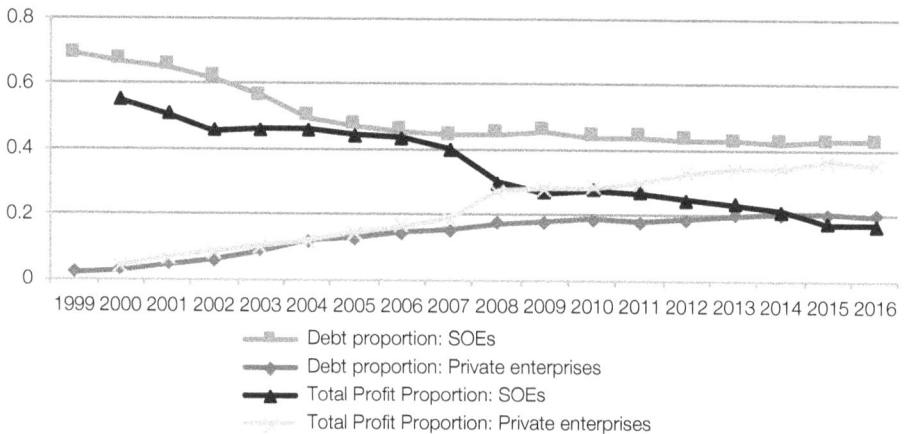

Figure 3.22 The contrast in total profit: State-owned versus private enterprises
Source: NBS.

It is worth mentioning that this gap between financial support and economic contribution is consistent with another important phenomenon arising after the GFC—that is, SOEs widely participated in various kinds of shadow banking activities. For example, using the data on entrusted loans published by the Shanghai

Stock Exchange and the Shenzhen Stock Exchange, Zhang et al. (2015) estimate that SOEs made 75 per cent of entrusted loans in 2013. This means these firms did not have good investment opportunities themselves but borrowed a substantial amount of money at a low cost from the financial system and then made loans to those companies that could not borrow from the formal financial system, at higher interest-rate-to-gain margins. Moreover, according to reports in the *Financial Times* on 16 August 2016, large Chinese SOEs were increasingly involved in entrusted loans when facing a downturn in their core business. The total stock of China's entrusted loans reached RMB12 trillion (US$1.8 trillion) in June 2016, increasing by 70 per cent since early 2014. In addition, entrusted loans became the fastest growing area of China's shadow banking industry. All these data prove that Chinese SOEs have borrowed too much money. Their debt ratio is too high and greatly beyond their ability to repay.

Therefore, to improve the efficiency of credit allocation, the first thing we should do is overcome the 'polarity' in financing activities between the state-owned and private sectors dating from 2008, so that the financial support to and economic contribution of the various sectors is roughly equal.

Conclusions and policy discussions

Recently, the demographic dividend that drove China's rapid economic growth over the past decades has been rapidly exhausted. Because of the family planning policies that began in the early 1980s, China's population will age rapidly in the next few years. If China wants to maintain high-speed economic growth in the ensuing period, it should first rely on the optimal allocation of capital, encouraging the efficient use of machinery and equipment, to increase the marginal output of the existing labour force. Second, China should rely on continuous innovation to move closer to the global technological frontier. To realise these two goals, the efficient allocation of resources in China's financial system is crucial. More specifically, can finance be allocated to enterprises with high efficiency and real productivity and to those early projects with innovative potential to support their development?

As mentioned at the beginning of this chapter, after 2008, the efficiency of credit in China declined significantly. One important reason for this is that those inefficient enterprises are receiving large amounts of funds. This constrains investment and innovation in the healthy and efficient enterprises and inhibits new enterprises from entering the industry. Furthermore, the phenomenon of 'finance does not support entities' has become more serious and, ultimately, has led to the inefficiency of the economy.

On the other hand, China's overall debt ratio has been rising continually; as a result, the pressure for deleveraging is increasing. Should the economy be deleveraged and, if so, how should we do it? Based on analysis of a dataset containing nearly 4 million above-scale Chinese industrial enterprises during the period 1998–2013, we attempted to provide some preliminary evidence to answer these questions. We focused on the following two issues.

First, the overall debt ratio of nonfinancial enterprises in China is at a high level, but where is the leveraging exactly? We find that most industrial enterprises were significantly deleveraged during the 16-year period, while only a small number of large, state-owned and listed enterprises increased their leveraging. Second, is the change in the debt ratio supported by the economic fundamentals? For this question, we first examine the changes in some key characteristics of the sample enterprises and find that the overall decline in the debt ratio is consistent with significant changes in certain characteristics, including an increase in operational risk and profitability, as well as a decline in the proportion of tangible assets. We further find in the regression analysis that the determination of the debt ratio in private enterprises basically accords with the findings in the Western literature; in contrast, SOEs are including fewer 'market-oriented' factors in their financial decision-making.

As for whether to deleverage and how to deleverage in China, our research is still preliminary. Nevertheless, the results and analysis in this chapter indicate that a complete answer should include at least two parts. First, for enterprises whose financial decision-making is consistent with the principle of marketisation (mainly private enterprises), sufficient capital supply should be ensured so the economic fundamentals support these enterprises obtaining adequate funds. Second, as for another group of enterprises, whose leveraging determinants contain more 'nonmarket' factors (mainly SOEs), funding 'transfusions' for such inefficient objects should be suspended, so that new loans can be allocated to the most efficient enterprises. Based on these results, we also have two specific suggestions for real implementation.

First, China's high rate of leveraging is a structural issue, with a large amount of debt concentrated in a few enterprises. In this case, a general and unified monetary policy—whether it is tight or loose—can be inefficient, and may even increase the severity of existing mismatches. The problem is not whether monetary policy should be loosened or tightened; rather, the transmission of monetary policy in China's financial system is seriously biased: credits are not allocated to those 'healthy' enterprises that need capital urgently. Therefore, effective policies must gradually correct the inefficiency of existing financial intermediaries, especially the allocation of funds in the banking system, and weaken the power of non-marketisation.

Second, for those SOEs that are inefficient and in deficit, debt is a 'stock', but new loans are 'flows', which should not be used to solve the stock problem. Paying off old debts with new loans can only lead to a rapid accumulation of total liabilities. According to the estimations from Wang and Zhong (2016), in 2015, between RMB1.5 trillion (US$240 billion) and RMB2 trillion (US$320 billion) of total new debt was used to repay previous interest expenses, which is equivalent to around 10 per cent of total new credit in that year. We suggest the problem of debt as stock should be settled by, for example, selling a portion of state-owned assets to repay debt, while restructuring the enterprises in deficit to enhance their capability.

For those enterprises with negative net assets, in particular, shutting down, suspending, merging or transforming them will increase the value of total state-owned assets rather than devaluing them. The point of selling assets is, in fact, to identify opportunities in the market to make full use of these assets. If these assets can be fully utilised, it will benefit the entire economy. With the current high debt ratio in China, new credit is a particularly valuable resource that needs to be used wisely and cautiously. Moreover, the allocation efficiency of incremental credits is directly related to China's medium and long-term potential economic growth.

To summarise, the high levels of leveraging in China are a structural issue that require 'structural' policies to be resolved. On the one hand, deleveraging is not right for most enterprises, but it is for inefficient areas, especially a few thousand highly leveraged firms. The main battlefield for deleveraging is the state-owned sector, especially inefficient and large enterprises, which usually have severe overcapacity. Thus, the Chinese Government should promote market-oriented reform of SOEs as well as a policy of 'shutting down, suspending, merging and transforming' firms to realise the goal of 'distinct property rights, well-defined power and responsibility, separation of government and enterprises, and scientific management', as proposed by the Third Plenary Session of the Fourteenth Central Committee more than two decades ago.

On the other hand, it is equally important to increase leveraging in efficient areas; efficient private enterprises should receive more support via new credit. For that, market-oriented reform of commercial banks and other financial intermediaries in China needs to be promoted further, so that valuable credit resources can be allocated to those enterprises with real productivity and sufficient returns on capital. In sum, the core aim of deleveraging is to keep deepening the reform of the state-owned sector so that new power and vitality can be generated for China's economic growth.

References

Bhabra, H.S., Liu, T. and Tirtiroglu, D. (2008), Capital structure choice in a nascent market: Evidence from listed firms in China, *Financial Management* 37(2): 341–64. doi.org/10.1111/j.1755-053X.2008.00015.x.

Caballero, R.J., Hoshi, T. and Kashyap, A.K. (2008), Zombie lending and depressed restructuring in Japan, *American Economic Review* 98(5): 1943–77. doi.org/10.1257/aer.98.5.1943.

Caixin (2016), Huang Yiping: Cracking down on China's high-leverage trap, *Caixin*, 14 March.

Chen, J.J. (2004), Determinants of capital structure of Chinese listed companies, *Journal of Business Research* 57(12): 1341–51. doi.org/10.1016/S0148-2963(03)00070-5.

Chen, J. and Strange, R. (2005), The determinants of capital structure: Evidence from Chinese listed companies, *Economic Change and Restructuring* 38(1): 11–35. doi.org/10.1007/s10644-005-4521-7.

China Business Journal (2011), The 'Inside Job' of banks in China, and shadow banking prevails, *China Business Journal Online*, available from: www.cb.com.cn/deep/2011_0910/271245_2.html.

China News (2012), Li Yang: Liabilities of Chinese enterprises have exceeded the warning line, *China News*, 18 May.

Cook, D.O. and Tang, T. (2010), Macroeconomic conditions and capital structure adjustment speed, *Journal of Corporate Finance* 16(1): 73–87. doi.org/10.1016/j.jcorpfin.2009.02.003.

Financial Times (2016), Large Chinese enterprises seeking higher returns from entrusted loans, *Financial Times*, 16 August, available from: www.ftchinese.com/story/001068932.

Flannery, M.J. and Rangan, K.P. (2006), Partial adjustment toward target capital structures, *Journal of Financial Economics* 79(3): 469–506. doi.org/10.1016/j.jfineco.2005.03.004.

Frank, M.Z. and Goyal, V.K. (2009), Capital structure decisions: Which factors are reliably important?, *Financial Management* 38(1): 1–37. doi.org/10.1111/j.1755-053X.2009.01026.x.

Frank, M.Z. and Goyal, V.K. (2003), Testing the pecking order theory of capital structure, *Journal of Financial Economics* 67(2): 217–48. doi.org/10.1016/S0304-405X(02)00252-0.

Huang, G. and Song, F.M. (2006), The determinants of capital structure: Evidence from China, *China Economic Review* 17(1): 14–36. doi.org/10.1016/j.chieco.2005.02.007.

Li, K., Yue, H. and Zhao, L. (2009), Ownership, institutions, and capital structure: Evidence from China, *Journal of Comparative Economics* 37(3): 471–90. doi.org/10.1016/j.jce.2009.07.001.

Lin, J.Y., Cai, F. and Li, Z. (1998), Competition, policy burdens, and state-owned enterprise reform, *American Economic Review* 88(2): 422–27.

National Bureau of Statistics of China (NBS) (various years), *Annual Survey of Industrial Enterprises*, Beijing: China Statistics Press.

Newman, A., Gunessee, S. and Hilton, B. (2012), Applicability of financial theories of capital structure to the Chinese cultural context: A study of privately owned SMEs, *International Small Business Journal* 30(1): 65–83. doi.org/10.1177/0266242610370977.

Rajan, R.G. and Zingales, L. (1995), What do we know about capital structure? Some evidence from international data, *Journal of Finance* 50(5): 1421–60. doi.org/10.1111/j.1540-6261.1995.tb05184.x.

Sina Finance (2017), Li Yang's view on de-leveraging: Monetary policy will be tight, *Sina Finance*, 23 September.

Sohu Finance and Economics (2017), Is it true that China's total debt exceeds 200 trillion and is ranked second worldwide?, *Sohu Finance and Economics*, 18 February.

Standard & Poor's (2014), Credit shift: As global corporate borrowers seek $60 trillion, Asia-Pacific debt will overtake US and Europe combined, *RatingsDirect*, June.

Tan, Y., Huang, Y. and Woo, W.T. (2016), Zombie firms and the crowding-out of private investment in China, *Asian Economic Papers* 15(3): 32–55. doi.org/10.1162/ASEP_a_00474.

Wang, T. and Zhong, J. (2016), What are the real problems with China's debt?, *UBS Global Research*, April.

Wu, L. and Yue, H. (2009), Corporate tax, capital structure, and the accessibility of bank loans: Evidence from China, *Journal of Banking & Finance* 33(1): 30–8. doi.org/10.1016/j.jbankfin.2006.10.030.

Zhang, W., Han, G., Ng, B. and Chan, S. (2015), *Corporate leverage in China: Why has it increased fast in recent years and where do the risks lie?*, HKIMR Working Paper No. 10/2015, Hong Kong: Hong Kong Institute for Monetary Research. doi.org/10.2139/ssrn.2597451.

4. A structural investigation of the Chinese economy with a hybrid monetary policy rule

Jiao Wang and Ran Li[1]

Introduction

Since about 2010, China has been experiencing a gradual and persistent slowdown in gross domestic product (GDP) growth, from an average of 10 per cent over the 30 years to 2010 to the latest figure, 6.6 per cent in 2018, making the latter the slowest growth rate for three decades. Chinese President Xi Jinping described this as the 'new normal' for the Chinese economy in May 2014. The slowing of China's economic growth has attracted a great deal of attention from policymakers and scholars. The release of the official data on GDP growth often makes headline news around the world. The seemingly persistent trend of the economic slowdown triggered worries and speculation about further slowing, and even economic collapse, in the future.[2] Given the increasingly important role the Chinese economy plays in the global supply chain and, in particular, in supporting demand for commodities and many intermediate goods from a number of resource-intensive economies including Australia, it is crucial to gain a better understanding of the causes of China's economic slowdown.[3]

What are the sources of China's economic slowdown since 2010? Researchers' answers to this question are diverse. From an international perspective, Eichengreen et al. (2012) show that rapidly growing economies slow significantly when their per capita incomes reach about US$17,000 in year-2005 constant international purchasing power parity (PPP) prices—a level China has recently reached. Their empirical

1   We are grateful to Ippei Fujiwara, Yiping Huang, Adrian Pagan, Peter Drysdale, Paul Kitney, Ligang Song, Shiro Armstrong and two anonymous reviewers for their useful suggestions and comments at various stages of this work. We are also thankful for all the comments and questions received at the Australian Conference of Economists at the Queensland University of Technology and a seminar at the Reserve Bank of Australia. All errors are those of the authors. Jiao Wang is grateful for the financial support of the University of Melbourne Early Career Researcher (ECR) Grant Themis Agreement Number 603760.

2   A separate but related issue to the release of GDP data is the reliability of the numbers released by the National Bureau of Statistics of China. Some argue that the official numbers might have overestimated economic growth, which, if true, would make the slowdown even larger. See, for example, Fernald et al. (2013) and Chen et al. (2019) for arguments for and against, respectively, the reliability of the official data.

3   Cashin et al. (2017) estimated that a 1 per cent permanent negative GDP shock in China could lead to a 0.23 percentage point growth loss in the short run and a surge in global financial market volatility. This could translate into a fall in world economic output of 0.29 per cent overall.

evidence from a sample including industrial and developing and emerging market economies shows that the fall in the productivity growth is the primary contributor to the economic growth slowdown, while the fall in the growth of labour share and capital investment play much smaller roles. The growth rate of human capital, on the other hand, even increased a little, so plays a positive role to economic growth (Eichengreen et al. 2012: 52–3). Cai and Lu (2013) estimate China's average annual growth potential to be 7.2 per cent over the Twelfth Five-Year Plan period and 6.1 per cent over the Thirteenth Five-Year Plan period, and highlight the diminishing demographic dividend as a result of the shrinking working-age population, which was a driver of China's rapid growth before 2010. From a business cycle perspective, there are studies that suggest that the Global Financial Crisis (GFC) was somewhat, if not solely, responsible for accelerating the slowdown process. For example, Gilchrist et al. (2009) argue that there is an evident cyclical component to Chinese growth rate dynamics and the observed slowdown since 2010 could be a temporary phenomenon tightly connected with the downswing phase of this cycle.

In this chapter, we aim to contribute to the discussion by conducting a structural investigation of the Chinese economy to better understand the sources of business fluctuations in China, especially fluctuations in output. There is, however, one puzzle that needs to be solved before we can proceed with the structural investigation. That is the unidentified rule governing China's monetary policy.

According to the Law of the People's Republic of China on the People's Bank of China, 'the objective of the monetary policy shall be to maintain stability of the value of the currency and thereby promote economic growth'. The People's Bank of China (PBC) is by no means an inflation-targeting central bank, like many other modern central banks, and its objectives extend far beyond price stability. As former PBC governor Xiaochuan Zhou has said, China's monetary policy has the following objectives: maintaining price stability, promoting economic growth, supporting employment and achieving a balance-of-payments equilibrium (Zhou 2016). In addition, the 2017 PBC Work Conference called for monetary policy to achieve a balance between economic growth, economic reform, economic structure, household welfare and financial stability (McMahon et al. 2018). Nevertheless, there is no consensus on the form of policy rules the PBC has been employing, let alone whether such rules can achieve their objectives.

Without a well-defined monetary policy rule, it will be difficult to accurately model China's macroeconomy. The transmission mechanism of a monetary policy shock to the economy is uncertain and the effects will be difficult to predict for the central bank. What is the PBC's monetary policy rule? Has the rule changed over time? What do the data say about the monetary policy rules in practice? What are the main sources of business fluctuations in the Chinese economy given what we know about the monetary policy rules? These are the questions this chapter aims to address.

To this end, we extend a standard new Keynesian dynamic stochastic general equilibrium (DSGE) model with financial friction shocks and investment-specific technology shocks to model the Chinese economy. The financial friction mechanism is of the type introduced by Bernanke et al. (1999) to model market imperfections in the financial sector. The investment-specific technology shock was suggested and developed by Greenwood et al. (1988, 1997) as a viable alternative to neutral technology shocks as sources of business cycles. Studies by Kaihatsu and Kurozumi (2014) and Justiniano et al. (2011) find that the financial friction shock and the investment-specific technology shock are important sources of business fluctuations in the United States. There are a number of studies applying DSGE models to the Chinese economy—for example, Xu and Chen (2009), Mehrotra et al. (2013), Yuan and Feng (2014) and Zhang et al. (2014). None of these studies has explicitly taken into account financial friction or shocks to investment.[4] It is reasonable to expect that these factors are significant drivers of China's business fluctuations.

We propose a hybrid form of monetary policy rule for the extended model. Past studies of China's monetary policy tend to make a choice between Taylor-type rules and quantity rules that have been used in studies of advanced economies.[5] For example, Zhang (2009) argues that a Taylor-type rule is likely to be more effective than a quantity-type rule in managing the economy. Liu and Zhang (2010) show that both rules outperform a single rule in a four-equation new Keynesian model.[6] Since there is no consensus on the specific form of the policy rules, we incorporate a general monetary policy rule that encompasses the pure Taylor-type or quantity-type rules for estimations, and let the estimated results using real-time data show which rule best represents China's monetary policy rule.

The main findings of the chapter are as follows. First, the PBC employed a hybrid monetary policy rule during the period 2001–17, during which the policy rate was adjusted in response to the inflation rate, output, output growth as well as the growth of real money in the economy. This finding sheds light on the functional form of the real monetary policy in operation during the sample period, even though there has been no consensus on what the rule is. Furthermore, the estimations for the possible breaking point of the rule before and after 2009 show clear existence of a change in weight of the quantity component of the monetary policy rule, which could

---

4   Yuan et al. (2011) and Kang and Gong (2014) incorporate financial friction shocks, but not investment-specific technology shocks in their models.

5   A quantity rule for monetary policy is a rule that sets the level or growth rate of money supply in the economy, it is so named because monetary policy directly controls the quantity of money in the economy. A Taylor-type rule for monetary policy is a rule that sets the nominal interest rate of the economy. It is a price rule as it sets the price of money, the interest rate on risk-free deposits, and it is a variant of the original Taylor rule, proposed by Taylor (1993).

6   Note that Liu and Zhang (2010) use the concept of a 'hybrid rule' in their study, which means that the central bank uses both the quantity rule and the Taylor rule to conduct monetary policy. Because of the small scale of their model, this is mathematically solvable.

be explained by the large increase in base money due to the significant fiscal and monetary stimulus after the GFC led the PBC to be more reactive to fluctuations in real money growth in the economy after 2009.

Second, the main sources of business fluctuations in output and consumption growth rates are neutral technology shocks and preference shocks, while fluctuations in investment and loans are driven primarily by investment-specific technology shocks and net-worth shocks. The structural investigation of China's business cycle shows the important contribution investment-specific technology shocks make to fluctuations in the financial sector. These investment-specific technology shocks differ from the nationwide neutral technology development shocks in affecting the economy and should be taken into account when examining economic fluctuations.

Third, while the consistently positive net-worth shocks explain the steady growth of investment, the negative neutral technology shocks have been the main contributor to the slowing of China's GDP growth since about 2010. This finding contributes to discussions of the GDP growth slowdown since that time, which has drawn huge attention from policymakers and researchers in China and among its trading partners. The finding supports the view that this phase of the slowdown is arising from a structural change in the nation's productivity, rather than a cyclical fluctuation, and policies that favour reform and industrial upgrading to address the change should be given higher priority at the leadership level.

The remainder of this chapter is organised as follows. Section two constructs the model, section three proceeds with the estimation, section four reports and discusses the results, while the concluding remarks are made in section five.

The model

The model is very close to that of Kaihastu and Kurozumi (2014), except for the central bank's behaviour. In this section, we will describe the behaviour of each agent in the economy in detail while presenting only a few mathematical equations. For details of system equations and derivations of optimal conditions, please see the working paper version of this chapter (Li and Wang 2018).

There are households comprising worker and entrepreneur members, financial intermediaries, intermediate-goods firms, consumption-goods firms, investment-goods firms, capital-goods firms and the central bank in the economy. The financial accelerator mechanism of Bernanke et al. (1999) is employed in the financial sector. The economy is subject to both technology shocks and financial shocks.

The representative household comprises a continuum of members normalised to unity. A proportion of members are workers, denoted by $m \in [0,1]$, and the rest are entrepreneurs. All members are assumed to pool their consumption and make joint consumption-saving decisions. The representative household's utility function consists of aggregate consumption with external habit formation—that is, previous aggregate consumption enters the utility function as an external inertia to the current consumption level, which smooths the effect of consumption on the utility of the representative households. Real money balance and labour efforts enter the utility function as standard in the DSGE model literature. The representative household consumes, works and saves via the financial intermediaries, which will be introduced shortly, receives dividends from firms that they own and pays taxes to the government. They also receive money transfers from the central bank in each period.

Workers—the designated proportion of household members—receive wages for working for production firms. The labour market is monopolistically competitive— that is, firms pay a markup above the base wage that measures the marginal productivity of workers. In the meantime, we assume that wages adjust sluggishly, according to a Calvo (1983) adjustment rule. In each period, a fraction of $1 - \xi_m \in (0,1)$ of workers are able to reoptimise their wages, while the wages of the remaining fraction, ξ_m, of workers are set by indexation to past inflation as well as the steady-state balanced growth rate, z^*.

Entrepreneurs—the remaining household members—enter period t with net worth, N_{t-1}, left from the previous period and obtain a loan, L_{t-1}, from financial intermediaries. They purchase capital, K_{t-1}, from capital-goods firms at a given price, Q_{t-1}, and choose the capital utilisation rate, μ_t. They then provide rental capital services to intermediate-goods firms and sell the rest of their capital back to capital-goods firms. After repaying their loan to the financial intermediary, a fraction, $1 - \eta_t \in (0,1)$, of entrepreneurs become workers, while the remaining, η_t, survive into the next period. This assumption is to ensure the relative population size of workers and entrepreneurs remains constant over time.

The loan rate, $E_t r_{t+1}^E$, consists of a deposit rate and the external finance (EF) premium, in the spirit of Bernanke et al. (1999) as Equation 4.1.

Equation 4.1

$$E_t r_{t+1}^E = E_t \left(\frac{r_t^n}{\pi_{t+1}} \right) F \left(\frac{Q_t K_t}{N_t} \right) \exp(z_t^\mu)$$

It shows that the loan rate is increasing with the leverage ratio and decreasing with the net worth of the debtor.

The intermediate-goods firms and consumption-goods firms follow the standard assumption and settings in DSGE models. Briefly, each intermediate-goods firm produces output according to nationwide technology with capital rented from entrepreneurs and the labour efforts of workers. The output is then sold in a monopolistically competitive market to consumption-goods firms. The price of the intermediate goods is again subject to the Calvo (1983) adjustment rule. Consumption-goods firms bundle the intermediate goods without cost into the final consumption goods for the households to consume. The price of the final goods is the consumer price index (CPI).

There are two other types of firms in the economy that are involved in capital-related production: investment-goods firms and capital-goods firms. The former convert one unit of consumption goods into differentiated investment goods according to an investment-specific technology, Ψ_t, which is a different technology from the intermediate-goods production technology, Z_t. The capital-goods firm takes the price of the investment goods and chooses an optimal combination of investment goods from all the investment-goods firms.

The central bank in the model is assumed to conduct monetary policy according to the rule proposed in Equation 4.2.

Equation 4.2

$$\log(r_t^n) = W\left(-\log\left(1 - \frac{1}{\lambda_t}\exp\left(z_t^b\right)\exp(z_t^m)\,m_t^{-\sigma}\right.\right.$$
$$+ (1-W)\left(\phi_r \log(r_{t-1}^n) + (1-\phi_r)\left(\log(r^n)\right.\right.$$
$$+ \frac{\phi_\pi}{4}\sum \log\left(\frac{\pi_{t-j}}{\pi}\right) + \phi_y \log\left(\frac{\frac{Y_t}{Z_t^*}}{y}\right)$$
$$+ \phi_{dy} \log\left(\frac{\frac{Y_t}{Y_{t-1}}}{z^*}\right) + z_t^r$$

This functional form consists of a linear combination of the part related to real money demand from the household, represented by the bracket associated with W and the part related to a typical Taylor rule, represented by the bracket associated with $(1 - W)$, and an exogenous shock, z_t^r. Setting the monetary policy rule in the above form allows us to feed the model with real-time Chinese data to obtain estimates of W. If $W = 1$, the above rule collapses to the condition describing the optimal demand for real money supply, which then determines the interest rate given mt. If $W = 0$, the above rule reduces to a typical Taylor-type rule with the interest rate responding to inflation and economic output. Finally, if $0 < W < 1$, the rule tells us that the policy rate responds to real money as well as inflation and economic output. We call the rule in this case a 'hybrid rule'. To close the model, we need another condition for the money supply in the economy. We follow Christiano et al. (2005) and define money growth following an AR(1) process, as in Equation 4.3.

Equation 4.3

$$M_t^s = \mu_t M_{t-1}^s \text{ and } \log(\mu_t) = \log(\mu_0) + z_t^{mg}$$

Estimation

We adopt a Bayesian likelihood approach from Kaihastu and Kurozumi (2014) with 12 Chinese quarterly time series: output, consumption, investment, labour (hours worked), the real wage, the price of consumption goods, the relative price of investment goods, the monetary policy rate, the loan rate, real loans, real net worth and real money balances. The data are obtained from the CEIC China Premium Database and the sample period is 2001–17 at quarterly frequency. Details of the sources of these data series are in the working paper version of this chapter (Li and Wang 2018).

Before taking the model to the estimation, a detrending of equilibrium conditions is needed since we allow for non-stationary technology in the economy. The stationary system is then log-linearised around its deterministic steady state with a capital utilisation rate of unity. We follow Smets and Wouters (2007) and Kaihastu and Kurozumi (2014) and use the Kalman filter to evaluate the likelihood function for the log-linear system and apply the Metropolis–Hastings algorithm to generate draws from the posterior distribution of model parameters.[7]

There are two sets of parameters: one to be estimated and the other calibrated to avoid any identification issues. To save space here, we do not present the table with calibration. The prior distribution of the 49 parameters to be estimated and the posterior estimates are reported in Table A4.1. Detailed discussions about the calibrated values and choices of prior distributions are in the working paper version of this chapter (Li and Wang 2018).

---

7   Our estimation is done using Dynare (Adjemian et al. 2011). In each estimation, 200,000 draws were generated, the first half of which were discarded. The scale factor for the jumping distribution in the Metropolis–Hastings algorithm was adjusted so that an acceptance rate of about 24 per cent was obtained.

Results

In this section, we present the results in three main parts. The first part reports the statistics of the posterior mean estimates of parameters over the sample period 2001Q1 – 2017Q4. A possible change of policy rule is also considered in this part. The second part of the section presents variance decompositions of output, consumption, investment and loans based on the estimated model. Both forecast error variance decompositions and historical decompositions are reported. Through this exercise, we are able to answer some fundamental questions about the main sources of economic fluctuations in China. The final part presents some discussions of the results.

Estimates of monetary policy rule

The first row of Table A4.1 reports the posterior mean of W and the 90 per cent confidence interval. Over the full sample period, W is estimated to be 0.0911 and is statistically significant from zero. Given the estimated value, the monetary policy rule in Equation 4.1 is indeed a hybrid rule. Over the past decade or more, the PBC conducted monetary policy by adjusting the policy rate according to the real money level, inflation rate, output level and output growth in the economy with assigned weights. Other macroeconomic conditions were subsequently pinned down through the interest rate channel in equilibrium. This finding could serve as a benchmark approach for estimating China's monetary policy rules as macro and financial conditions in China evolve over time.

We also conduct subsample estimations searching for possible policy rule changes. During the sample period, there was a breakdown of the global financial system, which might have caused some policy changes in the PBC. Recently, PBC officials have made several public speeches discussing the necessity of reforming monetary policy towards more price tool–based practices. We set 2009Q1 as the potential change point and estimate the model over the two subsamples. The results are reported in Tables A4.2 and A4.3. They show that the mean estimates of W are statistically and significantly different from each other before and after the breaking point in 2009Q1. Specifically, the posterior mean of W before 2009Q1 is equal to 0.0859, while after 2009Q1, it increases to 0.2466—both of which are statistically different from zero.[8]

This finding deserves some discussion. The different weights attached to the quantity part of the monetary policy rule before and after 2009 indicate that the GFC had a measurable impact on China's monetary policy. Despite the public speeches by

---

8　As a sensitivity check, we also use 2008Q1 and 2007Q1 as a potential breaking point for subsample estimations, and we obtain similar results to those using 2009Q1 as the breaking point.

PBC officials about moving towards more price tool–based practices, the actual monetary policy rule still places more weight on the quantity movements of real money balance in the economy. This is very likely considering the large fiscal and monetary stimulus that was put in place after the GFC. The PBC was aware of the increase in the money base in the economy and responded to a larger extent to the quantity component of the policy rule, everything else being equal, after the onset of the financial crisis.

Variance decompositions

Given the estimated monetary policy rule in the previous subsection, we can proceed with the investigation of the business cycle fluctuations in the Chinese economy in the period 2001–17. To see what accounts for the fluctuations in the key macroeconomic variables, we present the forecast error decompositions of the variances of output, consumption, investment and loans in Table A4.4 and historical decompositions of output and investment in Figures A4.1 and A4.2 based on the estimated model.

Table A4.4 shows the relative contribution of each shock to the variations in output growth, consumption growth, investment growth and real loan growth at forecast horizons T = 8, 32 quarters, evaluated at the posterior mean estimates of parameters. The main source of the output fluctuation is the exogenous demand shock. The next two important sources are the neutral technology shock and the preference shock. The investment-specific technology shock makes a small but increasing contribution to the output fluctuation from short-term (6 per cent) to long-term (11 per cent) horizons. The remainder of the shocks are negligible. The preference shock is the dominant source of the fluctuation in consumption, making up nearly 70 per cent of the variation. The neutral technology shock is the secondary source, while the remaining shocks all play minor roles. Half of the variation in investment growth is explained by the investment-specific shock, while 26 per cent is explained by the net-worth shock in the short run. The investment-specific shock becomes even more prominent in the long run (61 per cent). The intermediate-goods markup also plays a small role in affecting investment activities. The investment-specific and net-worth shocks also play a primary and secondary role, respectively, in explaining the fluctuations in real loans. The shock to the marginal efficiency of investment contributes marginally to the loan variation.

The results above reveal the main sources of business fluctuation in China. The real sectors—that is, consumption-goods sectors—are driven primarily by the neutral technology, preference and external demand shocks, while the financial sectors are dominated by the investment-specific technology and net-worth shocks.

To get a closer look at the fundamentals of business fluctuations in China, we present the historical decompositions of the percentage point deviations of output and investment from their respective steady states in Figures A4.1 and A4.2. Figure A4.1 shows a steadily decreasing trend of output growth from about 2011, with the neutral technology shock as the main negative contributor. This suggests that a structural break in neutral technological development—from consistently positive in 2001–07 to consistently negative in 2010–17—has been the primary driver of the slowing of China's GDP growth since 2010 that we discussed at the beginning of the chapter. There is a drastic fall in output growth from about mid-2008 to early 2009 in Figure A4.1. This corresponds to the onset of the GFC. The sudden meltdown of the global financial system and then of the real economy may affect technology and production through trade and financial channels.

Figure A4.2 shows that investment growth is, on average, positive and the net-worth shock is the primary positive contributor. Investment-specific technology is another key factor, but its contribution is volatile. This means that growth in investment is driven by the positive valuation of net worth while the volatility of investment is driven by its own technological development. Looking forward, we should be cautious about whether these valuation effects on net worth can continue and carefully monitor the evolution of investment activities.

Figures A4.1 and A4.2 together bring us another perspective on China's growth story: investment was steadily growing while economic growth showed clear signs of slowing over the past decade.

Discussions

Before closing this section, we would like to discuss the usefulness of the extended DSGE model we have used in this chapter and policy implications based on the results obtained. First, financial friction is indispensable in the model. We incorporate financial intermediaries and financial friction into the model as we expect them to be important sources of business fluctuations in China, as they are in the United States. The posterior mean estimation of the elasticity of the external finance premium (that is, μ in Table A4.1) shows that this premium equation is statistically significant in the model. The important role of the net-worth shock in explaining investment fluctuations also proves this point.

Second, we specify neutral technology and investment-specific technology as two types of technology for the consumption-goods sector and investment-goods sector. As demonstrated in the previous section, neutral technology is one of the main drivers of output growth fluctuations, while investment-specific technology and net-worth technology are the main drivers of investment activities. Without the specification of the two types of technologies, we would obtain misleading results of the main sources of business fluctuations in China.

Third, a hybrid monetary policy rule is obtained by constructing a generalised form of rule without imposing *ex ante* model restrictions and employing a Bayesian estimation strategy using real Chinese data. This approach can serve as a benchmark for future researchers to estimate China's monetary policy rule as macroeconomic and financial conditions evolve over time.

Last but not the least, the finding that negative development in neutral technology since about 2010 contributed to output variation provides important policy implications. As discussed in the introduction of the chapter, there are numerous explanations about the recent economic output slowdown without any consensus on the fundamental factors. Our result is supportive of the argument that it is mainly the technological slowdown that contributed to output fluctuations. Policies supporting technological innovations and industrial upgrading are then favourable in addressing such negative technological development. The 'new normal' of the Chinese economy would be sustainable if the future economic growth is supported by new industries and innovations in new and upgraded technology.

Conclusions

Policymakers and scholars are increasingly concerned with the recent economic slowdown in China. Our findings show that negative neutral technology development is what has caused this output fluctuation. After more than 30 years of driving high-speed economic development, the growth potential of neutral technological advancement has shown a clear sign of slowing. This has the important policy implication of encouraging technological innovation and industrial upgrading in China.

We construct a rich DSGE model in this chapter for the structural investigation of the Chinese economy. The results show that it captures important features of the economy that have not been found in previous studies using a simple model. Importantly, we find that China's monetary policy rule is a hybrid one. China's central bank conducts monetary policy by adjusting the policy rate in response to inflation, output conditions and real money growth. The policy rule changed after about 2009 towards placing more weight on responding to movements in the real money balance compared with before 2009. This suggests the quantity of money is strongly affecting monetary policy practices.

The variance decompositions of the key variables show the relative importance of various shocks in explaining the fluctuations of those variables. Specifically, financial friction shocks are indispensable sources of investment fluctuation. Neutral technology development was a consistently positive contributor to output growth during the period 2001–07 and became a negative contributor after 2010. This finding provides further evidence of the sources of the GDP slowdown in China since about 2010, pointing out that technological development has played a significant role in dragging down the pace of productivity growth. Future work on the causes of business fluctuations in China and China's monetary policy rule can draw on the results in this chapter.

References

Adjemian, S., Bastani, H., Juillard, M., Mihoubi, F., Perendia, G., Ratto, M. and Villemot, S. (2011), *Dynare: Reference Manual Version 4*, Dynare Working Papers 1, Paris: CEPREMAP.

Bernanke, B.S., Gertler, M. and Gilchrist, S. (1999), The financial accelerator in a quantitative business cycle framework, in J.B. Taylor and M. Woodford (eds), *Handbook of Macroeconomics: Volume 1A*, Amsterdam: Elsevier. doi.org/10.1016/S1574-0048(99)10034-X.

Cai, F. and Lu, Y. (2013), Population change and resulting slowdown in potential GDP growth in China, *China & World Economy* 21: 1–14. doi.org/10.1111/j.1749-124X.2013.12012.x.

Calvo, G.A. (1983), Staggered prices in a utility-maximizing framework. *Journal of Monetary Economics* 12(3): 383–98.

Cashin, P., Mohaddes, K. and Raissi, M. (2017), China's slowdown and global financial market volatility: Is world growth losing out?, *Emerging Markets Review* 31: 164–75. doi.org/10.1016/j.ememar.2017.05.001.

Chen, W., Chen, X., Hsieh, C.-T. and Song, Z.M. (2019), *A forensic examination of China's national accounts*, Brookings Papers on Economic Activity, Spring, Washington, DC: Brookings Institution. doi.org/10.3386/w25754.

Christiano, L.J., Eichenbaum, M. and Evans, C.L. (2005), Nominal rigidities and the dynamic effects of a shock to monetary policy, *Journal of Political Economy* 113: 1–45. doi.org/10.1086/426038.

Christiano, L.J., Motto, R. and Rostagno, M. (2010), *Financial factors in economic fluctuations*, ECB Working Paper No. 1192, Frankfurt am Main: European Central Bank.

Eichengreen, B., Park, D. and Shin, K. (2012), When fast-growing economies slow down: International evidence and implications for China, *Asian Economic Papers* 11: 42–87. doi.org/10.1162/ASEP_a_00118.

Fernald, J., Malkin, I. and Spiegel, M. (2013), On the reliability of Chinese output figures, *Federal Reserve Bank of San Francisco Economic Letter* 8: 1–5.

Gilchrist, S., Ortiz, A. and Zakrajsek, E. (2009), Credit risk and the macroeconomy: Evidence from an estimated DSGE model, 27 July, available from: ssrn.com/abstract=2088909.

Greenwood, J., Hercowitz, Z. and Huffman, G.W. (1988), Investment, capacity utilization, and the real business cycle, *The American Economic Review* 78(3): 402–17.

Greenwood, J., Hercowitz, Z. and Krusell, P. (1997), Long-run implications of investment-specific technological change, *The American Economic Review* 87(3): 342–62.

Justiniano, A., Primiceri, G.E. and Tambalotti, A. (2011), Investment shocks and the relative price of investment, *Review of Economic Dynamics* 14: 102–21. doi.org/10.1016/j.red. 2010.08.004.

Kaihatsu, S. and Kurozumi, T. (2014), Sources of business fluctuations: Financial or technology shocks?, *Review of Economic Dynamics* 17: 224–42. doi.org/10.1016/j.red. 2013.08.001.

Kang, L. and Gong, L. (2014), Financial frictions, net worth of bank and transmission of international crisis: Based on multi-sector DSGE model analysis, *Economic Research Journal* 49: 147–59.

Li, R. and Wang, J. (2018), A structural investigation of the Chinese economy with a hybrid rule, University of Melbourne, Mimeo, 2018.

Liu, L.-G. and Zhang, W. (2010), A new Keynesian model for analysing monetary policy in mainland China, *Journal of Asian Economics* 21: 540–51. doi.org/10.1016/ j.asieco.2010.07.004.

McMahon, M., Schipke, A. and Li, X. (2018), China's monetary policy communication: Frameworks, impact, and recommendations, IMF Working Paper No. WP/18/244.

Mehrotra, A., Nuutilainen, R. and Pääkkönen, J. (2013), Changing economic structures and impacts of shocks: Evidence from a dynamic stochastic general equilibrium model for China, *Pacific Economic Review* 18: 92–107. doi.org/10.1111/1468-0106.12012.

Smets, F. and Wouters, R. (2007), Shocks and frictions in US business cycles: A Bayesian DSGE approach, *American Economic Review* 97(3): 586–606.

Sun, L. and Sen, S. (2011), Monetary policy rules and business cycle in China: Bayesian DSGE model simulation, 9 April. doi.org/10.2139/ssrn.1806347.

Taylor, J.B. (1993), Discretion versus policy rules in practice, *Carnegie-Rochester Conference Series on Public Policy* 39: 195–214, North-Holland.

Wang, G. and Tian, G. (2014), Financial shocks and Chinese business cycle, *Economic Research Journal* 49: 20–34.

Xu, W. and Chen, B. (2009), Bank lending and economic fluctuations in China: 1993–2005, *China Economic Quarterly* 8: 969–94.

Yuan, P. and Feng, L. (2014), Research of housing price rise effects based on DSGE: Economic growth, income distribution and wealth gap widening, *Economic Research Journal* 49: 77–90.

Yuan, S., Chen, P. and Liu, L. (2011), Exchange rate system, financial accelerator and economical undulation, *Economic Research Journal* 2011-01: 57–70.

Zhang, W. (2009), China's monetary policy: Quantity versus price rules, *Journal of Macroeconomics* 31: 473–84. doi.org/10.1016/j.jmacro.2008.09.003.

Zhang, W., Zheng, J. and Huang, Y. (2014), An analysis on anticipated shocks of monetary policy and industrial transmission: Based on a multi-sectoral DSGE model, *Journal of Financial Research*: 33–49.

Zhou, X.C. (2016), Managing multi-objective monetary policy: From the perspective of transitioning Chinese economy, The 2016 Michel Camdessus Central Banking Lecture, 24 June, International Monetary Fund, Washington, DC.

Appendix A

Table A4.1 Prior and posterior distributions of parameters – full sample

	Prior mean	Post mean	90% HPD interval		Prior	Pstdev
alpha	0.500	0.0911	0.0179	0.1686	unif	0.2887
Csigma	2.000	0.8737	0.5647	1.1324	gamma	0.3750
Ctheta	0.700	0.5582	0.4176	0.6862	beta	0.1000
cchi	2.000	2.6598	1.5509	3.7217	gamma	0.7500
czeta	4.000	3.3357	2.2265	4.5573	gamma	1.5000
ctau	0.220	0.3155	0.1080	0.5033	gamma	0.1000
cphi	0.250	0.0531	0.0052	0.0986	beta	0.1250
calpha	0.600	0.1440	0.0860	0.2020	beta	0.1000
gammaw	0.500	0.2471	0.1017	0.3878	beta	0.1500
xiw	0.500	0.6422	0.5621	0.7186	beta	0.1000
gammap	0.500	0.3213	0.1461	0.4882	beta	0.1500
xip	0.500	0.8075	0.7412	0.8664	beta	0.1000
phir	0.750	0.7664	0.6873	0.8412	beta	0.1000
phipi	1.500	1.7688	1.3955	2.1307	gamma	0.2500
phiy	0.125	0.0440	0.0201	0.0681	gamma	0.0500
phidy	0.125	0.0579	0.0267	0.0869	gamma	0.0500
zstarss	1.163	1.2187	1.0790	1.3613	gamma	0.1000
psiss	0.077	0.0672	0.0144	0.1195	gamma	0.0400
hss	0.000	−0.1304	−2.4195	2.3909	norm	2.0000
piss	0.272	0.2660	0.1459	0.3955	gamma	0.1000

	Prior mean	Post mean	90% HPD interval		Prior	Pstdev
rnss	1.030	1.1060	0.9655	1.2442	gamma	0.1000
eta	0.973	0.9552	0.9276	0.9838	beta	0.0200
nkss	0.500	0.6077	0.5089	0.7027	beta	0.0700
cmu	0.070	0.0203	0.0141	0.0271	gamma	0.0200
ress	1.242	1.2177	1.1374	1.2929	gamma	0.0500
rho_b	0.500	0.7916	0.6060	0.9558	beta	0.2000
rho_g	0.500	0.9707	0.9470	0.9944	beta	0.2000
rho_w	0.500	0.2055	0.0349	0.3726	beta	0.2000
rho_p	0.500	0.9039	0.8407	0.9774	beta	0.2000
rho_i	0.500	0.8897	0.8323	0.9448	beta	0.2000
rho_r	0.500	0.2256	0.0632	0.3813	beta	0.2000
rho_z	0.500	0.1307	0.0295	0.2226	beta	0.2000
rho_psi	0.500	0.9568	0.9249	0.9909	beta	0.2000
rho_nu	0.500	0.9850	0.9774	0.9924	beta	0.2000
rho_mu	0.500	0.5413	0.4254	0.6784	beta	0.2000
rho_eta	0.500	0.8246	0.7015	0.9634	beta	0.2000
rho_mg	0.500	0.3782	0.1867	0.5541	beta	0.2000
e_b	0.500	2.8286	1.5204	3.8269	invg	Inf
e_g	0.500	0.8964	0.7581	1.0319	invg	Inf
e_w	0.500	0.4458	0.3527	0.5515	invg	Inf
e_p	0.500	0.1624	0.1037	0.2165	invg	Inf
e_i	0.500	1.1037	0.9333	1.2754	invg	Inf
e_r	0.500	0.1287	0.1088	0.1467	invg	Inf
e_z	0.500	1.7636	1.4635	2.0584	invg	Inf
e_psi	0.500	0.3763	0.2735	0.4741	invg	Inf
e_nu	0.500	4.1778	3.3739	4.9908	invg	Inf
e_mu	0.500	0.2854	0.2462	0.3230	invg	Inf
e_eta	0.500	0.8999	0.5881	1.2119	invg	Inf
e_mg	0.500	0.5839	0.5022	0.6575	invg	Inf

Note: Alpha is the weight on quantity rule.

Table A4.2 Prior and posterior distributions of parameters – subsample: before 2009Q1

	Prior mean	Post mean	90% HPD interval		Prior	Pstdev
alpha	0.500	0.0859	0.0005	0.1753	unif	0.2887
csigma	2.000	1.3525	0.8765	1.7459	gamma	0.3750
ctheta	0.700	0.5852	0.4222	0.8257	beta	0.1000
cchi	2.000	2.4886	1.1941	3.6389	gamma	0.7500
czeta	4.000	1.9989	0.6985	3.3205	gamma	1.5000

	Prior mean	Post mean	90% HPD interval		Prior	Pstdev
ctau	0.220	0.2622	0.0583	0.4580	gamma	0.1000
cphi	0.250	0.0471	0.0092	0.0847	beta	0.1250
calpha	0.600	0.3066	0.1694	0.4440	beta	0.1000
gammaw	0.500	0.2939	0.1110	0.4658	beta	0.1500
xiw	0.500	0.6172	0.5352	0.7205	beta	0.1000
gammap	0.500	0.3015	0.1326	0.4820	beta	0.1500
xip	0.500	0.7693	0.7071	0.8405	beta	0.1000
phir	0.750	0.6478	0.5332	0.7714	beta	0.1000
phipi	1.500	1.9313	1.5072	2.3432	gamma	0.2500
phiy	0.125	0.0430	0.0195	0.0683	gamma	0.0500
phidy	0.125	0.0963	0.0491	0.1404	gamma	0.0500
zstarss	1.163	1.2358	1.0650	1.3767	gamma	0.1000
psiss	0.077	0.0730	0.0163	0.1248	gamma	0.0400
hss	0.000	1.4090	−1.1566	4.3397	norm	2.0000
piss	0.272	0.3744	0.1941	0.5288	gamma	0.1000
rnss	1.030	1.0595	0.9096	1.2015	gamma	0.1000
eta	0.973	0.9717	0.9504	0.9917	beta	0.0200
nkss	0.500	0.4947	0.3934	0.5836	beta	0.0700
cmu	0.070	0.0224	0.0142	0.0317	gamma	0.0200
ress	1.242	1.2320	1.1524	1.3114	gamma	0.0500
rho_b	0.500	0.6454	0.3053	0.9043	beta	0.2000
rho_g	0.500	0.8943	0.8312	0.9641	beta	0.2000
rho_w	0.500	0.3522	0.0732	0.6039	beta	0.2000
rho_p	0.500	0.8405	0.7321	0.9461	beta	0.2000
rho_i	0.500	0.7362	0.5906	0.9162	beta	0.2000
rho_r	0.500	0.4865	0.2962	0.7321	beta	0.2000
rho_z	0.500	0.1716	0.0348	0.2960	beta	0.2000
rho_psi	0.500	0.9431	0.9056	0.9854	beta	0.2000
rho_nu	0.500	0.9747	0.9545	0.9960	beta	0.2000
rho_mu	0.500	0.8114	0.7099	0.9071	beta	0.2000
rho_eta	0.500	0.7650	0.6124	0.9208	beta	0.2000
rho_mg	0.500	0.2410	0.0441	0.4254	beta	0.2000
e_b	0.500	6.0075	2.3428	11.7735	invg	Inf
e_g	0.500	1.2548	0.8911	1.6161	invg	Inf
e_w	0.500	0.5312	0.3542	0.7339	invg	Inf
e_p	0.500	0.2457	0.1294	0.3331	invg	Inf
e_i	0.500	0.8898	0.6847	1.1021	invg	Inf
e_r	0.500	0.1507	0.1230	0.1822	invg	Inf
e_z	0.500	2.1435	1.6746	2.6424	invg	Inf

	Prior mean	Post mean	90% HPD interval		Prior	Pstdev
e_psi	0.500	0.4347	0.2928	0.5719	invg	Inf
e_nu	0.500	3.4362	2.1762	4.4342	invg	Inf
e_mu	0.500	0.1793	0.1365	0.2183	invg	Inf
e_eta	0.500	1.2113	0.7844	1.6362	invg	Inf
e_mg	0.500	0.4336	0.3271	0.5388	invg	Inf

Note: Alpha is the weight on quantity rule.

Table A4.3 Prior and posterior distributions of parameters – subsample: after 2009Q1

	Prior mean	Post mean	90% HPD interval		Prior	Pstdev
alpha	0.500	0.2466	0.0046	0.5121	unif	0.2887
csigma	2.000	1.0819	0.7355	1.3970	gamma	0.3750
ctheta	0.700	0.6755	0.5693	0.7927	beta	0.1000
cchi	2.000	2.2995	1.3164	3.3768	gamma	0.7500
czeta	4.000	4.8390	3.2622	6.4291	gamma	1.5000
ctau	0.220	0.2482	0.0801	0.4042	gamma	0.1000
cphi	0.250	0.1240	0.0181	0.2228	beta	0.1250
calpha	0.600	0.1712	0.1142	0.2296	beta	0.1000
gammaw	0.500	0.4677	0.2475	0.6837	beta	0.1500
xiw	0.500	0.6025	0.4935	0.7156	beta	0.1000
gammap	0.500	0.5818	0.3744	0.7944	beta	0.1500
xip	0.500	0.8019	0.7269	0.8755	beta	0.1000
phir	0.750	0.8010	0.6807	0.9109	beta	0.1000
phipi	1.500	1.6664	1.2879	2.0263	gamma	0.2500
phiy	0.125	0.0794	0.0267	0.1376	gamma	0.0500
phidy	0.125	0.1161	0.0576	0.1709	gamma	0.0500
zstarss	1.163	1.1451	1.0167	1.2853	gamma	0.1000
psiss	0.077	0.0763	0.0176	0.1353	gamma	0.0400
hss	0.000	−2.3959	−4.5247	−0.1487	norm	2.0000
piss	0.272	0.2334	0.1023	0.3559	gamma	0.1000
rnss	1.030	1.1051	0.9671	1.2318	gamma	0.1000
eta	0.973	0.9292	0.8976	0.9599	beta	0.0200
nkss	0.500	0.5809	0.4934	0.6743	beta	0.0700
cmu	0.070	0.0336	0.0223	0.0446	gamma	0.0200
ress	1.242	1.2259	1.1388	1.3026	gamma	0.0500
rho_b	0.500	0.3179	0.0456	0.5699	beta	0.2000
rho_g	0.500	0.9493	0.9213	0.9821	beta	0.2000
rho_w	0.500	0.2446	0.0481	0.4495	beta	0.2000
rho_p	0.500	0.8293	0.6927	0.9755	beta	0.2000

	Prior mean	Post mean	90% HPD interval		Prior	Pstdev
rho_i	0.500	0.8467	0.7585	0.9440	beta	0.2000
rho_r	0.500	0.4587	0.1000	0.8045	beta	0.2000
rho_z	0.500	0.1655	0.0381	0.2872	beta	0.2000
rho_psi	0.500	0.9619	0.9374	0.9900	beta	0.2000
rho_nu	0.500	0.9659	0.9472	0.9853	beta	0.2000
rho_mu	0.500	0.2073	0.0559	0.3554	beta	0.2000
rho_eta	0.500	0.5218	0.2850	0.7456	beta	0.2000
rho_mg	0.500	0.3737	0.1227	0.6500	beta	0.2000
e_b	0.500	1.8163	0.8817	2.7888	invg	Inf
e_g	0.500	0.7046	0.5510	0.8704	invg	Inf
e_w	0.500	0.3571	0.2584	0.4449	invg	Inf
e_p	0.500	0.1899	0.1141	0.2564	invg	Inf
e_i	0.500	1.2825	0.9970	1.5376	invg	Inf
e_r	0.500	0.1086	0.0855	0.1322	invg	Inf
e_z	0.500	1.7497	1.2774	2.2522	invg	Inf
e_psi	0.500	0.2778	0.1801	0.3815	invg	Inf
e_nu	0.500	3.4748	2.6189	4.3040	invg	Inf
e_mu	0.500	0.3267	0.2609	0.3989	invg	Inf
e_eta	0.500	0.8334	0.5687	1.1040	invg	Inf
e_mg	0.500	0.7029	0.5697	0.8478	invg	Inf

Note: Alpha is the weight on quantity rule.

Table A4.4 Forecast error decompositions of the variances of output, consumption, investment and loans

		Output		Consumption		Investment		Loan	
		T=8	T=32	T=8	T=32	T=8	T=32	T=8	T=32
z^b	Preference	23.78	21.85	69.44	68.13	0.02	0.02	0.05	0.04
z^g	Exogenous demand	34.84	32.37	0.61	0.63	0.33	0.27	0.02	0.03
z^w	Wage	0.01	0.01	0.03	0.03	0.04	0.03	0.05	0.04
z^p	Intermediate-good price markup	4.42	5.01	2.85	3.12	6.85	5.74	5.59	4.5
z^i	Investment-good price markup	0.15	0.18	0	0	0.87	0.7	0.21	0.24
z^z	Neutral technology	23.94	22.43	23.37	23.4	1.42	1.26	1.15	1.78
z^ψ	IS technology	6.09	11.08	2.2	2.48	50.15	61.28	51.78	55.21
z^ν	MEI	2.49	2.51	0.26	0.62	11.8	9.4	8.45	10.12
z^μ	EF premium	0.12	0.12	0	0	0.73	0.48	1.07	0.82
z^η	Net worth	3.16	3.44	0.63	0.96	26.05	19.6	30.05	25.96
z^m	Real money growth	0	0	0	0	0	0	0	0
z^r	Hybrid monetary policy	0.55	0.52	0.29	0.28	1.09	0.72	1.48	1.13
z^{mg}	Quantitative monetary policy	0.46	0.49	0.33	0.34	0.66	0.52	0.1	0.13

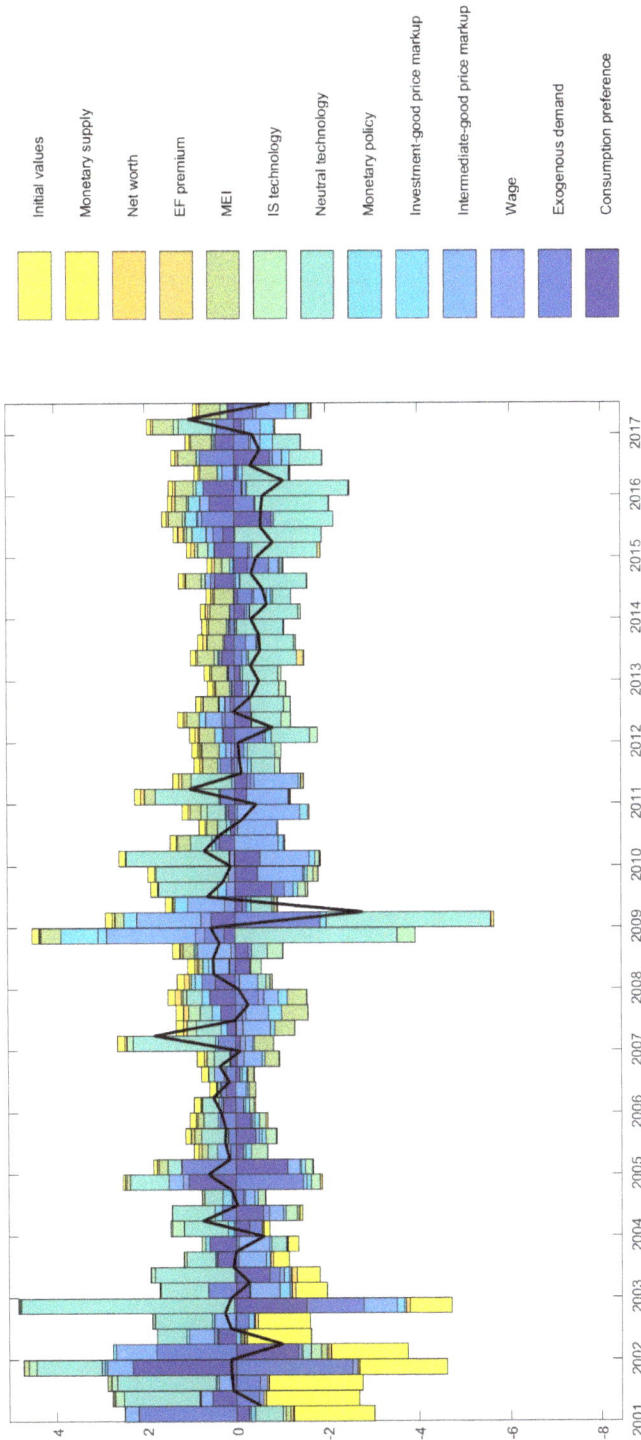

Figure A4.1 Historical decompositions of output

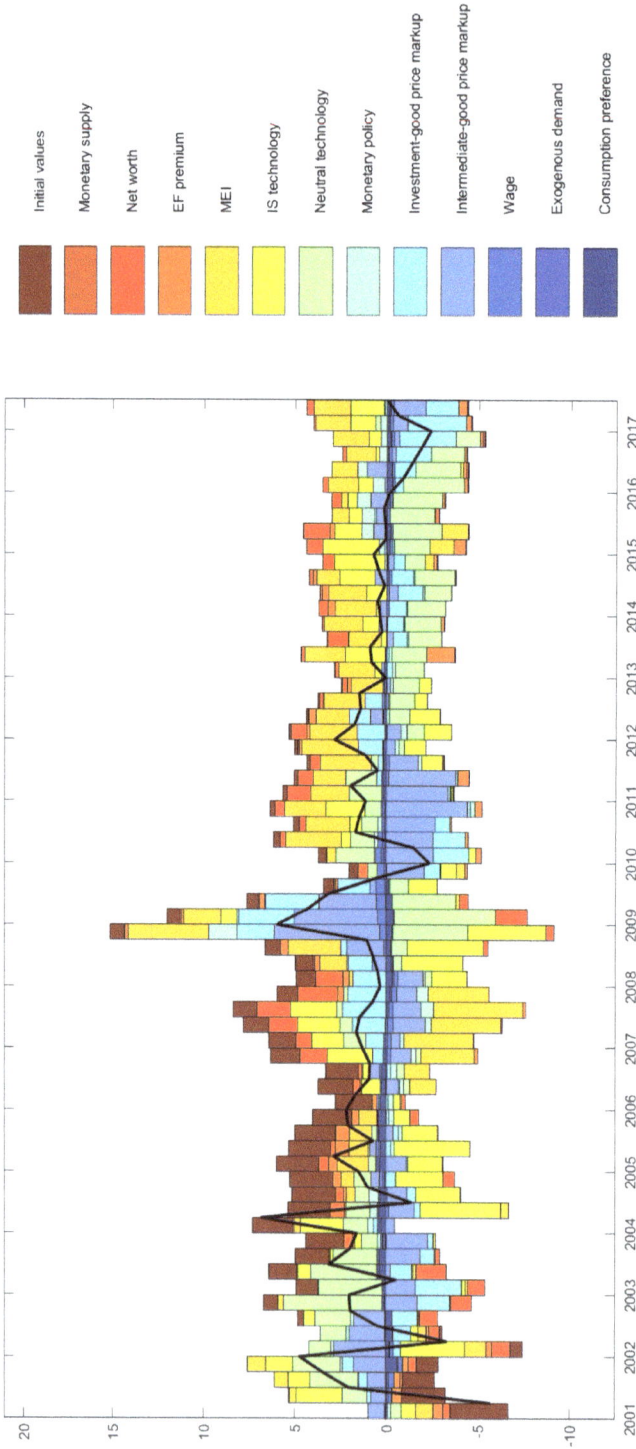

Figure A4.2 Historical decompositions of investment

5. Off-farm employment in rural China and the *hukou* system

Yuhan Zhao, Moyu Chen and Yu Sheng[1]

Over the past four decades, China has implemented a series of institutional and market-oriented reforms that have resulted in an integration of the rural and urban labour markets and substantially increased off-farm employment. In 1999–2000, only about 10 per cent of rural households in China were involved in off-farm work, while, by 2007–08, that share had risen to 22 per cent (Wang et al. 2017). The increase in off-farm employment has not only provided additional labour supply to support the industrialisation and urbanisation processes in China, but also facilitated the transformation and development of rural China through strengthening the rural non-agricultural sector. Between 1978 and 2015, real GDP per capita in China increased by 16.7 times, with 44 per cent of this coming from labour force reallocation from agriculture to non-agricultural sectors (Cai 2018).

Although non-agricultural sector growth and off-farm employment have significantly contributed to China's economic development, such activities have long been restricted by various institutional arrangements. The household registration system (*hukou*), initially established in the late 1950s, was designed to support urban development. However, as the rural and urban economies became more integrated over time, it became a barrier, restricting rural labour from working in urban areas. Under this system, China's population was divided into 'agricultural' and 'non-agricultural' sectors. As the system is not only a population registration system, but also a comprehensive policy system bundled with other institutional arrangements, it is believed to be one of the most important policies in preventing rural-to-urban migration and off-farm employment in the non-agricultural sector (Cai 2018).

To date, there have been many studies examining the impact of the household registration system on rural-to-urban migration and its economic and social consequences (Meng and Zhang 2010). Some studies suggest that rural and urban integration should be achieved under the constraint of the *hukou* system, since it gives privileges to urban residents to become rich first, which enlarges urban–rural income inequality and thus provides ongoing incentives for rural labour to move into cities (Lu and Chen 2004; Liu 2011). In contrast, other studies argue that the *hukou* system hinders rural-to-urban migration and reallocation of rural labour

1 The authors acknowledge financial support from the State Natural Sciences Foundation (No. 71873005 and No. 71742002); ATMAC (43643) Chinese Academy of Engineering (2018-ZD-07-1 and 2018-ZD-07-06-1); and the Data Centre for Management Science, PKU-NSFC (2018KEY06). All errors are the authors'.

(Seeborg et al. 2000; Démurger et al. 2009; Meng 2012). Although no consensus has been reached on the role of the *hukou* system on off-farm employment, gradual reforms have been made since 1984. While the *hukou* system's discrimination in the rights and privileges to off-farm employment and residence in rural areas has been gradually relaxed, discrimination relating to wages/incomes, job division, returns on education capital and social welfare protection for rural labourers working in urban areas remains (Seeborg et al. 2000; Démurger et al. 2009; Meng 2012).

The existing literature provides useful insights on the impact of the *hukou* system on rural-to-urban migration (Chan and Zhang 1999; Wan and Li 2013). Most of these studies, however, focus on the employment and wage status of rural migrants in urban China, and suffer from serious selection bias. This is because the majority of off-farm employment occurs in the non-agricultural sector of rural areas (who are not classified as rural migrants), and there is still a large amount of off-farm labour working in urban areas but not living there. Without properly accounting for this rural labour, the impact of the *hukou* system will not be adequately measured. In addition, although many empirical studies have been conducted, most use either pooled cross-sectional data or short-term panel data, which do not reflect the long-term changes in the *hukou* system and its potential impact on off-farm employment over the past 40 years.

This chapter investigates the evolution of the *hukou* system at the provincial level between 1981 and 2013, and examines its impact on off-farm employment in rural China from an empirical perspective. Off-farm employment is defined as rural labour (those holding rural *hukou*) who have worked in non-agricultural sectors in rural or urban areas, including rural-to-urban migrants, rural labourers working in rural non-agricultural sectors and rural labourers working in urban areas but living in rural areas.

The remainder of the study is structured as follows. Section two reviews China's *hukou* reforms before and after the reform and opening-up period, which began in 1978, along with relevant research on *hukou* policies and non-agricultural employment in the country. Section three constructs the empirical models and describes the data sources. Section four presents the empirical results, as well as the interpretation, while section five concludes the study.

Hukou system reforms and off-farm employment in China

Separate urban and rural household registration systems have been in place since the National People's Republic of China Registration Regulations were promulgated in 1958. The system has been changing over time alongside economic and institutional reforms. Taking the reform and opening-up policies that began in 1978 as a watershed, China's household registration system has experienced two major phases: before 1978 and after 1978. Before 1978, China's household registration system was rooted in a logical structure of 'family-birth-identity-order-control-distribution' (Lu 2002). Consequently, not only was there a need for rural labourers to complete a range of formalities (such as approval, certification and the payment of fees) to undertake off-farm employment, but also, rural workers faced significant restrictions on work and risks of detention. The strictness of the system distorted the allocation of labour resources and widened the gap between urban and rural economic development. The *hukou* system has gradually changed since 1978, when institutional and marketisation reforms were first implemented. In particular, after the mid-1990s, the government carried out a series of reforms to relax the *hukou* system, which allowed more rural migrants to work in urban areas (Song and Li 2014).

Although significant progress has been made by the central and local governments over the past four decades, the segregation of the rural and urban labour markets has continued. Incomplete reforms of the *hukou* system are regarded as one of the most important factors preventing the integration of the rural and urban labour markets by restricting off-farm labourers from gaining equal rights with their urban counterparts in access to basic public services, such as compulsory education for children, personal social insurance, minimum living security, housing and so on. There are two types of restriction policies in place: one restricts equal rights to employment and the other restricts equal rights to social welfare.

Given the importance of this issue, many studies have been conducted to analyse the impact of *hukou* reforms on rural-to-urban migration and off-farm employment in China over past decades. Four groups of related studies are summarised below.

The first group of literature explores the impact of *hukou* reforms on employment opportunities for off-farm labour. Before 1978, the *hukou* system severely restricted the occupational choice and work location of rural labour (Lu 2002). An extreme example of this was the campaign to send 'intellectual' urban youth to the countryside. Under this government-authorised anti-urbanisation movement, 18 million 16–20-year-olds migrated from urban to rural areas in the period 1962–78 (Bernstein and Olsen 2009; Kinnan et al. 2015). Since 1978, reforms to the *hukou* system have reduced the constraints on labour mobility, and a massive rural labour force has engaged in non-agricultural employment. However, compared with urban workers, rural migrant or off-farm workers are concentrated in the low-skill market, and face various discriminations (Meng and Zhang 2001; Li and Gu 2011; Démurger et al. 2012; Afridi et al. 2015).

The second group of research discusses the impact of the *hukou* system on rural labour's income levels. The post-reform era has witnessed a significant rise in the real wages of the rural population. However, compared with the urban labour force, rural labourers' wages are generally subject to discrimination because of the phenomenon of 'different compensation for equal work' (Knight et al. 1999; Dong and Bowles 2002; Démurger et al. 2009; Li and Gu 2011; Meng 2012). Meng and Zhang (2001) applied survey data for urban households from the Population Research Institute of Shanghai's Academy of Social Sciences for 1995–96 and found that household registration discrimination affected wages by 50 per cent, regardless of the difference in rural and urban labour distribution, and it influenced wages within the same industry as much as 82 per cent. Wang and Cai (2005) uses data from the fifth national census in 2000 to examine the impact of the household registration system on rural labour and found that, in the same occupation, it accounted for 39 per cent wage differences between rural and urban workers. However, Knight and Yueh (2004) argue that career conversion can significantly increase the income of rural labourers compared with urban residents. It is worth noting that the current research comparing wage differences between urban and rural labour is based more on the comparison of unit hourly wages than on the comparison of disposable income. Excluding personal income tax will seriously underestimate the degree of discrimination against migrant workers. Overall, although the income level of rural labour has increased since the *hukou* reforms, there is still notable income inequality between urban and rural labour.

The third group of literature focuses on how the *hukou* system influences the spatial migration of rural labour's employment. Dividing the labour market into urban and rural markets, non-agricultural employment and agricultural labour transfers can be achieved only at the margin (Cai 2018). Geographically, with the *hukou* reforms, rural labour transfers have been concentrated mainly in eastern China, followed by the central and western regions (NBS 2018). Moreover, after taking into account city size by using panel data from 123 major cities in China from 2000 to 2013, Yang (2017) finds that the *hukou* reforms in large cities did not attract labour inflows, but instead prompted labour outflows, which is a result of the relatively strict administrative constraints. The settlement threshold and household registration constraints of major cities in the eastern region were higher than those in the central and western regions, so that a massive amount of rural labour was transferred into the central and western regions.

The fourth group of studies contributes evidence of how *hukou* reform affects the social security and welfare of the rural labour force. The *hukou* system has created separate urban and rural social security systems and deepened the unfairness of such welfare in terms of the social insurance level, educational opportunities and housing inequality (Hertel and Zhai 2006; Sun et al. 2011; Tombe and Zhu 2019). Since the gradual relaxation of the family registration system, the opportunity for rural labour to settle in urban areas and obtain equal access to social security has increased (Meng 2000; Song 2014; Garriga et al. 2017; Chen and Yuan 2018).

In sum, most studies find that *hukou* (although it has been relaxed in the post-reform period) is still playing an important role in negatively affecting rural-to-urban migration. However, these studies focus mainly on the impact in urban areas, which leaves room for us to re-examine this issue from the perspective of rural areas.

Empirical model specification

Although rural-to-urban migration is influenced by the situations in both rural and urban areas, decision-making about migration is made mainly in the rural areas from which rural migrants originate. In this sense, it is essential to examine the impact of the *hukou* policies on the off-farm employment of rural labour, and one can start by looking at rural households.

Following previous literature such as Meng and Zhang (2001) and Démurger et al. (2009), we assume that the choice of off-farm employment by rural labour is a function of the *hukou* restriction policies (Equation 5.1).

Equation 5.1

$$Y_{hrt} = \alpha_0 + \beta_1 HP_{hrt} + \beta_2 HS_{hrt} + \gamma_1 age_{hrt} + \gamma_2 Marry_{hrt} + \gamma_3 lbr_{hrt} + \gamma_4 man_{hrt} \\ + \gamma_5 area_{hrt} + \gamma_6 lnWageGap_{hrt} + \gamma_7 T_t + \gamma_8 D_h + \gamma_9 D_r + \varepsilon_{hrt}$$

In this equation, Y_{hrt} denotes the share of off-farm employment in total household labour of rural household h in region r at time t. HP_{hrt} and HS_{hrt} denote the two types of household restriction policies in urban areas that could affect the choice of rural households' off-farm employment, respectively: the employment-related restriction policy and the settlement-related restriction policy. We distinguish between the two restriction policies because we expect they may impose different impacts.

The two variables, HP_{hrt} and HS_{hrt}, deserve further explanation, as they are the most important dependent variables in our study. First, to measure the change in employment-related restriction policies faced by rural farming households, we collect all migrant employment-related policy in the urban areas of each province and categorise them into three groups according to their level of restriction. A score of 1–3 is assigned to each group of policies, with 1 representing the most restrictive policy and 3 representing the least restrictive policy.[2] Second, how the household restriction policies in urban areas will affect rural labourers' choice of off-farm employment usually depends on where they are going for off-farm employment. To reflect this point, we need to consider the distance from the home village of

---

2   Please refer to Appendix 5.1 for a more detailed definition of the employment restriction and settlement restriction policies in each province and how we allocate the scores between different types of migration restriction policies.

the rural labourer to the capital city of each province. Third, the probability of rural labourers going to a particular city for off-farm employment is also important. According to China Centre for Agricultural Policy's (CCAP) farm household survey, more than 80 per cent of rural labourers choose to work off-farm within the same province in which they live. Thus, it is not appropriate for us to give the same weights within a province and between provinces. Consequently, we use the proportion of rural labourers in the same village moving for off-farm employment within and between provinces as weights (Equation 5.2).

Equation 5.2

$$HP_{hrt} = \sum_{P} \frac{HP_{pt}}{Dist_{rpt}} \times MigShr\_inprovince + \sum_{-P} \frac{HP_{-pt}}{Dist_{r-pt}} \times MigShr\_outprovince$$

In this equation, HP_{pt} is the comprehensive employment-related restriction policy indicator faced by rural labour in province p at time t. HP_{-pt} are the scores for the employment-related restriction policy in urban areas of other province $-p$ at time t. $Dist_{rpt}$ and $Dist_{r-pt}$ denote the distance between the sample village and the capital city of province p, with p and $-p$ representing within and between provinces, respectively. $MigShr\_inprovince$ and $MigShr\_outprovince$ denote the proportion of off-farm employment within province p, and between provinces $-p$.

A similar procedure is used to measure the change in the settlement-related restriction policy (Equation 5.3).

Equation 5.3

$$HS_{hrt} = \sum_{P} \frac{HS_{pt}}{Dist_{rpt}} \times MigShr\_inprovince + \sum_{-P} \frac{HS_{-pt}}{Dist_{r-pt}} \times MigShr\_outprovince$$

In this equation, HS_{pt} and HS_{-pt} represents the settlement-related restriction policies, while other notations are the same as in Equation 5.2.

In addition to the household restriction policies, there are many other factors affecting rural labourers' choice of off-farm employment. If we do not account for them in Equation 5.1, we will generate a significant measurement problem. In our study, we categorise those control variables into three groups and include them in Equation 5.1.

The first group of control variables includes the logarithm of urban–rural income differences, $ln\_WageGap_{hrt}$, which is calculated by taking a ratio of the per capita income of households at the farm level to the per capita disposable income of 28 capital cities across the country in the form of Equation 5.4.

Equation 5.4

$$ln\_WageGap_{hrt} = ln\left(\frac{rural\_wage_{hrt}}{urban\_wage_{hrt}}\right)$$

In this equation, $rural\_wage_{hrt}$ is the per capita income of households at the farm level. It should be noted that the per capita income for years other than the year of sampling (2000, 2008 and 2013) is imputed based on the per capita income of the province's rural population by using data from the *China Statistics Yearbooks* (NBS various years[a]) and *China Rural Statistical Yearbooks* (NBS various years[b]), while keeping the rural consumer price index (CPI) conversion in 2000 constant values. $urban\_wage_{hrt}$ refers to the per capita disposable income of 28 capital cities across the country. To be specific, applying the data from the statistical yearbooks while keeping the rural CPI conversion in 2000 constant prices, $urban\_wage_{hrt}$ is estimated by Equation 5.5 using distance and the proportion of rural labour as weights.

Equation 5.5

$$
\begin{aligned}
urban\_wage_{hrt} \\
= \sum_{P} \frac{city\_inc_{pt}}{Dist_{rpt}} \times MigShr\_inprovince \\
+ \sum_{-P} \frac{city\_inc_{r-pt}}{Dist_{r-pt}} \times MigShr\_outprovince
\end{aligned}
$$

The second group of control variables captures the characteristics of a rural household, which include age_{hrt} as the average age of all labour in each sampled farm household; $Marry_{hrt}$, which is the number of married persons per household as a percentage of the total number of persons per household; lbr_{hrt} refers to the ratio of the labour population aged 16 to 65 in the household to the total population of the household; and man_{hrt} denotes the proportion of males in the total population of the household.

The third group of control variables describes family agricultural production features: $area_{hrt}$ refers to the total land area operated by each farm household.

In addition to the above three groups of control variables, we also control the household-specific effects and the time-specific effects, by using the dummy variables, to reduce the impact of omitted variables. Specifically, D_h is a vector of rural household and location characteristics that are consistent over time, and T_t is a dummy variable to control the influence of macroeconomic conditions in each year on the off-farm employment of rural labour.

To effectively estimate Equation 5.1, we need to deal with two potential econometric problems. First, the two variables used to capture the employment-related restriction and the settlement-related restriction could be highly correlated and thus may generate the problem of multicollinearity. To deal with this, we use the ratio of the employment-related restriction variable over the settlement-related restriction variable, HS_{hrt}/HP_{hrt}, to replace HS_{hrt}. The estimated coefficient in front of the newly created variable will capture the difference in impact between the employment-related restriction relative to the settlement-related restriction. Second, the estimation of Equation 5.1 using the ordinary least squares (OLS) regression method may suffer from the omitted variable problem, since there are many other household-level or region-level factors affecting rural labourers' choice of off-farm employment that are not well reflected in our model specification. To deal with this problem, we adopt the panel data fixed effect model to estimate Equation 5.1. We acknowledge that this treatment may only help with reducing the omitted variable problem by eliminating those time-invariant factors so we use the time dummy to account for time-variant factors.

Finally, it is widely believed that *hukou* policies may generate different impacts on the different types of off-farm employment choice. In particular, part-time off-farm employment is unlikely to be affected by the settlement-related restriction, in theory. To capture this impact, we distinguish between two types of off-farm employment by using different dependent variables—namely, the ratios of full-time off-farm employment and part-time off-farm employment. Based on Equation 5.1, these two equations can be written as Equations 5.6 and 5.7.

Equation 5.6

$$ln\_OffFarm_{hrt}$$
$$= \alpha_0 + \beta_1 HP_{hrt} + \beta_2\,{}^{HS_{hrt}}/_{HP_{hrt}} + \gamma_1 age_{hrt} + \gamma_2 Marry_{hrt} + \gamma_3 lbr_{hrt}$$
$$+ \gamma_4 man_{hrt} + \gamma_5 area_{hrt} + \gamma_6 lnWageGap_{hrt} + \gamma_7 T_t + \gamma_8 D_h + \gamma_9 D_r + \varepsilon_{hrt}$$

Equation 5.7

$$ln\_FOffFarm_{hrt}$$
$$= \alpha_0 + \beta_1 HP_{hrt} + \beta_2\,{}^{HS_{hrt}}/_{HP_{hrt}} + \gamma_1 age_{hrt} + \gamma_2 Marry_{hrt} + \gamma_3 lbr_{hrt}$$
$$+ \gamma_4 man_{hrt} + \gamma_5 area_{hrt} + \gamma_6 lnWageGap_{hrt} + \gamma_7 T_t + \gamma_8 D_h + \gamma_9 D_r + \varepsilon_{hrt}$$

In Equation 5.6, $ln\_OffFarm_{hrt}$ refers to off-farm employment, estimated by using a ratio of off-farm employment to total population at the household farm level. Similarly, in Equation 5.7, $ln\_FOffFarm_{hrt}$ denotes full-time off-farm employment, measured by the proportion of full-time off-farm employment in the total labour at the household farm level. The employment-related restriction and the settlement-related restriction are defined by two variables, HP_{hrt} and ${}^{HS_{hrt}}/_{HP_{hrt}}$, with the latter concerning a multicollinearity between two categories of policies.

Based on Equations 5.6 and 5.7, we propose testing the following three hypotheses. First, a positive (negative) coefficient in front of HP_{hrt} and HS_{hrt}/HP_{hrt} may imply that the relaxation of the *hukou* policy in urban areas (or a higher score for the comprehensive household registration policy indicator) will tend to increase the willingness of rural labour to undertake off-farm employment, and vice versa. Second, a positive and significant coefficient in front of HS_{hrt}/HP_{hrt} implies that the settlement restriction is likely to impose a stronger impact on rural labour's off-farm employment choice. Third, when we distinguish between part-time and full-time off-farm employment, we can show how the relaxation of the household registration policies may affect rural labour's choice between the two types of off-farm employment.

Data sources and descriptive statistics

Data used in this study mainly come from two sources: microlevel farm household survey data collected by the Agricultural Policy Research Centre of the Chinese Academy of Sciences and the Peking University; and the province-level official statistics from various sources. These data are used mainly to measure the *hukou* system changes faced by rural labour and the rural–urban income gap. Both sets of data span the period from 1981 to 2013.

The CCAP farm household survey is a three-wave repetitive field survey conducted in 2000, 2008 and 2013. According to the ranking of the provincial per capita industrial output value, the survey used a multistage stratified sampling method to randomly select 30 counties, 60 villages and 1,200 farmers in six provinces in the major agricultural regions of China (that is, Hebei, Shaanxi, Liaoning, Zhejiang, Sichuan and Hubei). Figure 5.1 illustrates the geographical distribution of those sample regions.

The survey collects information including the characteristics of rural households, land usage, input usage, output of agricultural production, off-farm employment of each household member and their income, in six provinces. Among these, off-farm employment is divided into current employment status and off-farm employment history. Except for the households that could not be tracked due to uncontrollable reasons such as natural disasters, a total of 1,063 sample households were successfully tracked in the third phase. This chapter formed 33 years of balanced panel data from 1981 to 2013 (see Appendix 5.2 for more detailed information on the sampled farms).

Using the farm survey data, we first define rural labour's off-farm employment using each person's current employment status and their off-farm employment history. Specifically, according to the definition of off-farm employment by Brauw et al. (2002), we split part-time off-farm employment (which is defined as engaging in agricultural production and having off-farm income) from full-time off-farm employment (which is defined as being isolated from agricultural production, having no farming income and being fully engaged in non-agricultural industries). In addition, we have defined another eight variables: the employment-related household registration policy, the settlement-related household registration policy, the mean age of the household, the proportion of married people per household, the share of the labour force per household, the share of male agricultural labour per household, land area per household and the rural–urban wage gap.

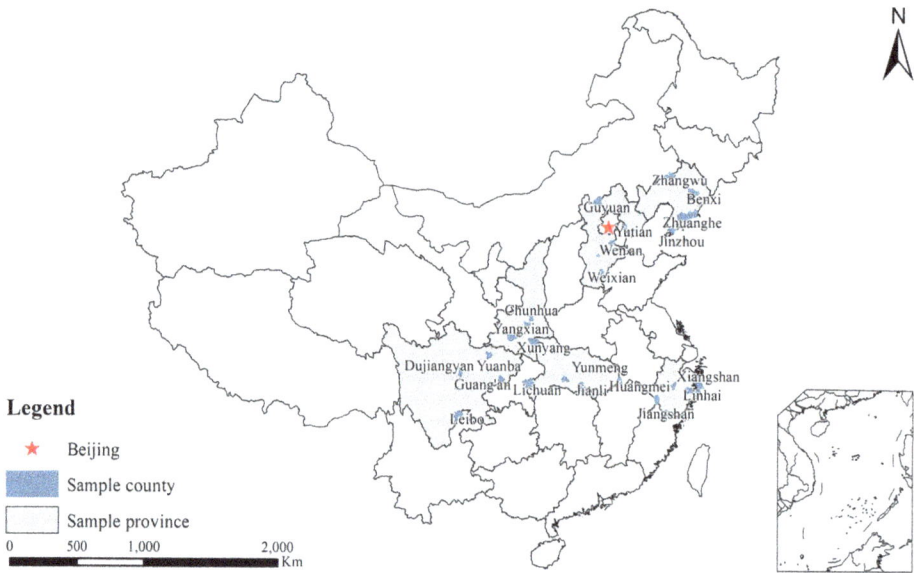

Figure 5.1 Geographical distribution of our sample farms, 2000, 2008 and 2015
Source: Summarised by the authors based on survey data.

Figure 5.2 shows the changing trend in the average proportion of off-farm employment in total rural labour at the household level between 1981 and 2013, while Figure 5.3 describes the relative proportion of part-time off-farm employment to that of full-time off-farm employment. Between 1981 and 2013, the proportion of off-farm employment in total rural labour increased from about 10 per cent to more than 60 per cent. Moreover, when we split full-time from part-time off-farm employment, the relative proportion of full-time off-farm employment to part-time off-farm employment increased over time, suggesting that the increase of off-farm employment comes mainly from the increase in full-time off-farm employment. It is notable that there are two 'cliffs' that appear at the junction of the three phases (in 2000 and 2008, respectively) of the trend in both Figure 5.2 and Figure 5.3. This is mainly due to the errors in farmers' recollection of their employment history, which does not affect the estimation of the overall trend of off-farm employment.

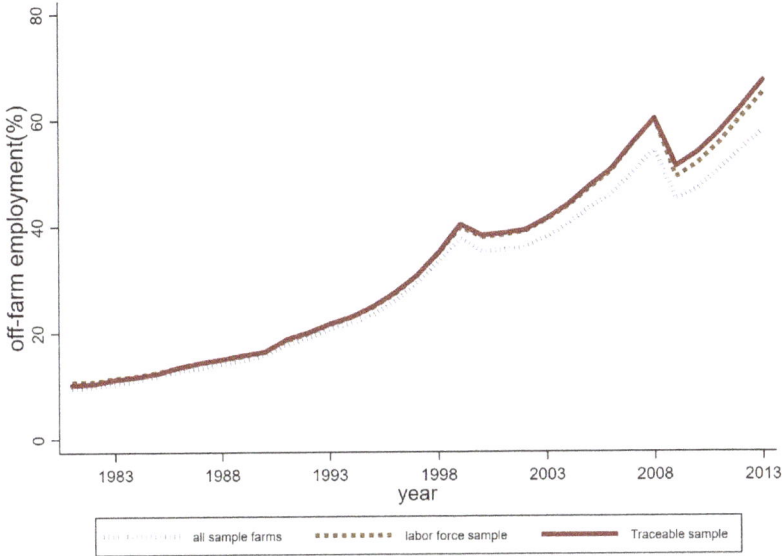

Figure 5.2 Change in relative proportion of off-farm employment in China, 1981–2013

Note: Although there are 'cliffs' in 2000 and 2008 in our time-series data due to the unreliable nature of recalled data, they do not affect our results. To test this, a robustness check has been made in Appendix 5.3, in which two dummy variables have been controlled in the regressions, and the results are consistent with our findings.

Source: Authors' estimations using CCAP farm survey data.

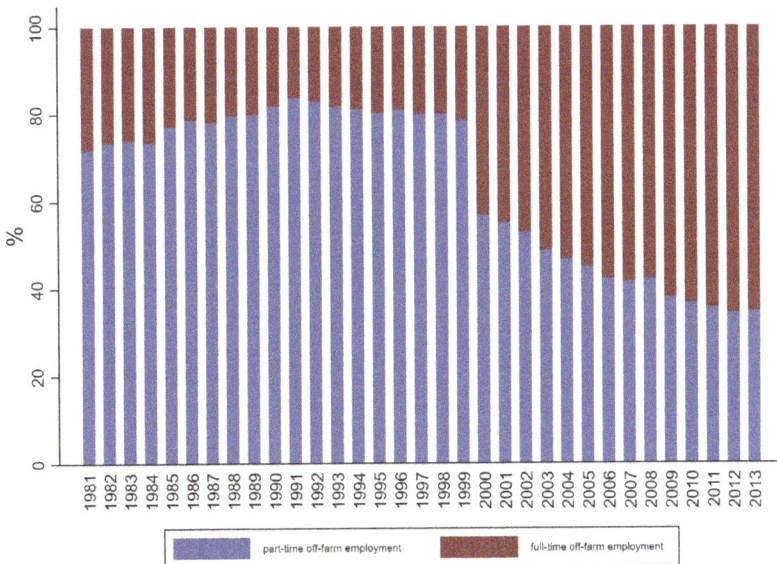

Figure 5.3 Part-time versus full-time off-farm employment, 1981–2013

Note: For the 'cliffs' in 2000 and 2008, please refer to the note under Figure 5.2.

Source: Authors' estimations using CCAP farm survey data.

It is widely believed that there are two important factors that may affect the choice of off-farm employment of rural labourers: the rural–urban wage gap and the household registration system. Before we conduct an analysis of the causal relationship, it is useful to look at the apparent relationship between these two factors and the average proportion of off-farm employment of rural labour at the farm level. As shown in Figures 5.4 and 5.5, the average proportion of off-farm employment has been increasing with the increasing rural–urban wage gap, as well as the relaxation over time of the *hukou* restrictions. This implies that further relaxing *hukou* restrictions is likely to increase the probability of rural labourers choosing off-farm employment. Although the visual relationship is informative, we need more thorough regression analysis to examine our hypotheses.

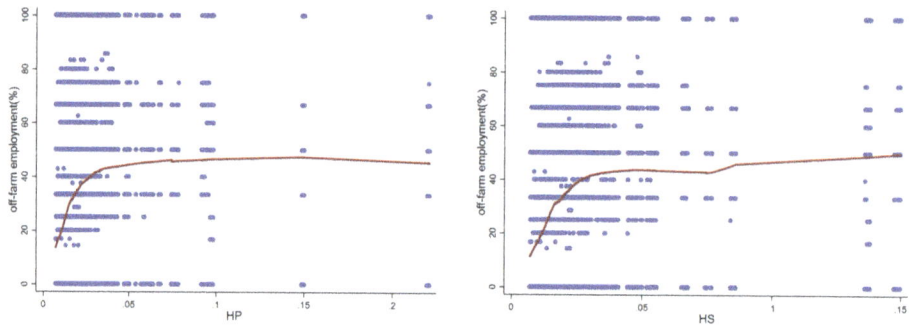

Panel (A) Household registration policy versus part-time non-agricultural employment

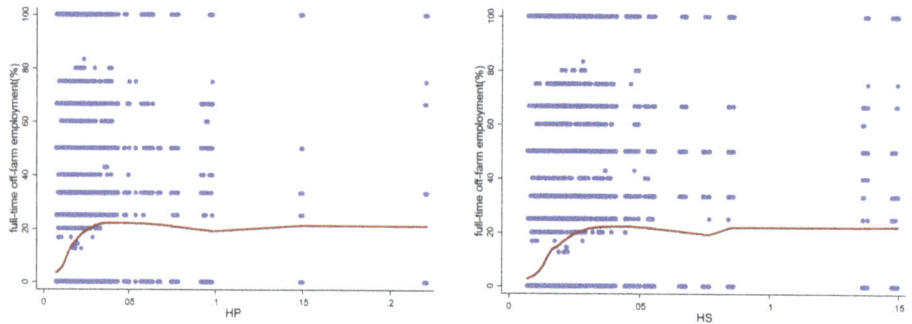

Panel (B) Household registration restrictions versus full-time non-agricultural employment

Figure 5.4 The apparent relationship between household registration restrictions and average off-farm employment

Source: Authors' estimations using CCAP farm survey data.

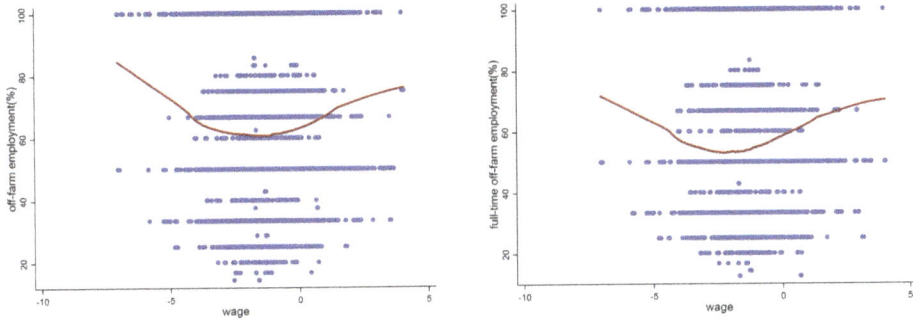

Figure 5.5 The apparent relationship between the urban–rural income gap and average off-farm employment

Source: Authors' estimations using CCAP farm survey data.

Finally, for other control variables, Table 5.1 provides some descriptive statistics on how they have changed over time between the three survey years: 2000, 2008 and 2013. Overall, it shows that a rise in the average scores of both categories of policies indicates the gradual relaxation of *hukou* policies, which is in accordance with the reform procedure. It is also notable that the degree of employment-related restrictions is relaxed more quickly than that of settlement-related restrictions. Since the wage variable is measured by the rural–urban income ratio, the increase in the mean of the wage variable, from 0.63 in 2000 to 0.31 in 2013, reveals an expansion in the urban–rural income gap over that time. The change in land area shows a decline from 6.34 mu to 5.61 mu across periods. The rise in the share of the labour force from 53.81 per cent to 56.92 per cent may facilitate non-agricultural employment.

Table 5.1 Descriptive statistics of key variables, 2000, 2008 and 2013

Year	1981–2013		2000		2008		2013	
Variable	Mean	SD	Mean	SD	Mean	SD	Mean	SD
Share of agricultural labour (%)	69.41	35.94	63.25	36.60	44.20	36.67	40.79	39.41
Share of part-time off-farm labour (%)	17.04	28.00	21.34	31.37	23.80	31.62	20.49	30.76
Share of full-time off-farm labour (%)	13.55	27.29	15.41	27.19	32.00	34.62	38.72	38.67
Employment-related household registration policy	0.02	0.02	0.02	0.01	0.03	0.02	0.04	0.03
Settlement-related household registration policy	0.02	0.02	0.02	0.01	0.03	0.03	0.03	0.03
Mean age of the household (year)	29.35	9.61	30.68	7.50	37.33	8.20	39.71	8.44
Share of married family members (%)	72.51	21.90	73.31	22.19	69.99	21.46	77.83	17.21
Share of labour force (%)	53.87	24.76	53.81	21.23	55.71	25.01	56.92	27.30
Share of male agricultural labour (%)	50.18	16.25	49.92	16.97	50.14	16.94	49.31	17.31
Land area (mu)	6.22	9.78	6.34	7.55	6.31	14.88	5.61	6.89
Ratio of rural–urban income (%)	0.62	2.02	0.63	1.71	0.40	2.01	0.31	1.17
Observations	35,079		1,063		1,063		1,063	

Source: Authors' estimations using CCAP farm survey data.

Empirical results: Impact of the *hukou* system on off-farm employment

The essential question we seek to answer is what are the impacts of the *hukou* policy on the off-farm employment of rural labour? To answer this question, we apply the panel data to estimate Equations 5.6 and 5.7 so as to quantify the impact of the employment-related and settlement-related policies, respectively, on the off-farm employment of rural labour. The estimation results obtained by using the OLS regression and the panel data regression with fixed effects are presented in Table 5.2.

Table 5.2 Regression results

Variables	Off-farm employment		Full-time off-farm employment		Part-time off-farm employment	
	(1) OLS	(2) Fixed effect	(3) OLS	(4) Fixed effect	(5) OLS	(6) Fixed effect
HP_{hrt}	0.378***	0.440***	0.305***	0.393***	0.050***	0.011
	(0.015)	(0.006)	(0.013)	(0.005)	(0.014)	(0.017)
HS_{hrt}/HP_{hrt}	0.254***	0.276***	0.157***	0.188***	0.084***	0.060**
	(0.022)	(0.009)	(0.019)	(0.007)	(0.024)	(0.025)
age_{hrt}	−0.000*	−0.000	−0.000	−0.000***	0.000***	0.005***
	(0.000)	(0.000)	(0.000)	(0.000)	(0.000)	(0.001)
$Marry_{hrt}$	−0.003***	−0.002***	−0.001**	−0.000***	−0.002***	−0.002***
	(0.000)	(0.000)	(0.000)	(0.000)	(0.000)	(0.000)
lbr_{hrt}	0.002***	0.001***	0.001***	0.001***	0.000	−0.000
	(0.000)	(0.000)	(0.000)	(0.000)	(0.000)	(0.000)
man_{hrt}	0.000	0.001***	0.000	0.001***	−0.000	−0.000
	(0.000)	(0.000)	(0.000)	(0.000)	(0.000)	(0.000)
$lnWageGap_{hrt}$	0.002	0.003***	0.002***	0.004***	0.005***	0.005***
	(0.002)	(0.001)	(0.001)	(0.000)	(0.001)	(0.001)
$area_{hrt}$	0.000	0.000	−0.000	−0.000*	0.001*	0.001**
	(0.000)	(0.000)	(0.000)	(0.000)	(0.000)	(0.000)
Constant	1.634***	1.878***	1.167***	1.508***	0.407***	0.187**
	(0.132)	(0.093)	(0.065)	(0.024)	(0.065)	(0.087)
Observations	33,355	33,355	33,355	33,355	33,355	33,355
Number of hhcode	1,011	1,011	1,011	1,011	1,011	1,011
R-squared		0.275		0.275		0.049

*** $p < 0.01$ statistically significant at the 10 per cent level
** $p < 0.05$ statistically significant at the 5 per cent level
* $p < 0.1$ statistically significant at 1 per cent level
Note: Standard errors in parentheses.

First, using the average proportion of off-farm employment in total labour at the farm household level, we examine the impact of the employment-related restriction policy and the settlement-related restriction policy on rural labour's choice of off-farm employment. Controlling household characteristics, the estimated coefficients in front of the employment-related restriction policy based on the panel regression with the household fixed effects is positive and significant at the 1 per cent level. This implies that the relaxation of the employment-related restriction policy positively contributes to an increase in the proportion of rural labour choosing off-farm employment. Moreover, the coefficients in front of the ratio between the settlement-related restriction policy and the employment-related restriction policy are also positive and significant at the 1 per cent level. This implies that relaxing the settlement-related restriction policy is likely to generate a larger impact on the off-farm choice of rural labour than relaxing the employment-related restriction policy.

Second, we further use the average proportion of full-time off-farm employment in total labour at the farm household level as the dependent variable and redo the exercise. As is shown in Table 5.2 (Columns 3 and 4), the impacts of both the employment-related restriction policy and the settlement-related restriction policy on the off-farm employment of rural labour are close to those obtained for total off-farm employment. The estimated coefficients in front of the employment-related restriction policy and the settlement-related restriction policy are positive and significant at the 1 per cent level. In addition, when compared with those estimates when the dependent variable is the proportion of part-time off-farm employment in total labour, the estimated impact seems to increase. This implies that the household restriction policies are likely to affect the full-time off-farm employment choices of rural labour much more than their part-time choices.

Third, although relaxing both the employment-related restriction policy and the settlement-related restriction policy will tend to increase average off-farm employment of rural labour at the farm level, the impact of the settlement restriction policy is more relevant to the increase of off-farm employment. According to the estimates in Table 5.2, in the scenario of the average proportion of off-farm employment (Columns 1 and 2), the positive and statistically significant coefficients in front of $^{HS_{hrt}}/_{HP_{hrt}}$ imply that the impact of the settlement-related restriction policy is 25.4 per cent to 27.6 per cent higher than that of the employment-related restriction policy. Meanwhile, in the scenario of the average proportion of full-time off-farm employment (Columns 3 and 4), the positive and statistically significant coefficients in front of $^{HS_{hrt}}/_{HP_{hrt}}$ indicate that the impact of the settlement-related restriction policy is 15.7 per cent to 18.8 per cent higher than the employment-related restriction policy.

As for control variables, a positive coefficient in front of the rural–urban wage gap, which implies that the rural–urban wage gap is one of the most important factors affecting the choice of off-farm employment. Comparing the estimates based on Equations 5.6 and 5.7, the coefficients in front of the wage gap when the dependent variable is the average proportion of full-time off-farm employment are greater than those in the case where the average proportion of off-farm employment in total labour is the dependent variable. This indicates that the wage gap is likely to exert more influence on full-time off-farm employment. The negative and statistically significant coefficients in front of the average age of a household indicate that average age negatively impacts on off-farm employment. The proportion of those married in the total population at the farm household level affects off-farm employment negatively and significantly based on Columns 1–4 in Table 5.2. Moreover, a positive and statistically significant coefficient in front of the share of the labour force in the total population at the farm household level implies that, with an increase in the share of the labour force, the average proportion of off-farm employment will increase as well. In addition, as is shown in Table 5.2, the positive and statistically significant coefficients in front of the average proportion of males in the total population at the farm household level imply that households with a higher proportion of males are more likely to participate in off-farm employment.

Concluding remarks

This chapter investigates the impact of household registration policies in urban areas on the off-farm employment of rural labour by using household-level data for the period 1981–2013. The study makes three main contributions. First, we construct a panel dataset of off-farm employment at the household level spanning 1981 to 2013, which allows us to examine the long-term effects of the *hukou* system on the off-farm employment of rural labour. Second, we compile a comprehensive indicator to capture the trans-temporal and cross-regional changes in the *hukou* system throughout the whole post-reform period and the potential impacts of policy reforms. Third, instead of conducting analysis from the perspective of urban areas, we concentrate on the rural side and attempt to investigate the behaviour of farm households under *hukou* reforms.

We show that the off-farm employment of rural labour tends to increase with the relaxation of *hukou* policies throughout the whole post-reform period, when the rural–urban wage gap and other farm household level characteristics are well controlled. In particular, when splitting full-time off-farm employment from part-time off-farm employment, we show that full-time off-farm employment is more likely to be restricted by the settlement-related policy. This implies that institutional barriers related to the *hukou* system are still important barriers to the integration of rural and urban labour markets. Further reforms are required to relax this system so as to facilitate rural-to-urban migration.

References

Afridi, F. Li, S. and Ren, Y. (2015), Social identify and inequality: The impact of China's hukou system, *Journal of Public Economics* 123(3): 17–29.

Bazzi, S., Gaduh, A., Rothenberg, A.D. and Wong, M. (2016), Skill transferability, migration, and development: Evidence from population resettlement in Indonesia, *American Economic Review* 106(9): 2658–98. doi.org/10.1257/aer.20141781.

Beegle, K., De Weerdt, J. and Dercon, S. (2011), Migration and economic mobility in Tanzania: Evidence from a tracking survey, *Review of Economics and Statistics* 93(3): 1010–33. doi.org/10.1162/REST_a_00105.

Bergmann, B.R. (1971), The effect on white incomes of discrimination in employment, *Journal of Political Economy* 79(2): 294–313. doi.org/10.1086/259744.

Bernstein, M. and Olsen, K.A. (2009), Identity deployment and social change: Understanding identity as a social movement and organizational strategy, *Sociology Compass* 3(6): 871–83.

Bonnin, M. (2014), The lost generation: The rustication of China's educated youth (1968–1980), *The China Quarterly* 218: 551–89.

Bosker, M., Brakman, S., Garretsen, H. and Schramm, M. (2012), Relaxing hukou: Increased labor mobility and China's economic geography, *Journal of Urban Economics* 72(2): 252–66. doi.org/10.1016/j.jue.2012.06.002.

Brauw A., Huang J. and Rozelle S. (2002), *The evolution of China's rural labor markets during the reforms*, Department of Agricultural and Resource Economics, UC Davis Working Paper (02-003).

Brown, R.S., Moon, M. and Zoloth, B.S. (1980), Incorporating occupational attainment in studies of male–female earnings differentials, *Journal of Human Resources* 28: 3–28. doi.org/10.2307/145344.

Bryan, G., Chowdhury, S. and Mobarak, A.M. (2014), Underinvestment in a profitable technology: The case of seasonal migration in Bangladesh, *Econometrica* 82(5): 1671–748. doi.org/10.3982/ECTA10489.

Cai, F. (2018), Perceiving truth and ceasing doubts: What can we learn from 40 years of China's reform and opening up?, *China & World Economy* 26(2): 1–22. doi.org/10.1111/cwe.12234.

Cai, F., Wang, D. and Du, Y. (2002), Regional disparity and economic growth in China: The impact of labor market distortions, *China Economic Review* 13(2): 197–212. doi.org/10.1016/S1043-951X(02)00072-X.

Cai, H., Chen, Y., Fang, H. and Zhou, L.-A. (2015), The effect of microinsurance on economic activities: Evidence from a randomized field experiment, *Review of Economics and Statistics* 97(2): 287–300. doi.org/10.1162/REST_a_00476.

Chan, K.W. and Zhang, L. (1999), The hukou system and rural–urban migration in China: Processes and changes, *The China Quarterly* 160: 818–55. doi.org/10.1017/S0305741000001351.

Chen, Y.P. and Yuan, Z. (2018), A decomposition method on employment and wage discrimination and its application in urban China (2002–2013), *World Development* 110: 1–12.

de Brauw, A.D. and Giles, J.T. (2006), *Migrant labor markets and the welfare of rural households in the developing world: Evidence from China*, IZA Discussion Papers No. 6765, Frankfurt am Main: Institute of Labor Economics.

Démurger, S., Gurgand, M., Li, S. and Yue, X. (2009), Migrants as second-class workers in urban China? A decomposition analysis, *Journal of Comparative Economics* 37(4): 610–28. doi.org/10.1016/j.jce.2009.04.008.

Démurger, S., Li, S. and Yang, J. (2012), Earnings differentials between the public and private sectors in China: Exploring changes for urban local residents in the 2000s, *China Economic Review* 23(1): 138–53. doi.org/10.1016/j.chieco.2011.08.007.

Dong, X. and Bowles, P. (2002), Segmentation and discrimination in China's emerging industrial labour market, *Chinese Economic Review* 13(2–3): 170–196.

Fan, Y. (2015), *Does adversity affect long-term consumption and financial behaviour? Evidence from China's rustication programme*, LSE Working Paper, London: London School of Economics.

Garriga, C., Tang, Y. and Wang, P. (2017), *Rural–urban migration, structural transformation, and housing markets in China*. CCAP Working Paper No. 2014-028.

Golley, J. (2002), Regional patterns of industrial development during China's economic transition, *Economics of Transition* 10(3): 761–801. doi.org/10.1111/1468-0351.t01-1-00133.

Greenwood, D.T. and Holt, R.P.F. (2010), Growth, inequality and negative trickle down, *Journal of Economic Issues* 44(2): 403–10. doi.org/10.2753/JEI0021-3624440212.

Hertel, T.W. and Zhai, F. (2006), Labor market distortions, rural–urban inequality and the opening of China's economy, *Economic Modelling* 23: 76–109.

Karlan, D., Osei, R., Osei-Akoto, I. and Udry, C. (2014), Agricultural decisions after relaxing credit and risk constraints, *The Quarterly Journal of Economics* 129(2): 597–652. doi.org/10.1093/qje/qju002.

Kinnan, C., Wang, S.Y. and Wang, Y. (2015), *Relaxing migration constraints for rural households*, NBER Working Papers No. 21314, Cambridge, MA: National Bureau of Economic Research. doi.org/10.3386/w21314.

Knight, J., Song, L. and Jia, H. (1999), Chinese rural migrants in urban enterprises: Three perspectives, *Journal of Development Studies* 35(3): 73–104.

Knight, J. and Yueh, L. (2004), Job mobility of residents and migrants in urban China, *Journal of Comparative Economics* 32(4): 637–60.

Krugman, P. and Venables, A.J. (1995), Globalization and the inequality of nations, *The Quarterly Journal of Economics* 110(4): 857–80. doi.org/10.2307/2946642.

Lewis, W.A. (1954), Economic development with unlimited supplies of labor, *The Manchester School* 22(2): 139–91. doi.org/10.1111/j.1467-9957.1954.tb00021.x.

Li, J. and Gu, Y. (2011), Hukou-based stratification in China's urban labour market, *Sociological Studies* 2011(2): 52–81.

Liu, Y. (2011), An econometric model of disequilibrium unemployment in urban China, *Econometrics* 101(9): 17–29.

Lu, J. (2002), Social development coming into a new stage: Analysis of societal situation 2001–2002, in X. Ru, X. Lu and P. Li (eds), *Blue Book of Chinese Society* (Analysis and Predictions of Chinese Society). Beijing: Social Science Publishing House.

Lu, M. and Chen, Z. (2004), Urban-biased economic policies and urban-rural inequality, *Economic Research Journal* 2004(6): 50–8.

Meng, X. (1998), Male–female wage determination and gender wage discrimination in China's rural industrial sector, *Labour Economics* 5(1): 67–89. doi.org/10.1016/S0927-5371(97)00028-6.

Meng, X. (2000), *Labour market reform in China*, Cambridge: Cambridge University Press.

Meng, X. (2012), Labour market outcomes and reforms in China, *Journal of Economic Perspectives* 26(4): 75–101. doi.org/10.1257/jep.26.4.75.

Meng, X., Gregory, R. and Wang, Y. (2005), Poverty, inequality, and growth in urban China, 1986–2000, *Journal of Comparative Economics* 33(4): 710–29. doi.org/10.1016/j.jce.2005.08.006.

Meng, X. and Kidd, M.P. (1997), Labour market reform and the changing structure of wage determination in China's state sector during the 1980s, *Journal of Comparative Economics* 25(3): 403–21. doi.org/10.1006/jcec.1997.1481.

Meng, X. and Zhang, D. (2010), Labour market impact of large-scale internal migration on Chinese urban 'native' workers, *IZA Discussion Paper* No. 5288.

Meng, X. and Zhang, J. (2001), The two-tier labour market in urban China: Occupational segregation and wage differentials between urban residents and rural migrants in Shanghai, *Journal of Comparative Economics* 29(3): 485–504. doi.org/10.1006/jcec.2001.1730.

National Bureau of Statistics (2018), Migrant workers monitoring survey report, available from: www.stats.gov.cn/tjsj/zxfb/201904/t20190429_1662268.html.

National Bureau of Statistics of China (NBS) (various years[a]), *China Statistics Yearbook*, Beijing: China Statistics Press.

National Bureau of Statistics of China (NBS) (various years[b]), *China Rural Statistical Yearbook*, Beijing: China Statistics Press.

Seeborg, M.C., Jin, Z. and Zhu, Y. (2000), The new rural–urban labour mobility in China: Causes and implications, *The Journal of Socio-Economics* 29(1): 39–56.

Song, J. and Li, S. (2014), Hukou's impact on labor occupation segmentation, *China Agricultural Economic Review* 6(3): 506–22. doi.org/10.1108/CAER-05-2013-0081.

Song, Y. (2014), What should economists know about the current Chinese *hukou* system?, *China Economic Review* 29: 200–12.

Sun W., Bai, C. and Xie, P. (2011), The effect on rural labor mobility from registration system reform in China, *Economic Research Journal* 2011(1): 28–41.

Todaro, M.P. (1969), A model of labor migration and urban unemployment in less developed countries, *American Economic Review* 59(1): 138–48.

Tombe T. and Zhu X. (2019), Trade, migration, and productivity: A quantitative analysis of China, *American Economic Review* 109(5): 1843–72.

Wan, H. and Li, S. (2013), The effects of household registration system discrimination on urban–rural income inequality in China, *Economic Research Journal* 9: 43–55.

Wang, M. and Cai, F. (2005), Gender wage differentials in China's urban labour market, *Economic Research Journal* 146: 1–25.

Wang, X.B., Huang, J.K. and Rozelle, S. (2017), Off-farm employment and agricultural specialization in China, *China Economic Review* 42: 155–65. doi.org/10.1016/j.chieco.2016.09.004.

Whalley, J. and Zhang, S. (2004), *Inequality change in China and (hukou) labor mobility restrictions*, NBER Working Papers No. 10683, Cambridge, MA: National Bureau of Economic Research. doi.org/10.3386/w10683.

Yang, X. (2017), The impact of household registration system reform on population immigration of big cities in China: An empirical study based on urban panel data from 2000 to 2014, *Urban Problems* 2017(1): 70–77.

Appendix 5.1 The household registration policy classification and score method

Based on the history of *hukou* reforms since 1958, we summarise all migrant policies in the urban areas of 28 provinces—excluding Tibet, Xinjiang, Gansu, Hong Kong, Macau and Taiwan—in each period of reform, and we find that employment-related and settlement-related restriction policies are essential administrative drivers of off-farm employment. Therefore, the *hukou* system referred to in this chapter is divided into two categories: the employment-related and settlement-related restriction policies. Each category is further divided into three groups, according to the level of restriction. A score of 1–3 is assigned to each policy group, with 1 representing the most restrictive policy and 3 representing the least restrictive policy. If the *hukou* system of a province in that year conforms to Category A, it will receive 1 point; if it conforms to Category B, it will receive 2 points; and if it conforms to Category C, it will be given 3 points. Since we define the category based on the quantified extent to which the *hukou* system evolves over time and is consistent between provinces, it allows us to make a quantitative comparison (although the method is simple). Table A5.1 provides the detailed definitions of the employment restriction and settlement restriction policies and scores for the two types of household registration systems in 28 provinces from 1981 to 2013.

Table A5.1 Household registration policy classification and score method

Level of policy relaxation	Employment-related policy	Settlement-related policy	Score of policy effects
A	Rural labourers are allowed to work outside household registration areas, but there are restrictions on the types of work, and the 'Mobile Personnel Employment Permit' and 'Mobile Personnel Employment Card' are required.	Rural labourers are allowed to register a residence permit if they are living legally and stably in this city; are employed legally and stably in this city and have been participating in the city's employee social insurance scheme for six months; are staying with relatives with local household registration; or have been studying for more than six months, etc.	1
B	Rural labourers are allowed to work outside the household registration area, there are no restrictions on the types of work, but a temporary residence permit is needed. The temporary residence permit requires workers to have a permanent place of residence (including a lease) and legal work. Basically, rural labourers cannot share the civil rights of urban residents.	If the holder of a residence permit continues to live in the same place and pays social insurance premiums for five years, has a stable occupation and meets the family planning policy, his or her children receive preschool education and compulsory education the same as permanent resident students.	2

Level of policy relaxation	Employment-related policy	Settlement-related policy	Score of policy effects
C	Temporary residence permit processing only requires resident ID card or other valid identification certificate. After processing, rural labourers can directly enjoy some citizen rights.	Rural workers with their spouses, unmarried children and parents living together are allowed to apply for registration of permanent residence if they are employed legally and stably for more than a year in a small or medium-sized city, have a legal and stable residence (including a lease) and participate in a social insurance scheme for a certain number of years.	3

Note: Two categories of the household registration policy are summarised according to the national household registration system policy from 1958 to the present, combined with the provincial household registration policy of 1981–2018 in 28 provinces, excluding Tibet, Xinjiang, Gansu, Hong Kong, Macau and Taiwan.

Appendix 5.2 The distribution of sample farms: 2008 and 2013

Table A5.2 summarises the distribution of sample farms in the second and third phases (2000 and 2008, respectively) of the CCAP farm household surveys.

Table A5.2 The distribution of sample farms, 2008 and 2013

Province	Number of sample farms	2008		2013	
		Field survey	Telephone survey	Field survey	Telephone survey
Nation	1,063	999	64	972	91
Hebei	177	173	4	173	4
Shaanxi	192	175	17	180	12
Liaoning	192	184	8	168	24
Zhejiang	180	177	13	153	27
Sichuan	150	147	3	143	7
Hubei	172	153	19	155	17

Source: Summarised by authors using CCAP farm survey data.

Appendix 5.3 Robustness check for the cliffs in 2000 and 2008

Table A5.3 Regression results incorporating dummy variables for 2000 and 2008

Variables	Off-farm employment		Full-time off-farm employment	
	(1) OLS	(2) Fixed effect	(3) OLS	(4) Fixed effect
HP_{hrt}	0.356***	0.420***	0.292***	0.382***
	(0.031)	(0.024)	(0.033)	(0.028)
HS_{hrt}/HP_{hrt}	0.250***	0.270***	0.164***	0.192***
	(0.033)	(0.031)	(0.030)	(0.030)
age_{hrt}	0.000	−0.000	−0.000	−0.000***
	(0.000)	(0.000)	(0.000)	(0.000)
$Marry_{hrt}$	−0.003***	−0.003***	−0.000**	−0.000
	(0.000)	(0.000)	(0.000)	(0.000)
lbr_{hrt}	0.002***	0.001***	0.001***	0.001***
	(0.000)	(0.000)	(0.000)	(0.000)
man_{hrt}	0.000	0.001	0.000	0.001*
	(0.000)	(0.001)	(0.000)	(0.000)
$lnWageGap_{hrt}$	0.002	0.003	−0.004**	−0.002
	(0.002)	(0.002)	(0.002)	(0.002)
$area_{hrt}$	0.000	0.000	−0.000	−0.000
	(0.000)	(0.001)	(0.000)	(0.001)
dum_2000_2008	0.036***	0.039***	0.005	0.009
	(0.009)	(0.009)	(0.008)	(0.008)
dum_2008_2013	0.066***	0.046***	0.072***	0.047***
	(0.009)	(0.009)	(0.010)	(0.008)
Constant	1.568***	1.821***	1.103***	1.456***
	(0.131)	(0.096)	(0.150)	(0.115)
Observations	33,355	33,355	33,355	33,355
Number of hhcode	1,011	1,011	1,011	1,011
R-squared		0.278		0.277

*** $p < 0.01$ statistically significant at the 10 per cent level

** $p < 0.05$ statistically significant at the 5 per cent level

* $p < 0.1$ statistically significant at the 1 per cent level

Note: Standard errors in parentheses.

6. Nonstandard employment: Global vision and evidence from China's urban labour market

Yongjie Wang

Nonstandard forms of employment have become a feature of contemporary labour markets around the world (ILO 2016). The growth of nonstandard employment (NSE) was noticed as early as the 1970s in developed economies such as Europe, the United States and Australia (Allan 2000; Kalleberg 2000; Adams and Deakin 2014). In Asia, there was also evidence of the development of NSE, the proportion of which increased from 17 per cent to 34 per cent from 1986 to 2008 in Japan, and from 27.4 per cent to 34.3 per cent from 2002 to 2011 in South Korea (Korea Labour Institute 2011; Asano et al. 2013, both cited in Cooke and Brown 2015). In recent years, new jobs and new forms of employment have tended to be more flexible and nonstandard. For example, in Organisation for Economic Co-operation and Development (OECD) countries, more than half of all jobs created since 1995 were nonstandard jobs and NSE accounted for about one-third of total employment in 2013 (OECD 2015). In Europe, the majority of new forms of employment generated since 2000 are nonstandard jobs, such as employee sharing, casual work, mobile work based on information and communication technology (ICT), portfolio work and crowd employment (Eurofound 2015). In the literature on NSE, it is explained as firms' strategies to save costs, attain flexibility and screen candidates for regular positions, and, at the structural level, it has been attributed to an expansion of the service sector, the availability of new technologies and labour market deregulation (Allan 2000; Houseman 2001; Bosch 2004; George and Chattopadhyay 2015). Some studies have described the growth of NSE as a response to strict labour laws and labour market regulations (Schömann et al. 1998; Adams and Deakin 2014; Cooke and Brown 2015; Aleksynska and Berg 2016).

NSE has also become an important feature of China's labour market. Nonstandard forms of employment—such as those based on ecommerce and virtual platforms and tasks—have become widespread and an important source of employment growth in China. In 2017, there were almost 7.2 million labourers employed in the shared economy (economic activities involving online services and transactions), accounting for 9.7 per cent of newly created jobs in China's urban labour market (Information Centre of the State Council and Internet Society of China 2018). In its people's wellbeing policy framework, the Chinese Government has given high priority to employment and pursued a proactive employment policy, supporting the development of flexible and new forms of employment (see Xi 2017; State Council of the People's Republic of China 2019).

Nevertheless, NSE is still a relatively new topic within both academic and policy debates in China. So far, there have been few studies of NSE in China. Some studies have investigated new forms of employment (Yang and Wang 2018; Yang et al. 2018; Zhang 2018) or have described NSE or nonstandard features of labour relations in China at a conceptual level (Dong 2008; Li 2011; Ma et al. 2011; Yang and Ma 2014; Qian 2018). There is limited knowledge of China's NSE, its proportion and characteristics. The aim of this chapter is to draw more academic attention to the growth of NSE in China. Studying China's NSE is timely, particularly in an era when forms of employment are becoming more diverse and flexible, and the Chinese Government is supporting the growth of new forms of employment to promote employment growth. A major dilemma accompanying the growth of NSE is how to adapt to and regulate NSE and build a more inclusive and integrated labour market. This is also a global challenge, since standard employment was the norm in past decades and the basis of labour market regulations (Kalleberg 2000). Given the juridical dimension of standard employment, its labourers not only earn regular wages, but also gain access to employment protection and social insurance, whereas NSE tends to be more precarious (Kalleberg 2003; Eichhorst and Tobsch 2014; Adams and Deakin 2014).

Based on its significance and the complexity and precarious nature of NSE, it is important to treat it as a separate employment category and produce targeted policies to adapt to the growth of NSE in China. To explore NSE in China, this chapter will address three questions: What is NSE from the global perspective and in terms of China's background? What are the scale and characteristics of NSE in China? Who are the people most likely to engage in NSE? This study draws on data from the China Urban Labour Survey (CULS) conducted in 2016. The policy implications of this study are summarised in the final section.

What is nonstandard employment?

Before discussing NSE in China, it is necessary to define NSE at the conceptual level. The term NSE has been used interchangeably with 'nontraditional employment', 'irregular employment', 'atypical employment' and 'nonregular employment'. When used to highlight its precarious and inferior status, NSE is also often labelled 'precarious employment', 'marginal employment' or 'alternative employment', despite the fact the scope of NSE is much wider than these last terms. This section reviews definitions of NSE by both academic and international organisations.

According to an earlier and widely cited definition of NSE, workers in the sector have limited temporal, physical and administrative attachment to organisations—unlike workers in standard employment, who have fixed working hours, indefinite employment contracts and work at a fixed location, under the direct supervision and administrative control of their employer (Pfeffer and Baron 1988). Standard employment relationships refer to

> a stable, socially protected, dependent, full-time job … the basic conditions of which (working time, pay and social transfers) are regulated to a minimum level by collective agreement or by labour and/or social security law. (Bosch 1986, cited in Bosch 2004)

Kalleberg (2009) maintains that, in a standard employment relationship, workers are assumed to work full-time for a particular employer at the employer's workplace, often progressing up the job ladder within internal labour markets. Adams and Deakin (2014) underscored the economic and juridical dimensions to distinguish between standard and nonstandard employment. Standard employment relationships provide labourers with access not just to income, but also to insurance against labour market risks, while NSE is associated with precariousness (Adams and Deakin 2014).

In reports on NSE released by international organisations, it is usually defined as a part-time, multiparty employment relationship and temporary work that deviates from a full-time, employer–employee bilateral employment relationship and indefinite labour contracts (Eurofound 2015; OECD 2015; ILO 2016). The International Labour Organization (ILO) defines NSE as work that falls outside the realm of standard employment relationships that are full-time, indefinite and part of a subordinate relationship between an employee and an employer (ILO 2016). If standard employment is defined as occurring at a set place of work outside the home, an even broader scope of tasks falls under NSE, including telework and remote work (ILO 2016). According to Eurofound (2015), NSE falls into one or more of the following categories: relationships between employers and employees that are different from the established one-to-one employment relationship; the provision of work on a discontinuous or intermittent basis or for very limited periods, rather than on a continuous or regular basis; and networking and cooperation arrangements between self-employed individuals.

There are common characteristics or essential dimensions of NSE across different contexts, manifested in the temporal, economic, juridical and employment relationship dimensions. Based on a review of definitions of NSE, the following characteristics of NSE are underlined. First, in the temporal dimension, NSE is distinguished by its working hours and the length of the employment relationship or labour contract. Standard employment refers to full-time employment on a regular, stable and continuing basis, whereas NSE refers to part-time employment or full-time work based on temporary or intermittent arrangements. Second, in the economic dimension, although employees in standard employment are paid regularly—usually on a biweekly or monthly basis—and have the right to a minimum wage, NSE workers are paid based on workload or tasks and may incur market risk. Third, in the juridical dimension, standard employment is based on the conclusion of legal labour contracts, be they written or verbal, depending on labour contract regulations in different countries. A standard employment relationship is legally and socially protected via employment protection, social insurance and the protection of employees' legal rights. Forth, standard employment is based on a direct and bilateral employment relationship between an employer and an employee. Multiparty employment relationships, such as labour dispatches or employee sharing, which involve three or more parties, are not standard employment arrangements. In addition to thresholds in the temporal, economic, juridical and labour relationship dimensions, NSE also includes a physical dimension and sometimes relies on the support of ICT—for example, mobile phones and personal computers—which may change work patterns and the nature of work relationships (Adams and Deakin 2014; Eurofound 2015).

Defining NSE in China

Even though there are general principles of NSE, as discussed above, in practice, there are multiple and emerging forms of this kind of employment. There is no official definition of NSE that could be applied across all contexts. Instead, there are variations of NSE across different economic contexts, legislative frameworks and labour market regulations. As noted by Bosch (2004), different legal and welfare regimes and variations in countries' welfare regimes might change the meaning of standard employment and NSE. In considering the employment characteristics and labour market regulations of China, this chapter defines standard employment in China as full-time work based on legal, written and stable labour contracts, be they fixed-term or indefinite, and direct bilateral employment relationships between an employer and an employee. The essential difference of this definition from that of the ILO is defining full-time fixed-term employment as standard. According to the ILO's classification, fixed-term employment is categorised as temporary employment, and is therefore considered as NSE.[1] Such a classification does not apply to the Chinese context. In China, full-time employment based on fixed-term labour contracts (excluding labour dispatches) should be considered as standard employment for two reasons.

---

1   According to the ILO (2016), there are four major types of NSE: temporary employment, part-time and on-call work, multiparty employment relationships and disguised employment/dependent self-employment. The category of temporary employment comprises employment based on fixed-term contracts, project or task-based contracts and seasonal and casual work, including daily work.

First, fixed-term employment is a mainstream and standard form of employment in China. The ILO categorises fixed-term employment as NSE, primarily because non-fixed-term employment is a prevalent employment arrangement in developed economies. Among OECD countries, the proportion of non-fixed-term employment is very high. The proportion of NSE in some OECD countries—including Australia, the United Kingdom, Norway, Denmark and another nine countries—was above 90 per cent in 2011 and 2012, whereas fixed-term employment is a non-mainstream form of employment (OECD 2014). In China, fixed-term employment is more prevalent. Drawing on data from the CULS for 2010, Wang (2013) finds that, in urban China, the proportion of non-fixed-term (indefinite) employment among migrant labourers and local urban labourers was 19.93 per cent and 44.58 per cent, respectively, whereas that of fixed-term employment was 75.36 per cent and 53.48 per cent, respectively (Wang 2013). This means that fixed-term employment is a common and standard employment arrangement in China.

Second, under current labour market regulations in China, workers under both fixed-term employment and non-fixed-term employment are subject to the same strict protections and have equal labour rights. According to China's Labour Contract Law, enacted in 2008, the establishment of a labour relationship between an employer and an employee occurs at the conclusion of a written labour contract.[2] The establishment of a labour relationship based on fixed-term and non-fixed-term contracts serves multiple purposes, including the provision of social protection, employment and income security, safe and healthy workplaces, equality of access, and so on (Rubery 2015; ILO 2016). Although China's Labour Contract Law also regulates three special employment arrangements—that is, collective contracts, labour dispatches and part-time employment—fixed-term and non-fixed-term employment are considered standard forms of employment. The strict labour market regulations regarding the conclusion of a labour contract, restrictions on the dismissal of workers, labour rights protection and identification of relevant responsibilities mainly target fixed-term and non-fixed-term employment groups. Du (2014) drew on the OECD's framework to investigate the level of protection and strictness of labour market regulations, examining regulations regarding the conclusion of labour contracts, requisite terms and content of labour contracts and regulations regarding the dismissal of workers and termination of a labour contract. Du (2014) found the framework of China's contemporary labour market regulations provides high-level employment and social protections, achieving a score of 3.3—higher than the average level of OECD countries (2.3). This means that, compared with developed economies, China's labour market regulations provide even stricter employment and legal protections. Based on this reality and its labour market regulations, fixed-term employment should be categorised as standard in China.

---

2 Labour Contract Law of the People's Republic of China, available from: www.npc.gov.cn/englishnpc/Law/2009-02/20/content_1471106.htm.

Given the above argument, this chapter defines standard employment and NSE in China according to the status of labour contracts. Standard employment refers to full-time employment based on non-fixed-term and fixed-term labour contracts (excluding labour dispatches) and employment of those who work for central and local governments and other jobs in the public sector. Employment falling outside the above realm should be categorised as NSE, such as part-time employment, multiparty employment relationships, temporary employment (project or task-based contracts, seasonal and casual work), platform or virtual employment and self-employment.

Data and sample

This study draws on data obtained from the CULS conducted by the Institute of Population and Labour Economics at the Chinese Academy of Social Sciences. So far, four rounds of CULS have been conducted. This study draws on the latest data, from the fourth round of the survey, in 2016. It was conducted in six provincial capital cities: Shanghai, Guangzhou, Fuzhou, Wuhan, Shenyang and Xi'an. It is a household-level survey covering labourers' education levels, employment status, previous experience, social protection status, skills, training and other personal information. A probability proportional to size (PPS) sampling method was utilised to select the samples.

This chapter focuses on working-age labourers—that is, those who are currently employed and are aged above 16 years. A study sample of 7,439 individuals was selected, including 1,044 respondents from Shenyang City, 1,335 respondents from Shanghai, 1,229 from Fuzhou, 1,254 from Wuhan, 1,478 from Guangzhou and 1,099 from Xi'an. Among the valid study sample, 57.59 per cent of respondents were male and 42.41 per cent were female. As for residence status, 63.15 per cent of respondents were local urban residents and 36.85 per cent were rural migrants. In terms of *hukou* (household registration) status, 25.83 per cent of respondents had rural *hukou*, while 74.17 per cent had urban *hukou*. The average age of the study sample was 39.04 years, and the average years of schooling among respondents were 12.88. The proportion of those married was 82.88 per cent, while the unmarried accounted for 17.12 per cent.

Main findings

Measurement and scale of NSE in China

In measuring the scale of NSE in China, this study categorises full-time employment based on non-fixed-term employment contracts and fixed-term contracts (excluding labour dispatches) as standard employment, including civil servants in central and local governments and those who are employed in other areas of the public and private sectors. Employment falling outside the above realm was taken as NSE.

Drawing on the CULS data, this study finds that the proportion of NSE among the six cities investigated in 2016 was 34.95 per cent, indicating that NSE has become an important feature of the labour market in China (Wang 2018). The result also reflects a significant regional gap. The proportion of NSE was highest in Wuhan City (43.9 per cent), while in Shenyang it was 43.29 per cent, 40.39 per cent in Guangzhou, 38.18 per cent in Xi'an and 34.39 per cent in Fuzhou. The lowest proportion of NSE was in Shanghai, at 22.73 per cent.

Characteristics of NSE in China

As indicated in the literature on NSE, this form of employment is often associated with precariousness. NSE workers tend to experience wage penalties, poor working conditions, long working hours, few training opportunities and a lack of labour rights and social security protections (Allan 2000; Cooke and Brown 2015). Due to limited temporal, physical and administrative attachments to organisations, NSE workers have weaker attachment to their employers, which may affect their behaviour and performance and may undermine organisational aims (Allan 2000; George and Chattopadhyay 2015). Based on the CULS data, NSE in China demonstrates the following characteristics: low levels of job satisfaction, low wage levels, high levels of overtime, low social insurance coverage and inadequate income protections (Wang 2018).

First, NSE workers tend to have lower levels of job satisfaction. As shown in Table 6.1, when asked about the degree of satisfaction with their current job, the proportion of NSE respondents who were very unsatisfied or unsatisfied with their employment was 0.91 per cent and 11.02 per cent, respectively—much higher than that for labourers in standard employment, which was 0.42 per cent and 5.8 per cent, respectively. The proportion of NSE labourers who were satisfied or very satisfied with their employment was 44.22 per cent and 4.41 per cent, respectively, which was lower than that of labourers in standard employment, which was 57.01 per cent and 6.74 per cent, respectively.

Second, NSE labourers have lower incomes. The average monthly income of NSE workers was RMB4,806.76 (US$716), which was RMB1,492.16 lower than that of standard workers. The average monthly income of NSE workers was 76.31 per cent of that of standard employees. The average hourly income of NSE workers was RMB23.34 (about US$16)—65.71 per cent of that of standard workers (Table 6.1).

Third, working overtime is common among labourers in NSE. The survey data show that urban labourers tend to work long hours—an average of 47.29 hours per week, which is much higher than the 40 hours per week standard regulated by the Chinese Government.[3] NSE workers put in even longer hours, 54.95 per week—11.74 hours more than labourers in standard employment. With 40 hours per week the standard as regulated by the Chinese Government, the proportion of NSE labourers who worked overtime was 71.32 per cent, while that of employees in standard employment was only 29.52 per cent (Table 6.1).

Table 6.1 Comparison of standard employment and NSE

	Overall (1)	Standard employment (2)	NSE (3)	(3) – (2)
Level of job satisfaction (%)				
Very unsatisfied	0.59	0.42	0.91	0.49
Unsatisfied	7.65	5.80	11.02	5.22
Neither good nor bad	33.36	30.04	39.43	9.39
Satisfied	52.49	57.01	44.22	−12.79
Very satisfied	5.92	6.74	4.41	−2.33
Work compensation and hours				
Monthly income (RMB)	5,781.04	6,298.92	4,806.76	−1,492.16
Hourly income (RMB)	31.29	35.52	23.34	−12.18
Average working hours (per week)	47.29	43.21	54.95	11.74
Proportion of overtime work (%)	45.57	29.52	71.32	41.80
Coverage of social insurance (%)				
Pension	71.43	90.41	36.09	−54.32
Basic medical insurance	69.46	88.77	33.50	−55.27
Unemployment insurance	59.15	79.45	21.38	−58.07
Industrial injury insurance	58.87	78.87	21.66	−57.21
Maternity insurance	52.32	71.02	17.52	−53.50

Source: IPLE-CASS (2016).

3   According to regulations on working hours released by the State Council of China in 1994, the regular working hours of a full-time employee are 8 hours per day and 40 hours per week (MoHRSS 1994).

Fourth, social insurance coverage among NSE workers is lower than that among workers in standard employment. The proportion of employees in standard employment who were covered by a basic pension was 90.41 per cent, while that of NSE employees was only 36.09 per cent. The coverage rates for basic medical insurance, unemployment insurance, industrial injury insurance and maternity insurance for NSE workers were 55.27 per cent, 58.07 per cent, 57.21 per cent and 53.5 per cent lower, respectively, than those of labourers in standard employment, as shown in Table 6.1. The low level of social security coverage is a major area requiring change to improve the status of NSE workers.

Fifth, the proportion of labour union members is lower among NSE labourers. The proportion of labour union members in standard employment was 33 per cent, while that of NSE workers was only 3.68 per cent—implying a low level of representation of NSE workers in such organisations. The proportion of labour union members among workers in standard employment varied across cities, and was highest in Shenyang City, at 58.03 per cent, and lowest in Guangzhou, at 21.19 per cent. As shown in Table 6.2, the proportion of labour union members among NSE labourers was much lower. In spite of the differences between cities, the average proportion of labour union members among those in NSE was only 3.68 per cent. Even in Wuhan, where the proportion of labour union members among NSE workers was the highest, it was only 6.15 per cent. The low proportion of NSE workers in labour unions is not conducive to improving the bargaining power of those workers. Measures should be taken to increase the proportion of labour union membership among NSE employees, to strengthen the diversity of labour unions and include representatives of part-time and dispatch workers in labour unions.

Table 6.2 Proportion of labour union members in standard employment and NSE (per cent)

City	Standard employment	NSE	Overall
Shenyang	58.03	5.17	35.15
Shanghai	32.97	4.24	26.44
Fuzhou	33.66	5.40	23.95
Wuhan	31.63	6.15	20.45
Guangzhou	21.19	0.47	12.82
Xi'an	35.43	3.85	23.37
Overall	33.00	3.68	22.75

Source: IPLE-CASS (2016).

Sixth, among the six cities investigated, the proportion of NSE labourers whose wage was lower than the local minimum standard (7.25 per cent) was higher than that of workers in standard employment (2.42 per cent) (Table 6.3).

Table 6.3 Proportion of labourers earning less than the local minimum wage (per cent)

City	Standard employment	NSE	Overall
Shenyang	5.26	8.20	6.53
Shanghai	2.41	6.14	3.25
Fuzhou	0.61	2.23	1.17
Wuhan	3.63	11.83	7.20
Guangzhou	1.07	5.96	3.02
Xi'an	1.74	5.46	3.17
Overall	2.42	7.25	4.10

Source: IPLE-CASS (2016).

Who are the workers most likely to engage in NSE in China?

According to reports from the ILO (2016) and OECD (2015), women, young workers, migrants and those with a low level of educational achievement are most likely to engage in NSE. There are multiple reasons behind the choices of NSE workers. For example, women choose NSE to fit in around their care tasks, while migrant workers choose NSE primarily because of their poor human capital, poor linguistic capability, poor professional networks or weak bargaining power (OECD 2015; ILO 2016).

This chapter finds that, in China's urban labour market, the proportions of senior workers, males, migrant labourers and those with low levels of educational achievement were higher among NSE workers. First, the proportion of senior-age workers is higher among NSE than among standard workers. Drawing on the CULS (IPLE-CASS 2016), the average age of standard workers was 38.35 years, while that of NSE workers was 40.33 years. As shown in Table 6.4, in terms of age distribution, the proportion of workers over the age of 35 among NSE workers is higher than that among workers in standard employment. In particular, for those aged between 45 and 54, the proportion in standard employment was 21.86 per cent, while that in NSE was 28.03 per cent.

Second, the proportion of men in NSE was higher than that of women. The survey data show that 57.22 per cent of nonstandard employees were men while 42.78 per cent were women. However, gender distribution in NSE was similar to that in standard employment. The proportion of men in standard employment (57.78 per cent) was also higher than that of women (42.22 per cent). The regression analysis shows that gender had no significant impact on the possibility of engaging in NSE (Table 6.6).

Table 6.4 Worker age distribution in standard employment and NSE (per cent)

Age	Standard employment	NSE	Overall
16–24	5.13	5.98	5.43
25–34	36.24	26.44	32.81
35–44	29.90	30.96	30.27
45–54	21.86	28.03	24.02
55 and above	6.88	8.59	7.47
Overall	100.00	100.00	100.00

Source: IPLE-CASS (2016).

Third, labourers with a low level of educational attainment accounted for a higher proportion of labourers in NSE. Data analysis shows the average years of schooling among all workers were 12.88. The average years of schooling among standard employees were 13.97, while among NSE labourers it was only 10.85. As indicated in Table 6.5, 77.87 per cent of NSE labourers had achieved high school education or below, which was much higher than the proportion of those in standard employment (37.24 per cent). The proportion of labourers with tertiary education (college level and above) among NSE labourers was only 22.14 per cent, while that among standard employment labourers was 62.75 per cent (Table 6.5).

Table 6.5 Education distribution of standard employment and NSE labourers (per cent)

Education level	Standard employment	NSE	Overall
Primary school	1.73	9.07	4.29
Junior high school	11.96	39.71	21.65
Senior high school or technical secondary school	23.55	29.09	25.48
College	23.02	12.52	19.36
Undergraduate	33.66	9.31	25.16
Masters degree and above	6.07	0.31	4.06
Overall	100.00	100.00	100.00

Source: IPLE-CASS (2016).

Fourth, the proportion of NSE workers with rural *hukou* was higher than those with urban *hukou*. The survey data show that the proportion of workers with rural *hukou* in standard employment was 16.17 per cent, while that in NSE was 43.81 per cent. From the regression analysis results shown in Table 6.6, if other conditions are the same and we control the variables of type of employer, industrial sector and city, the following trends are observed. First, the lower the level of educational achievement, the higher is the possibility of labourers engaging in NSE. The probability of engaging in NSE increased by 4.52 per cent for each one-year reduction of schooling. Second, with the increase in workers' age, the probability of engaging in NSE increased by

0.21 per cent. Third, the possibility of engaging in NSE among unmarried labourers was 8.38 per cent higher than among married labourers. Fourth, gender did not have an evident effect on the probability of engaging in NSE. Finally, *hukou* status also impacted on the probability of labourers engaging in NSE. If other conditions were the same, the probability of labourers with rural *hukou* engaging in NSE was 8.85 per cent higher than that of urban *hukou* holders.

Given the characteristics of labourers who are more likely to engage in NSE, targeted policies and actions are required to broaden the employment opportunities and improve the job quality of those with lower levels of educational achievement, those who are older and unmarried and workers holding rural *hukou*.

Table 6.6 Factors influencing labourers' participation in NSE (probit model)

	Dependent variable: Whether or not to engage in NSE (Yes = 1) (marginal effects)	
	Coefficient	Standard error
Gender (male = 1)	−0.0053	0.0166
Years of schooling	−0.0452***	0.0030
Age	0.0021**	0.0010
Marital status (married = 1)	−0.0838***	0.0232
Hukou status (rural *hukou* = 1)	0.0885***	0.0216
Type of employer	Controlled	
Industrial sector	Controlled	
City	Controlled	
Study sample	7,367	

*** significant at 1 per cent
** significant at 5 per cent
* significant at 10 per cent
Source: IPLE-CASS (2016).

Conclusion

This study has three major findings, which fill existing knowledge gaps regarding NSE in China and provide evidence for policymakers considering further strategies to adapt to and regulate the growth of NSE in China. First, the proportion of NSE in China's urban labour market was 34.95 per cent, demonstrating the significance of this form of employment in China. The result also reflects a significant regional gap. The proportion of NSE in advanced regions, such as Shanghai, which leads in realising economic transformation and upgrading, was lower than that in other cities. Second, NSE in China demonstrated the following characteristics: low levels of job satisfaction, low wages, high levels of overtime, low social insurance coverage and poor wage protection. Third, in China's urban labour market, the proportions of senior-age workers, males, migrants and those with low levels of educational achievement were higher among NSE workers, and workers with these characteristics were more likely to engage in NSE.

Based on these findings, three key issues are highlighted to deal with the growth of NSE in China. First, NSE should be treated as a separate employment category in the design of employment policy and labour market regulations. Although in recent years there has been significant progress, current employment policies and protections mainly target labourers in standard employment, whereas NSE labourers are not subject to employment protection under contemporary labour laws and market regulations. There is still no legal reference for the management of NSE and the protection of the rights of NSE labourers.

Second, job quality assessment and improvement should be emphasised. Compared with standard employment, in NSE, job quality tends to be lower, characterised by low job satisfaction, low wages, high levels of overtime, low social insurance coverage, poor protection of wage rights and interests, and so on. Measures are required to assess and monitor job quality in terms of working hours, wages and social insurance coverage. Regular evaluation and monitoring should be carried out to determine the trends in NSE and form more dynamic monitoring. Multiple measures are required, including legislation, the justice system and labour supervision. Nevertheless, due to the large scale of NSE and its multiple forms, such activities will incur high management costs. How to achieve a balance between improving job quality and promoting employment growth also needs careful consideration.

Third, targeted policies and actions are required to broaden the employment choices for those who are most likely to engage in NSE. It is also necessary to take measures to strengthen the collective bargaining power of NSE workers by enhancing labour union membership at all levels, improving the representation of organisations and absorbing nonstandard workers into labour unions.

There are also a few limitations of this study. Due to the complex and heterogeneous nature of NSE and its emerging forms with the development of new technology, measuring NSE is difficult. The definition of NSE may vary across different contexts or with modifications in the legal framework within one country. The limited availability of data on NSE (Barrientos 2011) is a global challenge to the study of NSE trends. This chapter provides an overview of NSE in China based on evidence from China's urban labour market; nevertheless, multiple sources of data are needed for future studies to observe the trends of NSE in China.

References

Adams, Z. and Deakin, S. (2014), Institutional solutions to precariousness and inequality in labour markets, *British Journal of Industrial Relations* 52(4): 779–809. doi.org/10.1111/bjir.12108.

Aleksynska, M. and Berg, J. (2016), *Firms' demand for temporary labour in developing countries: Necessity or strategy?*, Conditions of Work and Employment Series No. 77, Geneva: International Labour Organization.

Allan, C. (2000), The hidden organisational costs of using non-standard employment, *Personnel Review* 29(2): 188–206. doi.org/10.1108/00483480010295989.

Barrientos, S. (2011), *'Labour chains': Analysing the role of labour contractors in global production networks*, BWPI Working Paper No. 153, Manchester: Brooks World Poverty Institute. doi.org/10.2139/ssrn.1895292.

Bosch, G. (2004), Towards a new standard employment relationship in Western Europe, *British Journal of Industrial Relations* 42(4): 617–36. doi.org/10.1111/j.1467-8543.2004.00333.x.

Cooke, F. and Brown, R. (2015), *The regulation of non-standard forms of employment in China, Japan and the Republic of Korea*, Conditions of Work and Employment Series No. 64, Geneva: International Labour Organization.

Dong, B. (2008), Nonstandard labor relations, *Academic Research* 7(July): 50–7.

Du, Y. (2014), International comparison of labor market institutions and its implications for China, *Studies in Labor Economics* 4(August): 161–92.

Eichhorst, W. and Tobsch, V. (2014), *Not so standard anymore? Employment duality in Germany*, IZA Discussion Paper No. 8155, Bonn: Institute of Labor Economics.

Eurofound (2015), *New Forms of Employment*, Luxembourg: Publications Office of the European Union.

George, E. and Chattopadhyay, P. (2015), *Non-standard work and workers: Organizational implications*, Conditions of Work and Employment Series No. 61, Geneva: International Labour Organization.

Houseman, S. (2001), Why employers use flexible staffing arrangements: Evidence from an establishment survey, *Industrial and Labor Relations Review* 55(1): 149–70. doi.org/10.1177/001979390105500109.

Information Centre of the State Council and Internet Society of China (2018), *Annual Report of the Development of Share Economy in China 2018*, available from: www.sic.gov.cn/archiver/SIC/UpFile/Files/Default/20180320144901006637.pdf.

Institute of Population and Labor Economics, Chinese Academy of Social Sciences (IPLE-CASS) (2016), *The China Urban Labour Survey (CULS) 2016*, Beijing: IPLE-CASS.

International Labour Organization (ILO) (2016), *Non-Standard Employment around the World: Understanding challenges, shaping prospects, Geneva*: ILO.

Kalleberg, A. (2000), Nonstandard employment relations: Part-time, temporary and contract work, *Annual Review of Sociology* 26(1): 341–65. doi.org/10.1146/annurev.soc.26.1.341.

Kalleberg, A. (2003), Flexible firms and labor market segmentation: Effects of workplace restructuring on jobs and workers, *Work and Occupations* 30(2): 154–75. doi.org/10.1177/0730888403251683.

Kalleberg, A. (2009), Precarious work, insecure workers: Employment relations in transition, *American Sociological Review* 74(1): 1–22. doi.org/10.1177/000312240907400101.

Li, P. (2011), Explorations of nonstandard labor relations in China, *Human Resource Development of China* (March): 84–6.

Ma, Y., Chen, M. and Yang L. (2011), Investigation and analysis of nonstandard labor relations against circumstances of new law, *Human Resource Development of China* 8(August): 88–93.

Ministry of Human Resources and Social Security (MoHRSS) (1994), *State Council Regulations on Working Hours of Employees*, Beijing: MoHRSS, available from: www.mohrss.gov.cn/SYrlzyhshbzb/zcfg/flfg/xzfg/201604/t20160412_237909.html.

Organisation for Economic Co-operation and Development (OECD) (2014), *OECD Employment Outlook 2014*, Paris: OECD Publishing.

Organisation for Economic Co-operation and Development (OECD) (2015), *In It Together: Why less inequality benefits all*, Paris: OECD Publishing.

Pfeffer, J. and Baron, J. (1988), Taking the workers back out: Recent trends in the structuring of employment, in B. Staw and L. Cummings (eds), *Research in Organizational Behavior. Volume 10*, Greenwich: JAI Press.

Qian, Y. (2018), Nonstandard employment and informal employment: Distinction, overlapping and adjustment, *China Labor* 4(April): 57–62.

Rubery, J. (2015), *Re-regulating for inclusive labor markets*, Conditions of Work and Employment Series No. 65, Geneva: International Labour Organization.

Schömann, K., Rogowski, R. and Kruppe, T. (1998), *Labour Market Efficiency in the European Union: Employment protection and fixed-term contracts*, London: Routledge.

State Council of the People's Republic of China (2019), *Annual Government Work Report 2019*, 5 March, Beijing, available from: www.gov.cn/premier/2019-03/16/content_5374314.htm.

Wang, M. (2013), The implementation of China's Labor Contract Law: Problems and policy suggestions, *Journal of Guizhou University of Finance and Economics* 1(January): 23–31.

Wang, Y. (2018), Non-standard employment in international perspective and China's interpretation: Scale and characteristics of non-standard employment in China, *Studies in Labor Economics* 6(December): 95–115.

Xi, J. (2017), *Report to the 19th National Congress of the Communist Party of China*, 18 October, Beijing, available from: www.gov.cn/zhuanti/2017-10/27/content_5234876.htm.

Yang, H. and Ma, Y. (2014), On the defects of workers' rights protection system and its improvement under non-standard labor relations, *Journal of Hunan University of Science & Technology* (Social Science Edition) 1(January): 74–9.

Yang, W. and Wang, Q. (2018), Patterns and determinants of labor supply of digital platform workers: An analysis based on U car-hailing platform drivers, *Population Research* 4(July): 78–90.

Yang, W., Zhang, C. and Xin, X. (2018), A study on the digital economy paradigm and working relations revolution, *Journal of China University of Labor Relations* 5(October): 56–60.

Zhang, C. (2018), A study on the current situation of employment and labor relations of the sharing-economy platform: A survey based on platforms in Beijing, *Journal of China University of Labor Relations* (June): 61–70.

7. E-commerce development in rural China

Sherry Tao Kong

General introduction of e-commerce in China

Against the backdrop of its remarkable economic progress, China has seen rapid development in the application of information and communication technology (ICT). With the provision of extensive telecommunication infrastructure, China is digitalising rapidly. As a direct result of the expansion of digital networks, the rate of internet penetration in China has been increasing steadily, currently approaching 60 per cent of the total Chinese population. Given China's population size, this signifies a huge market of consumers, many of whom are ready to embrace the digital world in an enthusiastic and innovative manner. China therefore provides uniquely fertile ground for experiments with and commercialisation of digital business models.

There has been remarkable growth in digitalisation over the past decade. From 2007 to 2016, the rate of internet penetration in China increased from 16 per cent to 53.2 per cent overall, surging from 26 per cent to 69.1 per cent in urban areas and from 7.4 per cent to 33.1 per cent in rural areas (China Internet Network Information Center 2017). Along with greater internet penetration in China, the number of internet users increased at an average pace of nearly 20 per cent per annum for at least a decade after 2006. By 2018, the total number of internet users in China reached 828.5 million and broadband networks had connected 378 million households, of which 87.5 per cent were using optical fibre. Alongside this remarkable digitalisation process, a defining feature of Chinese internet users is their utilisation of mobile devices. By mid-2018, 788 million Chinese were using mobile devices to access the internet, accounting for 98.3 per cent of all internet users.

Along with the rapid expansion and upgrading of internet infrastructure, as well as the formation of the enormous internet user population, the digital economy has become an increasingly important part of China's economic landscape. Based on the *2018 China's Internet Industry Report* (iResearch Global 2018), the gross value of the digital economy reached RMB27.2 trillion in 2017, accounting for 32.9 per cent of national gross domestic product (GDP)—2.6 percentage points higher than in

2016.[1] Moreover, it is particularly noteworthy that the digital economy contributed approximately 55 per cent of overall GDP growth, serving as a powerful engine of growth and encouraging a range of socioeconomic developments in China.

E-commerce constitutes a considerable part of the digital economy. Admittedly, China was not an early starter in e-commerce development compared with other countries. The very first online transaction in China was completed in April 1998 and growth during the subsequent decade was slow (Cao and Zhang 2009). The take-off in China's e-commerce came in 2008 when it exhibited exponential growth. Over the course of the subsequent decade, the total transaction value of e-commerce achieved a remarkable tenfold growth, from RMB3.14 trillion to RMB31.63 trillion (Xinhua News Agency 2019). Today, China has become a leading force in the global digital economy. The country is home to 42 per cent of global e-commerce and its total annual e-commerce transaction value is greater than that of France, Germany, Japan, the United Kingdom and the United States combined (Wang et al. 2017).

During the same period, the annual transaction value of online retail grew sharply. In 2008, online accounted for only 1.3 per cent of total retail sales in China. This share was considerably lower than that in the United States (3.72 per cent) and the United Kingdom (4.5 per cent). However, this modest position quickly became history. The total value of online sales in China reached RMB1.89 trillion in 2013—a more than tenfold rise from the modest RMB130 billion in 2008. China, for the first time, surpassed the United States and became the largest e-commerce market in the world (China E-commerce Research Centre 2016)—a position that has since been further consolidated. In 2016, China's total value of online sales rose to RMB5.33 trillion, accounting for 14.9 per cent of the country's total retail sales. By 2018, the annual online retail sales value reached a staggering RMB9 trillion. In the meantime, the population of online business owners grew from 7.9 million in 2008 to 50 million in 2016. Regardless of the measure one uses, China is by far the world's largest online retail market.

It is not simply the astounding economic value or the remarkable growth rates that make e-commerce development in China a topic worthy of discussion. More importantly, as a form of business activity, e-commerce provides exciting opportunities for job creation, increasing household incomes and skill formation. In particular, e-commerce, especially online retail sales, has sparked hopes about its potential benefits for more inclusive rural development.

---

1   During its presidency of the G20 in 2016, China supported global efforts to define the digital economy within the G20 Digital Economy Development and Cooperation Initiative. That initiative defined the digital economy as 'a broad range of activities that include using digitalised information and knowledge as the key factor of production, modern information networks as an important activity space, and the effective use of ICT as an important driver of productivity growth and economic structure optimisation'.

Traditionally, retail businesses attached a great deal of importance to their physical establishment—a precondition for development. For example, a shopfront is required to display goods for sale and advertise services provided; bank branches or ATMs are required to enable payments and process financial transactions. Such development preconditions generally left rural areas in a less advantageous position compared with cities. However, the same need not apply in the context of e-commerce. In contrast to the traditional offline business model, e-commerce is arguably location-neutral; as long as there is internet access and logistical systems are in place, rural areas are not immediately disadvantaged because of a lower level of general development. Because of this, e-commerce seems to be able to offer a more level playing field for rural areas to catch up with urban levels of development. As a result, there is much hope that the digital economy—in particular, e-commerce—can serve as an effective vehicle to generate growth, alleviate poverty, reduce inequality and improve various dimensions of social development in rural China.

However, while e-commerce in rural China holds much exciting potential, in practice, the actual level of e-commerce remains seriously underdeveloped in rural areas compared with cities. Over the past decade, despite an increase in the number of internet users in rural China—from 23.11 million in 2006 to 201 million in 2016—the value of online sales in rural China grew only modestly, reaching RMB353 million in 2015 and RMB482 million in 2016. Based on data from the Ministry of Commerce, rural online retailing increased by 39.1 per cent in 2017. The total value of online sales of agricultural products reached RMB243.7 billion—increasing by 53.3 per cent. By the end of 2017, the number of online stores being run from rural areas was 9.86 million—an increase of 20.7 per cent.

However, it remains to be investigated whether, and to what extent, rural e-commerce can realise its promise of delivering prosperity and reducing inequality. Against the backdrop of the general development of e-commerce in China, this chapter focuses on the important area of development of rural e-commerce, particularly that of 'Taobao villages' (administrative villages where both the aggregate transaction value of e-commerce and the total number of online businesses registered in the village have reached a certain threshold). In addition, by considering the related research findings and national- and subnational-level policies, we provide some initial thoughts on the impacts of rural e-commerce development and the policies required to unleash the potential of the digital economy.

E-commerce development in rural China and related research

General assessment of the extant literature

Rural e-commerce essentially means using the internet to purchase products from and sell goods to rural areas. The possibility of engaging the rural population in both production and consumption brings great development potential. Indeed, as early as 1984, the International Telecommunication Union proposed eradicating poverty through developing telecommunications infrastructure. A number of academic studies also demonstrated that the application of ICT had significant effects on education, poverty reduction and employment opportunities (Sumanjeet 2009).

In the case of China, it is generally accepted that the development of rural e-commerce is improving both local economies and household livelihoods, especially by providing opportunities for the economic advancement of people living in rural and remote areas (Lin et al. 2016). The belief that poverty alleviation can be achieved through the development of rural e-commerce is widely held, to the extent that the Chinese Government and organisations such as the World Bank have engaged in the active promotion of rural e-commerce. In the meantime, while the value of rural online sales accounts for only a small fraction of the total in China, rural areas are widely seen as a great untapped market. Moreover, in anticipation of the gradual saturation of online markets in urban areas, a large number of e-commerce enterprises have begun expanding their businesses into rural markets. As such, the opportunities for rural e-commerce development have become apparent and have been enthusiastically embraced by both the private sector and the government. Recent studies such as Liu et al. (2018) provide valuable overview and analysis on the development of rural e-commerce.

While from a business perspective the importance of rural e-commerce may be more than obvious, research on the actual impact of rural e-commerce remains limited. Furthermore, existing studies often rely on anecdotal evidence or are based on analyses conducted by enterprises within the industry.

In contrast, formal studies based on reliable microlevel data are rare, with a small number of exceptions, including, notably, Couture et al. (2018) and Fan et al. (2018). This probably has much to do with the fact that online sales data are too often available only from the platform on which the transactions take place. Consequently, although a sizeable body of case studies has been produced by scholars and commentators, academically rigorous research on China's rural e-commerce remains scarce.

Moreover, when assessing the actual impact of rural e-commerce development, the findings are revealing. As one of the only few academic studies that investigates this topic, Couture et al. (2018) found that rural e-commerce resulted in stronger consumption-side effects as e-commerce terminals offered lower prices, greater convenience and increased product variety. For households, gains in household purchasing power were strongest for durable products. However, rural e-commerce was found to have no significant effects on the local economy and fewer pro-competition effects on local retail prices. Furthermore, production-side effects are less immediate: in the absence of complementary interventions—such as business training, access to credit or targeted online promotions—few production-side effects are likely to materialise for the average rural marketplace in the short to medium runs.

The above results demonstrate that realisation of the promise of e-commerce for rural development is not automatic. Reliable internet access, trustworthy digital transaction methods and convenient parcel delivery and logistics services are necessary but insufficient conditions to realise the promise of e-commerce in less-developed areas. The development of e-commerce in rural areas requires a combination of grassroots organic growth and supportive government policies.

In sum, when entrepreneurship encounters conducive conditions, rural e-commerce flourishes.

An important area of rural e-commerce development: Taobao villages

Taobao villages are a powerful example of the development of rural e-commerce in China. The official definition of a Taobao village is an administrative village where the total annual value of e-commerce transactions—or gross merchandise volume (GMV)—is no less than RMB10 million (approximately, A$2 million) and there are at least 100 active online stores or a minimum of 10 per cent of local households are operating online stores (AliResearch 2016). In short, a Taobao village is a cluster of e-commerce businesses operating in a rural area.

Such villages are called 'Taobao' because the statistics used to calculate the GMV of online retailing are taken from Taobao.com as the primary marketplace. Taobao.com and the associated Tmall.com—both provided by the Alibaba Group Holding Limited—are the largest e-commerce platforms on which to buy and sell products online. In 2014, Taobao and Tmall accounted for 81.5 per cent of the total value of GMV in China. As the e-commerce market expands at a staggering pace, competition between various online platforms has become increasingly heated. Despite strong rivalry from JD.com and others, Alibaba remains by far the largest e-commerce platform provider, accounting for 58.2 per cent of market share in 2018—more than three times larger than the next player, JD.com. As a result, the development of Taobao villages illustrates the general patterns of growth of rural e-commerce.

The first Taobao village was officially approved by Alibaba in 2009 and, by 2013, the number of such villages slowly climbed to 20. What followed then was mindboggling: within a year, the total number of Taobao villages increased to 212—a tenfold growth. In addition, for the first time, 17 Taobao townships emerged. These are townships formed by the congregation of at least three Taobao villages. As is shown in Table 7.1, during the period 2014–18, the number of Taobao villages and townships grew dramatically, along with rapid overall expansion of e-commerce in China. In these Taobao villages, the number of active online stores also increased, from 70,000 in 2014 to 660,000 in 2018.

Table 7.1 Number of Taobao villages and Taobao townships

		2014	2015	2016	2017	2018
Taobao village	Total number	212	778	1,311	2,118	3,202
	Growth rate (%)		267	69	62	51
Taobao township	Total number	17	71	135	242	363
	Growth rate (%)		318	90	79	50

Source: Nanjing University Space Planning Research Centre and Ali New Village Research Centre (2018).

While it is easy to be impressed by these figures, it is important to put them into perspective. There were 671,729 administrative villages in China in 2016; only 0.2 per cent of them qualified as Taobao villages. Taobao villages account for only a tiny fraction of villages in China as a whole, and so there remains room for further growth of rural e-commerce. With that in mind, it is now useful to extend our study beyond the impressive rates of growth of Taobao villages and distil a number of distinctive patterns that have emerged, particularly over the past five years.

First, the number of provinces with Taobao villages expanded from seven in 2012 (Zhejiang, Guangdong, Jiangsu, Shandong, Fujian, Hebei and Jiangxi) to 24 by 2017, including remote and economically underdeveloped provinces such as Guizhou, Shaanxi, Ningxia and two ethnic autonomous regions, Xinjiang and Guangxi. To some extent, this shows the vitality and reach of e-commerce. At the same time, the greatest increase in Taobao villages was in areas where they first took root, such as Zhejiang, Guangdong, Jiangsu and Shandong provinces. In stark contrast, the increase in the number of Taobao villages in the other provinces has been slow and, in some places, even negative. For example, there were two Taobao villages in Yunnan Province in 2015, but this was reduced to one in 2016 and 2017. This growth pattern seems to suggest that the development of rural e-commerce reinforces early advantages and builds on successful initial conditions.

Second—not dissimilar to other aspects of China's economic development—the distribution of Taobao villages exhibits clear regional disparities. Taobao villages are highly concentrated in the eastern coastal region, whereas only a small number are scattered across other regions. In fact, more than 90 per cent of Taobao villages are located in the east, which is also where the fastest growth is observed compared with the rest of China. In contrast, other regions are lagging far behind, with the central region leading the west and north-east by a small margin. Within the eastern region, the provincial distribution is also uneven. The number of Taobao villages in Zhejiang Province is 1,172, accounting for just over one-third of the total number of Taobao villages in the whole country.

While it is probably unsurprising that the distribution and growth patterns reveal clear regional disparities, this is a particularly interesting angle from which to assess the relationship between the development of the digital economy and that of the traditional economy. Theoretically, e-commerce should be free of geographical limitations, as it operates on the internet and does not depend on any physical presence like traditional brick-and-mortar businesses. However, Taobao villages are clearly clustered in the coastal region, where the economy is generally more developed compared with the rest of the country. This seems to imply that the development of e-commerce is not decoupled from the real economy or the traditional sectors.

Third, the formation and growth processes of Taobao villages can reveal the impact of important laws governing rural e-commerce development. The first generation of Taobao villages all had fairly humble beginnings. They initially appeared on the periphery of cites where residents with relatively low socioeconomic status concentrated. These Taobao storeowners were resourceful and adventurous enough, but the types of products sold were mainly low-cost manufacturing goods targeted at low-income consumers.

Many case studies show that the identification of popular products by one or two individuals heralds the subsequent proliferation of online businesses within their community. Diffusion of information and knowledge is particularly effective and rapid within these 'acquaintance societies' in rural villages at the city fringes. Inspired by successful examples, more people find ways to take advantage of the available conditions to drive online sales. For example, some will discover that existing industrial production in nearby areas offers low-cost products; some find that, by moving deeper into rural areas, they can access more labour and greater production and warehousing space at lower costs. The logistics industries attracted by the expansion of e-commerce into rural areas effectively address the issue of the 'last mile' of parcel delivery. Combined with the powerful market integration enabled by online platforms that allow sellers to access the entire national market, reliable shipping services in turn provide further impetus to the growth of rural e-commerce.

In sum, through the lens of the development of Taobao villages, one can see how the traditional rural economy is undergoing digitalisation. As business clusters, Taobao villages are able to take advantage of existing industries, such as processing and manufacturing, and stimulate upgrading and further development of new sectors, such as logistics and e-commerce services. In this process, job opportunities are created, income levels are improved and the wider local community benefits. However, despite their internet origins, the formation and subsequent growth of Taobao villages do not seem to be entirely independent of traditional sectors and the prevailing socioeconomic conditions. As always, there seems to be a set of preconditions. Nevertheless, rural e-commerce clearly offers innovative and proven business models that allow third-party online business platforms to work productively in a rural setting, creating fresh opportunities for the upgrading of the rural economy and better integration into wider markets.

Government policies

The extraordinary development of rural e-commerce in China is a product of the great vitality of e-commerce as a business model, the vast and underserved domestic demand, the rapid progress of digital technology—particularly the development of digital finance—and a range of other factors. However, it is arguable that this extraordinary development would not have occurred had the government not played a highly supportive and facilitating role. The rest of this section briefly reviews national and subnational policies.

National policies

At the national level, policies related to rural e-commerce development can be traced back as far as 2001 when the State Council issued the 'Framework for the Technological Development of Agriculture (2001–2010)',[2] which stressed the need to develop agricultural information technology. In response, the Ministry of Agriculture issued the tenth Five-Year Plan (2001–05), outlining national policies for agricultural and rural economic development.[3] Consistent with the State Council's framework, this plan emphasised the acceleration of the building of rural economic information systems, the establishment of comprehensive information

---

2   The State Council issued the official document in April 2001.
3   The document was issued by the Ministry of Agriculture in July 2001.

networks for agriculture and the further expansion and completion of information networks for the marketing of agricultural products. In the same year, both the Ministry of Technology and the Ministry of Finance issued plans to promote the development of information networks in rural areas. These policies set the scene for many subsequent policies focused on promoting the development of agricultural information networks. Many other national-level organisations also responded with specific policies to promote agricultural development through informatisation.

In 2006, the 'No. 1 Central Document' that outlined the annual strategic priorities for the country made clear the agenda for the development of rural informatisation. This was immediately followed by the release of the National Strategy of Informatisation (2006–20), in which specific goals were announced for the development of internet coverage and information services and systems to serve the rural population and agriculture. It is fair to say the central government attached great importance to rural informatisation and, in response, various line ministries and institutions crafted a wide range of policies to achieve this goal.

Between 2006 and 2013, the national government set a policy agenda that laid out the necessary foundations for rural e-commerce to take root in China, including building and improving the logistics industry, encouraging traditional businesses to engage in online operations, improving the e-commerce environment and developing related service industries. In 2007, the central policymaking agency, the National Development and Reform Commission and the Information Office of the State Council jointly issued the first national plan for e-commerce development, the 'E-Commerce 11th Five-Year Plan'. This plan identified two focal points for development: promoting the coverage and intensity of e-commerce applications and strengthening the development of e-commerce service industries. In addition, a supportive environment, more technical innovation, effective rules and regulations as well as education and public promotion were identified as four important areas to lend fundamental support to e-commerce development. It is also worth mentioning the Broadband China Strategy and Implementation Plan announced by the State Council in 2013. It charted a clear technical path, schedule and milestones as well as supportive measures, which were combined with an additional series of policies aimed at improving e-commerce credit systems and electronic payment processes as well as transaction security, allowing rural e-commerce development to gather further momentum.

Over the past five years, rural e-commerce has become increasingly important. In 2014, the expansion of e-commerce to the countryside was set as a national policy priority in its own right to promote rural economic development, alleviate rural poverty and reduce rural–urban economic disparity. In early 2015, the Poverty Alleviation Office of the State Council listed 'Poverty Alleviation through E-Commerce' as one of the key projects for targeted poverty reduction. Given that China set eradicating poverty by 2020 as a national goal, it is evident the central government has great expectations for rural e-commerce as an effective means of income generation in economically backward areas. The degree of policy significance attached to rural e-commerce was even more pronounced in 2017 when, for the first time, the 'No. 1 Central Document' dedicated an entire section to accelerating the development of rural e-commerce. Subsequently, in the 'Opinion on the Implementation of the Rural Revitalisation Strategy' of 2018, the central government outlined a clear plan for the implementation of rural e-commerce development, which indicated that e-commerce was expected to play a major role in promoting rural socioeconomic development, eradicating rural poverty and revitalising the countryside.

Local policies

At the subnational level, most of the policies that actively promote the development of rural e-commerce were crafted and implemented over the past five years. This is in line with the greater importance placed on rural e-commerce by the central government. The State Council's 'Opinion on Further Developing E-Commerce and Fostering New Driving Forces of the Economy' provided the defining impetus for subnational—particularly county-level—governments to devise specific policies to promote local e-commerce development.

While policies rolled out by county-level governments vary from one locality to another, a central element is their compatibility with the existing conditions and their clear focus on rural e-commerce development. We use Wuyi county as an example to illustrate the range of policies that can be devised by county governments. Wuyi is a small, typical rural county in central Zhejiang Province that has traditionally relied on agriculture. Due to its mountainous location, transportation infrastructure was underdeveloped and the county was economically backward and poverty-stricken. However, the development of rural e-commerce has turned it into a successful example of how this sort of development can promote growth and help transform the countryside. In 2018, six new Taobao villages and one new Taobao township emerged, and the GMV of Wuyi exceeded RMB11.6 billion—a 30 per cent increase.

Over the years, the Wuyi County Government has issued a wide range of policies that can be summarised into four areas. First, a designated organisation was established with a full-time staff and authority to craft and implement e-commerce policies. Second, the county government invited independent consultants to draft a five-year plan for the development of Wuyi's e-commerce. The expertise of independent professionals provided valuable guidance over the strategies for and direction of e-commerce development. Third, the county government offered a range of supports for e-commerce startups. For example, it allocated RMB15 million as an annual grant to fund e-commerce activities, while an e-commerce service centre and association and e-commerce industrial parks were established to lend support to online businesses. Fourth, the county government mobilised the media and organised public events to popularise the idea of e-commerce, promote entrepreneurs and create a favourable environment for related innovation.

In addition, the Wuyi County Government built up a coordinated service mechanism, including township and village-level governments, so e-commerce businesses can receive support at all stages of development. For instance, one county-level logistics centre is in Wuyi and an additional 18 township-level branches and 398 village-level service stations have spread to all corners of the county, forming a network to facilitate the operation of e-commerce.

To take advantage of the positive spillover effects and economies of scale, Wuyi has made significant efforts to foster the creation of Taobao villages. The county government first identified promising projects in particular villages and provided facilities, such as incubators, to help them take shape. Successful individuals would then inspire others to emulate them and become involved in rural e-commerce. For example, Louwang was the first Taobao village in Wuyi county. It was started by one individual, selling electronic tools online. With the support of the local e-commerce office, the business expanded and a large number of villagers and returned migrants began to participate in other e-commerce activities, bringing genuine returns to the community. In 2018, the total value of online retailing in Louwang amounted to RMB200 million and the average annual villagers' income reached RMB30,000. Louwang village has since been recognised as one of the top 10 specialised Taobao villages in Zhejiang Province.

Implications

Since the mid-2000s, China has experienced exceptional growth in rural e-commence and has established a rich digital ecosystem, expanding beyond just a few large companies. The development of rural e-commerce—by accessing highly integrated markets via online platforms—is expected to bring significant economic advantages, not least inclusive growth, poverty alleviation and inequality reduction. Motivated by such desirable potential, the Chinese Government not only allowed space for digital companies to experiment, but also introduced a wide range of policies and projects to improve the country's internet infrastructure to promote the development of e-commerce. Today, China has become a significant investor in and consumer of digital technologies.

One area with important policy implications for other developing countries is the role of rural e-commerce as an effective tool to combat poverty. Since 2014, 756 counties have been recognised by the national government as model counties for their introduction of e-commerce into the countryside. Among these, 60 per cent (499) are rated poverty-stricken counties by national standards. By 2017, 832 nationally declared poverty-stricken counties had engaged in e-commerce and the transaction value increased by 52.1 per cent, totalling RMB120.8 billion. However, despite the exciting development of e-commerce in rural China, numerous challenges remain before its potential to address rural poverty is fully realised.

To start with, there are different causes of poverty—for example, unfavourable geography, underdeveloped infrastructure or lack of labour and human capital. A common feature of such areas is weak business infrastructure, which manifests itself in a number of ways, all of which translate into concrete obstacles to the development of e-commerce. For example, many of these areas are endowed with high-quality agricultural products; however, their production is often uncoordinated and output is subject to much uncertainty due to weather and other factors, and is therefore unstable. Due to their remote location, these types of poverty-stricken areas face exceedingly high transportation and warehousing costs and low-quality internet services. Statistics show that the cost of logistics is at least four times higher for villages in western China than for those in the coastal region. Another important factor is human capital. Most talent is attracted to economically developed areas, where they can enjoy higher incomes. Poorer areas therefore routinely experience a shortage of skilled labour to operate online businesses and related services. The relatively low levels of education in these areas also make training less effective. The absence of expertise in branding, marketing and retail limits sales. Consequently, the income effects and positive externalities of e-commerce do not automatically lead to a reduction in poverty.

To better unleash the potential of e-commerce, a number of policy implications can be drawn from the development experiences so far. First, leadership and accountability are important. As the experience of Wuyi county demonstrates, the formation of a designated governmental body like its e-commerce development office—with full-time staff and appropriate authority and funding support—is key to e-commerce policymaking and development. Second, it seems the first-mover effects are critical in the expansion of e-commerce. The example provided by successful individuals is powerful and can inspire others. Therefore, it is useful to identify a small number of promising projects and focus limited resources on fostering these projects. Third, logistics, warehousing, transport and internet connectivity are particularly important for underdeveloped rural areas. Only by effectively reducing the costs of trade can the benefits of access to the entire domestic market through online trading platforms be realised. Lastly, for the above three areas to work, training, education and funding support are needed. In this regard, governments at all levels will need to be decisive and innovative in crafting policies to address the shortage of talent and funding for rural e-commerce development.

References

AliResearch (2016), *China Taobao Village Research Report (2016)*, [Online], Alibaba Group, available from: www.aliresearch.com/Blog/Article/detail/id/21242.html.

Cao, L. and Zhang, Z. (2009), *The research report of the twelve years of China's e-commerce: 1997–2009*, available from: tech.qq.com/2009921e/ebaogao.doc.

China E-commerce Research Centre (2016), The annual monitoring report of Online retail sales of China, available from: www.100ec.cn/zt/upload_data/wllsbg/wllsbg.pdf.

China Internet Network Information Center (2017), *China statistical report on internet development.*

Couture, V., Faber, B., Gu, Y. and Liu, L. (2018), *E-commerce integration and economic development: Evidence from China*, NBER Working Paper No. 24384, Cambridge, MA: National Bureau of Economic Research. doi.org/10.3386/w24384.

Fan, J., Tang, L., Zhu, W. and Zou, B. (2018), The Alibaba Effect: Spatial consumption inequality and the welfare gains from e-commerce. *Journal of International Economics* 114: 203–20. doi.org/10.1016/j.jinteco.2018.07.002.

iResearch Global (2018), *2018 China's internet industry report (the full edition)*, available from: www.iresearchchina.com/content/details8_40769.html.

Lin, G., Xie, X. and Lv, Z. (2016), Taobao practices, everyday life and emerging hybrid rurality in contemporary China, *Journal of Rural Studies* 47: 514–23. doi.org/10.1016/j.jrurstud.2016.05.012.

Liu, M., Huang, J., Zhang, Q. and Gao, S. (2018), What drives the development of e-commerce in rural China—the empirical evidence from the emergence of Taobao Villages. International Association of Agricultural Economists 2018 Conference, 28 July – 2 August. Vancouver, British Columbia.

Nanjing University Space Planning Research Centre and Ali New Village Research Centre (2018), *China Taobao Village Development Report (2014–2018)*, [Online], available from: dy.163.com/v2/article/detail/E4MPSS3H0511B3FV.html.

Sumanjeet (2009), Social implications of electronic commerce, *Journal of the Social Sciences* 21(2): 91–7. doi.org/10.1080/09718923.2009.11892757.

Wang, K.W., Woetzel, J., Seong, J., Manyika, J., Chui, M. and Wong, W. (2017), Digital China: Powering the economy to global competitiveness, *McKinsey Global Institute*, December, available from: www.mckinsey.com/featured-insights/china/digital-china-powering-the-economy-to-global-competitiveness.

Xinhua News Agency (2019), China's total e-commerce transactions increased 10 times in 10 years, *CCTV News*, 12 April, available from: jingji.cctv.com/2019/04/12/ARTIW9X jnXSiq2QxKCUPA4MC190412.shtml.

8. Innovation of Chinese listed enterprises: Evaluation and policies[1]

Zhongyu Ma, Huiqing Gao, Weihua Yin and Zhichao Wen

At the end of 2012, the report of the eighteenth National Congress of the Communist Party of China proposed that, by 2020, China would become one of the most innovative countries in the world. This was the first time such a goal had been set since China's period of reform and opening-up began; it was also the first time in the thousands of years of China's history.

Over the years, the Chinese Government has carried out reforms designed to delegate power to enterprises, streamline administration and optimise government services, to promote large-scale entrepreneurship and encourage cultural and educational innovation. As a result, an atmosphere of innovation has taken hold in Chinese society; the innovation system has been continuously improved, levels of innovation have been growing and new modes of business have emerged. According to the 2018 Global Innovation Index, published by the World Intellectual Property Organization (WIPO), Cornell University and other institutions, mainland China has moved up five positions to seventeenth place since 2017. This is the first time mainland China has featured in the top 20—signalling that it is becoming one of the world's most innovative economies.

Behind the rapid improvement of China's overall innovative competency is the improvement of the innovative competency of Chinese companies, with listed companies the main force of company innovation and development. With the help of 'big data' technology, China has built a system to evaluate technological and model innovation competency, which is the first integrated system anywhere that integrates technological and model innovation competency in one index. The results of the evaluation show that, although China's national innovation competency is ranked among the top 20 in the world, Chinese listed companies are generally in the preliminary stages of innovation and development, and the potential for future progress is great.

It can be foreseen that, with the continuous implementation of innovation-driven strategies, Chinese companies will gradually become the main body driving innovation, and the national science and technological innovation system will be greatly improved. In addition, the goal of China becoming one of the most innovative countries in the world by 2030, as well as establishing a world-class innovation centre by 2050, can be achieved.

---

1   Based on the data of listed enterprises in 2017.

Theories and methods

Drawing on previous theoretical findings and considering the characteristics of innovation, we propose a method to establish the first index evaluation system for listed companies' technological and model innovation competency.

Relevant theories of evaluation of listed companies' innovation

Two basic theories

Theory of innovation ecology

According to theory, a sound innovation ecosystem should include the following components. First, a broad awareness and culture of innovation in the society, strict property rights and an intellectual property protection system, transparent business rules, fair market order and a complete mechanism for talent flow. Second, it must provide resources for education, scientific research, talent and capital to meet the needs of innovative companies. Third, it must produce a mechanism that promotes effective and integrative development of policies, production, learning and research, as well as advancing the role of the government and the market in resource allocation, accelerating industrialisation of scientific and technological achievements and maximising the realisation of economic and social benefits. Fourth, the government must pay close attention to innovation in economic development and, according to the needs at different stages of innovation and development, carry out policymaking and strategic planning to effectively promote innovation.

Theory of innovation competency

The innovation competency of companies is their ability to achieve innovation, improvement and advancement in all aspects of production and operation. It comprises the following six competencies:

1. Innovation input competency, which refers to the quantity and quality of the resources invested in a company's innovation activities, which is, in turn, the basis of that company's innovation activities. According to the internationally accepted method, company innovation input is divided into research and development (R&D) input and non–R&D input.

2. Innovation of R&D competency, which is a key factor influencing a company's innovation, including its competency of R&D in terms of creating new technology and new products.

3. Market innovation competency—that is, any innovative activity must ultimately be recognised by the market and be commercialised, so that all innovation input can be transformed into real economic and social benefits. This includes the competence to marketise new products and to adopt new technologies to transform existing markets.

4. Organisational innovation competency, which mainly includes the innovation competencies of the organisational system and function, the organisational management system and its rules and regulations.

5. Innovation of motivation competency, which helps stimulate a company's desire for innovation and encourages it to make this a reality. This competency can encourage employees to take the initiative and be forward-looking in their approach to innovation.

6. Innovation output competency, which refers to the capability to reduce costs, create markets and generate revenue through technological innovation, demonstrating the economic benefits and technological advances brought by such innovation.

Two basic forms of innovation

The term 'technological innovation' in this chapter refers to innovative activities in which new technologies are researched and developed; these technologies are directly utilised to establish new processes and produce new products. The term 'model innovation' refers to the innovative activities in which new models of production (excluding the establishment of new processes), organisational models and business models are researched and developed. Based on these definitions and the comparison of various international methods of innovation classification, we believe that almost all forms of innovation can be categorised as one of three types: 1) technological innovation, 2) model innovation or 3) hybrid innovation, which combines the first two types of innovation.

Construction of an evaluation index for innovation competency of listed companies in China

Drawing on the above theories and the research findings of similar projects in China, this chapter is a response to the need to promote the innovation and development of Chinese listed companies. Moreover, this chapter establishes, with the support of big data technology, the first evaluation index for Chinese listed companies' technological and model innovation. The research data mainly comes from three sources: the Wind Database (innovation inputs and innovation outputs), the Guotaian Database (technological innovation patent) and data mining from annual reports and announcements of listed companies (innovation environment, technological innovation, model innovation).

Composition of the index

The innovation index system of Chinese listed companies consists of five major sectors: the innovation environment, innovation inputs, technological innovation, model innovation and innovation outputs. It should be noted that in this framework, technological innovation and model innovation are regarded as the intermediate processes between innovation input and innovation output.

Table 8.1 Index system of technological and model innovation competency of listed companies

Primary indicator	Secondary indicator
Innovation environment	Industry–university–research innovation alliance
	Innovative culture
	Innovation incentive mechanism
Innovation inputs	R&D investment quantity and intensity
	Number and proportion of R&D personnel
	Government funding for innovation
Technological innovation	Number of patents (including application and authorisation)
	Technological innovation awards
	New product quantity and proportion
Model innovation	Innovative organisation
	New marketing and new business
Innovation outputs	Full labour productivity
	Company value–benefit ratio
	Operating profit margin

Index synthesis methods

The system consists of five primary indicators: innovation environment, innovation inputs, technological innovation, model innovation and innovation outputs (Table 8.1). First, all secondary indicators of one primary indicator are non-dimensionalised. The value of the secondary indicators and their associated weights are calculated according to the weighted average formula to obtain a score for the primary indicator. The score for each primary indicator is then weighted and averaged again to obtain an overall score for the index.

Evaluation of innovation competency of listed companies in China

Among industries in China, the most active and competitive companies are domestic listed companies. Therefore, evaluation of the innovation competency of listed companies in China can provide a good picture of the structural distribution and overall trend of China's innovation competency.

Overall analysis of innovation competency

Innovation competency of listed companies is generally low

China's securities market has long been oriented towards finance, and there is no effective incentive mechanism for company innovation and development. In addition, the lag in the reform of the securities market system has seen many internet innovation companies, represented by 'BAT',[2] target overseas markets. The innovation competency of listed companies in China is generally weak and the total innovation competency score in the index is currently 43.94 (Table 8.2).

Most listed companies in China are in the preliminary stage of innovation and development

The innovation and development of listed companies in China reveal a development trend of 'relatively high input and relatively low output'.

Table 8.2 Innovation competency index of listed companies in China, 2017

Overall indicator		Primary indicator				
Innovation index	Innovation competency	Innovation environment	Innovation input	Technological innovation	Model innovation	Innovation output
Overall	43.94	53.42	45.8	40.77	39.09	40.61

The scores for the technological innovation index, model innovation index and innovation output index of listed companies in China are significantly smaller than that of the innovation input index, which has a twofold importance: first, most of the listed companies in China are still in the preliminary stages of innovation, marked by high inputs, and only a few companies have entered the later innovation stage marked by high benefits. Second, there is a relatively low conversion efficiency of China's listed companies' innovation inputs. In the future, as China increases innovation inputs, it must also pay more attention to increasing the conversion efficiency of these inputs.

---

2   'BAT' is the acronym formed by the names of the three major Chinese internet companies: Baidu, Alibaba and Tencent.

Analysis of innovation competency according to region

Innovation activities of listed companies in China are highly concentrated in the east

The regional distribution of China's top 500 companies in terms of innovation competency shows there are more innovative companies in the east and fewer in the west of the country. Among the top 500 companies, more than 80 per cent are in the east. The numbers of listed companies in the central, western and north-eastern regions account for 11.4 per cent, 6.2 per cent and 2 per cent, respectively, of the total (see Figure 8.1).

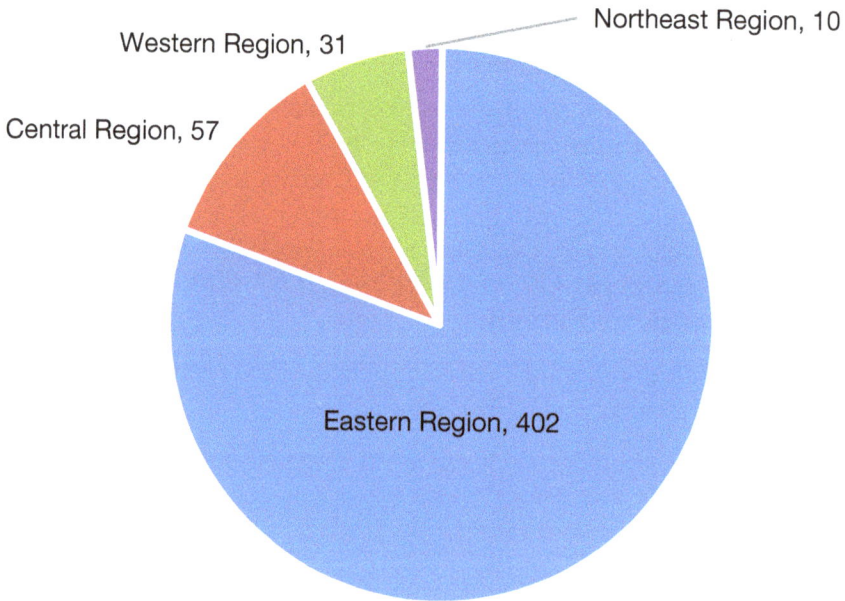

Figure 8.1 Distribution of top 500 listed enterprises for innovation capability in China, 2017

Source: Authors' calculation.

Spatial distribution of innovation competency by municipality and province takes a gradient descent

The provinces and municipalities with a total innovation competency score of 63 or above are identified as the 'first echelon' (Table 8.3). Those in the first echelon have strong innovation competency and include Beijing, Guangdong Province, Zhejiang Province, Shanghai, Jiangsu Province, Fujian Province and Shandong Province.

The provinces and municipalities with a total innovation competency score of 53–63 form the 'second echelon', and their innovation competency is relatively strong. The second echelon includes 14 provinces and municipalities: Sichuan Province, Hubei Province, Anhui Province, Henan Province, Hunan Province, Liaoning Province, Tianjin, Hebei Province, Chongqing, Shaanxi Province, Jiangxi Province, Guizhou Province, Jilin Province and Yunnan Province.

The provinces and municipalities with a total innovation competency score of 53 or less are identified as the 'third echelon', and their innovation competency is relatively weak. The third echelon includes 10 provinces and municipalities: Xinjiang Uygur Autonomous Region, Guangxi Zhuang Autonomous Region, Heilongjiang Province, Gansu Province, Shanxi Province, Hainan Province, Inner Mongolia Autonomous Region, Tibet Autonomous Region, Qinghai Province and Ningxia Hui Autonomous Region.

The gradient distribution makes it obvious that innovation competency follows a descending pattern from eastern China to the central and then the western regions. All provinces and municipalities in the first echelon are in eastern China. The majority of places in the second echelon are in the central region, while in the third echelon—except for Hainan Province and Heilongjiang Province—all provinces and municipalities are in the west.

Table 8.3 Regional innovation advantages and shortcomings in innovative competency of Chinese listed companies, 2017

Region	Overall indicator (X) Innovation competency	Primary indicator (X1) Innovation environment	Primary indicator (X2) Innovation input	Primary indicator (X3) Technological innovation	Primary indicator (X4) Model innovation	Primary indicator (X5) Innovation output
Beijing	68.88	66.79 (4)	84.90 (1)	69.02 (3)	76.26 (2)	47.41 (5)
Guangdong Province	68.40	65.48 (4)	83.19 (1)	76.18 (2)	71.08 (3)	46.09 (5)
Zhejiang Province	66.50	54.61 (4)	81.24 (1)	69.58 (3)	78.33 (2)	48.72 (5)
Shanghai	66.20	58.89 (4)	82.67 (1)	67.48 (3)	74.39 (2)	47.57 (5)
Jiangsu Province	66.04	64.84 (4)	71.95 (2)	71.71 (3)	75.88 (1)	45.82 (5)
Fujian Province	64.64	65.42 (3)	78.23 (1)	61.89 (4)	73.38 (2)	44.28 (5)
Shandong Province	63.59	61.95 (4)	77.13 (1)	66.59 (3)	70.32 (2)	41.95 (5)
Sichuan Province	62.49	65.41 (3)	73.49 (1)	62.75 (4)	66.41 (2)	44.37 (5)
Hubei Province	61.58	61.12 (4)	76.36 (1)	62.21 (3)	66.31 (2)	41.89 (5)
Anhui Province	61.50	60.53 (4)	68.01 (2)	63.43 (3)	70.37 (1)	45.16 (5)
Henan Province	60.73	59.41 (4)	70.18 (1)	63.61 (2)	63.02 (3)	47.45 (5)
Hunan Province	60.13	63.96 (2)	70.59 (1)	58.23 (4)	60.32 (3)	47.53 (5)
Liaoning Province	58.79	58.09 (3)	74.36 (1)	56.56 (4)	59.05 (2)	45.87 (5)
Tianjin	57.86	57.35 (4)	67.77 (1)	62.96 (2)	60.68 (3)	40.57 (5)
Hebei Province	56.28	58.98 (2)	57.39 (4)	64.50 (1)	56.93 (3)	43.61 (5)
Chongqing	55.72	59.52 (2)	59.26 (3)	60.76 (1)	58.78 (4)	40.27 (5)
Shaanxi Province	54.03	61.46 (2)	62.35 (1)	49.71 (4)	57.72 (3)	38.93 (5)
Jiangxi Province	53.14	61.53 (2)	51.52 (4)	62.37 (1)	53.42 (3)	36.84 (5)
Guizhou Province	52.45	65.14 (1)	49.83 (4)	55.65 (2)	51.66 (3)	39.98 (5)

Region	Overall indicator (X) Innovation competency	Primary indicator (X1) Innovation environment	Primary indicator (X2) Innovation input	Primary indicator (X3) Technological innovation	Primary indicator (X4) Model innovation	Primary indicator (X5) Innovation output
Jilin Province	52.16	58.40 (2)	63.13 (1)	45.12 (5)	47.36 (3)	46.80 (4)
Yunnan Province	51.35	65.11 (1)	55.21 (2)	50.11 (3)	48.82 (4)	37.52 (5)
Xinjiang Uygur Autonomous Region	49.96	58.26 (1)	48.37 (4)	50.50 (3)	52.04 (2)	40.61 (5)
Guangxi Zhuang Autonomous Region	48.83	57.43 (1)	50.84 (2)	45.56 (3)	45.42 (4)	44.92 (5)
Heilongjiang Province	48.77	51.61 (2)	54.21 (1)	49.49 (3)	48.39 (4)	40.15 (5)
Gansu Province	48.14	54.79 (1)	44.12 (4)	52.44 (2)	51.07 (3)	38.26 (5)
Shanxi Province	47.39	57.45 (1)	47.41 (3)	52.30 (2)	44.70 (4)	35.08 (5)
Hainan Province	46.75	51.71 (2)	57.33 (1)	42.68 (4)	43.27 (3)	38.74 (5)
Inner Mongolia Autonomous Region	45.37	48.58 (1)	42.64 (4)	46.17 (3)	46.81 (2)	42.64 (5)
Tibet Autonomous Region	44.02	55.06 (1)	45.13 (3)	33.63 (4)	33.19 (5)	53.10 (2)
Qinghai Province	39.44	52.34 (1)	34.23 (5)	37.92 (2)	35.93 (4)	36.75 (3)
Ningxia Hui Autonomous Region	38.57	51.84	34.35	38.02	38.12	30.52

Note: The number in parentheses indicates the ranking of the subindicators.

Analysis of innovation competency according to industry

High-tech manufacturing industries and modern service industries have strong innovation competency, and traditional industries have relatively weaker innovation competency

According to the comparative analysis of the overall index of innovation competency, industries with a higher total innovation competency index are mainly high-tech manufacturing and modern service industries (Table 8.4). Industries with lower innovation competency are mainly traditional manufacturing and traditional service industries. The innovation competency scores of high-tech manufacturing and modern service industries are 48.52 and 48.56, respectively.

Innovation competency scores for traditional manufacturing and service industries are 41.96 and 37.07, respectively, which are 6.56 and 11.49 points less than the high-tech manufacturing and modern service industries, respectively.

Service industries focus on model innovation and manufacturing industries focus on technological innovation

Innovation in service industries is dominated by model innovation. The score for the model innovation index of service industries is 3.74 points higher than the technological innovation score. The scores for model innovation for information transfer, software and information technology services, culture, sports and entertainment, leasing and commercial services, finance and board and lodging services are 6 points higher than the scores for the technological innovation index.

Innovation in manufacturing industries is dominated by technological innovation. The technological innovation index score for manufacturing is 5.17 points higher than the model innovation score. The technological innovation index scores for the comprehensive utilisation of waste resources, processing of timber, manufacturing of wood, bamboo, rattan, palm and straw products, smelting, rolling and pressing of ferrous metals and smelting, rolling and pressing of nonferrous metals are 10 points higher than their model innovation scores.

Table 8.4 Innovative competency scores of Chinese listed companies, 2017

Industry	Overall indicator (X) Innovation competency	Primary indicator (X1) Innovation environment	Primary indicator (X2) Innovation input	Primary indicator (X3) Technological innovation	Primary indicator (X4) Model innovation	Primary indicator (X5) Innovation output
Manufacture of measuring instruments and machinery	54.48	58.09 (2)	67.66 (1)	46.65 (4)	53.44 (3)	46.56 (5)
Information transfer, software and information technology services	53.36	53.76 (2)	70.34 (1)	43.40 (5)	55.26 (3)	44.01 (4)
Manufacture of computers, communication equipment and other electronic equipment	50.20	55.72 (2)	61.29 (1)	48.36 (3)	46.11 (4)	39.51 (5)
Manufacture of special machinery	48.71	54.88 (2)	57.44 (1)	47.16 (3)	44.07 (4)	40.01 (5)
Manufacture of electrical machinery and equipment	48.29	52.38 (2)	53.42 (1)	50.28 (3)	46.19 (4)	39.16 (5)
Manufacture of medicines	46.59	55.35 (1)	50.80 (2)	42.34 (4)	37.95 (5)	46.49 (3)
Scientific research and technical services	45.93	55.09 (1)	54.64 (2)	37.98 (4)	37.10 (5)	44.85 (3)
Manufacture of general-purpose machinery	45.55	55.14 (1)	52.32 (2)	42.87 (3)	39.32 (4)	38.12 (5)
Printing and reproduction of recording media	45.37	54.54 (1)	45.40 (3)	43.18 (4)	37.97 (5)	45.74 (2)
Comprehensive utilisation of waste resources	45.23	53.98 (1)	48.34 (2)	47.93 (3)	30.68 (5)	45.20 (4)

Industry	Overall indicator (X) Innovation competency	Primary indicator (X1) Innovation environment	Primary indicator (X2) Innovation input	Primary indicator (X3) Technological innovation	Primary indicator (X4) Model innovation	Primary indicator (X5) Innovation output
Manufacture of culture, education, handicraft, fine arts, sports and entertainment articles	44.48	58.72 (1)	49.09 (2)	38.23 (4)	34.68 (5)	41.65 (3)
Manufacture of furniture	44.45	56.76 (1)	43.20 (3)	43.67 (2)	38.91 (5)	39.71 (4)
Manufacture of motor vehicles	44.34	53.50 (1)	49.91 (2)	43.57 (3)	37.03 (5)	37.71 (4)
Manufacture of rubber and plastics	44.28	53.96 (1)	46.81 (2)	43.57 (3)	38.27 (5)	38.78 (4)
Manufacture of railway, ship, aviation and other transport equipment	44.09	53.05 (1)	52.34 (2)	42.38 (3)	34.41 (5)	38.26 (4)
Manufacture of metal products	43.81	54.12 (1)	45.44 (2)	44.70 (3)	36.48 (5)	38.33 (4)
Public health and social work	43.17	59.65 (1)	40.61 (3)	36.29 (5)	37.93 (4)	41.38 (2)
Culture, sports and entertainment	42.91	55.94 (1)	39.51 (4)	31.89 (5)	39.96 (3)	47.26 (2)
Construction	42.43	52.81 (1)	41.60 (3)	42.25 (2)	36.29 (5)	39.19 (4)
Manufacture of raw chemical materials and chemical products	42.27	51.29 (1)	46.12 (2)	39.59 (4)	34.73 (5)	39.60 (3)
Manufacture of nonmetal ores	42.25	52.15 (1)	42.69 (2)	41.46 (3)	36.83 (5)	38.14 (4)
Textiles and garments	42.09	52.41 (1)	37.16 (4)	40.22 (3)	44.00 (2)	36.64 (5)
Manufacture of food	41.85	55.01 (1)	36.46 (4)	42.23 (2)	35.12 (5)	40.40 (3)
Water conservation, environment and public facilities management	41.36	53.00 (1)	38.68 (3)	37.12 (4)	33.16 (5)	44.82 (2)

Industry	Overall indicator (X) Innovation competency	Primary indicator (X1) Innovation environment	Primary indicator (X2) Innovation input	Primary indicator (X3) Technological innovation	Primary indicator (X4) Model innovation	Primary indicator (X5) Innovation output
Leasing and commercial services	41.15	54.13 (1)	33.90 (4)	33.41 (5)	40.28 (3)	44.03 (2)
Manufacture of paper and paper products	40.69	52.95 (1)	41.38 (2)	39.53 (3)	35.25 (4)	34.34 (5)
Wood, bamboo, rattan, palm and straw products	40.32	44.33 (2)	34.90 (4)	48.88 (1)	34.24 (5)	39.26 (3)
Smelting, rolling and pressing of nonferrous metals	39.92	49.74 (1)	41.72 (3)	42.15 (2)	30.42 (5)	35.57 (4)
Other manufacture	39.64	49.04 (1)	37.41 (4)	38.05 (3)	32.03 (5)	41.66 (2)
Manufacture of textiles	39.53	50.17 (1)	39.34 (2)	37.25 (3)	36.25 (4)	34.61 (5)
Liquor, beverages and refined tea	39.33	53.58 (1)	30.71 (5)	35.32 (3)	34.76 (4)	42.26 (2)
Food processing from agricultural products	38.92	55.10 (1)	32.33 (5)	36.85 (2)	35.08 (4)	35.24 (3)
Manufacture of leather, fur, feather and related products, and shoes	38.88	56.26 (1)	31.58 (5)	34.77 (4)	36.56 (2)	35.22 (3)
Smelting, rolling and pressing of ferrous metals	38.83	49.87 (1)	39.08 (3)	44.38 (2)	31.19 (4)	29.65 (5)
Comprehensive	38.63	49.34 (1)	33.21 (4)	36.90 (3)	32.69 (5)	41.00 (2)
Manufacture of chemical fibres	38.40	52.60 (1)	39.50 (2)	36.34 (3)	27.68 (5)	35.91 (4)
Finance	38.32	52.18 (2)	23.03 (5)	27.36 (4)	34.08 (3)	54.95 (1)
Mining	37.58	50.91 (1)	33.52 (4)	37.92 (2)	30.12 (5)	35.43 (3)

Industry	Overall indicator (X) Innovation competency	Primary indicator (X1) Innovation environment	Primary indicator (X2) Innovation input	Primary indicator (X3) Technological innovation	Primary indicator (X4) Model innovation	Primary indicator (X5) Innovation output
Agriculture, forestry, animal husbandry and fisheries	37.28	48.27 (1)	33.59 (5)	33.60 (4)	36.70 (2)	34.22 (3)
Electricity, heat, gas and water production and supply	37.20	53.06 (1)	28.22 (5)	34.13 (3)	28.62 (4)	41.97 (2)
Transport, warehousing and postal industries	37.02	52.72 (1)	27.50 (5)	30.17 (4)	32.46 (3)	42.27 (2)
Real estate	36.83	51.78 (1)	23.05 (5)	32.08 (3)	31.05 (4)	46.17 (2)
Wholesale and retail	36.75	52.85 (1)	27.14 (5)	31.20 (4)	36.24 (3)	36.33 (2)
Petroleum processing, coking and nuclear fuel processing	35.77	49.85 (1)	33.16 (4)	35.03 (2)	27.28 (5)	33.54 (3)
Board and lodging	34.65	52.46 (1)	19.96 (5)	30.66 (4)	37.19 (2)	32.97 (3)
Education	31.22	50.53 (1)	30.92 (3)	18.78 (5)	20.47 (4)	35.42 (2)
Mean	43.94	53.42	45.80	40.77	39.09	40.61

Note: The number in parentheses indicates the ranking of the subindicators.

Conclusions

Chinese company innovation is still in the early stage of development

The process of company innovation and development consists of an early high-input stage and a late high-yield stage. At the end of 2017, China's strategy for innovation-driven development had been in operation for only five years, and the innovation and development of Chinese companies remain in the early stages. The innovation competency of listed companies is generally low, which is in line with the general trend of innovation and development. The evaluation results show that, with the implementation of the innovation-driven strategy, the continuous promotion of the government's reforms to delegate power, streamline administration and optimise government services and to promote large-scale entrepreneurship and innovation have led to significant improvements in the external environment for the innovation and development of Chinese companies. This has laid a robust foundation for the sustainable and sound development of company innovation.

It should be noted that the level of innovation and development of Chinese companies is due mainly to a small number of leading companies, while the innovation competency of most listed companies can, and should, be improved. A favourable pattern in which leading companies help smaller ones so as to achieve coordinated development has not yet been established.

Distribution of China's listed companies according to innovation competency follows a gradient descent

This study shows that, compared with the traditional factor-driven economy, an innovation-driven economy can lead to a concentration of resources. China's eastern region has the advantage of many resources—such as talent, capital, culture, internationalisation, reform and opening-up—and has become an area of concentration for Chinese company innovation and development. Among the top 500 innovative companies, those in the east account for 80 per cent of the total, with 44.6 per cent in Guangdong and Beijing alone. Guangdong and Beijing have assumed leading positions in company innovation and development on a national scale.

At the same time, the central region has become the main area for industrial transfer from the east and is strongly influenced by innovation activities in the eastern region. The central region has relatively good resources in terms of talent, capital and culture, and its innovation competency is ranked second in the country. In contrast, the mid-west and north-east regions have relatively few innovative resources, and therefore overall company innovation competency is weak.

Active innovation in high-tech manufacturing and modern service industries

Company innovation activities are often carried out based on new technologies and models of operation. In recent years, to accelerate the upgrading and transformation of China's industrial structure, the central government has implemented a number of supporting policies that have effectively promoted the innovation and development of China's high-tech manufacturing industries and modern service industries. Among these industries, information transfer, software and information technology services, the manufacturing of computers, communication equipment and other electronic equipment, the manufacturing of electrical machinery and equipment, the manufacturing of special equipment and pharmaceutical manufacturing have become the five major innovative industries.

Comments on innovation policies for firms in China

In China, the rudiments of capitalism were already evident as long ago as the Song Dynasty. In the Ming Dynasty, there was a large-scale coal industry, which included exploration for and utilisation of natural gases, and a rather advanced iron and steel industry, which had already solved technical problems around the casting of iron and steel that Europeans were not able to figure out until the nineteenth century. However, the Industrial Revolution did not take place in China. The key reason was the long-term suppression of Chinese entrepreneurs' innovative spirit throughout history.

In September 2017, the State Council issued a policy document entitled 'Opinions Regarding Making a Healthy Growing Environment for Entrepreneurs, Spreading Excellent Entrepreneurial Spirit and Better Exercising Entrepreneurs' Roles'. The chairman of the board of Alibaba Group noted that this document marked 'a great leap forward in thinking since 2,000 years ago in China' (Sina Technology 2017). This document and the gradual introduction of relevant supporting policies will undoubtedly shape China's future development.

To encourage enterprise innovation, the Chinese Government has over the years issued hundreds of relevant policies, with the number reaching the tens of thousands when coupled with policies introduced by local governments. These policies can be grouped into the following categories:

1. Increasing efforts to protect intellectual property and establish and perfect the legal system governing intellectual property.
2. Promoting reforms to delegate power, streamline administration and optimise government services, and build a market environment in which entrepreneurs can compete fairly. Propelling the system of negative listing of market access

and guaranteeing that all kinds of market subjects can legally and equally enter industries, fields and services outside the negative list. Opposing local protectionism, revising local regulations that hinder fair competition and establishing a unified market that allows the free flow of production factors.

3. Encouraging local governments to be bold and establishing a mechanism that tolerates mistakes and is adventurous.

4. Promoting close cooperation between universities, research institutes and enterprises, integrating three-party resources, improving innovation capacities and increasing the conversion efficiency of technological achievements.

5. Establishing and perfecting service platform systems that support entrepreneurial innovation. There are more than 5,500 maker spaces in China, along with more than 4,000 high-tech business incubators and over 970 innovation and startup platforms built by central government enterprises.

6. Some 120 innovation and startup model bases have been established. Through exploration and practise, successes can be promoted nationwide.

7. Boosting the construction of an innovation mechanism that involves cooperation between large, medium and small enterprises. Through an industry chain, these enterprises can co-establish innovation platforms, open innovation resources and engage in cooperative innovation activities.

8. Increasing efforts to support innovation-based enterprises in terms of finance and taxation policies and offering favourable fiscal terms to these enterprises.

9. Broadening the direct financing channels of innovation-based enterprises, and prioritising bond issues, financing and public offerings of medium and small tech enterprises.

As can be seen, to effectively promote the innovative development of enterprises, the Chinese Government has not only offered innovation-based enterprises taxation and financial support, but also introduced a series of supportive legal, social and administrative policies. These efforts have yielded remarkable results.

Based on various local surveys, there are two major flaws in the policies aimed at encouraging entrepreneurial innovation in China. The first is that some policies have not yet been fully formulated, such as the imperfect system of intellectual property protection. And the second is that some policies are not completely implemented due to various interruptions. These problems are bound to occur in the development process of a transitional country. Along with the continual and thorough implementation of innovation-driven strategies, these problems will gradually be effectively alleviated or resolved.

With the perfecting of the policy system that supports entrepreneurial innovation, Chinese enterprises will move from the early innovation stage of high investment to the late stage of high yields. This is the main reason the innovation of Chinese enterprises enjoys a rosy prospect.

References

Breschi, S., Malerba, F. and Orsenigo, L. (2010), Technological regimes and Schumpeterian patterns of innovation, *Economic Journal* 110(463): 388–410. doi.org/10.1111/1468-0297.00530.

Cao, H.J., Zhao, X. and Huang, S.J. (2009), Research on assessment systems of enterprises' independent innovation, [in Chinese], *China Industrial Economies* 9: 105–14.

Chen, K. and Guan, J. (2011), Mapping the functionality of China's regional innovation systems: A structural approach, *China Economic Review* 22(1): 10–27. doi.org/10.1016/j.chieco.2010.08.002.

Chung, S. (2002), Building a national innovation system through regional innovation systems, *Technovation* 22(8): 485–91. doi.org/10.1016/S0166-4972(01)00035-9.

Cooke, P. (1997), Regional innovation systems: Institutional and organizational dimensions, *Research Policy* 26(4–5): 475–91. doi.org/10.1016/S0048-7333(97)00025-5.

Cooke, P. (2011), Transition regions: Regional–national eco-innovation systems and strategies, *Progress in Planning* 76(3): 105–46. doi.org/10.1016/j.progress.2011.08.002.

Dang, W.J., Zhang, Z.Y. and Kang, J.J. (2008), The impact of the regional innovation environment on regional innovation capability, [in Chinese], *China Soft Science* 3: 52–7.

Edwards, G. (2013), Regions and innovation: A reflection, in S. Kinnear, K. Charters and P. Vitartas (eds), *Regional Advantage and Innovation: Achieving Australia's national outcomes*, Heidelberg: Springer-Verlag.

Fagerberg, J.E. and Verspagen, B. (2009), Innovation studies: The emerging structure of a new scientific field, *Research Policy* 38(2): 218–33. doi.org/10.1016/j.respol.2008.12.006.

Godoe, H. (2012), Innovation theory, aesthetics, and science of the artificial after Herbert Simon, *Journal of the Knowledge Economy* 3(4): 372–88. doi.org/10.1007/s13132-011-0055-6.

Gössling, T. and Rutten, R. (2007), Innovation in regions, *European Planning Studies* 15(2): 253–70. doi.org/10.1080/09654310601078788.

Guan, J. and Chen, K. (2012), Modeling the relative efficiency of national innovation systems, *Research Policy* 41(1): 102–15. doi.org/10.1016/j.respol.2011.07.001.

Guan, J. and Ma, N. (2003), Innovative capability and export performance of Chinese firms, *Technovation* 23(9): 737–47. doi.org/10.1016/S0166-4972(02)00013-5.

Huang, L. (2000), Approach to the main content of regional innovation systems, *Science Research Management* 21(2): 43–8.

Jacobsson, S. and Bergek, A. (2011), Innovation system analyses and sustainability transitions: Contributions and suggestions for research, *Environmental Innovation & Societal Transitions* 1(1): 41–57. doi.org/10.1016/j.eist.2011.04.006.

Jia, Y.N. (2001), Theory and analysis of regional creative milieus, [in Chinese], *Areal Research & Development* 20(1): 5–8.

Li, W., Chang, J., Wang, M.J., Zhu, X.Y. and Jin, A.M. (2014), Innovation 3.0 and innovation ecosystems, [in Chinese], *Studies in Science of Science* 13(1): 39–63.

Martin, R. and Simmie, J. (2008), Path dependence and local innovation systems in city-regions, *Innovation* 10(2–3): 183–96. doi.org/10.5172/impp.453.10.2-3.183.

Motohashi, K. and Yun, X. (2007), China's innovation system reform and growing industry and science linkages, *Research Policy* 36(8): 1251–60. doi.org/10.1016/j.respol.2007.02.023.

Pekkarinen, S. and Harmaakorpi, V. (2006), Building regional innovation networks: The definition of an age business core process in a regional innovation system, *Regional Studies* 40: 401–13. doi.org/10.1080/00343400600725228.

Phan, P., Zhou, J. and Abrahamson, E. (2010), Creativity, innovation, and entrepreneurship in China, *Social Science Electronic Publishing* 6(2): 175–94. doi.org/10.1111/j.1740-8784.2010.00181.x.

Ronde, P. (2005), Innovations in regions: What does really matter?, *Research Policy* 34(8): 1150–72. doi.org/10.1016/j.respol.2005.03.011.

Simmie, J. (2003), Innovation and urban regions as national and international nodes for the transfer and sharing of knowledge, *Regional Studies* 37(6–7): 607–20. doi.org/10.1080/0034340032000108714.

Sina Technology (2017), This document from the central government makes entrepreneurs very excited! Wang Jianlin says he is reassured, [in Chinese], *China Business News*, 30 September, available from: cj.sina.com.cn/article/detail/1650111241/424211?column=china&ch=9.

Tian, Z.K., Zhao, X.J. and Tong H.Q. (2008), Comparison and assessment of China's technology innovation ability, [in Chinese], *China Soft Science* 7: 155–60.

Tong, J.S. (2003), The cooperative innovation system of industry, universities and research institutes and independent intellectual property, [in Chinese], *China Soft Science* (1): 113–16.

Wang, H.Q. and Hou, Y. (2017), Evaluation study on technological ability of high-tech industry in China, [in Chinese], *Forum on Science and Technology in China* 3: 58–63.

Wang, Z.H. and Liu, L. (2015), A comparative analysis of the national innovative evaluation indexes, [in Chinese], *Science Research Management* 1: 162–8.

Yin, W.H. and Zhang, Y.X. (2016), Analysis of independent innovation capability of industrial enterprises in China, [in Chinese], *The World of Survey and Research* 2: 36–47.

Zeng, G.P., Gou, Y.Z. and Liu, L. (2013), From innovation system to innovation ecosystem, [in Chinese], *Studies in Science of Science* 31(1): 4–12.

Zhou, B.X., Ding, Y.B. and Ren, C.M. (2007), Study on regional innovation systems structure model and operation mechanism, [in Chinese], *China Soft Science* (3): 135–8.

9. The effects of financial sector opening on financial constraints in China

Liqing Zhang, Yan Zhang and Zhixiao Dong

As the threat of a Sino–US trade war continues, China has made new moves towards financial services liberalisation.[1] In his speech to the seventeenth Boao Forum in April 2018, Chinese President Xi Jinping announced a plan to further liberalise China's financial markets. The Governor of the People's Bank of China, Gang Yi, promulgated details of policies to open up the financial services sector, including removal of restrictions on foreign ownership of banks and asset management companies. China is determined to liberalise its financial services sector at this critical stage in its broader opening-up and domestic reforms.

There is considerable evidence that financial constraints are a key impediment to investment and the efficiency and growth of firms (Stein 2003; Li and Huang 2015). This is particularly important in developing countries such as China, where imperfections in capital markets remain. Financial constraints can arise from various sources. The literature identifies information asymmetries and agency problems as the most important factors influencing the allocation of financial resources to firms. Our chapter revisits the relationship between financial service liberalisation and financial constraints in China. We aim to investigate whether the financial constraints on Chinese firms have eased with financial sector liberalisation and through what channels financial sector openness has an impact.

Empirical studies of the effects of financial sector opening on developing countries have produced ambiguous results and are therefore not helpful in providing any clear policy guidelines. A transitional economy such as China's inherits from its previous central-planning phase a repressed financial system in which active directed credit programs channelled funds at a subsidised price to large state-owned enterprises (SOEs). Financial sector opening and the entry of foreign financial institutions—aimed at phasing out these practices—are expected to lead to more efficient allocation of funds to business.

1　There are two aspects of financial liberalisation: financial sector opening and financial market liberalisation. In this chapter, we focus only on financial sector, which includes the banking services, insurance and securities sectors.

Our chapter first reviews the policies of China's financial sector opening. And, by using a foreign direct investment (FDI) restrictiveness index as an exogenous policy measure of China's financial services sector and a Chinese regional input–output table, we calculate China's financial sector opening with variations according to region, industry and year. By using the panel data for listed firms for 2010–15, four indices are used to measure China's firm-level financial constraints through internal and external finance channels. We then examine how financial liberalisation in China alleviates the financing constraints on Chinese firms.

We find that financial sector opening can significantly reduce the financial constraints on enterprises, mainly through external financing—especially bank credit. Opening of the financial sector will encourage enterprises to substitute trade credits with bank credits and upgrade their financing structure. By examining heterogeneity effects according to firm ownership and return on assets (ROA), we find that financial sector opening can eliminate financial discrimination and promote financing efficiency. Financial sector opening is most conducive to alleviating the financial constraints on private and profitable enterprises. The mechanisms of financial sector opening affect financial constraints mainly through collateral channels and by eliminating information asymmetry between financial institutions and listed enterprises.

Section two of this chapter provides a brief literature review. Section three reviews the impact of China's financial sector opening on the bank, insurance and security sectors. Measures of China's financial constraints are contained in section four, while sections five and six present and discuss the empirical results, before the final section provides a conclusion.

Literature review

Financial sector opening is an important step in the liberalisation of financial services—which usually refers to the process by which the operation of a country's financial services sector and the allocation of financial resources gradually cast off government regulation and open up to market determination. Williamson and Mahar (1998) define the scope of financial liberalisation in six aspects: relaxing financial regulations, eliminating loan controls, providing free access to financial services, respecting financial institution autonomy, bank privatisation and liberalisation of international capital flows. In an ideal market without friction, enterprises can choose between internal and external financing without any difference in impact. The investment behaviour of an enterprise will not be restricted by its financial status and will be related only to its investment needs.

However, in the real economy, due to information asymmetry and principal–agent problems, financial markets are not completely efficient. Financing costs vary considerably, according to whether internal or external financing is chosen.

Fazzari et al. (1988) define the difference between external financing costs and internal financing costs as the financial constraints on a business. Financial sector liberalisation—especially the entry of foreign banking—could reduce information asymmetries, promote the market-oriented operation of financial institutions, improve financing efficiency and ease firms' financial constraints.

More empirical research investigates the effects of financial services liberalisation on financial constraints, but the results are still not consistent. Some research finds positive and significant effects from financial liberalisation on the alleviation of firms' financial constraints, such as Harris et al. (1994), Love (2003), Beck et al. (2005), Naeem and Li (2019) and Zhang and Zheng (2019). Early work was conducted by Harris et al. (1994), who empirically studied the relationship between financial liberalisation and financial constraints in Indonesia from 1981 to 1988. They compared conditions before and after financial liberalisation in Indonesia and found the external financial costs decreased and financial constraints improved. Love (2003) uses Euler's equation and structural equations to investigate the determinants of financial constraints and finds that, after controlling other factors—such as scale effects, business cycles and the legal environment—financial liberalisation reduces enterprises' financial constraints. Bekaert et al. (2005) show that liberalisation of the stock market will promote real economic growth by 1 per cent per year. Beck et al. (2005) find that financial liberalisation has much bigger effects on small firms, and financial liberalisation will alleviate financial constraints due to the institutional environment, such as laws and levels of corruption. Naeem and Li (2019) argue that financial sector reform can alleviate financial constraints and improve investment efficiency. Zhang and Zheng (2019) argue that financial constraints have significant impacts on innovation and the effects are stronger for non-SOEs and foreign-owned enterprises.

Some research—most of which focuses on developing countries—produces results with negative or heterogeneous effects. Haramillo et al. (1996) use panel data of manufacturing companies for the period 1983–88 in Ecuador and find that the country's financial reforms have no effects on the financial constraints of domestic companies. The imperfect development of capital markets has a greater impact on small and medium-sized enterprises (SMEs), but less impact on large enterprises. Laeven (2003) shows that financial liberalisation does not reduce financial constraints for large firms, and only reduces financial constraints on SMEs in 13 developing countries. According to Dell'Ariccia and Marquez (2004), financial liberalisation has intensified competition among banks, which has led to a continuous reduction in lending rates, making it easier for companies to obtain funds. But this has also increased the systemic risk of the entire economy. Koo and Maeng (2005) show that, although financial liberalisation can alleviate the financial constraints on South Korean companies, it mainly benefits SMEs. For large enterprises, financial liberalisation has not brought much improvement.

Some research has investigated the characteristics of China's financial markets. External (indirect) financing and banking finance are the main financing channels in China. Historically in China's banking sector, all banks were state-owned and credit was more inclined to go to SOEs. Non-SOEs face more serious financial constraints than their state-owned counterparts. According to Batra et al. (2003), although China has the largest banking system in the world, private companies face bigger financial constraints than SOEs. Huang (2005) also shows that financial constraints are among the biggest hindrance to the development of private companies. After its accession to the World Trade Organization (WTO) in 2001, China accelerated its financial liberalisation, gradually liberalising the local currency business of foreign banks on the mainland. Lin (2011) uses China's WTO accession policies to investigate the effects on financial constraints and finds that, on average, the entry of foreign banks had no significant impact on financial constraints, while different types of enterprises were affected differently and those with higher profitability and higher ROA as well as private firms were more likely to obtain loans.

Other studies have tried to explore the effects of financial opening on the performance of banks and enterprises. Berger et al. (2009) collected China's bank data for the period 1994–2003 and found that Chinese state-owned banks were less efficient than foreign banks. The entry of foreign banks had a positive and significant effect, enhancing the efficiency of Chinese domestic banks. Huang (2005) also used this policy shock in the banking sector and a difference-in-differences method to study its impacts on total factor productivity (TFP). The final regression results show that the entry of foreign banks increased the TFP of all enterprises by 2.03 per cent. However, the entry of foreign banks reduced the TFP of SOEs and collective enterprises and increased the TFP of private enterprises. Meanwhile, Lai et al. (2016) find the entry of foreign banks in a certain region had no significant impact on the aggregate productivity of that region; companies in that region that relied more on financial support in the production process would be better developed. The impact of foreign banks on domestic enterprises comes more through the improvement of technological upgrading, rather than through efficiency enhancement of the redistribution of resources in the region.

China's financial sector opening

Financial sector opening has played a very important role in the development of the domestic economy and the efficient allocation of production factors. China entered the WTO in 2001. The establishment of the China (Shanghai) Pilot Free-Trade Zone in 2013 was another key node of China's financial service liberalisation. With 2001 and 2013 as the dividing years, we introduce China's financial sector opening policies in two stages after 2001.

Development stage (2001–13)

China's entry to the WTO was a landmark event in bringing China into the global economy. It adopted a model of gradual opening and made corresponding commitments within the WTO to liberalise its financial institutions such as banks and the securities and insurance sectors.

WTO commitments

Bank services sector

China made a commitment that immediately on its accession to the WTO it would allow foreign banks to conduct foreign currency business without any limitations on market access or national treatment. Within two years of China's accession, foreign banks were able to conduct domestic currency business with Chinese enterprises, subject to certain geographical restrictions. After entry into the WTO in 2001, China committed to a five-year phase-in period for foreign banking services. Specifically, China would cancel the geographical restrictions on foreign banks gradually over five years. The geographical restrictions on Shanghai, Shenzhen, Tianjin and Dalian were lifted in 2001, followed later in the same year by those on Guangzhou, Zhuhai, Qingdao, Nanjing and Wuhan. The geographical restrictions on Kunming, Beijing and Xiamen were lifted before 2003, as were those on Shantou, Ningbo, Shenyang and Xi'an the following year. Within five years of China's accession, foreign banks were able to conduct domestic currency business with Chinese enterprises and individuals, and all geographical restrictions were lifted (Tables 9.1 and 9.2).

Table 9.1 China's WTO commitments on banking services I

	Cross-border supply	Consumption abroad	Commercial presence	Presence of natural persons
Limitations on market access	Unbound, with exceptions[1]	None	a. Geographic coverage b. Clients c. Licensing	Unbound except as indicated in horizontal commitments
Limitations on national treatment	None		Except for geographical restrictions and client limitations on local currency business	Unbound except as indicated in horizontal commitments
Additional commitments	Foreign financial leasing corporations will be permitted to provide financial leasing services at the same time as domestic corporations			

[1] Unbound except for the following: Provision and transfer of financial information, financial data processing and related software by suppliers of other financial services; advisory, intermediation and other auxiliary financial services on all activities listed in subparagraphs (a) through (k), including credit reference and analysis, investment and portfolio research and advice, advice on acquisitions and on corporate restructuring and strategy.

Source: WTO (n.d.).

Table 9.2 China's WTO commitments on banking services II

	2001	2002	2003	2004	2005	2006
Clients for foreign currency business	No limitation	No limitation	No limitation	No limitation	No limitation	No limitation
Clients for renminbi	Chinese enterprises	Chinese enterprises	Chinese enterprises	All Chinese clients	All Chinese clients	All Chinese clients
Geographical limitation for operation of foreign exchange	No limitation	No limitation	No limitation	No limitation	No limitation	No limitation
Geographical limitation for operation of renminbi	Four cities: Shenzhen, Shanghai, Dalian, Tianjin	Nine cities: Guangzhou, Zhuhai, Qingdao, Nanjing, Wuhan	12 cities: Kunming, Beijing, Xiamen	16 cities: Shantou, Ningbo, Shenyang, Xi'an	No limitation	No limitation
Qualifications for engaging renminbi	Three years of business operation in China and being profitable for two consecutive years prior to the application; otherwise, none.					
Licensing criteria for establishing a subsidiary	Total assets of more than US$10 billion at the end of the year prior to filing the application.					
Licensing criteria for establishing a branch	Total assets of more than US$20 billion at the end of the year prior to filing the application.					
Licensing criteria for establishing a Chinese–foreign joint bank or a Chinese–foreign joint finance company	Total assets of more than US$10 billion at the end of the year prior to filing the application.					

Source: WTO (n.d.).

Insurance services sector

China has also gradually liberalised its insurance sector. According to China's WTO commitment on insurance services, foreign non–life insurance providers are permitted to set up a branch or a joint venture in China and may hold a 51 per cent equity share of that. Within two years of China's WTO accession, foreign non–life insurance providers were permitted to establish whole ownership of a joint venture. On accession, large-scale insurance and reinsurance for commercial risk, international marine, aviation and transport and joint ventures with foreign equity of no more than 50 per cent were permitted; within three years of accession, foreign equity shares could increase to 51 per cent; and, within five years of accession, wholly foreign-owned subsidiaries were permitted.

The geographical restrictions on foreign insurance companies were also phased out. Relative to the open stage of the banking industry, liberalisation of the insurance sector has been relatively brief. In 2003, China released the geographical restrictions on Shanghai, Dalian, Shenzhen and Foshan, and, in 2004, on another 10 cities (Beijing, Chengdu, Chongqing, Fuzhou, Suzhou, Xiamen, Ningbo, Shenyang, Wuhan and Tianjin). All geographical restrictions on foreign insurance companies were lifted before 2005 (Tables 9.3 and 9.4).

Table 9.3 China's WTO commitments on insurance services I

	Cross-border supply	Consumption abroad	Commercial presence	Presence of natural persons
Limitation on market access	Unbound except for: reinsurance, international transport insurance and brokerage for large-scale commercial risks	Unbound for brokerage. Other, none	a. Establishment form b. Geographic coverage c. Business scope d. Licences	Unbound except as indicated in horizontal commitments
Limitation on national treatment	None	None	None, with exceptions[1]	Unbound except as indicated in horizontal commitments

[1] None, except for: Foreign insurance institutions shall not engage in the statutory insurance business; on accession, a 20 per cent cession of all lines of primary risk for non-life, personal accident and health insurance businesses with an appointed Chinese reinsurance company shall be required; one year after accession, 15 per cent shall be required; two years after accession, 10 per cent shall be required; and three years after accession, 5 per cent shall be required; and four years after accession, no compulsory cession shall be required.

Source: WTO (n.d.).

Table 9.4 China's WTO commitments on insurance services II

		2001–03	2004–06	
Form of establishment	Non-life insurance	Foreign insurers allowed to establish as a branch or as a joint venture with 51 per cent foreign ownership	Foreign insurers allowed to establish as a wholly owned subsidiary	
	Life insurance	Foreign insurers allowed 50 per cent ownership in a joint venture with the partner of their choice		
	Insurance brokerage	Joint venture with foreign equity of no more than 50 per cent allowed	Joint venture with foreign equity of 51 per cent allowed	
Geographic coverage		2003: Shanghai, Guangzhou, Dalian, Shenzhen and Foshan	2004: Beijing, Chengdu, Chongqing, Fuzhou, Suzhou, Xiamen, Ningbo, Shenyang, Wuhan, Tianjin	2005: No geographical restrictions

		2001–03	2004–06
Business scope	Non-life insurance	Provide 'master policy' insurance/insurance of large-scale commercial risk	Provide the full range of non-life insurance services to both foreign and domestic clients
	Life insurance	Provide individual (not group) insurance to foreigners and Chinese citizens	Provide health insurance, group insurance and pension/annuities insurance to foreigners and Chinese citizens
	Reinsurance	Provide reinsurance services for life and non-life insurance as a branch, joint venture or wholly foreign-owned subsidiary, without geographical or quantitative restrictions on the number of licences issued	
Licence qualifications		Investor shall be a foreign insurance company established for more than 30 years and a WTO member; shall have had a representative office for two consecutive years in China; shall have total assets of more than US$5 billion at the end of the year prior to application, except for insurance brokers.	
Total assets requirement		2002: more than US$400 million / 2003: more than US$300 million	2005: more than US$200 million

Source: WTO (n.d.).

Security services sector

China's WTO commitments on the securities sector relate mainly to limitations on market access: joint ventures are allowed to manage investment funds, but their stakes cannot exceed 33 per cent, relaxing three years after accession (Table 9.5).

Table 9.5 China's WTO commitments on securities

Limitations on market access	
Cross-border supply	Unbound except for the following: Foreign securities institutions may engage directly (without a Chinese intermediary) in B-shares business
Consumption abroad	None
Commercial presence	Unbound, except for the following: On accession, representative offices of foreign securities institutions in China may become 'special members' of all Chinese stock exchanges
	On accession, foreign service suppliers will be permitted to establish joint ventures with foreign investment up to 33 per cent to conduct domestic securities investment fund management
	Within three years of China's accession, foreign investment shall be increased to 49 per cent
	Within three years of accession, foreign securities institutions will be permitted to establish joint ventures, with foreign minority ownership not exceeding one-third, to engage (without a Chinese intermediary) in underwriting A shares and in underwriting and trading B and H shares as well as government and corporate debt, and launching of funds
	Criteria for authorisation to deal in China's financial industry are solely prudential (that is, containing no economic needs test or quantitative limits on licences)
Presence of natural persons	Unbound except as indicated in horizontal commitments

Relevant policies after WTO accession

Since entering the WTO, China has accelerated the pace of reform in its financial sector to comply with its accession commitments, implementing active liberalisation policies in the areas of banking, insurance and securities.

Banking services sector

In line with its WTO commitments on the banking services sector, China published its 'Regulations of the People's Republic of China on the Administration of Foreign-Funded Financial Institutions (Amended)' in December 2001. The geographical and customer restrictions on foreign-funded banks' handling of foreign exchange business were cancelled. Foreign banks are allowed to operate foreign exchange business for Chinese companies and Chinese residents and also local currency business in four cities: Shanghai, Shenzhen, Tianjin and Dalian.

In January 2002, 'The Rules for Implementing the Regulations of the People's Republic of China on the Administration of Foreign Financial Institutions (Amended)' were published, and in December of the same year, renminbi business was opened to foreign banks in five cities: Guangzhou, Qingdao, Zhuhai, Nanjing and Wuhan. In December 2003, 'The Regulations on Equity Investment of Foreign Financial Institutions in Chinese Financial Institutions' was promulgated, allowing foreign banks to operate in local currency business in four cities—Jinan, Fuzhou, Chengdu and Chongqing—and operate renminbi business for domestic enterprises in areas where renminbi business has been opened for local currency business. The state-owned commercial banks in China also started to reform their shareholding system in the same year.

In 2004 and 2005, foreign banks were allowed to operate local currency business in Kunming, Beijing, Xiamen, Shenyang, Xi'an, Shantou, Ningbo, Harbin, Changchun, Lanzhou, Yinchuan and Nanning. On 27 October 2005, China Construction Bank Corporation was listed on the Hong Kong Stock Exchange. Subsequently, the Bank of China and the Industrial and Commercial Bank of China were also listed. Finally, in 2006, with the promulgation of the 'Regulations on the Administration of Foreign-Funded Banks' and their implementation rules, the geographical and nonprudential restrictions on foreign investment essentially disappeared, the banking sector achieved comprehensive liberalisation and WTO commitments were successfully completed.

China continued to maintain an open attitude and expand the operating scope for foreign banks. In June 2007, foreign corporate banks with qualifications to operate renminbi retail business were allowed to issue bank cards satisfying the Chinese bank card business and technical standards, and enjoying the same treatment as

Chinese banks. In December 2008, foreign banks were allowed to trade on the interbank bond market and underwrite financial bonds and nonfinancial corporate debt financing instruments, but they were required to report to the local banking regulatory bureau. In June 2010, the 'Notice on the Relevant Matters Concerning the Establishment of Sub-Branches of Foreign-Funded Banks in Cities and Counties with High Density of Foreign-Oriented Enterprises' was issued, allowing foreign-invested banks to set up branches in the qualifying cities and counties. After China's WTO accession in 2001, the speed of liberalisation for foreign banks improved significantly. However, development slowed with the impact of the Global Financial Crisis in 2008. As shown in Table 9.6, the number of foreign banks in China is constantly expanding.

Table 9.6 Development of foreign banks in China

	2003	2004	2005	2006	2007	2008	2009	2010	2011	2012
Number of foreign banks	192	211	254	312	274	311	338	360	387	412
Total assets of foreign banks (RMB billion)	4,159	5,823	7,155	9,279	12,525	13,448	13,492	17,423	21,535	23,804

Note: The data series starts in 2003 as this is the year the China Banking Regulatory Commission began to provide detailed statistics on foreign banks in China.
Source: CBRC (various years).

Insurance services sector

Under China's WTO accession commitments, the transition period for the insurance services sector was only three years, which was shorter than that for the banking sector. At the same time as China entered the WTO, in December 2001, the 'Regulations of the People's Republic of China on the Administration of Foreign-Invested Insurance Companies' were announced by the State Council. China's insurance sector has since entered a new era of comprehensive reform and liberalisation.

On 11 December 2004, China liberalised the operations of foreign-invested insurance companies, allowing foreign life insurance companies to provide health insurance, group insurance and pension/annuity insurance business, and cancelling geographical restrictions on the establishment of foreign-invested insurance institutions. The proportion of foreign equity in insurance brokerage companies can now exceed 51 per cent.

In the life insurance sector, foreign ownership is restricted to a maximum of 50 per cent. Apart from the market entry restrictions on non–life insurance businesses, the geographical restrictions and business scope have been gradually liberalised after China's accession to WTO, the ratio of statutory reinsurance will be reduced by 5 per cent every year until cancelled. The insurance sector was the first of the financial sectors to liberalise. Since 2005, except for foreign ownership restrictions (to a maximum of 50 per cent), foreign insurance companies have enjoyed national treatment basically. In 2012, China and the United States signed the 'Joint Statement on Strengthening Sino–US Economic Relations', which liberalised compulsory liability insurance for motor vehicle accidents and has already surpassed China's WTO commitments.

After China entered the WTO, its insurance services sector experienced stable and rapid development (Table 9.7). The proportion of foreign capital in China's insurance sector has remained about 5 per cent.

Table 9.7 Development of foreign insurance companies

	2005	2006	2007	2008	2009	2010	2011	2012
Number of head offices	40	41	43	48	52	53	51	52
Number of provincial branches	47	67	90	117	150	168	360	212

Source: NBS (various years[a]).

Security services sector

After China's accession to the WTO, the representative office of a foreign securities institution in China could apply for special membership of Chinese stock exchanges. Foreign-invested institutions were allowed to set up joint venture securities companies and foreign securities institutions could directly engage in B-share transactions.

In July 2002, the 'Rules for the Establishment of Foreign-Funded Securities Companies' were implemented to clarify the conditions and procedures for the establishment of foreign-invested securities companies and to stipulate the scope of their business. The rules stipulated that 'the proportion of shares held by foreign shareholders (the proportion of equity held by a shared securities company) should not exceed one-third'. In 2012, the maximum limit on foreign capital in joint venture securities companies was increased to 49 per cent.

In October 2002, the China Securities Regulatory Commission (CSRC) promulgated the 'Measures for the Administration of the Acquisition of Listed Companies' and the 'Measures for the Administration of Information Disclosure of Shareholders' Changes in Listed Companies'. Foreign-invested companies were allowed to participate in the merger and acquisition of listed companies. In November 2002, the CSRC and the People's Bank of China jointly promulgated the 'Interim Measures for the Administration of Domestic Securities Investment by Qualified Foreign Institutional Investors', introducing qualified foreign institutional investors (QFII) into the Chinese securities market, taking effect in July 2003. The first QFII,

UBS Securities Asia Limited, placed an order to buy four A shares, marking the first step for foreign investment to enter the Chinese A-share market. In June 2007, the CSRC issued the 'Pilot Measures for the Administration of Overseas Securities Investment by Qualified Domestic Institutional Investors' and related notices. In 2011, the Renminbi Qualified Foreign Institutional Investors (RQFII) scheme was launched, based on the QFII scheme.

Accelerated stage (2013 – today)

The establishment of the China (Shanghai) Pilot Free-Trade Zone in 2013 was not only an important measure in the liberalisation of the financial services sector, but also indicated that China's service industry had entered a new stage.

Banking services sector

In September 2014, the 'Implementation Measures for Administrative Licensing of Foreign-Invested Banks' were promulgated, unifying the market access standards for Chinese and foreign banks. In addition, the regulations requiring foreign banks to apply to establish branches one at a time were cancelled, and the minimum requirements for working capital for a sub-branch were cancelled. In November 2014, the 'Regulations on the Administration of Foreign-Invested Banks' were amended to allow foreign banks, Sino–foreign joint venture banks and foreign bank branches to engage in bond trading on the interbank market in accordance with the business scope approved by the China Banking Regulatory Commission.

In July 2017, the 'Measures for Administrative Licensing of Chinese Commercial Banks' were revised, further relaxing the threshold for foreign banks to invest in Chinese banks. On 24 February 2018, the 'Measures for Administrative Licensing of Foreign-Invested Banks (Revised)' stipulated that the procedures for the establishment and mergers of sub-branches shall be reviewed, and only the approval of the opening of branches shall be retained. On the same day, the 'Measures for Administrative Licensing of Foreign-Funded Banks (Revised)' stipulated that 'foreign-invested legal banks and joint venture banks in China may invest in Chinese financial institutions', abolishing the relevant restrictions in the 2003 measures. As shown in Table 9.8, after 2013, the number of foreign-invested banks continued to grow.

Table 9.8 Development of foreign banks, 2013–17

	2013	2014	2015	2016	2017
Number of foreign banks	419	437	464	475	483
Total assets of foreign banks (RMB billion)	25,577	27,921	26,820	29,286	32,438

Source: CBRC (various years).

Insurance services sector

In September 2013, the Shanghai Free-Trade Zone was officially listed and the China Pacific Insurance (Group) and Public Insurance became the first enterprises to settle in the new zone. In September 2014, Shanghai Life Insurance received approval from the China Insurance Regulatory Commission to raise funds. There are plans to expand the foreign currency policy and other businesses in the free-trade zone in future.

Shanghai Life Insurance was the first national insurance company approved after the promulgation of the 'Opinions of the State Council on Accelerating the Development of the Modern Insurance Services Industry'. It was also the first legal personal finance institution registered in the Shanghai Free-Trade Zone. On 30 May 2018, the 'Regulations on the Administration of Foreign-Invested Insurance Companies (Draft for Comment)' were proposed, stipulating that the maximum for foreign-invested shares in joint venture life insurance companies should be increased to 51 per cent, relaxing the stipulation in the 2004 'Foreign Investment Insurance Company Regulations' that 'the proportion of foreign-invested shares in joint venture life insurance companies must not exceed 50 per cent'.

After 2013, the number and assets of foreign-invested insurance companies continued to grow, but the scale of foreign-invested companies remained relatively stable (Table 9.9).

Table 9.9 Number of Sino–foreign joint venture insurance institutions, 2013–17

	2013	2014	2015	2016	2017
Number of head offices	55	57	57	57	57
Provincial branches	224	276	304	327	354
Total assets of foreign-invested insurance companies (RMB100 m)	82,886.95	101,591.47	123,597.76	153,764.66	169,377.32

Source: NBS (various years[a]).

Securities services sector

In May 2014, the State Council issued the 'Opinions on Further Promoting the Healthy Development of the Capital Market', which outlined the overall plan for cross-border investment and financing, liberalisation of the securities and futures sectors and strengthening of cross-border supervision and coordination. On 28 April 2018, the 'Administrative Measures for Foreign-Invested Securities Companies' provided new regulations for foreign-invested securities companies, deleting the shareholder requirements that the proportion of foreign-owned shares not exceed China's WTO commitments, and stipulating that the restriction of foreign-invested shares to 51 per cent would be relaxed in three years.

Measures of financial sector opening

FDI regulatory restrictiveness index

The FDI regulatory restrictiveness index (FDIR index) gauges the restrictiveness of a country's FDI rules by looking at the four main types of restrictions on FDI: 1) foreign equity limitations; 2) discriminatory screening or approval mechanisms; 3) restrictions on the employment of foreigners as key personnel; and 4) other operational restrictions—for example, restrictions on branching, capital repatriation or landownership by foreign-owned enterprises. Restrictions are evaluated on a scale from 0 (open) to 1 (closed). Financial sector opening was measured based on this index, covering financial sectors and three subsectors of banking, insurance and securities. The FDI index is drawn from the Organisation for Economic Co-operation and Development (OECD) database.

As shown in Figure 9.1, China's total FDI index and financial services FDIR index decreased over time, indicating that China was continuing to liberalise its markets. After joining the WTO in 2001, China accelerated its opening-up. After 2013, the FDIR index began to decline rapidly, while the financial services sector declined relatively slowly. This shows that China has maintained a relatively cautious attitude towards the liberalisation of financial services. Although China is constantly promoting its opening to the world, it still has a large gap compared with the average openness of OECD countries, as shown in Figure 9.2.

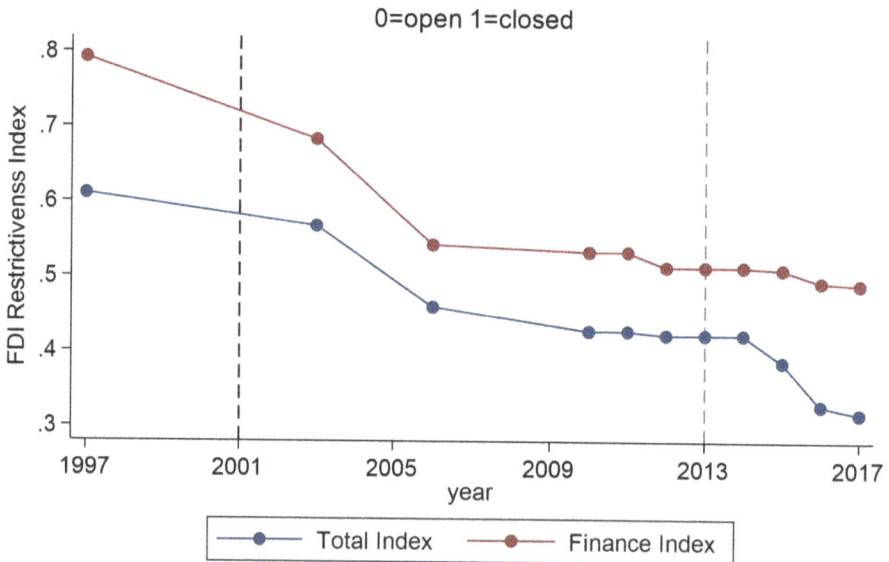

Figure 9.1 FDI restrictiveness index of China

Source: OECD (n.d.).

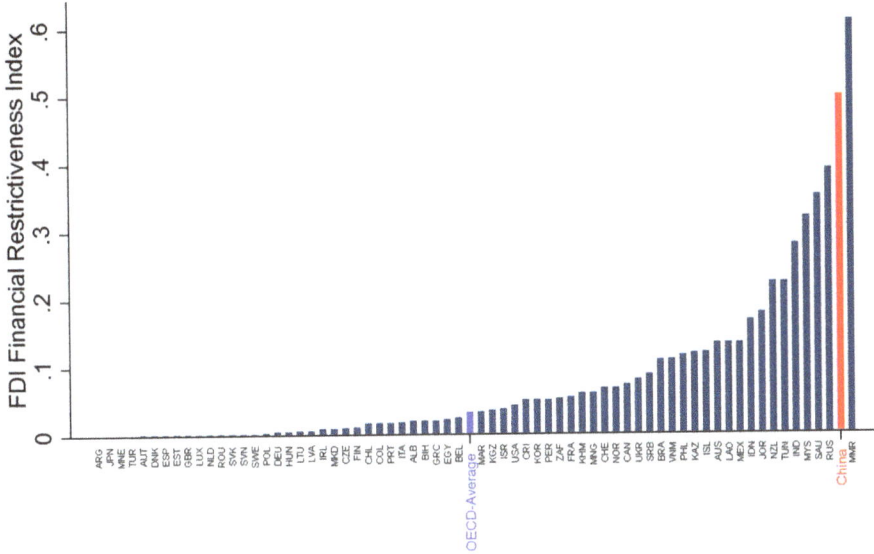

Figure 9.2 FDI restrictiveness index in financial services, 2017
Source: OECD (n.d.).

China's financial sector opening index

The FDIR index can only measure China's financial sector openness over time, but financial liberalisation could have different effects on firms in different locations and different sectors. So, utilising China's regional input–output table (for 2012, published by the National Bureau of Statistics), we calculate the financial services input ratio (α_{cr}) for 42 industries in 31 provinces in China. The financial services input ratio (α_{cr}) is the financial services input divided by the total intermediate inputs. China's financial sector openness is calculated in Equation 9.1.

Equation 9.1

$$FL_{crt} = \alpha_{cr}{}^{*}(1 - FDIR_{t})$$

FL is financial sector openness. The larger the FL index, the more open is the financial sector in that industry in that region.

Financial constraints in China

Measures of financial constraints

First, from the perspective of business operations, companies with good business conditions generally have greater cash flow, meaning a considerable proportion of projects could be financed through the company's internal finance. At the same time, companies with good business practices have lower credit risk and less chance of defaulting. Wang and Lu (2018) uses corporate cash flow indicators to measure financial constraints, with the method (operating profit + depreciation)/total assets. The greater the cash flow, the greater is the amount of financing the company can obtain through its own operations, and the lower is the financial constraint the enterprise suffers. Han and Wang (2012) use the operating cash flow as an indicator to measure the internal financial constraints on enterprises. The higher the net profit of enterprises, the stronger is their internal financing ability and the fewer financial constraints they encounter.

Besides internal finance, external finance is an important way for enterprises to obtain finance. The interest paid can reflect the external financing situation of the enterprise. Altman et al. (1977) believe the interest coverage ratio can be used as an indicator of corporate liquidity and corporate financial information, and can be used to measure the financial constraints on an enterprise. The formula for calculating the interest coverage ratio is the enterprise's earnings before interest and tax/interest expense. Li and Yu (2013) use the logarithm of corporate interest payments as an indicator to measure corporate financial constraints. The greater the interest expenses, the lower are the financial constraints.

Banks are not the only source of external financing for Chinese companies. Informal financing, such as trade (commercial) credit, is an important source of financing for most companies. Enterprises in the upstream supply chain can increase their accounts payable by using their strong market position and provide financial support for the development and operation of the company. Wang (2012) finds commercial credit is an important channel through which Chinese export enterprises can obtain external financing. This measure is (accounts payable/current sales). The higher the indicator, the lower are the financial constraints suffered by the company.

Many scholars estimate the financial constraints on enterprises by constructing a series of indices. Kaplan and Zingales (1997), Cleary (1999) and Whited and Wu (2006) constructed indices called KZ, ZFC and WW, respectively. The common feature of these indices is that they contain more information from enterprises and are more comprehensive than the single measure of financial constraints. However, the selection of some variables in the process of construction includes qualitative and quantitative information on corporate financial constraints, which are easily influenced by personal subjectivity, producing measurement errors. Hadlock and Pierce (2010) cast serious doubt on the validity of the KZ index as a measure of financial constraints, while offering mixed evidence on the validity of other common measures of such constraints. They also find that firm size and age are particularly useful predictors of financial constraint levels, and propose a measure of financial constraints called the 'SA index' based solely on these firm characteristics.

Measures of financial constraints in China

According to the literature above, our chapter uses the following four indicators to measure the financial constraints on Chinese listed companies.

Financial constraint 1: Internal financing

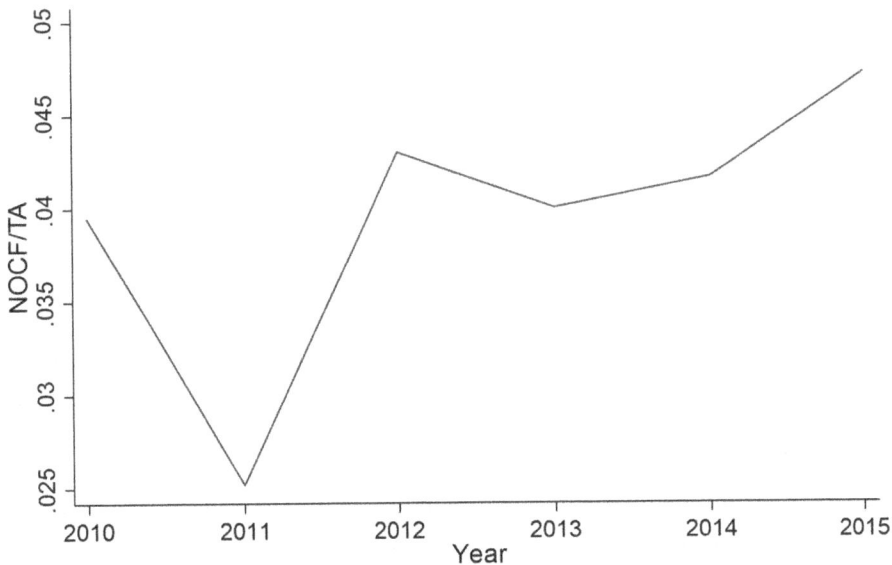

Figure 9.3 Internal financing of Chinese listed companies, 2010–15
Source: Calculated by the authors.

Internal financing refers mainly to a company's own funds and the accumulation of funds in the production and operating processes. In the long run, enterprises can obtain internal financing by improving their operational efficiency, which is a fundamental of guaranteeing the source of production. We use the ratio of net operating cash flow (NOCF) to total assets (TA) to measure the internal financing of enterprises. As can be seen from Figure 9.3, internal financing is greatly affected by the business conditions of the enterprise, and there was significant fluctuation during the period 2010–15.

Financial constraint 2: External financing

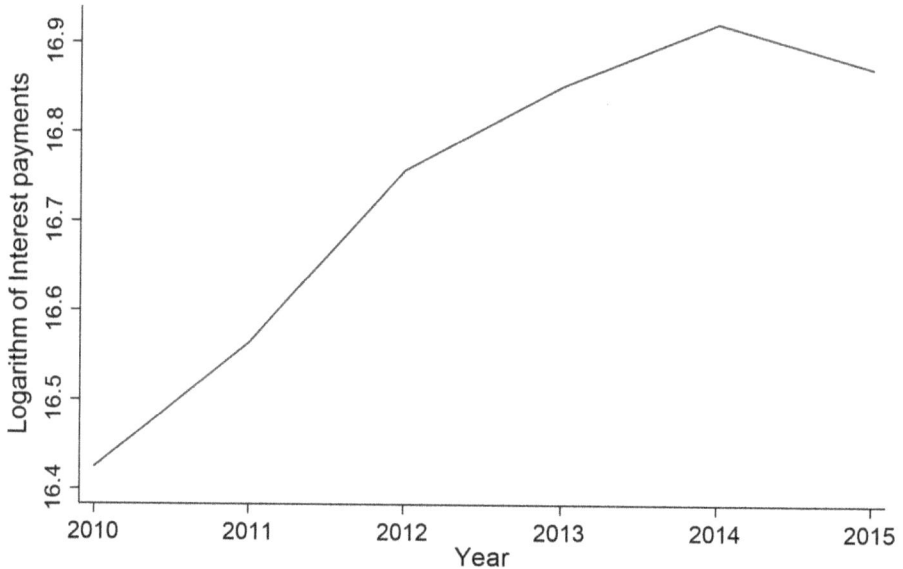

Figure 9.4 External financing of Chinese listed companies, 2010–15
Source: Calculated by the authors.

We follow Li and Yu (2013) by using the logarithm of interest expenses as an indicator to measure external financial constraints. The more interest payments a company makes, the greater is its external financing support and the lower are the external financial constraints. The level of interest payments made by Chinese companies significantly increased after 2010 (see Figure 9.4). This shows that the number of funds obtained by Chinese listed companies through external financing channels has increased.

Financial constraint 3: Trade credit

We use trade credit (accounts payable/operating income) as another measure of the external financial constraints on enterprises. The accounts payable of the enterprise refer to the debt caused by time inconsistencies between obtaining materials and paying for goods. The larger the indicator, the higher is the amount of finance the company can obtain from its partner companies. By using the money of its partner companies, an enterprise can alleviate its own financial constraints. To eliminate differences in company size from the measurement indicators, we divide the accounts payable by the company's operating income.

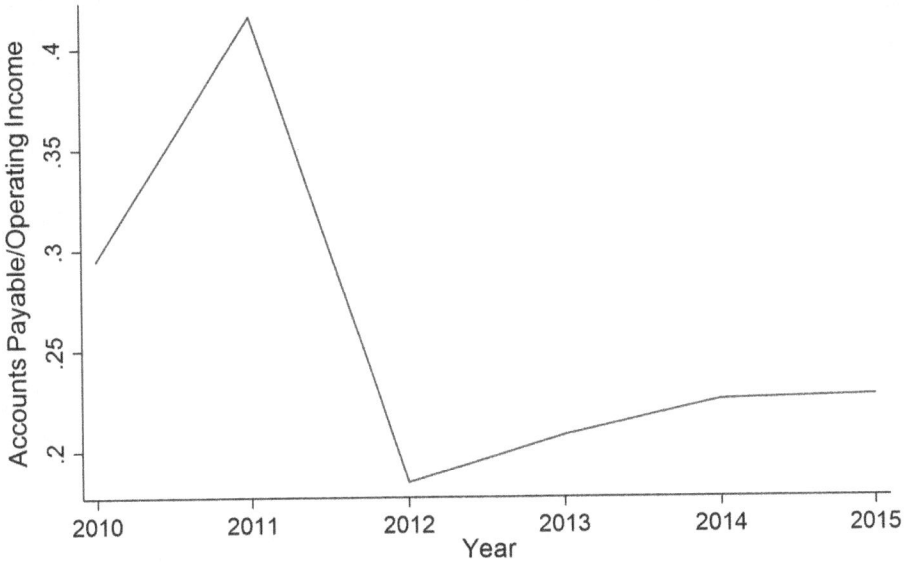

Figure 9.5 Trade credit of Chinese listed companies, 2010–15
Source: Calculated by the authors.

As can be seen from Figure 9.5, from 2010 to 2015, the average proportion of accounts payable in the current year's sales was 0.25. In 2011, the highest value was 0.415, and in 2012, the lowest value was 0.19—indicating a significant downward trend. On the one hand, this shows that the market environment in China has improved and the problem of arrears between enterprises has gradually eased. On the other hand, in Chinese listed companies, the role of trade credit in erasing corporate financial constraints continues to decrease.

Financial constraint 4: SA index

Finally, we chose the SA index followed by Wu and Huang (2017) as an indicator of financial constraints. Compared with a single financial indicator, index-based indicators use more information to measure the financial constraints on enterprises. The formula for calculating the SA index is Equation 9.2.

Equation 9.2

$$SA = -0.737size + 0.043size^2 - 0.04age$$

Size=ln (total assets/1,000,000) and age represents the company's listing period. The result calculated by SA is negative. The greater the absolute value of SA, the more serious are the financial constraints faced by the company.

Estimation and results

Empirical model specification

This chapter studies the average effects of China's financial sector opening on financial constraints. We estimate the following linear regressions (Equation 9.3).

Equation 9.3

$$Y_{icjt} = \beta_0 + \beta_1 FL_{cjt} + \theta X'_{icjt} + \alpha_i + \delta_t + \epsilon_{icjt}$$

In this equation, i, c, j and t represent firm, region, industry and year, respectively. The dependent variable is a firm-level financial constraint. The baseline regression uses four measures of financial constraints as the dependent variables. FL is the financial sector opening index, as denoted before. Here, we want to look at the direct impact of financial sector opening, so we control only for firm fixed effects, α_i, which absorb any unobserved time-invariant firm effects; δ_t is year fixed effects and X_{icjt} controls for time-varying firm-level variables such as firm size and profitability. The average impact of financial sector opening is captured by β_1. If β_1 is negative, financial sector opening has improved the financial constraints in China.

Data

Data for Chinese firms listed on the Shanghai and Shenzhen stock markets are obtained from the China Stock Market & Accounting Research Database. Following the literature, financial firms are excluded from the sample; we Winsorize the variables at the first and ninety-ninth percentile of their distribution to eliminate the effect of extreme values. The sample period for the whole dataset is 2010–15, with the number of firm observations ranging from 1,838 (in 2010) to 2,601 (in 2015). The data report detailed financial information on enterprises and their ownership type, location and industry code. FDI restrictiveness index is from the OECD database. The industry classification has been coordinated with that of China's input–output table for 2012, according to the two-digit industry division standards of the CSRC in 2006. Table 9.10 provides some summary statistics for the key variables scaled by capital stock.

Table 9.10 Summary of listed company indicators

Variable	No.	Mean	SD	Min.	Max.
Account/operating income	14,000.00	0.25	3.90	0.00	419.95
Log of fixed assets	14,000.00	19.98	1.79	7.59	27.32
Ownership	14,000.00	0.73	0.44	0.00	1.00
SA index	13,000.00	3.44	0.28	2.74	4.16

Variable	No.	Mean	SD	Min.	Max.
NOCF/TA	13,000.00	0.04	0.08	−1.28	0.88
ln(interest)	12,000.00	16.75	2.26	2.37	21.65
ln_size	13,000.00	21.88	1.20	19.24	25.81
ROA	13,000.00	0.04	0.10	−2.07	8.44
Survey	14,000.00	0.64	0.48	0.00	1.00
FL	14,000.00	0.03	0.05	0.00	0.30

Empirical results

This chapter aims to investigate the effects of financial sector opening on financial constraints in China. Using measures of financial constraints, we can identify the channels through which FL could improve firms' financial constraints. The estimation results for Equation 9.3 are shown in Table 9.11. Financial sector opening can significantly reduce the SA index as shown in Column (4), but the internal financing situation of enterprises is not significantly affected by FL, as shown in Column (2). FL also enhances external financing through bank credits, which are measured by the interest expense, as in Column (2). FL has significant, negative effects on trade credit in Column (3), which means FL could provide more formal financing channels for financial institutions and will substitute informal finance with trade credit.

Table 9.11 Baseline results

Variables	(1) Internal finance FC1	(2) Bank credit FC2	(3) Trade credit FC3	(4) SA index FC4
FL	−0.3275	18.2239**	−15.8121*	−6.2624***
	(0.6391)	(9.0205)	(8.8590)	(0.3044)
ln_size	−0.0044**	1.1307***	0.0015	0.0517***
	(0.0020)	(0.0302)	(0.0288)	(0.0010)
ROA	0.0540***	−0.6218***	0.5961***	0.0097***
	(0.0074)	(0.1183)	(0.1074)	(0.0037)
Constant	0.1391***	−8.7081***	0.5711	2.3880***
	(0.0467)	(0.6878)	(0.6570)	(0.0226)
Firm fixed effect	YES	YES	YES	YES
Year fixed effect	YES	YES	YES	YES
Observations	12,739	11,763	13,179	13,181
R-squared	0.4647	0.8743	0.4094	0.9898

FC = financial constraint

*** $p < 0.01$ ** $p < 0.05$ * $p < 0.1$

Note: Standard errors are in parentheses.

Robustness checks

This chapter examines firms' heterogeneity by ownership type and ROA. Financial sector opening could reduce information asymmetry, promote the market-oriented operation of financial institutions, improve financing efficiency and ease firms' financial constraints. We then try to investigate two channels by which FL alleviates financial constraints—through collateral and information asymmetry.

First, we investigate whether FL will have a heterogeneous effect according to firm ownership. We generate an ownership dummy with non-SOEs as 1 and SOEs as 0. We then introduce the interaction terms of FL and the ownership dummy in our baseline specification. The results in Table 9.12 show that FL has stronger effects for private firms for bank loans, and FL could also improve private firms' financial structure, with the substitution of informal trade credit. With the opening of China's financial sector, the degree of Mercerization of the finance sector has been continuously accelerating. The decision-making of financial institutions no longer follows the ownership attributes of the company as a single indicator. With competition from foreign financial institutions, domestic financial banks and institutions could learn how to increase the efficiency of their loans. Private firms with higher productivity and better performance could then be targeted by foreign and domestic banks.

Table 9.12 Results by firm ownership type

Variables	(1) Internal finance FC1	(2) Bank credit FC2	(3) Trade credit FC3
Ownership*FL	1.4413	40.4255***	−54.9765***
	(0.9457)	(13.4688)	(12.9541)
ln_size	−0.0046**	1.1276***	0.0070
	(0.0020)	(0.0302)	(0.0288)
ROA	0.0539***	−0.6231***	0.5957***
	(0.0074)	(0.1183)	(0.1073)
Constant	0.1159***	−8.6411***	0.7353
	(0.0449)	(0.6630)	(0.6325)
Firm fixed effect	YES	YES	YES
Year fixed effect	YES	YES	YES
Observations	12,739	11,763	13,179
R-squared	0.4648	0.8744	0.4102

FC = financial constraint

*** $p < 0.01$ ** $p < 0.05$ * $p < 0.1$

Note: Standard errors are in parentheses.

Second, we investigate the heterogeneous effects of ROA. The return rate of the project is one of the most important indicators for investors. We use ROA to represent the profitability of the company: the higher the ROA, the stronger is the business capability. We then also introduce the interaction term of ROA with FL. The results in Table 9.13 show financial sector opening has stronger effects for firms with better operating performance and eases financial constraints through both bank credit and trade credit. China's financial sectors have become more and more market-oriented, and companies with better operating performance could have received more external financing support. Companies with higher profit have better expected returns and could raise funds more easily through external financing.

Table 9.13 Results by firms' ROA

Variables	(1) Internal finance	(2) Bank credit	(3) Trade credit
ROA*FL	0.4681	8.4049*	51.7222***
	(0.2910)	(4.4884)	(4.1156)
ln_size	−0.0045**	1.1352***	0.0003
	(0.0020)	(0.0302)	(0.0286)
ROA	0.0359***	−0.9095***	−1.3590***
	(0.0135)	(0.1959)	(0.1885)
Constant	0.1316***	−8.2808***	0.1854
	(0.0438)	(0.6510)	(0.6147)
Firm fixed effect	YES	YES	YES
Year fixed effect	YES	YES	YES
Observations	12,739	11,763	13,179
R-squared	0.4648	0.8743	0.4179

*** $p < 0.01$ ** $p < 0.05$ * $p < 0.1$

Note: Standard errors are in parentheses.

Third, we try to explore the mechanisms of FL on financial constraints. A company's fixed-asset investment plays an important role in that company's development. On the one hand, fixed-asset investment is accompanied by an expansion of scale, updating of production equipment and an increase in productivity. In a market-oriented environment, productivity improvement is conducive to enterprises obtaining greater profits and improving their internal financing capacity. On the other hand, in the process of external financing, fixed assets can be used as collateral to reduce the default risk of corporate borrowing and improve the probability of successful financing. We use the logarithm of fixed assets as an indicator of the collateral status of an enterprise, and introduce the interaction term of fixed assets to FL. The results in Table 9.14 show that all the coefficients of the interaction term are positive and significant. With the opening of the financial sector, a company with much collateral can effectively alleviate its financial constraints through both internal and external channels.

Table 9.14 Results by firms' collateral

Variables	(1) Internal finance	(2) Bank credit	(3) Trade credit
Collateral*FL	0.0522***	0.9257***	−1.1998***
	(0.0150)	(0.2188)	(0.2076)
ROA	0.0537***	0.6081***	0.5989***
	(0.0074)	(0.1182)	(0.1073)
In_size	−0.0059***	1.1066***	0.0339
	(0.0021)	(0.0309)	(0.0295)
Constant	0.1335***	−8.1821***	0.0835
	(0.0440)	(0.6540)	(0.6214)
Firm fixed effect	YES	YES	YES
Year fixed effect	YES	YES	YES
Observations	12,737	11,761	13,177
R-squared	0.4653	0.8745	0.4111

*** $p < 0.01$ ** $p < 0.05$ * $p < 0.1$

Note: Standard errors are in parentheses.

Fourth, we try to investigate channels of information asymmetry, which is one of the main causes of financial constraints on enterprises. Financial institutions cannot clearly understand the operating situation of those demanding capital (enterprises), which causes a huge gap between the cost of internal financing and the cost of external financing. It is important for financial institutions to investigate listed companies to eliminate information asymmetry between these institutions and enterprises. By surveying listed companies, financial institutions can verify the publicly disclosed information of those companies, and also have direct communication with the company's managers, eliminating barriers to information-sharing. We generate a dummy variable with the unit of whether the listed companies have been surveyed by financial institutions (such as banks and insurance and securities institutions), and 0 otherwise. The results in Table 9.15 show that a company surveyed by a financial institution is more likely to receive financial support from a bank and less likely to rely on credit finance. Surveys by financial institutions could well solve the problem of information asymmetry between enterprises and those institutions and alleviate the financial constraints on enterprises. We have not, however, found significant effects of financial opening on internal financing.

Table 9.15 Results by finance institution survey

Variables	(1) Internal financing	(2) Bank credit	(3) Trade credit
Survey*FL	0.0242	0.1067**	−2.3075***
	(0.0459)	(0.0468)	(0.6348)
ln_size	−0.0046**	−0.0306***	0.0087
	(0.0020)	(0.0021)	(0.0289)
ROA	0.0539***	−0.0587***	0.5965***
	(0.0074)	(0.0079)	(0.1073)
Constant	0.1329***	0.8758***	−0.0135
	(0.0440)	(0.0458)	(0.6211)
Firm fixed effect	YES	YES	YES
Year fixed effect	YES	YES	YES
Observations	12,739	13,181	13,179
R-squared	0.4647	0.8658	0.4100

*** $p < 0.01$ ** $p < 0.05$ * $p < 0.1$

Note: Standard errors are in parentheses.

Last but not least, we change another measure of financial sector opening in our robustness checks. According to the policy summary in section three, China has gradually liberalised its banking sector since its entry to the WTO in 2001. The Chinese Government agreed to remove restrictions on foreign banks' local currency business in a number of cities every year during the first five years after accession (2001–06), with no restrictions on foreign banks anywhere in the country beyond that. This step-by-step deregulation of foreign banking provides a suitable policy experiment for analysing the effects of banking sector liberalisation on financial constraints. Following Lin (2011), we use a dummy variable, *FBLct*, indicating the timing and geographic variation of foreign bank entry into local currency business with firms in a particular city. For example, in the City of Beijing, *FBLc;2004 = 0* and *FBankc;2005 = FBankc;2006 = 1*, since Beijing opened to foreign bank entry at the end of 2004.

The model specification is Equation 9.4.

Equation 9.4

$$Y_{icjt} = \beta_0 + \beta_1 FBL_{ct} * Ownership + \theta X'_{icjt} + \alpha_i + \delta_t + \epsilon_{icjt}$$

In this robustness test, we use Chinese firm-level data from the *Annual Survey of Industrial Enterprises* for1998 to 2007, conducted by the National Bureau of Statistics of China (NBS various years[b]). This dataset covers all state-owned and non-state-owned industrial firms with more than RMB5 million in revenue. The regression results are shown in Table 9.16. We find that banking liberalisation alleviates financial constraints by improving both bank credit and trade credit for private firms, while the ratio of bank credit to trade credit also increases. This is consistent with our previous results, and shows that banking liberalisation upgrades the financing structure by substitution of trade credit with more bank credit.

Table 9.16 Regression results with banking sector liberalisation on WTO commitments

Variables	(1) Bank credit FC2	(2) Trade credit FC3	(3) Ratio FC2/FC3
FL*Ownership	0.165***	0.0953***	0.0482***
	(0.00536)	(0.00384)	(0.00699)
ln_size	0.626***	0.470***	0.140***
	(0.00308)	(0.00234)	(0.00407)
Constant	1.647***	4.290***	−2.610***
	(0.0181)	(0.0136)	(0.0241)
Observations	1,038,451	1,433,281	967,787
R-squared	0.849	0.842	0.752
Firm fixed effect	YES	YES	YES
Year fixed effect	YES	YES	YES

FC = financial constraint

*** $p < 0.01$ ** $p < 0.05$ * $p < 0.1$

Note: Standard errors are in parentheses.

Conclusions

This chapter investigates the effects of China's financial sector opening on financial constraints on Chinese listed firms. We first systematically review the policies on China's financial sector opening and set up a relatively exogenous policy measure based on the OECD's FDI restrictiveness index. Then, based on the latest panel data for listed firms for the period 2010–15, we calculate four indices to measure China's firm-level financial constraints through internal and external financing channels. We find that China's financial sector opening alleviates financial constraints and upgrades the financing structure for China's listed firms. Financial openness also eliminates ownership discrimination and promotes financing efficiency, alleviating the financial constraints on private and profitable enterprises. The mechanisms of the effects of financial sector opening on financial constraints occur mainly through collateral channels and the elimination of information asymmetry.

This chapter has some important policy implications. On the one hand, China's financial sector opening could alleviate financial constraints and upgrade the financing structure. On the other hand, policymakers should be aware that once they open their financial services trade to foreign competition, they may also invite more capital flows into their economies, which will bring greater competition to domestic financial institutions and tend to render the existing capital control regime less effective. As China is expected to accelerate its financial services liberalisation, the impact on financial markets and capital flows will become substantial, which implies that China's capital controls will become more porous in the future. Therefore, the pace of China's capital account liberalisation will proceed faster than expected.

References

Altman, E.I., Haldeman, R.G. and Narayanan, P. (1977), ZETATM analysis: A new model to identify bankruptcy risk of corporations, *Journal of Banking and Finance* 1(1): 29–54. doi.org/10.1016/0378-4266(77)90017-6.

Batra, G., Kaufmann, D. and Stone, A.H. (2003), *Investment Climate Around the World: Voices of the firms from the World Business Environment Survey*, Washington, DC: The World Bank. doi.org/10.1596/0-8213-5390-X.

Beck, T., Demirgüç-Kunt, A. and Maksimovic, V. (2005), Financial and legal constraints to growth: Does firm size matter?, *Journal of Finance* 60(1): 137–77. doi.org/10.1111/j.1540-6261.2005.00727.x.

Bekaert, G., Harvey, C.R. and Lundblad, C. (2005), Does financial liberalization spur growth?, *Journal of Financial Economics* 77(1): 3–55. doi.org/10.1016/j.jfineco.2004.05.007.

Berger, A.N., Hasan, I. and Zhou, M. (2009), Bank ownership and efficiency in China: What will happen in the world's largest nation?, *Journal of Banking and Finance* 33(1): 113–30. doi.org/10.1016/j.jbankfin.2007.05.016.

China Banking Regulatory Commission (CBRC) (various years), *Annual Report of China Banking Regulatory Commission*, Beijing: China Banking Regulatory Commission Press.

Cleary, S. (1999), The relationship between firm investment and financial status, *Journal of Finance* 54(2): 673–92. doi.org/10.1111/0022-1082.00121.

Dell'Ariccia, G. and Marquez, R. (2004), Information and bank credit allocation, *Journal of Financial Economics* 72(1): 185–214. doi.org/10.1016/S0304-405X(03)00210-1.

Fazzari, S.M., Hubbard, R.G., Petersen, B.C., Blinder, A.S. and Poterba, J.M. (1988), Financing constraints and corporate investment, *Brookings Papers on Economic Activity* 1988(1): 141–206. doi.org/10.2307/2534426.

Fisman, R. and Love, I. (2007), Financial dependence and growth revisited, *Journal of the European Economic Association* 5(2–3): 470–9. doi.org/10.1162/jeea.2007.5.2-3.470.

Greenaway, D., Guariglia, A. and Kneller, R. (2007), Financial factors and exporting decisions, *Journal of International Economics* 73(2): 377–95. doi.org/10.1016/j.jinteco. 2007.04.002.

Hadlock, C.J. and Pierce, J.R. (2010), New evidence on measuring financial constraints: Moving beyond the KZ index, *The Review of Financial Studies* 23(5): 1909–40. doi.org/ 10.1093/rfs/hhq009.

Han, J. and Wang, J. (2012), Why Chinese local enterprises are far-reaching: Explanation based on financial credit constraints, *Journal of World Economy* 35(1):98–113.

Haramillo, F., Schiantarelli, F. and Weiss, A. (1996), Capital market imperfections before and after financial liberalization: A Euler equation approach to panel data for Ecuadorian firms, *Journal of Development Economics* 51(2): 367–86. doi.org/10.1016/S0304-3878(96)00420-8.

Harris, J.R., Schiantarelli, F. and Siregar, M.G. (1994), The effect of financial liberalization on the capital structure and investment decisions of Indonesian manufacturing establishments, *The World Bank Economic Review* 8(1): 17–47. doi.org/10.1093/wber/ 8.1.17.

Huang, Y. (2005), *Institutional environment and private sector development in China*, Asia Program Special Report No. 129, Washington, DC: Woodrow Wilson International Center for Scholars.

Kaplan, S.N. and Zingales, L. (1997), Do investment-cash flow sensitivities provide useful measures of financing constraints?, *Quarterly Journal of Economics* 112(1): 169–215. doi. org/10.1162/003355397555163.

Koo, J. and Maeng, K. (2005), The effect of financial liberalization on firms' investments in Korea, *Journal of Asian Economics* 16(2): 281–97. doi.org/10.1016/j.asieco.2005.02.003.

Laeven, L. (2003), Does financial liberalization reduce financing constraints?, *Financial Management* 32(Spring): 5–34. doi.org/10.2307/3666202.

Lai, T., Qian, Z. and Wang, L. (2016), WTO accession, foreign bank entry, and the productivity of Chinese manufacturing firms, *Journal of Comparative Economics* 44(2): 326–42. doi.org/10.1016/j.jce.2015.06.003.

Li, R. and Huang, Y. (2015), How does financial opening affect industrial efficiency? The case of foreign bank entry in the People's Republic of China, *Asian Development Review* 32(1): 90–112. doi.org/10.1162/ADEV_a_00046.

Li, Z. and Yu, M. (2013), Exports, productivity, and credit constraints: A firm-level empirical investigation of China, *Economic Research Journal* 48(6):85–99. doi.org/10.2139/ssrn.1461399.

Lin, H. (2011), Foreign bank entry and firms' access to bank credit: Evidence from China, *Journal of Banking and Finance* 35(4): 1000–10. doi.org/10.1016/j.jbankfin.2010.09.015.

Love, I. (2003), Financial development and financing constraints: International evidence from the structural investment model, *The Review of Financial Studies* 16(3): 765–91. doi.org/10.1093/rfs/hhg013.

Naeem, K. and Li, M.C. (2019), Corporate investment efficiency: The role of financial development in firms with financing constraints and agency issues in OECD non-financial firms, *International Review of Financial Analysis* 62: 53–68. doi.org/10.1016/j.irfa.2019.01.003.

National Bureau of Statistics of China (NBS) (various years[a]), *China Statistical Yearbook*, Beijing: China Statistical Publishing House Press.

National Bureau of Statistics of China (NBS) (various years[b]), *Annual Survey of Industrial Enterprises*, Beijing: China Statistics Press.

Organisation for Economic Co-operation and Development (OECD) (n.d.), *OECD FDI regulatory restrictiveness index*, available from: stats.oecd.org/Index.aspx?datasetcode=FDIINDEX#.

Stein, J.C. (2003), Agency, information and corporate investment, *Handbook of the Economics of Finance*, Vol. 1, Part A. doi.org/10.1016/s1574-0102(03)01006-9.

Wang, Y. (2012), Export behavior of private and the relationship: An analysis based on reputation mechanism, *The Journal of World Economy* 35(2): 98–119.

Wang, Y. and Lu, B. (2018), Exchange rate movement, financial constraints and exporter's R&D, *The Journal of World Economy* 41(7): 75–97.

Whited, T.M. and Wu, G. (2006), Financial constraints risk, *The Review of Financial Studies* 19(2): 531–59. doi.org/10.1093/rfs/hhj012 .

Williamson, J. and Mahar, M. (1998), *A Survey of Financial Liberalization*, Princeton, NJ: International Finance Section, Department of Economics, Princeton University.

World Trade Organization (WTO) (n.d.), *China*, available from: www.wto.org/english/thewto_e/acc_e/a1_chine_e.htm.

Wu, Q. and Huang, X. (2017), The function display of finance company and financing constraints relieve of the group's listed companies, *China Industrial Economic* (9): 156–73. doi.org/10.19581/j.cnki.ciejournal.2017.09.009.

Zhang, D. and Zheng, W. (2019), Does financial constraint impede the innovative investment? Micro evidence from China, *Emerging Markets Finance and Trade* (January): 1–24. doi.org/10.1080/1540496X.2018.1542594.

10. Financing support schemes for SMEs in China: Benefits, costs and selected policy issues

Qin Gou and Yiping Huang

Until the Global Financial Crisis (GFC) in 2008, China had achieved 9.75 per cent annual GDP growth since its economic reforms began in 1978, making it one of the fastest-growing economies in the world—sometimes described as the 'China miracle' (Lin et al. 1996). Small and medium-sized enterprises (SMEs) played an important role in that economic growth. According to the National Bureau of Statistics of China (NBS), 99.6 per cent of enterprises in China were SMEs at the end of 2005 and they accounted for 59 per cent of GDP, 60 per cent of total sales, 48.2 per cent of taxes paid and about 75 per cent of employment in urban areas (Shen et al. 2009). Since 2008, the Chinese economy has switched to a slower lane of economic growth (Huang et al. 2013; Zhang and Gou 2016). To promote economic growth and create more job opportunities, the sound development of SMEs is vital. But, in contrast to their contribution to economic growth, SMEs' difficulty in obtaining external financing from formal financial institutions is widely recognised (Allen et al. 2005; Chong et al. 2013; Gou et al. 2018).

In fact, the major external source of SMEs' financing is bank loans (Beck et al. 2008), but the problems of information asymmetry, moral hazard and adverse selection that typically plague lending (Stiglitz and Weiss 1981) affect SMEs most severely. And this seems to be even more true in China, where, according to the World Bank's Investment Climate Survey in 2012, 49.1 per cent of surveyed SMEs were credit rationed (Gou et al. 2018). A lack of appropriate financing channels and credit unavailability have become the main hurdles for the development of SMEs (Bai et al. 2006; Shen et al. 2009; Du et al. 2012).

The Chinese Government has long recognised the problem and even raised it to the national development agenda, resulting in the Law of the People's Republic of China on Promotion of Small and Medium-sized Enterprises in 2003 and amendments to this law in 2018. This law was enacted to improve the business environment for SMEs, promoting their sound development, creating more job opportunities and promoting entrepreneurship and innovation. One of the important amendments to this law in 2018 was to place separate emphasis on support from the financial sector—which had been included with fiscal funding supports in the original version of the law—to meet the demands of the SMEs and better match their financial structure.

A set of specific financing support schemes for the banking sector was authorised. Among them, the China Banking Regulatory Commission (CBRC) implemented a policy in 2008 aimed at increasing credit support to SMEs, which is usually referred to as the 'double no-lower-than' policy. This policy required that the growth rate of SME loans should not be lower than the growth rate of the total loans and the increase of SME loans should not be lower than that in the previous year. This policy was dynamically adjusted by relaxing the requirements in 2011 and tightening them again in 2015.

In light of SMEs' financing problems and the policy implications, this chapter aims to analyse whether the financing support scheme for SMEs in China has effectively promoted banks' credit allocation to SMEs. Specifically, we focus on the impact of the policy that assesses banks' SME loans since 2008, based on bank branch–level survey data from China. Following the CBRC's regulations on SME loans, more banks began to evaluate the loans to SMEs internally, to meet the new regulations. This provides us with the possibility of event studies on how the SME financing support policy affects banks' decisions on loans to SMEs.

In regard to lending to SMEs, small banks have a comparative advantage while large banks tend to favour transaction-based lending to non-SMEs. This is because small banks tend to interact much more personally with their borrowers, are able to utilise more soft information and provide more relationship loans to SMEs (Berger et al. 2002). The 'small bank advantage' hypothesis is supported by many empirical studies (Berger and Udell 1995, 1996; Peek and Rosengren 1998; Cole et al. 1999).

However, China's banking sector is still dominated by large banks—in particular, the four largest state-owned banks, known as the 'big four': Bank of China, China Construction Bank, the Industrial and Commercial Bank of China and the Agricultural Bank of China. With the implementation of China's reform and opening-up policies in 1978, other types of banks were set up, including regional banks (which, in large part, are owned by local governments), rural credit cooperatives and joint-stock banks that have comparatively low levels of government ownership and have progressively increased their market share (Allen et al. 2012). In November 2013, the Third Plenary Session of the eighteenth Central Committee of the Communist Party of China allowed qualified private capital to establish financial institutions, such as small and medium-sized banks; five banks entirely funded by private capital were given the green light by authorities in 2014. However, domination by the large state-owned commercial banks continues and the entry of new players is still extremely limited. According to the CBRC, in 2017, the asset share of the largest commercial banks was still 36.8 per cent, the national equity banks held 17.8 per cent and rural and city commercial banks held 25.6 per cent.

Therefore, one concern about the above CBRC policy is that it may bring costs to the large banks as they are disadvantaged in lending to SMEs. In this chapter, we investigate the influence of the policy on banks of different size. More importantly, we investigate whether this policy brings costs for banks in terms of credit risk and reduced profits.

The rest of the chapter is organised as follows: section two describes the sources of the data used in our empirical analysis and presents some summary statistics; sections three to five present the results of how financing schemes affect banks' credit allocation to SMEs, banks' credit risk and their profits, respectively. Section six summarises and section seven provides conclusions.

Bank-level statistics of SME financing schemes

Data source

The data used in this study are from the Financial Ecological Environment Survey (FEES), conducted by the research group of the National School of Development at Peking University in 2014. The survey is retrospective, with most of the variables covering the period 2005–13. Fourteen provinces were selected from the survey on the basis of their economic development and geographical location: Zhejiang, Jiangsu, Guangdong, Fujian and Shandong to represent provinces in the more developed eastern coastal region; Hubei, Jilin, Hunan and Jiangxi to represent the central provinces; and Shaanxi, Sichuan, Chongqing, Guizhou and Ningxia Autonomous Region for western China.

Our data cover county-level districts (hereafter referred to as counties) in both rural and urban areas, which greatly reduces the possibility of selection bias and justifies the representativeness of the data (Shen et al. 2009). The final survey sample covers 90 counties—47 rural and 43 urban counties—according to the standard county codes provided by the NBS.

The survey covered 892 financial institutions in the 90 sampled counties, belonging to 185 legal institutions. Among them, there are 315 branch offices of the four big state-owned commercial banks (a share of 38.7 per cent). There are 84 branches of the Postal Savings Bank of China, 160 branches of the national joint-stock commercial banks, 105 city commercial banks, 141 rural financial institutions (including rural commercial banks, rural credit cooperatives and rural banks) and 10 branches of foreign banks. The survey covered all types of banking institutions in China. The sample distribution of the institutions is shown in Table 10.1.

Table 10.1 Sample distribution by institution

Type of institution	Number	Share (%)
Big four state-owned banks	315	38.70
Equity banks	160	19.60
Postal savings banks	84	10.30
City commercial banks	105	12.90
Rural commercial banks	50	6.10
Rural credit cooperatives	44	5.40
Village banks	47	5.80
Foreign banks	10	1.20
Total	815	100.00

Source: Authors' calculations using FEES.

The survey data are rich in detail, containing not only detailed financial information, such as balance sheet and bank credit outcomes, but also nonfinancial variables, such as evaluations of the SME loans ratio and basic information about financial institutions.

The data provide us with information on whether and when an institution started to evaluate its share of SME loans, the specific requirements and whether the branch met those requirements. Excluding financial institutions that did not report information on SME loan evaluations, we obtain a panel dataset spanning 2005 to 2013, for 756 institutions.

Summary statistics of SME financing schemes at bank level

The key variable of this study is whether and when a bank begins to implement evaluation of SME loan shares. Table 10.2 provides an illustration of the evaluation of SME loan shares for the surveyed institutions. In total, 446 of the total 756 financial institutions surveyed implemented an evaluation of SME loan shares during our sample period (see Column 1 in Table 10.2), accounting for 58.99 per cent (Column 2 in Table 10.2).

Among the institutions that implemented such an evaluation, only 34 (7.62 per cent) provided the SME loan evaluation before 2008, with the majority (92.38 per cent) beginning to adopt this evaluation in 2008 or after (see Column 3 in Table 10.2). Since 2008, there have been 68 institutions, on average, adopting this evaluation each year, with a peak in 2010 of 103 institutions. The data also show that the initial year of evaluation of SME loans was centred on the period between 2008 and 2014. This is mainly due to the exogenous shock of the new CBRC regulations from 2008. During our sample period (2005–13), 438 branches implemented the evaluation of SME loans, accounting for 57.94 per cent of the total sample.

Table 10.2 Number of branches starting to evaluate SME loans, by year

Initial year of evaluation	(1) No. of branches	(2) Share of branches adopting evaluation (100%)	(3) Share of initial year (100%)
1986	1	0.13	0.22
1990	1	0.13	0.22
2001	1	0.13	0.22
2002	1	0.13	0.22
2003	2	0.26	0.45
2004	1	0.13	0.22
2005	6	0.79	1.35
2006	4	0.53	0.90
2007	17	2.25	3.81
2008	28	2.25	6.28
2009	49	3.70	10.99
2010	103	6.48	23.09
2011	80	13.62	17.94
2012	92	10.58	20.63
2013	59	12.17	13.23
2014	1	7.80	0.22
Before 2008	34	4.50	7.62
After 2007	412	54.49	92.38
Total	446	58.99	100

Source: Authors' calculation using FEES.

In terms of the different categories of commercial banks, the proportion of domestic commercial banks adopting evaluation of SME loans is much higher than that of foreign banks (see Table 10.3). The ratios of the city commercial banks, the big four state-owned banks and rural commercial banks are significantly higher than the sample average, while those of rural credit cooperatives and postal savings banks are significantly below the sample average.

For those institutions that evaluate SME loans, the requirements on the SME loans share are obviously different, as shown in Figure 10.1. The share of SME loans is required to be above or close to 50 per cent for village banks, foreign banks, city commercial banks and rural commercial banks, while it is required to be about 30 per cent for equity banks, rural credit cooperatives, the big four state-owned banks and postal savings banks.

Table 10.3 Number of branches starting to evaluate SME loans, by institution type

Type	Before 2008	2008–13	Total	Total sample	Ratio (%)	Rank
Big four state-owned banks	24	170	194	297	65.32	2
Equity banks	5	74	79	142	55.63	5
Postal savings banks	4	28	32	80	40	6
City commercial banks	1	67	68	97	70.10	1
Rural commercial banks		29	29	45	64.44	3
Rural credit cooperatives		14	14	40	35	7
Village banks		27	27	45	60	4
Foreign banks		2	2	10	20	8

Source: Authors' calculations using FEES.

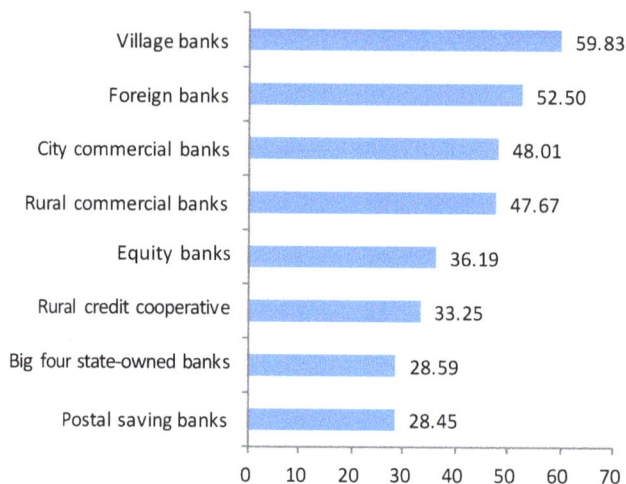

Figure 10.1 The lower bound requirement for SME loan shares for reformed branches (per cent)
Source: Authors' calculations using FEES.

Since the evaluation on SME loan shares was introduced, the proportion of branches that do not meet the evaluation requirements has significantly decreased across all institutions—from 90.71 per cent to 46.38 per cent, on average, as indicated in the last row of Table 10.4. This reduction is almost 40 per cent for all types of institutions, except for the postal savings banks. The postal savings banks managed a reduction of only 24.2 per cent, while they had the highest proportion of branches among the domestic banks falling short of the evaluation requirements both before and after evaluations began. Overall, Table 10.4 indicates that the evaluation of SME loan shares has a strong effect in increasing SME loans, while it was challenging for the postal savings banks to meet the evaluation requirements during our sample period.

Table 10.4 The proportion of branches not meeting the evaluation requirements for SME loan shares, by institution

Type of institution	Before evaluation (%)	Since evaluation (%)	Difference (%)	Rank
Big four state-owned banks	81.63	41.88	39.75	7
Equity banks	97.79	51.90	45.89	2
Postal savings banks	99.20	75.00	24.20	8
City commercial banks	91.55	45.93	45.62	3
Rural commercial banks	85.99	43.96	42.03	5
Rural credit cooperatives	87.64	38.82	48.82	1
Village banks	97.95	52.38	45.57	4
Foreign banks	100.00	60.00	40.00	6
Total	90.71	46.38	44.33	

Source: Authors' calculations using FEES.

In summary, there are differences in whether and when different types of financial institutions implemented evaluations of SME loan shares. The staggered adoption of the evaluations provides rich variation with which to identify its effects on SME loans as well as on other bank lending outcomes.

Do SME financing schemes increase loans to SMEs?

Empirical model specification

We begin our analysis by examining whether the evaluation of SME loan shares effectively increases lending to SMEs. To identify the effect of SME financing schemes on the origination of bank loans to SMEs, we employ a difference-in-differences (DID) strategy and compare a group of financial institutions before and after they adopted the evaluations with those institutions that had not yet adopted it during the same period. Thus, the baseline empirical specification is given by Equation 10.1.

Equation 10.1

$$SME\_loan_{it} = \beta_0 + \beta_1 Evaluation_{it} + \beta_2 X_{it} + v_i + \tau_t + \varepsilon_{it}$$

In this equation, i, c and t indicate bank, county and year, respectively. The independent variable SME_loan_{ict} represents banks loans to SMEs indexed by two variables: the growth rate of SME loans (GSME) and the share of SME loans (SME). $Evaluation_{it}$ is the regressor of interest, standing for the incentive design of bank i in year t. Specifically, $Evaluation_{it} = Treatment_i \bullet Post_{it}$, where $Treatment_i = 1$ if bank i carried out the SME scheme during the sample period, and 0 otherwise. $Post_{it} = 1$ is a post-treatment indictor, taking a value of 1 if $t \geq tc0$, where $tc0$ is the year bank i implements the evaluation, and 0 otherwise.

X_{it} represents other important bank-level variables that may affect banks' loan allocations. In the baseline model, we include bank size, indexed by the logarithm of total assets (Lnassets). The bank fixed effects (v_i) capture all the time-invariant bank characteristics that might influence the outcome of interest. Year fixed effects (τ_t) control for nationwide shocks in a particular year that are likely to have affected all banks in a similar manner. ε_{it} is the error term. To address the potential serial correlation and heteroskedasticity, we cluster the standard errors at the county level. Detailed variable definitions and descriptive statistics are presented in Table 10.5.

This strategy identifies how the evaluations of SME loans affect bank loans to SMEs, controlling for other important influencing variables and time and bank-invariant effects. The coefficient β_1 is our DID estimate of the effect of interest.

Table 10.5 Variable definitions and summary statistics

Variable	Definition	Obs	Mean	SD	p50	Min.	Max.
GSME	Growth rate of SME loans (%)	2,233	0.101	0.2279	0	−1	1.189
SME	SME loan share (%)	2,981	71.530	37.0740	95.700	0	100.000
NPLR	Nonperforming loans ratio (%)	1,691	2.576	4.6790	0.632	0	26.130
Lnasset	Logarithm of total assets	2,981	12.118	1.2280	12.054	5.995	16.750
ROA	Return over total assets	2,981	0.019	0.0260	0.018	−0.364	0.857
NII	Net interest rate income over total loan outstanding	2,880	0.075	0.3320	0.048	−1.365	10.530

For the banks that implemented the evaluation of SME loan shares in 2005 and previous years, it is impossible to obtain the comparison data for the pre-treatment period. For the banks that implemented evaluations in 2013, it is impossible to obtain the comparison data for the post-treatment period. We therefore remove these banks to allow at least one year before and one year after the evaluation adoption, as required by the DID method.

Empirical results

Table 10.6 reports the baseline results of the impact of the evaluation of SME loans on banks' credit allocation to SMEs. Column (1) shows the results of how implementing the evaluation impacts the growth rate of SME loans and it shows an insignificant effect. Column (3) examines the impacts of the evaluation on the share of SME loans in total loans outstanding, and the effect of the evaluation is still insignificant. Therefore, on average, it seems that the evaluation is ineffective in enhancing banks' loan originations to SMEs.

Table 10.6 Impacts of evaluation of SME loans: Total effect

	(1)	(2)	(3)	(4)
Variables	Growth rate of SME loans		Share of SME loans	
Evaluation	0.1160	0.1073	1.6334	1.1839
	(0.0990)	(0.1349)	(1.0258)	(1.2918)
L.SME	−0.0259***	−0.0280***	0.5258***	0.4957***
	(0.0029)	(0.0037)	(0.0178)	(0.0214)
lnasset	0.0003	−0.0136	−1.1115	−0.5041
	(0.1393)	(0.1986)	(1.3093)	(1.6527)
Year effect	YES	NO	YES	NO
Institute*Year	NO	YES	NO	YES
Province*Year	NO	YES	NO	YES
Branch FE	YES	YES	YES	YES
Constant	YES	YES	YES	YES
Observations	2,227	1,776	2,451	1,992
R-squared	0.2420	0.3461	0.9033	0.9104

*** $p < 0.01$ ** $p < 0.05$ * $p < 0.1$

Note: Standard errors are in parentheses.

Source: Authors' estimations.

One concern with the above models might be that some local credit demand shocks and institutional credit supply shocks (such as policy and technology shocks) might coincide with the banks' adoption of the evaluation. To account for this and other similar concerns, in Columns (2) and (4), we modify the model by including an interacted year with province fixed effects and an interacted year with legal institutional fixed effects. This specification controls for all time variations within those provinces and within those legal institutions. In such a specification, one compares the growth rate of SME loans and SME loan shares of a bank adopting evaluation with a bank of the same legal institution not adopting it in the same province and in the same year. As a result, we exploit the intraprovincial and intra-legal institutional variations between treated and non-treated branches. To the extent that local shocks affect all banks at a provincial level and internal shocks affect all branches of the same legal institution, such shocks are differenced out in our specification. Columns (2) and (4) indicate an insignificant impact from the evaluation on both the growth rate of SME loans and the share of SME loans.

As elaborated in the previous section, before implementing the evaluation, some banks had already met the requirements, although most had not. Banks that met the requirements before implementing the evaluation did not need to increase their loans to SMEs following implementation. Therefore, the estimations in Table 10.6 may underestimate the effect of evaluation as they mix all the treated banks in the same way. In this regard, we modify the model by distinguishing between the initial conditions of banks in terms of whether they meet the evaluation requirements. The results for how implementing evaluation of SME loan shares affects the growth rate of SME loans are presented in Table 10.7 and the impacts on the shares of SME loans are presented in Table 10.8.

In the first columns of Table 10.7, we include the interaction of the variable *Evaluation* with the lag term of the share of SME loans (*L.SME*). This shows a significantly positive effect of the evaluation and a significantly negative effect of its interaction with the lag term of the share of SME loans. This indicates that implementing the evaluation increases the growth rate of SME loans, while this effect weakens as the initial share of SME loans increases. The results imply that the initial conditions when implementing evaluation are important in determining its overall effectiveness. As the initial SME loans share is low, the effect of the evaluation in enhancing loans to SMEs is strong. The results are robust in the model of Column (2), as shocks from the region and legal institutions are controlled.

Furthermore, we identify whether the initial SME loans share meets the evaluation requirements and construct a dummy variable, *below*, to indicate the initial conditions. If the initial SME loans share is below the evaluation requirement, *below* equals 1 and we call these 'constrained' banks; otherwise, it equals 0, and these banks are 'unconstrained'. We then include both the variable *below* and its interaction with the evaluation in Column (3). The results indicate significantly positive effects from both the interaction term and the variable of initial conditions (*L.Below*), and positive but insignificant effects of the variable *Evaluation*. For the unconstrained banks, the evaluation has no significant effect on the growth rate of SME loans. For the constrained banks, the effect of the evaluation is determined by both the coefficients of *Evaluation* and the interaction term (*Evaluation*L.Below*). The overall effect of evaluation for these banks is significant, around 0.37 per cent, which implies that, after evaluation, the growth rate of SME loans increases by 0.37 per cent, on average. As the sample mean of the growth rate is 0.101 per cent, this overall effect of 0.37 per cent is comparably very strong. The modified model specification in Column (4) does not affect the qualitative nature of our results other than a slightly increased overall effect for the constrained banks.

Table 10.7 Impacts of evaluation on the growth rate of SME loans

Variables	(1)	(2)	(3)	(4)
	Growth rate of SME loans			
Evaluation	0.6204***	0.6384**	0.0453	0.0472
	(0.2190)	(0.2834)	(0.1123)	(0.0761)
L.SME	−0.0239***	−0.0260***		
	(0.0030)	(0.0038)		
Evaluation*L.SME	−0.0064***	−0.0070**		
	(0.0025)	(0.0033)		
Evaluation*L.Below			0.3276*	0.3641***
			(0.1816)	(0.1203)
L.Below			1.0346***	1.2209**
			(0.2487)	(0.5866)
Lnasset	0.0366	0.0096	0.0038	−0.0201
	(0.1398)	(0.1986)	(0.1413)	(0.1163)
Year effect	YES	NO	YES	NO
Institute*Year	NO	YES	NO	YES
Province*Year	NO	YES	NO	YES
Branch FE	YES	YES	YES	YES
Constant	YES	YES	YES	YES
Observations	2,227	1,776	2,227	1,776
R-squared	0.2448	0.3485	0.2226	0.3309
Overall effect when below			0.3729**	0.4113***
Standard error			0.1653	0.0761

*** $p < 0.01$ ** $p < 0.05$ * $p < 0.1$

Note: Standard errors are in parentheses.

Source: Authors' estimations.

In Table 10.8, we investigate how the evaluation affects banks' shares of SME loans. Results in the first two columns show robust evidence that the evaluation significantly increases the share of banks' SME loans, and this effect is stronger for banks with higher initial shares of SME loans. In Columns (3) and (4), the coefficient of *Evaluation* is significantly negative while the interaction term (*Evaluation*L. Below*) is significantly positive. This reveals that, for banks with an initial share of SME loans above the requirement, their share of SME loans falls significantly—by more than 4 per cent. But for banks with an initial share of SME loans below the requirement, the share of SME loans increases by more than 6 per cent.

Table 10.8 Impacts of evaluation on the share of SME loans

Variables	(1)	(2)	(3)	(4)
	Share of SME loans			
Evaluation	10.5757***	6.8199***	−4.5368***	−4.2711***
	(1.8290)	(2.2015)	(1.4100)	(1.6123)
L.SME	0.5543***	0.5142***		
	(0.0183)	(0.0221)		
Evaluation*L.SME	−0.1245***	−0.0826***		
	(0.0212)	(0.0262)		
Evaluation*L.Below			11.7152***	10.3552***
			(1.8777)	(2.6879)
L.Below			−16.4225***	−20.7308***
			(1.8551)	(3.6403)
Lnasset	−0.8912	−0.6454	0.1271	−1.1991
	(1.2990)	(1.6482)	(1.3871)	(2.9591)
Year effect	YES	NO	YES	NO
Institute*Year	NO	YES	NO	YES
Province*Year	NO	YES	NO	YES
Branch FE	YES	YES	YES	YES
Constant	YES	YES	YES	YES
Observations	2,451	1,992	2,805	2,248
R-squared	0.9050	0.9110	0.8589	0.8788
Overall effect when below			7.1783***	6.08407**
Standard error			1.5988	2.4405

*** $p < 0.01$ ** $p < 0.05$ * $p < 0.1$

Note: Standard errors are in parentheses.

Source: Authors' estimations.

In Table 10.9, we further check the effects of the evaluation on banks of different size. We classify the big four state-owned banks and the national equity banks as large banks and the remainder as small banks. Results in Table 10.9 show that the evaluation has no effect on the unconstrained small banks while it significantly decreases the share of SME loans for the unconstrained large banks. For the constrained banks, the evaluation significantly increased the share of SME loans for both small and large banks, with a slightly larger effect for small banks than for larger banks. These results indicate that the evaluation effectively promotes the constrained banks to allocate more loans to SMEs.

Table 10.9 Impacts of evaluation on the share of SME loans, by bank size

Variables	(1)	(2)	(3)	(4)
	Share of SME loans			
	Small banks	Large banks	Small banks	Large banks
Evaluation	−0.9499	−4.6540***	1.0763	−4.9057***
	(1.9064)	(1.6226)	(1.8447)	(1.6550)
Evaluation*L.Below	8.7482***	10.7829***	6.9654*	10.4752***
	(2.6435)	(2.1694)	(3.9017)	(2.7140)
L.Below	−5.8593***	−21.6008***	−3.2827	−22.1151***
	(2.2509)	(2.3042)	(3.6485)	(3.9876)
lnasset	5.8558***	−1.7280	9.4113*	−0.8208
	(2.2316)	(1.6415)	(5.3561)	(3.3182)
Year effect	YES	YES	NO	NO
Institute*Year	NO	NO	YES	YES
Province*Year	NO	NO	YES	YES
Branch FE	YES	YES	YES	YES
Constant	YES	YES	YES	YES
Observations	732	1,903	755	1,926
R-squared	0.8698	0.8666	0.8959	0.8885
Overall effect when below	7.7983***	6.1288***	8.041733**	5.5696**
Standard error	2.3436	1.8528	3.901827	2.372877

*** $p < 0.01$ ** $p < 0.05$ * $p < 0.1$

Note: Standard errors are in parentheses.

Combining the results in Tables 10.7–10.9, we find that implementing evaluation of SME loans has increased banks' loan originations to SMEs, especially for banks that have low shares of SME loans. In this regard, the evaluation is effective and beneficial.

How do SME financing schemes affect banks' credit risk?

So far, we have shown that evaluation of SME loans effectively increases the number of loans to SMEs. But usually more serious information asymmetry between banks and SMEs results in higher credit risk for SME loans (Stiglitz and Weiss 1981). To assess the overall influence of this evaluation of SME loans on banks, we go further to investigate the impact of the evaluation on banks' credit risk in Equation 10.2, with the DID strategy.

Equation 10.2

$$NPLR_{it} = \alpha_0 + \alpha_1 Evaluation_{it} + \alpha_2 Evaluation_{it} * L.Below$$
$$+ \alpha_3 X_{it} + v_i + \tau_t + \varepsilon_{it}$$

In Equation 10.2, credit risk is measured by *NPLR*, following Zhang et al. (2016) and subject to data availability. We control bank size, the SME loan ratio, time-invariant fixed effects and bank-invariant fixed effects. The baseline results are presented in Table 10.10.

The results in Column (1) show a significant and negative effect of *Evaluation* on the *NPLR*, and the interaction term (*Evaluation*L.Below*) is robustly significant and positive. These results indicate that, for banks with an initial share of SME loans at or above the requirements (unconstrained banks), the evaluation decreases their *NPLR*.

However, these results imply that for banks with an initial share of SME loans below the evaluation requirement (constrained banks), their *NPLR* increases by 0.23 per cent (–1.0971 per cent + 1.3265 per cent) following the evaluation. This overall effect is not significant. Results are robust, as we control for regional and legal institutional shocks in Column (2).

We believe there is a competition effect between the unconstrained and constrained banks, which may help explain the above findings. The unconstrained banks face no pressure to increase their SME loans and have the space to increase non-SME loans. Meanwhile, restrained by both the regulated requirements for SME loans and lending capacity, the constrained banks move partly to the SME loans market, which increases competition in that market and decreases competition in the non-SME loans market. The reduction of competition in the non-SME loans market facilitates the unconstrained banks decreasing their *NPLR*. The constrained banks struggle to expand their loans to SMEs, which puts them into the more competitive and higher-risk SME market.

In Columns (3) and (4) of Table 10.10, we further check the heterogeneous effect of the evaluation on credit risk for small and large banks. Results indicate significantly negative effects of *Evaluation* and positive effects of the interaction term (*Evaluation*L.Below*) for both small banks and large banks, except that the coefficient of *Evaluation* is insignificant for small banks.

For the unconstrained banks, the evaluation has no significant effect on small banks' *NPLR*, while it significantly decreases the *NPLR* of large banks. For the constrained large banks, the overall effect of the evaluation on *NPLR* is 0.18 per cent (1.4123 per cent – 1.2370 per cent) but is insignificant. However, it is significant and about 2.1 per cent (2.2593 per cent – 0.1726 per cent) for the constrained small banks. These findings imply that the SME loans requirement significantly exacerbates the credit risk of constrained small banks while it improves the credit quality of unconstrained large banks.

There are two possible interpretations that may help explain the above results. On the one hand, there is another competition effect, which is between small banks and large banks. Although small banks usually have a greater advantage in providing loans to SMEs (Berger and Udell 2006), they suffer from more severe competition from large banks after the policy shock. Under the policy shocks of the CBRC's regulations on SME loans, large banks start to compete more in the SME loans market, which crowds out some high-quality SMEs to large banks from small banks and then worsens the credit quality for small banks. On the other hand, large banks have greater diversification opportunities and higher levels of management of credit risk.

Table 10.10 Impacts of evaluation on branches' nonperforming loans

Variables	(1) NPLR	(2) NPLR	(3) NPLR	(4) NPLR
	Whole sample	Whole sample	Small bank	Large bank
Evaluation	−1.0971**	−1.3347***	−0.1726	−1.2370*
	(0.5236)	(0.2770)	(0.1109)	(0.5979)
Evaluation*L.Below	1.3265*	1.4569***	2.2593***	1.4123*
	(0.7162)	(0.3924)	(0.4128)	(0.7065)
L.Below	−0.7779	−1.3898***	−2.2313***	−1.0286
	(0.7902)	(0.2297)	(0.0109)	(0.5856)
SME	0.0136	0.0102	−0.0063	0.0157
	(0.0099)	(0.0082)	(0.0042)	(0.0124)
lnasset	−0.9489	0.6479	−2.6830	1.2713
	(0.8013)	(0.7671)	(2.6271)	(1.1394)
Year	YES	NO	NO	NO
Institute*Year	NO	YES	YES	NO
Province*Year	NO	YES	YES	NO
Branch FE	YES	YES	YES	YES
Observations	1,800	1,800	468	1,361
R-squared	0.6255	0.9246	0.9972	0.7981
Overall effect when below	0.2295	0.1222	2.0867***	0.1753
Standard error	0.4139	0.2209	0.3464	0.1753

*** $p < 0.01$ ** $p < 0.05$ * $p < 0.1$

Note: Standard errors are in parentheses.

Source: Authors' estimations.

To combine results in the previous section, our findings highlight that the evaluation of SME loans is a double-edged sword for the constrained banks: although it pushes these banks to expand their SME loans, it also brings higher credit risk to small banks. Banks that increase their loans to SMEs incur a cost by bearing more credit risk, especially small banks.

How do SME financing schemes affect banks' profits?

To complete the picture, we also check how the evaluation of SME loans affects banks' profits. The empirical specification is given by Equation 10.3.

Equation 10.3

$$Profits_{it} = \gamma_0 + \gamma_1 Evaluation_{it} + \gamma_2 Evaluation_{it} * L.Below$$
$$+ \gamma_3 X_{it} + v_i + \tau_t + \zeta_{it}$$

We measure banks' profits with two variables: net interest rate income over total loans outstanding (NII) and the return on assets (ROA). The former variable indicates banks' profitability on the business of deposits and loans, and the latter represents banks' overall profitability.

Table 10.11 reports the impacts of the evaluation on net interest income and returns over bank assets. The results of Columns (1) and (2) show that the coefficient of *Evaluation* is significantly positive and the coefficient of the interaction term (*Evaluation*L.Below*) is significantly negative. These results imply that, for unconstrained banks, the evaluation improves their net interest income. For banks that are constrained by the evaluation requirements, the evaluation has an overall negative influence on their net interest income, but it is not significant.

For Columns (3) and (4), results are similar. While evaluation increases the return on assets for unconstrained banks, it has a negative but insignificant impact on the constrained banks that fell short of the requirements before the evaluation.

Table 10.11 Impacts of evaluation on branches' performance

Variables	(1) NII	(2) NII	(3) ROA	(4) ROA
Evaluation	0.0097***	0.0057***	0.0040***	0.0045***
	(0.0033)	(0.0018)	(0.0011)	(0.0010)
Evaluation*L.Below	−0.0161***	−0.0097*	−0.0056***	−0.0047***
	(0.0047)	(0.0051)	(0.0014)	(0.0017)
L.Below	0.0111***	0.0091**	0.0039***	0.0033***
	(0.0032)	(0.0045)	(0.0011)	(0.0006)
Lnasset	0.0017	0.0003	−0.0018	−0.0041**
	(0.0060)	(0.0057)	(0.0015)	(0.0017)
Year	YES	NO	YES	NO
Institute*Year	NO	YES	NO	YES
Province*Year	NO	YES	NO	YES
Branch FE	YES	YES	YES	YES
Observations	3,348	2,716	3,517	2,875
R-squared	0.7597	0.8097	0.7157	0.7865
Overall effect when below	−0.0064	−0.004	−0.0016	−0.0003
Standard error	0.0040	0.0044	0.0010	0.0012

*** $p < 0.01$ ** $p < 0.05$ * $p < 0.1$

Note: Standard errors are in parentheses.

Source: Authors' estimations.

We then go through the different effects of the evaluation on the profitability of small and large banks in Table 10.12. Interestingly, we find that the evaluation significantly increases profits for unconstrained large banks, while it has no effect on unconstrained small banks. This also relates to the two competition effects between constrained and unconstrained banks and between constrained small and constrained large banks. The unconstrained large banks improve their profitability as they do not have to compete for SME loans, but they enjoy less competitive non-SME loans. For the unconstrained small banks, they face more severe competition in the SME loans market and meanwhile have more space to provide services to non-SME loans. Therefore, the overall effect of the evaluation on these small unconstrained banks is ambiguous, and it is insignificant in our sample.

For constrained banks, the evaluation decreases net interest income for both the small and the large banks, while it decreases the return on assets for small banks only.

Table 10.12 Impacts of evaluation on branches' performance, by bank size

Variables	(1) NII	(2) NII	(3) ROA	(4) ROA
	Small bank	Big bank	Small bank	Big bank
Evaluation	0.0028	0.0043**	0.0002	0.0039***
	(0.0025)	(0.0016)	(0.0013)	(0.0009)
Evaluation*L.Below	−0.0091**	−0.0094***	−0.0032*	−0.0050***
	(0.0045)	(0.0015)	(0.0019)	(0.0014)
L.Below	0.0068**	0.0141***	0.0005	0.0029***
	(0.0032)	(0.0020)	(0.0016)	(0.0009)
Lnasset	0.0071	0.0091	0.0044	−0.0056**
	(0.0047)	(0.0055)	(0.0032)	(0.0020)
Institute*Year	YES	YES	YES	YES
Province*Year	YES	YES	YES	YES
Branch FE	YES	YES	YES	YES
Observations	711	1,756	673	1,615
R-squared	0.8001	0.7334	0.7243	0.7337
Overall effect when below	−0.0054*	−0.0050*	−0.0030*	−0.0011
Standard error	0.0031	0.002746	0.0018	0.0012

*** $p < 0.01$ ** $p < 0.05$ * $p < 0.1$

Note: Standard errors are in parentheses.

Source: Authors' estimations.

Benefits and costs of SME financing schemes: A summary

In the previous three sections, we investigate the impacts of the evaluation of banks' SME loans on their lending outcomes, including banks' shares of SME loans, credit risk and profits. We summarise these effects in Table 10.13 and analyse them in the benefit and cost framework.

The expected benefit of the evaluation of the SME loans is to effectively increase the number of loans to SMEs, as the evaluation aims to boost bank loans to SMEs. But from this perspective, the overall benefit is uncertain, because the evaluation has the opposite impact on the initially unconstrained and constrained banks. It effectively increases the share of SME loans for the constrained banks, which initially fell short of the evaluation requirements, while it decreases that share for the unconstrained banks, which initially exceeded the requirements (see the first two rows of Column (1)). For banks of different size, the impacts are also different: the evaluation increases the share of SME loans for both constrained small and constrained large banks, but it decreases the share only for constrained large banks. Thus, overall, the evaluation increases the SME loans for small banks but the impact is unclear for large banks as a whole.

The evaluation also has some spillover effects on banks' credit risk and profits. The evaluation significantly increased the credit risk for the constrained small banks, while it decreased the credit risk for the unconstrained large banks (see the third and fourth rows of Table 10.13). While the evaluation increased profits for unconstrained large banks, it decreased profits for both small constrained and large constrained banks.

Overall, the evaluation has different influences for banks with different initial conditions regarding SME loans and banks of different size. For the constrained small banks, the evaluation increased their SME loans while raising some costs by increasing their credit risk and decreasing their profits. For the unconstrained small banks, there are no significant effects. For the constrained large banks, the evaluation increased their share of SME loans, but decreased their net interest income. The evaluation benefits the unconstrained large banks by decreasing their credit risk and improving their profits.

Table 10.13 The effect of evaluation of SME loans on banks' lending outcomes

Row	Lending outcome	Initial condition	Sample		
			Whole sample	Small banks	Large banks
			(1)	(2)	(3)
1	SME loans	Unconstrained	Decrease	No	Decrease
2		Constrained	Increase	Increase	Increase
3	Credit risk	Unconstrained	Decrease	No	Decrease
4		Constrained	No	Increase	No
5	Profits-NII	Unconstrained	Increase	No	Increase
6		Constrained	No	Decrease	Decrease
7	Profits-ROA	Unconstrained	Increase	No	Increase
8		Constrained	No	Decrease	No

Note: 'Decrease' and 'Increase' indicate that the evaluation significantly decreases and increases, respectively, the lending outcomes separately, and 'No' indicates that the evaluation has no significant impact on lending outcomes.

Conclusion and policy implications

The sound development of SMEs in China is of primary importance for promoting economic growth, job creation and innovation. A lack of appropriate financing channels and credit unavailability are the main hurdles for the development of SMEs. The Chinese Government has authorised a set of schemes to solve the financing problems of SMEs. Yet, to date, there has been little evidence of the effectiveness of these schemes in increasing the number of loans to SMEs. The literature is similarly quiet on the cost to the banks of these financing schemes.

In this chapter, we investigate the benefits and costs of one of these financing schemes in China, which was initiated by the CBRC in 2008 to force commercial banks to meet certain requirements on SME loans. Based on a unique county branch–level survey dataset, our empirical analysis finds that the evaluation policy has different influences on banks with different initial conditions regarding SME loans and banks of different size. Although the evaluation policy increases lending to SMEs for banks that initially fell short of the requirements, it decreases SME loans for banks that initially exceeded the requirements. The overall benefit of this policy in terms of increasing SME loans depends on the distribution of the constrained and unconstrained banks. In regard to the cost, the evaluation increases credit risk and decreases the profits for constrained small banks, and it decreases net interest income for constrained large banks.

The empirical findings in this chapter have important policy implications. Based on our findings, financing support schemes for SMEs bring both benefits and costs for banks. One of the notable problems of this SME financing scheme is that it increases the credit risk of small banks and decreases their profits. To fix this problem, the government needs to introduce policies to fundamentally improve the business, financial and innovation environments and the service system for SMEs. The efficient enforcement of the 2018 amendments to the law on the promotion of SMEs is an important and necessary step.

References

Allen, F., Qian, J. and Qian, M. (2005), Law, finance, and economic growth in China, *Journal of Financial Economics* 77: 57–116. doi.org/10.1016/j.jfineco.2004.06.010.

Allen, F., Qian, J., Zhang, C. and Zhao M. (2012), *China's financial system: Opportunities and challenges*, NBER Working Paper No. 17828, Cambridge, MA: National Bureau of Economic Research. doi.org/10.3386/w17828.

Bai, C.E., Lu, J. and Tao, Z. (2006), Property rights protection and access to bank loans, *Economics of Transition* 14: 611–28. doi.org/10.1111/j.1468-0351.2006.00269.x.

Beck, T., Demirgüç-Kunt, A. and Maksimovic, V. (2008), Financing patterns around the world: Are small firms different?, *Journal of Financial Economics* 89: 467–87. doi.org/10.1016/j.jfineco.2007.10.005.

Berger, A.N., Miller, N.H., Petersen, M.A., Rajan, R.G. and Stein, J.C. (2002), *Does function follow organizational form? Evidence from the lending practices of large and small banks*, NBER Working Papers No. 8752, Cambridge, MA: National Bureau of Economic Research. doi.org/10.3386/w8752.

Berger, A.N. and Udell, G.F. (1995), Relationship lending and lines of credit in small firm finance, *Journal of Business* 68: 351–82. doi.org/10.1086/296668.

Berger, A.N. and Udell, G.F. (1996), Universal banking and the future of small business lending, in A. Saunders and I. Walter (eds), *Financial System Design: The case for universal banking*, Chicago: Irwin Publishing.

Berger, A.N. and Udell, G.F. (2002), Small business credit availability and relationship lending: The importance of bank organizational structure, *Economic Journal* 112: 32–53. doi.org/10.1111/1468-0297.00682.

Berger, A.N. and Udell, G.F. (2006), A more complete conceptual framework for SME finance, *Journal of Banking & Finance* 30(11): 2945–66. doi.org/10.1016/j.jbankfin.2006.05.008.

Chong, T.T., Lu, L. and Ongena, S. (2013), Does banking competition alleviate or worsen credit constraints faced by small- and medium-sized enterprises? Evidence from China, *Journal of Banking and Finance* 37: 3412–24. doi.org/10.1016/j.jbankfin.2013.05.006.

Cole, R., Goldberg, L. and White, L. (1999), Cookie-cutter versus character: The micro structure of small business lending by large and small banks, in J. Blanton, A. Williams and S. Rhine (eds), *Business Access to Capital and Credit: A Federal Reserve System research conference*, Washington, DC: Board of Governors of the Federal Reserve System.

Du, J., Lu, Y. and Tao, Z. (2012), Bank loans vs. trade credit, *Economics of Transition* 20: 457–80. doi.org/10.1111/j.1468-0351.2012.00439.x.

Gou, Q., Huang, Y. and Xu, J. (2018), Does ownership matter in banking credit allocation in China?, *European Journal of Finance* 24(16): 1409–27. doi.org/10.1080/1351847X.2016.1190391.

Huang, Y., Cai, F., Xu, P. and Gou, Q. (2013), The new normal of Chinese development, in R. Garnaut, F. Cai and L. Song (eds), *China: A new model for growth and development*, Canberra: ANU E Press. doi.org/10.22459/CNMGD.07.2013.03.

Lin, J.Y., Cai, F. and Li, Z. (1996), *The China Miracle: Development strategy and economic reform*, Hong Kong: The Chinese University Press.

Peek, J. and Rosengren, E.S. (1998), Bank consolidation and small business lending: It's not just bank size that matters, *Journal of Banking and Finance* 22: 799–819. doi.org/10.1016/S0378-4266(98)00012-0.

Shen, Y., Shen, M., Xu, Z. and Bai, Y. (2009), Bank size and small- and medium-sized enterprise (SME) lending: Evidence from China, *World Development* 37(4): 800–11. doi.org/10.1016/j.worlddev.2008.07.014.

Stiglitz, J. and Weiss, A. (1981), Credit rationing in markets with imperfect information, *American Economic Review* 71: 181–214.

Zhang, D., Cai, J., Dickinson, D. and Kutan, A. (2016), Non-performing loans, moral hazard and regulation of the Chinese commercial banking system. *Journal of Banking & Finance* 63: 48–60. doi.org/10.1016/j.jbankfin.2015.11.010.

Zhang, L. and Gou, Q. (2016), Demystifying China's economic growth: Retrospect and prospect, in A. Calcagno, S. Dullien, A. Márquez-Velázquez, N. Maystre and J. Priewe (eds), *Rethinking Development Strategies after the Financial Crisis. Volume II: Country studies and international comparisons*, New York: United Nations. doi.org/10.18356/daa61e24-en.

11. Modelling the economic impact of the Sino–US trade dispute: A global perspective

Deborah H.Y. Tan and Chen Chen[1]

Introduction

The global economy works best when goods, services, people and ideas flow freely across administrative boundaries. The current prosperity we all enjoy is due, in no small part, to the benefits of international trade, which unlocks the positive benefits of national and regional comparative advantage. The position of our employer, BHP, on this point is clear.

Quoting directly from the six-monthly update that BHP publishes with its financial results:

> While we stress that an increase in trade protection alone is not a recessionary level shock for the global economy, it is an exceedingly unhelpful starting point for the pursuit of broad based growth across regions, expenditure drivers and industries. That observation highlights the importance of continued advocacy for free trade and open markets by corporations, governments and civil society … As the true economic costs of trade protection are progressively recognised by global consumers, we anticipate a popular mandate for a more open international trading environment will eventually emerge. (McKay 2019)

Exactly how large might those costs be and what can be done to mitigate them? That is what this chapter is about.

The current trade dispute between the United States and China stems from the Trump administration's long-held commitment to adopt a tougher stance against China to change what it regards as unfair trade practices. These practices are, in the administration's view, the reason for the US trade deficit with China. At a deeper level, the trade dispute can also be seen as a surface manifestation of the emerging superpower rivalry between the United States and China.

At the time of writing, talks between US and Chinese trade negotiators are under way and have gained traction in recent months. However, it is difficult to foresee the final outcome of the negotiations—or, indeed, if there will be an end or whether this

---

1   The authors thank Warwick McKibbin, Larry Liu and Huw McKay for helpful suggestions on an earlier draft.

issue is best seen as a continuum. Therefore, rather than presenting a single set of results, we have instead prepared a number of different scenarios, of varying intensity and duration, with varying counterpolicies in play, to capture the range of potential outcomes for the US, Chinese and global economies in the coming decade.

The scenarios have been simulated in the G-cubed multicountry model. A key reference for this chapter is McKibbin and Stoeckel (2017), who use the G-cubed model to simulate the effects of a range of multilateral trade war scenarios.

Our conclusion is that a trade war will, unsurprisingly, leave both the Chinese and the American people less prosperous than they would otherwise have been. Our definition of a full-blown Sino–US trade war will be costly for both countries and could reduce the size of both economies by 0.5 per cent, on average, over the next decade. While the impact on China is initially greater due to China's higher trade exposure, the cost to the United States increases over time. However, bystander countries stand to gain, at the margin, from the diversion of activity, with market share gains in both China and the United States for the likes of Germany, Japan and South Korea. It also appears to be strongly in China's interests to resolve the dispute through negotiation, while simultaneously pursuing a set of sensible countercyclical policies to cushion the Chinese domestic economy in the near to medium terms.

The economic priorities of President Trump and President Xi

President Donald Trump's major economic policy priorities have been to raise economic growth and create jobs by boosting investment. The levers used to do this have been lowering taxes (especially corporate taxes) and reducing regulation, while providing protection for US manufacturing by raising tariffs and renegotiating trade agreements. This platform has had mixed success, both legislatively and in terms of economic outcomes. The biggest legislative achievement to date—the *Tax Cuts and Jobs Act*, signed into law in December 2017—is arguably the most sweeping overhaul of the US tax system in more than 30 years. The tax package lifted growth above potential in 2018, and we estimate that it will continue to support investment, employment and wages above a counterfactual baseline for a half-decade or so. However, it is not self-financing and the Joint Committee on Taxation (2017) argues it will add an extra US$1.1 trillion to the budget deficit over 10 years. The boost to domestic demand relative to that of the United States' trading partners also suggests that the US trade balance will worsen, running counter to the administration's efforts to reduce the nation's trade deficit.

On trade, President Trump has been able to use national security provisions in trade legislation to expedite measures, rather than seeking congressional approval. The basic line from the administration is that the large bilateral trade deficits the United States runs with its major partners are a sign that US exporters are being treated unfairly and that these partners should be buying more American exports. While China has not been alone in receiving US criticism on trade,[2] China has arguably been the primary target. This has also extended beyond the bilateral relationship to shape US dealings with other nations. For instance, the new US–Mexico–Canada Agreement to replace the North American Free Trade Agreement includes a 'poison pill' provision allowing the United States to veto Canada's and Mexico's choices of other trading partners, and appears to be a clear effort to single out China.

While US policymaking has grown more nationalistic under the current administration, China is pursuing a broader long-run economic growth strategy and a more influential role regionally. The Chinese authorities continue to view economic growth as a key priority under the guidance of the thirteenth Five-Year Plan, which aims to double China's per capita income by 2020. At the same time, reforms have been promoted to a similar level of importance over the past five years as the maturing economy is confronted with various structural issues, mainly in the areas of industrial capacity, financial risk and the environment. Over the past five years, the Chinese Government has navigated a gradual growth slowdown alongside the implementation of various supply-side structural reforms. China has also pursued some unilateral trade reforms while negotiations with the United States have been proceeding, such as lower tariffs on cars, and it also passed a new foreign investment law at the most recent National People's Congress.

China's long-run goal to become a 'modernised and prosperous economy' by the mid-twenty-first century has also catalysed the pursuit of industrial policies that would drive its sizeable manufacturing sector (currently low to middle in terms of value added) up the value chain. 'Made in China 2025' is a well-known government-backed industrial policy focused on advancing China's manufacturing sector into a technological superpower and targeting key sectors such as information, communication and telecommunication, machinery and equipment and industrial materials. More broadly, China has been growing in influence in the Asia-Pacific over the past few years through establishing closer bilateral economic linkages. The Belt and Road Initiative, for instance, has become the backbone of the incumbent administration's foreign policies. The establishment of the Beijing-headquartered Asian Infrastructure Investment Bank highlighted China's commitment to play a serious role in terms of providing support for regional economic development. The sum of these moves presents a clear strategy to move China up the value chain while increasing China's role in international governance, particularly in the development financing sphere.

---

2   Elsewhere, President Trump has threatened to impose tariffs of up to 25 per cent on European car imports if he is unable to reach a deal with the bloc following findings from the US Commerce Department in February this year. Also, steel and aluminium tariffs have been global in nature, with only a few exemptions offered, and with countries in the Americas the most heavily impacted.

State of play on trade negotiations

Concerns about Chinese trade practices, the treatment of foreign companies in China and questions about intellectual property rights protection are not new. According to the US Trade Representative (2019) and European Commission (European Chamber of Commerce 2018), many policymakers believe the Chinese Government has not met all its World Trade Organization (WTO) accession commitments. Claims include 'unfair' support for Chinese domestic companies, alleged forced technology transfers and denial of market access to international competitors. The American Chamber of Commerce in Shanghai (2017) notes significant barriers to entry in five key industries: financial services, information and communications technology, health care, agriculture and the automotive industry. Meltzer and Shenai (2019) and Hass and Balin (2019) from The Brookings Institution also observe that China's ambition to become a technology superpower has caused bipartisan consternation in the United States, centred on whether China would use industrial policy to provide, once again, 'unfair' support to domestic players. The rapid escalation in tensions in recent months has built on the foundations created by these perceptions.

From China's point of view, the US merchandise trade deficit reflects a number of structural factors. First, the current trade deficit is a reflection of the low level of US national savings, across the public and private sectors. The dollar's role as the global vehicle funding currency also necessitates the provision of US dollar liquidity through perpetual trade deficits—also known as the Triffin dilemma. Finally, the comparative advantage of Chinese goods production and the redistribution and fragmentation of the global supply chain have led to major shifts in the country of origin of products American consumers buy, both from established brands and in terms of increases in indigenous Chinese firms' market share.

Tensions between the world's two largest economies have escalated rapidly following the US decision to impose tariffs on steel and aluminium imports in March 2018. Figure 11.1 provides a timeline of developments to date. So far, the United States has imposed duties on more than half of its imports of Chinese goods and China has retaliated with tariffs on more than 70 per cent of its imports of US goods. Between 30 November and 1 December 2018, a 'truce' agreement was reached between both countries at the G20 summit in Buenos Aires. As part of the temporary ceasefire, the United States agreed to postpone raising tariffs from 1 January 2019 and set a 90-day time frame for the two sides to make progress on key structural issues. On 24 February, President Trump decided to postpone the implementation of the more punitive tariffs that were due to come into effect on 1 March. At the time of writing, in early April 2019, talks are still under way between US and Chinese trade negotiators. While both governments have been keen to point out the highly productive nature of their talks, it remains to be seen whether substantive progress has truly been made.

March 2018

US imposed 25% tariffs on steel and 10% tariffs on aluminum imports from China

China retaliated with tariffs on 128 US products

April 2018

US proposed 25% tariffs on $50b of Chinese goods, relating to intellectual property theft and forced technology transfer

China proposed 25% tariffs on $50b imports from the US, including aircraft, soybeans and autos

US proposed tariffs on an additional $100b of imports as China did not 'remedy its misconduct'

At the Boao Forum, President Xi shared plans to increase China's imports demand, broaden market access to foreign capital, reduce tariffs in certain sectors and enhance intellectual property protection

May 2018

US senior officials travelled to Beijing to resume trade negotiations

June 2018

Despite several rounds of trade talks, the US announced tariffs on $50b on Chinese imports. The tariffs would come into force in two tranches, $34b from 6 July and the rest from 23 August

China retaliated like for like

In response to Chinese retaliation, President Trump directed the US Trade Representative to identify an additional $200b Chinese imports to be targeted with 10% tariffs

July 2018

US Trade Representative released list of Chinese imports worth $200b, President Trump threatened to increase tariffs from 10% to 25%

September 2018

US imposed 10% tariffs on an additional $200b Chinese goods

China retaliated with 5–10% tariffs on $60b US imports

November 2018

At the first China International Import Expo, Chinese authorities pledged to open its domestic market and improve business environment

President Trump and President Xi spoke by phone and both parties expressed goodwill

December 2018

At the sidelines of the G20, the US and China agreed to hold back further tariff increases until 1 March 2019 and restart trade talks

February 2019

President Trump postponed the tariff increases due on 1 March given progress on trade talks

April 2019

US and Chinese officials conclude latest round of high-level trade talks with further consultation to follow on outstanding issues

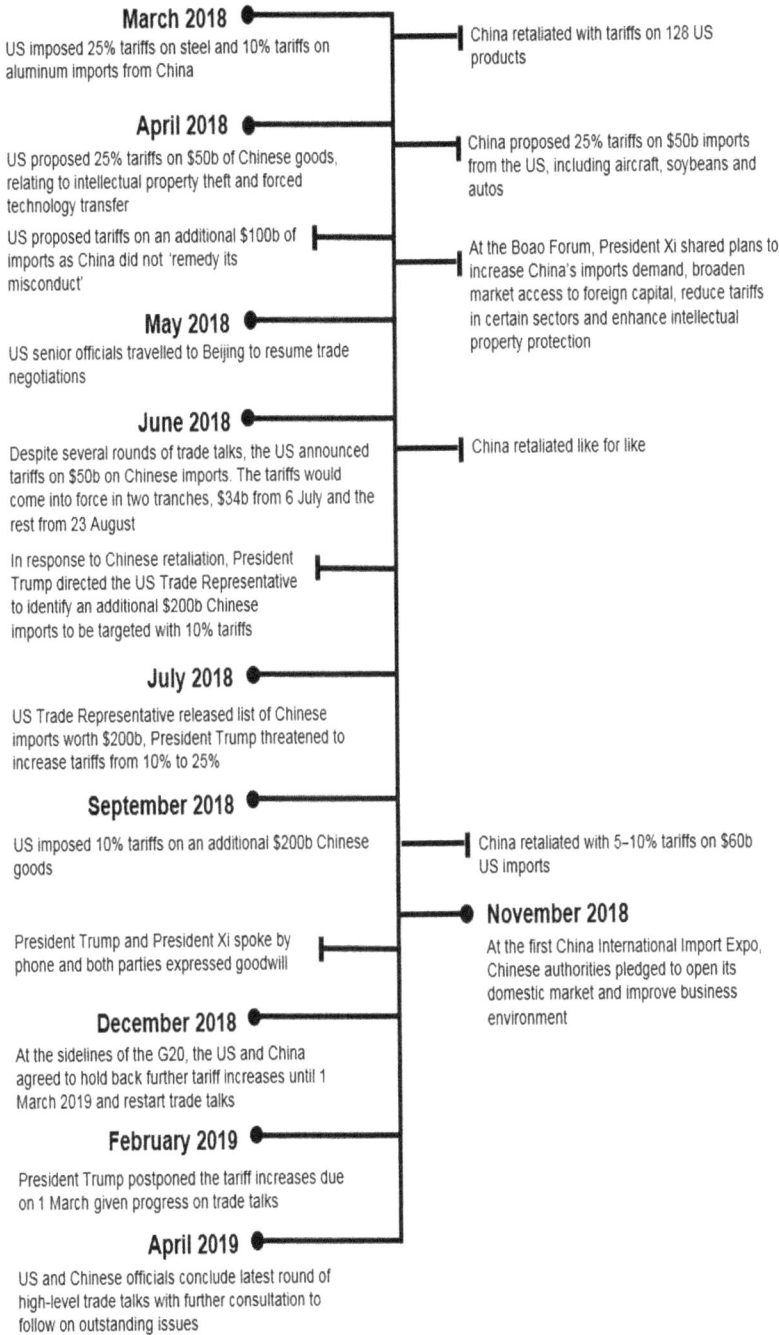

Figure 11.1 Sino–US trade developments timeline

Source: BHP analysis.

It is difficult to foresee the final outcome of the negotiations and what the United States might expect from China in exchange for either continued suspension of increased tariffs or removal of those tariffs that are in place. Other questions—such as those relating to industrial policy, market access and intellectual property—will also need to be resolved. In the unlikely event that negotiations fail completely, the United States has the upper hand in both the breadth and the volume of tariffs that it could impose, while China is unable to match like for like given its lower level of imports from the United States (Figure 11.2). Although China has insisted it does not wish to escalate the dispute, there are other policy tools the Chinese leadership could deploy to stabilise the economy, albeit with intertemporal trade-offs.

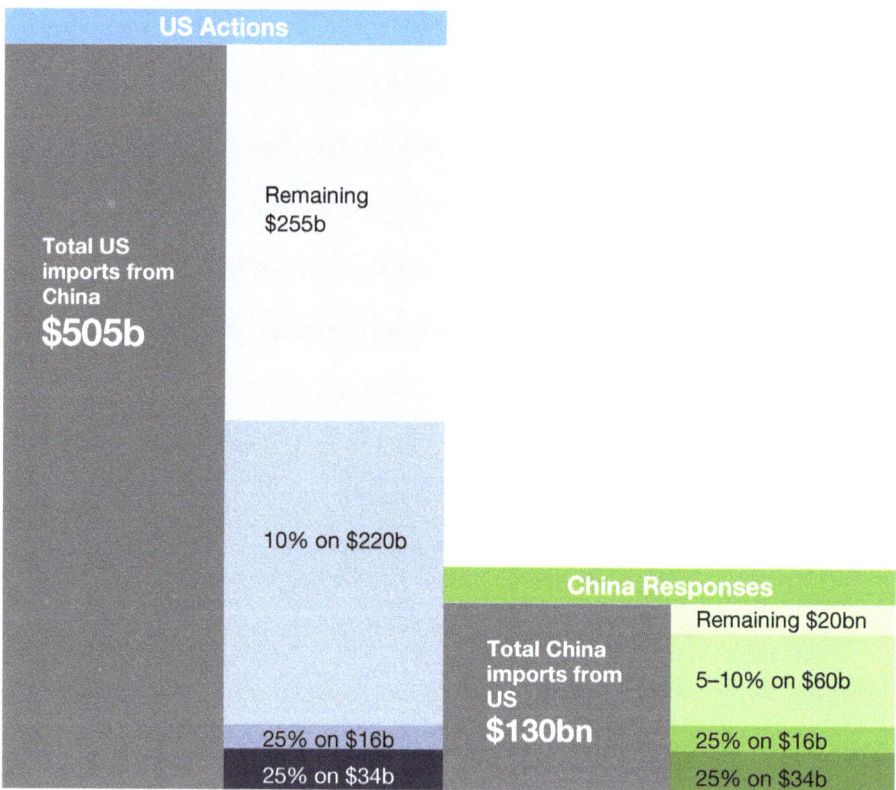

US Actions

Total US imports from China **$505b**

Remaining $255b

10% on $220b

25% on $16b

25% on $34b

China Responses

Total China imports from US **$130bn**

Remaining $20bn

5–10% on $60b

25% on $16b

25% on $34b

Figure 11.2 Trade policy actions from the United States and China
Source: BHP analysis.

To assess the range of impacts of the conflict, we use a set of scenarios to capture three possible outcomes of the Sino–US trade dispute. At the time of writing, two scenarios have been overtaken by the pace of events. Taking the outcomes of the first set of scenarios into account, we then examine the impact of three Chinese policy countermeasures. Some of these countervailing measures have already been implemented, while others may yet be adopted.

The model

The policy choices of the United States and China have a strong influence on their own domestic economies, each other's trade performance as well as the economic opportunities faced by their other trading partners. Protectionism increases operating costs for firms in import destination markets, reduces the purchasing power of consumers, reduces the rate of return on capital and leads to lower investment. Employment falls as businesses downsize and slack in the labour market depresses wages and spending. A full-blown Sino–US trade war will certainly be costly for both countries. Meanwhile, bystander countries such as Germany and Japan stand to gain from the diversion of activity. While Chinese stimulus policies could stabilise the economy in the near term, that would be at the expense of a higher fiscal deficit and the need for consolidation in the future.

To capture all of these influences and interactions, we have used the comprehensive dynamic global model originally developed by McKibbin and Wilcoxen (1999, 2013). The G-cubed model incorporates all of these interactions in a dynamic and global setting, with sectoral detail. The version used in this chapter is outlined in more detail in McKibbin and Stoeckel (2017). Specifically, the model version used here has six sectors (energy, mining, agriculture, manufacturing durables, manufacturing nondurables and services) plus a capital goods–producing sector and 17 countries/regions, as set out in Table 11.1. Each region's central bank is assumed to adjust short-term nominal interest rates following the Henderson–McKibbin–Taylor rule,[3] as set out in Henderson and McKibbin (1993) and Taylor (1993). In this model version, all central banks, with the exception of China's, target inflation and GDP growth. Compared to most central banks, the People's Bank of China has several policy targets, including price stability, economic growth, employment, balance of payments, financial markets reform and liberalisation (Zhou 2016). China's central bank targets inflation, GDP growth and the nominal exchange rate. In the first set of scenarios, the US and Chinese central banks automatically respond to macroeconomic outcomes according to the monetary rule. In the second set of scenarios, the Chinese central bank cuts short-term interest rates independently and subsequently responds to macroeconomic outcomes following the monetary rule. As for fiscal policy, government spending here is assumed to be exogenous and the government collects taxes to service its debt interests.

---

3   The nominal interest rate set by the central bank should respond to divergences of actual inflation from target inflation and of actual economic output from potential economic output.

G-cubed features businesses that are forward looking in their investment and spending decisions, which are made based on current and past rates of return and future expected rates of return. Here, we expect businesses to invest less given expectations of lower returns in the future due to the imposition of tariffs. As such, it is an ideal tool with which to assess the potential impacts of these wideranging trade policies on the global economy.

Table 11.1 G-cubed model countries/regions in v.144

United States	China
Japan	India
United Kingdom	Indonesia
Germany	Other Asia
Rest of euro area	Latin America
Canada	Other emerging economies
Australia	Eastern Europe and former Soviet Union
South Korea	OPEC
Rest of advanced economies	

OPEC = Organization of the Petroleum Exporting Countries

Literature review

Over the past year, there has been increased attention on the potential adverse economic impacts of a trade war. The scope of these studies varies to a substantial degree and depends on the countries that are involved in the scenario analyses as well as the assumptions in general. A global trade war has far more negative repercussions, whereas a bilateral trade war leads to leakages to third countries. The upside to our analysis is that we have realistically focused on the two countries involved. In addition, we have included a suite of possible Chinese policy responses in a full-escalation scenario.

McKibbin and Stoeckel (2017) used the G-cubed model to simulate the effects of a range of multilateral trade war scenarios. They find that tariffs imposed by the United States on all imports from all countries would leave all countries and regions worse off. The United States itself is also worse off under this scenario, with GDP falling by 0.3 per cent in the first year, and the impact on China is three times larger, at −0.9 per cent. In a global trade war, all countries are worse off—some more than others due to their trade exposure. The losses to China, Germany and other countries in Asia are some three times larger than for the United States.

Freund et al. (2018) from the World Bank used a computable general equilibrium model and considered three scenarios, all of which included mutual tariffs between the United States and China, with the third scenario including a decline in investor confidence. The authors find that third-party countries benefit from trade diversion when the two trading partners impose tariff surcharges. But, when investor confidence is shaken, these gains are more than offset for all regions by negative income effects. In this scenario, income losses range between 0.9 per cent for South Asia and 1.7 per cent for Europe and Central Asia. The biggest declines in incomes are recorded by China and the United States—up to 3.5 per cent and 1.6 per cent, respectively. The sectors most affected include agriculture, chemicals and transport equipment in the United States, and electronic equipment, machinery and other manufacturing in China.

Li et al. (2018) used a multicountry global general equilibrium model to simulate the effects of possible Sino–US trade wars, including both tariff and nontariff measures. The authors find that the United States can gain under unilateral sanctions measures on China, but it will lose if China takes retaliatory measures. Under a mutual trade war, China will lose more than the United States. Additionally, trade wars between China and the United States will hurt most countries and the world, especially in terms of GDP and manufacturing employment.

The trade war scenario analysis by the European Central Bank (ECB) is published as part of their economic bulletin dating from September 2018. By using the model of the International Monetary Fund (IMF) as well as their own global model, the ECB assesses both the trade and the confidence channels by which the economy might be impacted by the current trade war. The study examines a global trade war in which the United States imposes tariffs on all imports and all trading partners reciprocate these protectionist US measures. This explains the relatively higher impact on the US economy compared with China, as the latter can benefit from substitution effects. Furthermore, the study assumes that the trade tensions will ease going forward and will last for only two years.

Simulations

The first set of scenarios assesses the impact of three different outcomes of the trade dispute, excluding any Chinese policy response. The tariff shocks are assumed to be permanent. The second set considers the impact of three different Chinese policy responses in the event of a bilateral trade war. Table 11.3 summarises the key assumptions in each scenario.

The first set of scenarios is chosen to reflect the observed evolution of the trade dispute as well as a plausible intensification. Our first scenario, 'Symbolic retaliation', mirrors the first tit for tat between the United States and China in March 2018 after

President Trump invoked Section 232 of the *Trade Act* (1962) and imposed tariffs of 25 per cent on steel and 10 per cent on aluminium imports. We find this scenario to have a largely neutral impact on long-term growth prospects. The second scenario, 'Escalated tensions', mirrors the tit for tat between the United States and China in July–August 2018, following the findings of the Section 301 investigation under the *Trade Act* (1974). The US Trade Representative then targeted US$50 billion of imported Chinese products that were deemed instrumental in helping China achieve its goals of becoming a global leader in the advanced technology sector, prompting China to retaliate like for like. In September 2018, the United States imposed a further 10 per cent tariff on an additional US$200 billion of Chinese imports, with China responding with 5–10 per cent tariffs on an additional US$60 billion of US imports. Prior to the truce achieved at the G20 meeting in December 2018, a further escalation of the dispute was a distinct possibility. As such, we assume the worst-case scenario of a bilateral trade war in our third scenario, 'Trade war'.

The trade shocks in the simulations are designed to be close to the announced policies but will not capture the precise measures. With this caveat in mind, we compare the impact of each simulation against a baseline before the United States and China openly engaged in tit for tat. Given the six-sector setting in the G-cubed model, we convert the industry-specific tariffs to an aggregate rate that can be applied to the entire sector, based on the industry's share in that sector. We use 2016 bilateral import data from the World Integrated Trade Solution Trade Stats database to estimate the industry shares. We then apply the industry weights to the new tariffs and arrive at a sector-wide tariff rate.

A more detailed description of the three scenarios is as follows.

Symbolic retaliation

In March 2018, US metals importers faced higher duties following the imposition of tariffs on steel and aluminium (25 per cent and 10 per cent, respectively) sourced from several countries. China retaliated by raising duties (ranging from 15 per cent to 25 per cent) on its imports of US food, animal products and metal articles. In this simulation, we apply a sector-wide average tariff on US imports of Chinese durable manufacturing goods to reflect the higher levies on the metals industry. We also apply a sector-wide average tariff on Chinese imports of US nondurable manufacturing, agricultural, fishing and hunting and durable manufacturing goods to reflect higher levies on the affected industries.

Escalated tensions

In July 2018, the US administration imposed 25 per cent tariffs on US$50 billion of Chinese goods, covering industrial, transport and medical products. China retaliated with 25 per cent tariffs on US$50 billion of US goods, including soybeans, automobiles and aircraft. In this simulation, the sector-wide incremental tariff rate on US imports of Chinese durable manufacturing goods is revised to include new levies on machinery and equipment, transportation and other miscellaneous manufactured articles. For China, the sector-wide tariffs on US agricultural, fishing and hunting, durable manufacturing and nondurable manufacturing goods are also updated to reflect the new levies on agricultural products, transport equipment and chemicals and plastics.

Trade war

In a fully fledged trade war, the United States and China are assumed to raise tariffs on all bilateral imports. In this simulation, we apply 25 per cent tariffs on all sectors.

In 2018, China rolled out several supportive measures in response to not only a weaker external outlook arising from trade tensions, but also the slowing domestic economy (Table 11.2). In the second set of scenarios, we assess the efficacy of a package of Chinese policy responses in the event of a trade war against the same pre-dispute baseline. In the first scenario, 'Drip irrigation', the policy shocks are designed to be similar to the announced stimulus but will not fully capture the precise measures. In the second scenario, 'Pump priming', we assume the Chinese authorities provide much more aggressive policy support to shore up short-term growth. In the third scenario, 'Sell-off', we hypothesise that China counters US aggression through other nontariff means—namely, through a sell-off of its substantial holdings of US Treasuries.

Table 11.2 Chinese policy package in 2018

Date announced	Policy measures
March 2018	China announced import tariff cuts focused on consumer goods— e.g. automobiles, pharmaceuticals.
May 2018	A value-added tax cut (1 per cent) applied to manufacturing, transport and construction firms.
April, June, October 2018	The central bank cumulatively lowered commercial banks' required reserve ratio from 17 per cent to 14.5 per cent. The interbank offered rate was lowered by approximately 25 basis points since Q2 2018, partly as a result of a round of required-rate-of-return cuts, as well as proactive market operations by the People's Bank of China through its mid-term lending facility and reverse repurchase.
October 2018	Individual tax threshold raised to RMB5,000 from RMB3,500, as well as policies on income tax deductions. Effective from January 2019.
November 2018	Chinese authorities increased export tax rebates on about 400, mainly capital, goods.

Source: MoFCOM, BHP analysis.

Drip irrigation

This simulation captures major policies implemented in 2018 to stabilise the economy. Between March and October, the Chinese authorities lowered the required reserve ratio on three occasions (in April, July and October). Although the People's Bank of China did not engage in an outright reduction in the policy rate, the interbank offer rate—or what we would interpret as the shadow rate—fell by 25 basis points over the same period in response to the liquidity injection. Accordingly, we reduce the short-term interest rate to reflect monetary easing. We also lower the personal income tax rate at the margin to reflect the increase in the tax-free personal income band. We also use a tax credit to proxy the package of tax rebates, tariff cuts and sales tax reductions offered to firms in durable and nondurable manufacturing.

Pump priming

In this simulation, the tax shocks are unchanged from the first simulation; however, monetary policy easing is assumed to be more aggressive (in our case, the cut to short-term interest rates is doubled). Government spending is also increased to reflect higher future expenditures on indigenous research and development to meet the authorities' long-term strategic objectives.

Sell-off

In this simulation, the tax and monetary policy shocks are unchanged from the first simulation. In addition, we assume that Chinese authorities withdraw their capital from the US Government bond market and redeploy this capital in domestic investment and other parts of the world. Presently, China's holdings of US Treasuries (worth US$1 trillion) is equivalent to about 5 per cent of US nominal GDP. The shock is set up such that the United States will face a capital outflow equivalent to 5 per cent of GDP over the next 20 years—that is, a loss of 0.25 per cent of GDP per year. This $1 trillion from the United States is then reallocated to the rest of the world in proportion to GDP.

Table 11.3 Overview of scenario assumptions

Aspect	Symbolic retaliation	Escalated tensions	Trade war	Drip irrigation	Pump priming	Sell-off
US tariffs on Chinese imports	25% on steel, 10% on aluminium (permanent)	25% on steel, 10% on aluminium, 25% on machinery and equipment, transportation and other miscellaneous manufactured articles (permanent)	25% on all goods (permanent)	25% on all goods (permanent)	25% on all goods (permanent)	25% on all goods (permanent)
Chinese tariffs on US imports	15–25% on food, animal products and metal articles (permanent)	15–25% on food, animal products and metal articles, 25% on agricultural products, transport equipment and chemicals and plastics (permanent)	25% on all goods (permanent)	25% on all goods (permanent)	25% on all goods (permanent)	25% on all goods (permanent)
Chinese taxes				2 percentage point cut to headline personal tax rate (permanent), investment tax credits for durable and nondurable manufacturing (government starts unwinding policy from 2025)	2 percentage point cut to headline personal tax rate (permanent), investment tax credits for durable and nondurable manufacturing (government starts unwinding policy from 2025)	2 percentage point cut to headline personal tax rate (permanent), investment tax credits for durable and nondurable manufacturing (government starts unwinding policy from 2025)
Chinese short-term interest rate				25 basis point cut to short-term interest rate (central bank starts unwinding policy from 2023)	50 basis point cut to short-term interest rate until 2022 (central bank starts unwinding policy from 2023)	25 basis point cut to short-term interest rate until 2022 (central bank starts unwinding policy from 2023)
Chinese Government spending					GDP share of government spending increases by 1 percentage point (permanent)	
US capital account						Outflow equivalent to 0.25% of GDP per year (next 20 years)

Model results: Scenario set 1

In the first set of simulations, we assess the impact of three different trade outcomes relative to a benchmark before the trade dispute. In the most benign of the three simulations, 'Symbolic retaliation', GDP deviates only slightly from the baseline (Figure 11.3, Exhibits 5–1). In the 'Escalated tensions' simulation, US and Chinese GDP fall by 0.2 per cent and 0.3 per cent, respectively, over the next decade. In the worst-case scenario, 'Trade war', both US and Chinese GDP decline by 0.5 per cent on average over the next 10 years. The initial impact on China is greater than that on the United States across all scenarios due to China's higher trade exposure. However, the cost to the United States becomes larger over time. On the other hand, third countries such as Germany and Japan will benefit from rising exports as activity is diverted away from the combatants. This is a positive for GDP in these countries (Figure 11.3, Exhibit 2) and, to some extent, this cushions the overall negative impact on the global economy.

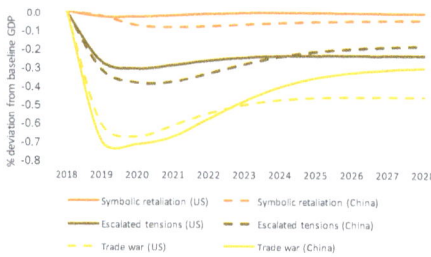

Exhibit 1 Impact on GDP from three simulated shocks

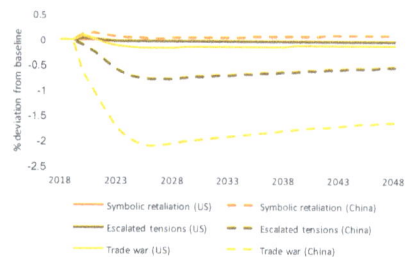

Exhibit 4 Impact on average wage

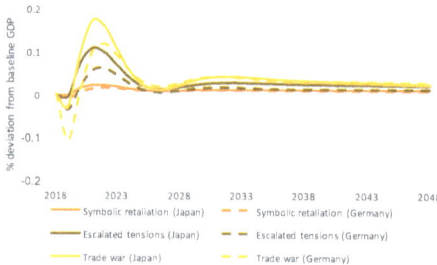

Exhibit 2 Impact on GDP

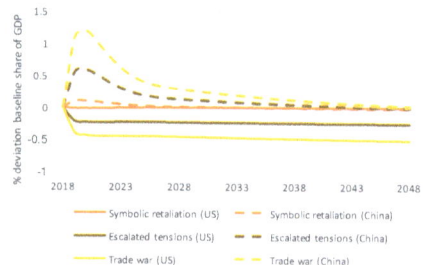

Exhibit 5 Impact on trade balance

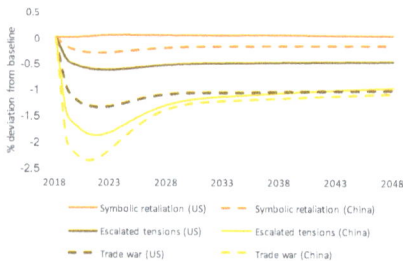

Exhibit 3 Impact on durable manufacturing output

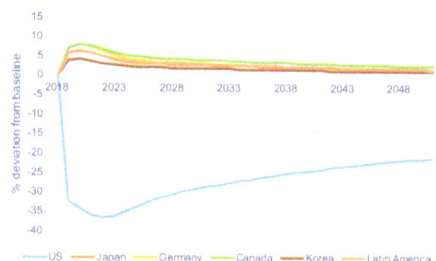

Exhibit 6 Imports of Chinese durable manufacturing goods from key trading partners

Figure 11.3 Impact of trade tensions

Source: BHP analysis based on G-cubed model.

Sectors facing protectionism will lose out, with durable manufacturing taking the biggest hit. This is a key sector targeted explicitly by both governments and accounts for the bulk of bilateral imports. The impact on China's durable manufacturing will also be much larger relative to the United States, due to the sector's bigger relative trade exposure (Figure 11.3, Exhibit 3). Tariffs increase the price of imported capital goods and lower firm profits and rates of return on investment. While an increase in tariffs may encourage a switch from foreign to domestic goods, the higher operating costs and lower returns on investment actually outweigh the benefits of an extra boost to domestic demand. As a result, investment and output fall in the United States and China, with a greater impact on China. The short to medium-term impact is greater on China but the difference narrows over time.

In the 'Trade war' scenario, wages could be –0.1 per cent and –1.5 per cent lower on average in the United States and China, respectively, over the next decade (Figure 11.3, Exhibit 4). The durable manufacturing sectors that are most impacted by the trade barriers will see the sharpest fall in employment. Businesses are expected to lower their demand for labour and wages will be driven down as they start to downsize operations. The slowdown in real activity dampens the effects of higher imported inflation. The United States and China are expected to see mildly higher inflation.

In China, the decline in return on capital discourages new investment and leads to an internal rebalancing in overall savings and investments. The sharp drop in investment could stem from reduced demand for imported raw materials and equipment. This change in the savings–investment balance leads to an improvement in China's trade position (Figure 11.3, Exhibit 5). The renminbi is also expected to weaken in the medium term as China experiences a sharper capital outflow given a reduced domestic need for investment. The weaker renminbi in turn increases the competitiveness of Chinese exports and encourages demand from other trading partners, such as Germany and Japan, mitigating some of the overall decline in exports (Figure 11.3, Exhibit 6). In contrast, the US trade position deteriorates, reflecting a slight worsening of its savings–investment balance. The United States experiences a drop in investment demand and a bigger drop in domestic savings. The change in relative rates of return between the United States and China attracts some capital inflow into the United States, which supports a stronger US dollar through the medium term. The stronger dollar encourages more consumption and domestic savings falls, leading to a weaker trade position. The strength of the US dollar also reduces the export competitiveness of US goods and services. While we mainly discuss the changes to nominal exchange rates, the change to real exchange rates largely follows a similar profile given the limited inflationary impact.

Model results: Scenario set 2

In the second set of scenarios, we assess the effectiveness of a range of Chinese policy responses in the event of a trade war. In all three scenarios, the policy stimulus buffers a negative trade shock and leads to a smaller decline in China's medium-term output (Figure 11.4, Exhibit 1). Monetary easing lowers borrowing costs for domestic firms. Tax credits to the export-oriented manufacturing sector also increase after-tax profits and rates of return on investment, making it more attractive to expand business operations in these sectors. The change in relative return on investment also results in some capital being drawn away from the United States. Indeed, in all three scenarios, the United States experiences a steeper decline in investment, but the outcomes are not materially different from those absent a policy response.

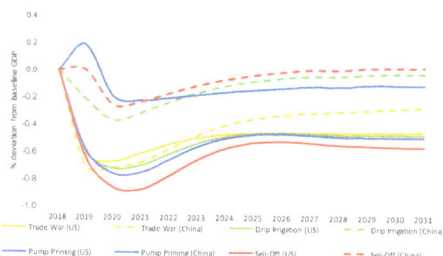

Exhibit 1 GDP: China and the United States

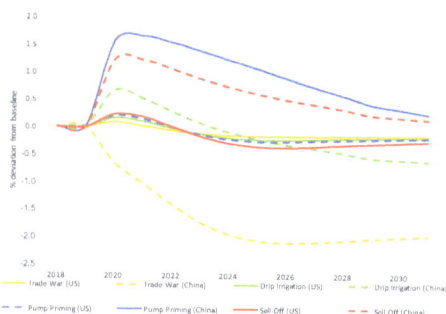

Exhibit 4 Average wage: China and the United States

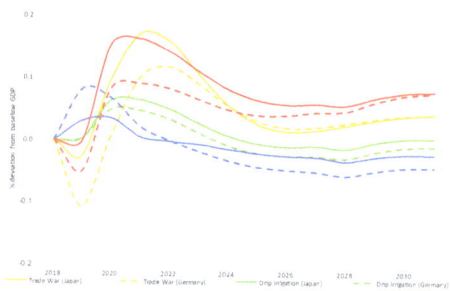

Exhibit 2 GDP: Japan and Germany

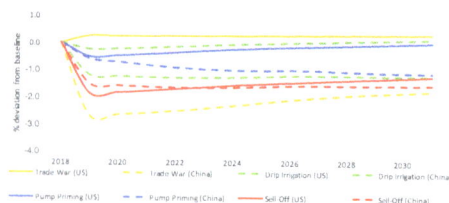

Exhibit 5 Nominal exchange rate: China and the United States

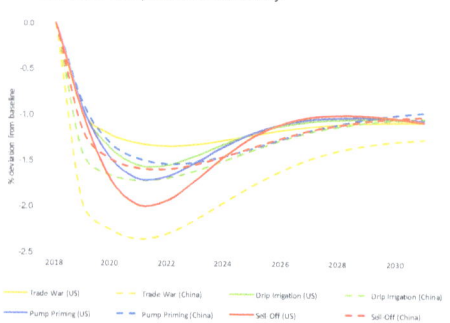

Exhibit 6 Trade balance: China and the United States

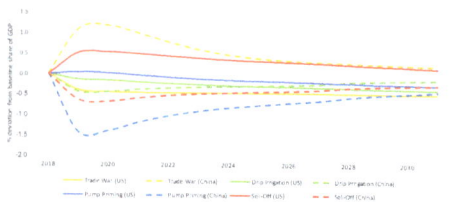

Exhibit 3 Durable manufacturing output: China and the United States

Figure 11.4 Impact of Chinese policies
Source: BHP analysis based on G-cubed model.

China's choice of policies also leads to differentiated outcomes in the short and medium terms. A stronger stimulus under 'Pump priming' lends the greatest support in the short term, but this comes at the expense of lower output in the longer term as higher government spending necessitates some form of fiscal consolidation in the future. While the 'Sell-off' scenario is slightly less effective at offsetting the near-term shocks, the Chinese economy benefits from increased domestic investment from a redeployment of Chinese capital (away from US Treasuries) and sees a stronger pickup in real activity over the longer term.

From China's perspective, the 'Sell-off' scenario is expected to be as effective as 'Pump priming' in cushioning the impact of a bilateral trade war over the next decade, with GDP expected to be 0.1 per cent lower on average over the next 10 years in both cases. This compares with an average decline in China's GDP over the next decade by 0.5 per cent in a trade war and 0.2 per cent under the 'Drip irrigation' scenario. Over the next 10 years, US GDP is expected to decline by 0.5 per cent in a trade war and will worsen marginally with 'Drip irrigation' and 'Pump priming'. Under the 'Sell-off' scenario, US GDP is expected to fall by 0.7 per cent. These outcomes show that such retaliatory measures can be quite limited in their capacity to inflict economic damage on the United States. The limited economic damage and the politically explosive nature of a sell-off appear to support the views of some Chinese policymakers.[4]

Bystander countries such as Germany and Japan continue to benefit as trade activity and capital flows are diverted away from the combatants (Figure 11.4, Exhibit 2). However, ongoing EU–US trade talks have yet to make decisive progress and the threat of US auto tariffs remains tangible. If auto tariffs were to materialise, the boost to auto exporters from diverted trade is likely to fall significantly, with Japan experiencing a greater loss (compared with Germany) given its larger relative exposure to US final demand. In 2017, the United States imported US$40 billion worth of Japanese-made cars and US$20 billion worth of German-made cars.

Figure 11.4, Exhibit 3 shows that countercyclical measures can mitigate some of the negative impacts on investment from a trade war. Specifically, the stimulus increases the after-tax return from investing in China and reduces the relative attractiveness of investing in the United States. The more expansionary the policy ('Pump priming' being the most aggressive), the better the investment outcome for China is. For the United States, the pullback in investment is the largest under the 'Sell-off' scenario. For decades, foreign purchases of US Government securities have subsidised the borrowing costs of the US Government, relative to what it would have had to pay if it only had access to US domestic savings. This has also driven down the borrowing costs of US corporations in domestic markets. Under the 'Sell-off' scenario, the

---

4 Chinese ambassador Cui Tankai compared selling US Treasuries to playing with fire and thought the authorities in Beijing would not wish to cause any financial instability in global markets (Lee 2018).

outflow of capital leads to a drop in the US dollar and a rise in long-term US bond yields and borrowing costs; these two mutually reinforcing forces are expected to weigh on investment sentiment.

The stimulus also cushions the impact on Chinese employment from a trade war (Figure 11.4, Exhibit 4). Chinese businesses are expected to lower their demand for labour as operations are downsized. The slowdown in activity is moderated, leading to a milder decline in Chinese wages. Under a highly expansionary stance ('Pump priming'), wages could even rise as stronger government spending and investment activity bid up labour demand. In the United States, 'Sell-off' places the largest cap on US wage growth prospects in the medium term. These wage dynamics are expected to mirror investment decisions.

While the stimulus is in itself inflationary, economic activity generally remains below potential in all three scenarios, so China experiences only mildly higher inflation. The size of the stimulus under the 'Pump priming' scenario imparts the strongest inflationary impulse in the early years. In the United States, 'Sell-off' has the largest impact on inflation. Specifically, the combined effect of lower demand for US Treasuries and a redirection of these capital flows towards other competitors leads to a depreciation in the US dollar relative to its major trading partners and the United States experiences higher imported inflation.

The stimulus raises the relative rate of return of investing in China and attracts capital inflows, so even with outright monetary easing, the renminbi falls by less in all three scenarios (Figure 11.4, Exhibit 5). In 'Sell-off', recipients of Chinese capital see their exchange rates appreciate so this to some extent dampens the strength of the renminbi against its non-US trading partners. However, the renminbi strengthens relative to the US dollar. On a trade-weighted basis, the renminbi depreciates the least in 'Pump priming', under which overall demand for Chinese capital is the highest. Across the three scenarios, capital flight out of the United States in 'Sell-off' leads to the weakest outcome for the US dollar.

The first set of scenarios showed that the drop in investment demand in China rebalances domestic savings and investment and leads to an improvement in China's trade balance (Figure 11.4, Exhibit 6). With a policy stimulus and higher investment needs, however, the improvement in China's trade balance will be reduced. In the case of 'Pump priming', the trade balance actually deteriorates as higher investment demand spurs capital inflows, which strengthen the renminbi. The stronger renminbi is expected to weaken the export competitiveness of Chinese goods and services. In 'Sell-off', demand for investment falls and capital flows out of the United States. Reduced support for the US dollar increases the export competitiveness of US goods and services and, taken together with lower demand for imports, moves the US trade position closer to balance.

Conclusion

A trade war is costly for both the United States and China. While the United States will impose a larger cost on China in the initial years, it will suffer a similar medium-term adverse impact on growth. While both countries have a strong incentive to avoid a trade war because of the economic consequences, there may be circumstances in which policymakers are willing to accept some economic pain to try to change the behaviour of the other party in the pursuit of long-term strategic interests.

From China's perspective, while aggressive fiscal expansion appears to be an attractive policy option in the near term, by offering the most short-term relief, output in the longer term will be compromised. Further, a sharp increase in credit is inconsistent with China's strategic focus on deleveraging. While a diversification of Chinese foreign assets through a redeployment of its US holdings appears to be an attractive strategy prima facie, given it does not compromise the government's balance sheet or long-term prospects, the risks of further escalation makes it a strategy that one would not recommend. The Chinese Government, while occasionally adopting strong rhetoric, has consistently said it is committed to not escalating tensions, so such a provocative move appears relatively unlikely. However, it is wrong to say that China's options for retaliation are solely related to matching tariffs should it be pushed into a very tight corner. All up, we think the current policy approach by the Chinese Government is a sensible and conservative option that cushions the economy adequately in the near to medium terms, while reducing the chances of international repercussions.

References

American Chamber of Commerce in Shanghai (2017), *Market Access Challenges in China*, October 2017, Shanghai: AmCham.

David, J.E. (2019), Trump says he will delay additional China tariffs originally scheduled to start on March 1, *CNBC*, 24 February.

Erken, H., Giesbergen B. and Vreede, I. (2018), Re-assessing the US–China trade war, *Rabobank*, 26 November.

European Central Bank (ECB) (2018), Macroeconomic implications of increasing protectionism, *ECB Economic Bulletin*, June, Frankfurt am Main: ECB.

European Chamber of Commerce (2018), *China: Certain measures on the transfer of technology—Request for consultations by the European Union*, June, Brussels: Directorate-General Trade, European Commission.

Freund, C., Ferrantino, M.J., Maliszewska, M. and Ruta, M. (2018), *Impacts on global trade and income of current trade disputes*, MTI Practice Note No. 2, Washington, DC: World Bank Group.

Hass, R. and Balin, Z. (2019), *US–China relations in the age of artificial intelligence*, Artificial Intelligence and Emerging Technologies Initiative Report, 10 January, Washington, DC: The Brookings Institution.

Henderson, D.W. and McKibbin, W.J. (1993), *A comparison of some basic monetary policy regimes for open economies: Implications of different degrees of instrument adjustment and wage persistence*, International Finance Discussion Papers 458, Washington, DC: Board of Governors of the Federal Reserve System. doi.org/10.1016/0167-2231(93)90011-K.

International Monetary Fund (IMF) (2018), *World Economic Outlook: Challenges to steady growth*, January, Washington, DC: IMF.

Joint Committee on Taxation (2017), *Macroeconomic analysis of the Conference Agreement for H.R.1, the 'Tax Cuts and Jobs Act'*, 22 December, JCX-69-17, Washington, DC: US Congress.

Lee, J. (2018), Exclusive: China not seriously considering U.S. Treasuries as trade war weapon—envoy, *Reuters*, 28 November.

Li, C., He, C. and Lin, C. (2018), Economic impacts of the possible China–US trade war, *Emerging Markets Finance and Trade* 54(7): 1557–77. doi.org/10.1080/154049 6X.2018.1446131.

McKay, H. (2019), *BHP's Economic and Commodity Outlook*, Melbourne: BHP, available from: www.bhp.com/media-and-insights/prospects/2019/02/bhps-economic-and-commodity-outlook.

McKibbin, W.J. (2018), How countries could respond to President Trump's trade war, *Australian Financial Review*, 5 March.

McKibbin, W.J. and Stoeckel, A. (2017), *Some global effects of President Trump's economic program*, Centre for Applied Macroeconomic Analysis Working Paper 53/2017, Canberra: The Australian National University. doi.org/10.2139/ssrn.3028388.

McKibbin, W.J. and Wilcoxen P. (2013), A global approach to energy and the environment: The G-cubed model, in P.B. Dixon and D.W. Jorgenson (eds), *Handbook of Computable General Equilibrium Modeling SET. Volumes 1A and 1B*, Amsterdam: North Holland. doi.org/10.1016/B978-0-444-59568-3.00015-8.

McKibbin, W.J. and Wilcoxen, P.J. (1999), The theoretical and empirical structure of the G-cubed model, *Economic Modelling* 16(1)(January): 123–48. doi.org/10.1016/S0264-9993(98)00035-2.

Meltzer, J.P. (2019), Developing a mutually beneficial US–China economic relationship, *Up Front*, 28 February, Washington, DC: The Brookings Institution.

Meltzer, J.P. and Shenai, N. (2019), *The US–China economic relationship: A comprehensive approach*, Report, 28 February, Washington, DC: The Brookings Institution. doi.org/10.2139/ssrn.3357900.

Politi, J. (2018), Trump's 'poison pill' in China trade fight, *Financial Times*, 9 October.

Sink, J. and Talev, M. (2019), Trump signs spending bill and declares emergency to build wall, *Bloomberg*, 15 February.

State Council Information Office of the People's Republic of China (2018), The facts and China's position on China–US trade friction, 24 September, Beijing.

State Council of the People's Republic of China (2015), Notice on printing and distributing 'Made in China 2025', 8 May, Beijing.

Taylor, J.B. (1993), *Discretion versus policy rules in practice*, Carnegie-Rochester Conference Series on Public Policy 39, Amsterdam: North Holland. doi.org/10.1016/0167-2231(93)90009-L.

United States Trade Representative (2019), *2018 Report to Congress on China's WTO Compliance*, February, Washington, DC: Office of the United States Trade Representative.

Zhou, X. (2016), Managing Multi-Objective Monetary Policy: From the Perspective of Transitioning Chinese Economy. The 2016 Michel Camdessus Central Banking Lecture, International Monetary Fund, Washington, DC, 24 June.

12. Inequality of opportunity and gender discrimination in China's labour income

Jane Golley, Yixiao Zhou and Meiyan Wang

Income inequality has been a persistent feature of China's rapid growth and development since the late 1970s. A vast literature has emerged to explain these inequalities along a number of dimensions, including regional and rural–urban disparities and intergenerational persistence in virtually all measures of 'economic advantage', be they per capita GDP, household income and wealth, individual earnings or educational attainment.[1] While Deng Xiaoping famously justified these inequalities by arguing that some regions and people would need to become rich first before all could eventually prosper, he surely did not envisage, nor seek to justify, a gender divide in this argument—in which men would become rich first and women would only eventually prosper. Yet a growing body of evidence suggests that this gender divide not only exists, but also is widening.

A gender earnings gap has persisted in urban China throughout the reform period—and has, in fact, grown since the mid-1990s—despite a narrowing of the gender gap in educational attainment in recent years, to the point where women now out-educate men, on average.[2] A wide literature has confirmed that most of the earnings gap is attributable to gender discrimination, rather than observable factors such as gender differences in human capital or occupational choices.[3] In rural China, gaps in both education and earnings are even more substantial.[4] Rozelle et al. (2002) find that market reforms did little to affect the gender earnings gap in the rural economy, and they attribute much of the (relatively stable) gap between 1988 and 1995 to 'unexplained factors' or wage discrimination. Meng (1998), while finding some reduction in wage discrimination in the most marketised sectors of Chinese rural industry in the mid-1980s, found that it still accounted for two-thirds of the wage differential in these sectors, leading her to conclude that China's

---

1   We cannot do justice to this literature here. See Knight (2014) and Zhou and Song (2016) for recent overviews; Gustafsson et al. (2008) and Li et al. (2013) for comprehensive discussions across many dimensions; Kanbur and Zhang (2005) and Golley (2007) on regional inequalities; Sicular et al. (2007) on rural–urban inequalities; Piketty et al. (2017) on wealth inequality; and Golley and Kong (2018) on intergenerational inequalities in education.
2   For evidence, see Golley and Kong (2018); Li (2010); and Zhang and Chen (2014).
3   See, for example, Li et al. (2011); Wang and Cai (2008); and Zhang et al. (2008a).
4   See, for example, Hannum et al. (2009); Zhang et al. (2007); and Zhang et al. (2012).

gender wage discrimination was much more serious than in other industrial and developing economies. We have found no evidence to suggest that the situation for rural Chinese women has improved since then.

Female participation in the labour market has deteriorated during the reform period as well, with, for example, the urban female labour force participation rate dropping to 57 per cent in 2009 from 78 per cent in 1988 (Zhang et al. 2008a). Cook and Dong (2011) attribute this to the intensified pressures on women arising from their dual responsibilities as (unpaid) family carers and income earners during the economic transition. Zhang et al. (2008b) concur on this point, demonstrating that the observed gender earnings gap is strongly related to family status, with married women and mothers facing the most significant disadvantages in the (urban) labour market. Liu et al. (2010) likewise demonstrate the reduction in employment probability and hours of paid work for Chinese women, with the most striking costs being imposed by caring for one's parents-in-law, not one's own parents. The costs of child and elder care imposed on China's female labour force vary across urban, migrant and rural groups, but there is ample recent evidence that none of these groups is immune (Connelly et al. 2018; Ding et al. 2018; Song and Dong 2018).

There is also evidence of a growing gender bias in the political realm. During the 1980s and 1990s, women accounted for one-third of Communist Party members, while by 2017 they accounted for just one-quarter. Shu and Bian (2003) examine the importance of 'political capital'—proxied by Communist Party membership—as a determinant of the gender earnings gap. Noting that party members are more likely to be promoted and receive sponsorship for further education and training, they show that Communist Party membership was associated with earnings that were 6 per cent and 10 per cent higher for men and women, respectively, in 1995. However, the higher return for women did not reduce the earnings gap because of lower female membership numbers overall. Appleton et al. (2009) reveal an increasing wage reward for party membership—from 29 per cent in 1988 to 33 per cent in 1999—despite their initial expectations that they would fall, as market forces became more dominant. These findings suggest that party membership still matters for earnings, and it matters in different ways for men and for women.

Against this background, this chapter sets out to explore the factors that have contributed to inequality of opportunity in China's individual labour income, with a particular focus on gender. Inequality of opportunity is broadly defined as the component of overall inequality that can be explained by 'circumstances' beyond the control of an individual, as distinct from 'efforts' or choices that those individuals make. This distinction is crucial because, while inequality stemming from the latter can be justified as being fair and reasonable, inequality stemming from the former— for example, being born male or female—cannot. We utilise the standard method in a burgeoning literature on inequality of opportunity to reveal that China's inequality of opportunity in labour income is alarmingly high. Furthermore, we show that gender is the number one determinant of unequal opportunities, ahead of socioeconomic, regional and urban–rural divides.

We complement this analysis with a more standard micro-level analysis of the underlying causes of gender earnings inequality. We use a standard Oaxaca–Blinder decomposition, in which differences between male and female incomes are apportioned into differences between male and female coefficients (the 'unexplained' portion, broadly interpreted as gender discrimination) and differences between male and female characteristics (the 'explained' portion), which comprise the circumstance and effort variables used in the inequality of opportunity analysis.[5] This reveals that discrimination explains the dominant proportion of differences in average labour income between males and females, with gender differences in the rewards associated with marriage being the most significant contributing factor.

Inequality of opportunity, circumstances and effort

Background

The economic literature on 'inequality of opportunity' begins with the premise that the observed inequality in any particular economic outcome, or 'advantage', can be attributed to two components. The first component derives from the different circumstances in which individuals find themselves and over which they have no control—for example, their gender, place of birth or the socioeconomic status of their parents. The second derives from the different levels of effort that individuals may exert to influence a given outcome—for example, how hard they study, the occupation they choose or whether they choose to migrate or marry. This distinction is critical for assessing the extent to which equal opportunity does or does not prevail.

Roemer (1993, 1998) defines equal opportunity as a situation in which the distribution of a given outcome is independent of circumstances—that is, all individuals who exert the same level of effort will achieve the same outcome, regardless of their circumstances. Partitioning the population into groups of people—or 'types'—with identical circumstances and measuring the extent to which this condition is *not* satisfied provide one measure of inequality of opportunity. This involves suppressing 'intra-type' inequality (the inequality that can be explained by variation within each type, attributed to variation in 'effort') and calculating the extent of 'inter-type' inequality based on the mean levels for each type as an absolute measure of inequality

---

5   See Oaxaca (1973) and Blinder (1973), along with three examples of applications to China by Song et al. (2017), Su and Heshmati (2011) and Démurger et al. (2007).

of opportunity. For comparability across different datasets and countries, it is more common to focus on the share of 'inter-type' inequality in overall inequality or the 'relative inequality of opportunity' (IOR).

A variety of empirical methods has been used to estimate inequality of opportunity for a wide range of outcomes, including household per capita income and consumption expenditure (as in Marrero and Rodríguez 2012); individual annual, monthly and long-run incomes (for example, by Bourguignon et al. 2007; Checchi et al. 2010; Björkland et al. 2012); educational attainment (as in the application to China in Golley and Kong 2016); and health outcomes (as in Jusot et al. 2013). Those focusing specifically on income inequality reveal significant variation in the share of inequality of opportunity in total income inequality (at both the household and the individual levels), ranging from close to one-third in Brazil and Guatemala (Ferreira and Gignoux 2011) to one-quarter for India (Singh 2012) and below 5 per cent in Norway, Denmark, Finland, Germany, the Netherlands and Slovakia (Marrero and Rodríguez 2012).[6]

While a number of different circumstances have been identified in these studies, a predominant set has emerged. These include father's (or parents') occupation and education; geographical location (region of birth, for single-country analyses; country of birth for cross-country ones); race, ethnicity or caste (in the case of India); and gender. Gender, however, has not been the primary focus in any of these works. Instead, for individual-level analyses, male-only samples tend to be used, with only a few exceptions. For example, Ferreira and Gignoux (2011) include gender as a circumstance in their analysis of individual labour earnings for five Latin American countries, and find that the share of overall inequality attributed to gender is small— from just 0.2 per cent in Colombia to 5.8 per cent in Guatemala—with other family background circumstances being more important, particularly parental education and father's occupation. De Barros et al. (2009) find a similar share for gender in the inequality of individual labour earnings in Mexico, at 3–4 per cent. Martinez et al. (2017) also use gender as a circumstance in their analysis of Australian individual income inequality between 2001 and 2013, revealing rising gender disparities over that period, but still a relatively small contribution of gender to overall income inequality, of less than 6 per cent (compared with more than 50 per cent for father's occupation—the most important circumstance). These small contributions contrast starkly with the dominant role we find for gender in the empirical analysis for China that follows.

In these cited works, the role of 'effort' has been largely overlooked, with the predominant estimation method (explained further below) subsuming this into the error term. One notable exception is Bourguignon et al. (2007), a much-cited

---

6 See Brunori et al. (2013) and Ferreira and Peragine (2015) for more comprehensive surveys of the methods used and results found.

paper that examines individual (male) real hourly earnings across seven birth cohorts in Brazil. Their analysis explicitly considers the relationship between circumstances (race, region of birth, parental schooling and father's occupation) and three 'effort' variables—the individual's own schooling attainment, a migration dummy and a variable for labour market status—all of which are assumed to be determined, in turn, by circumstances. Despite some subsequent problems with the paper (conceded in a 2011 corrigendum), this paper was seminal in its attempt to identify both the direct effect of circumstances on earnings (or other outcomes) and the indirect effect as it operated through 'effort'.

Measuring inequality of opportunity

To formalise the ideas discussed above, we follow Roemer (1998) and begin with a finite population of individuals, $i \in \{1,...,N\}$, each of whom has achieved an economic outcome (in our case, annual labour earnings), y_i, with distribution $\{y_i\}$. Earnings are assumed to be determined by a vector of circumstances, C_i, and a vector of efforts, E_i, which will be at least partially determined by circumstances, implying that $y_i = f(C_i, E_i(C_i, v_i), u_i)$. The sample population can then be divided into 'types', which by definition contain individuals with identical circumstances.

In principle, it is straightforward to calculate an *absolute* scalar measure of inequality of opportunity, *IOA*, by assigning to every individual the mean for their type (and thereby suppressing all intra-type inequality) and measuring the inequality in the distribution of those means using an appropriate index of inequality. The associated relative measure, *IOR*, is then *IOA* as a share of total inequality. However, this simple nonparametric method requires a sample size far beyond what is available to us, or a significant reduction in the number of circumstances so as to limit the number of 'types'—a trade-off we are not willing to make. Instead, we use the standard parametric method, explained at length in Bourguignon et al. (2007) and Ferreira and Gignoux (2011), and summarised here.

We begin by approximating the relationship between earnings, circumstances and effort with the following structural forms (Equations 12.1 and 12.2).

Equation 12.1

$$\ln(y_i) = a + bC_i + cE_i + u_i$$

Equation 12.2

$$E_i = d + eC_i + v_i$$

Substituting Equation 12.2 into Equation 12.1 yields the reduced-form regression of Equation 12.3.

Equation 12.3

$$\ln(y_i) = \alpha + \beta C_i + \varepsilon_i$$

In Equation 12.3, $\alpha = a + cd$, $\beta = b + ce$, $\varepsilon = cv_i + u_i$; y is labour earnings and C is a vector of discrete circumstance variables, which can be partitioned into 'types'. Using the estimated coefficients, $\hat{\beta}$, and the actual values of circumstances, we construct a distribution, $\{\hat{y}\}$, where $\hat{y}_i = \exp[\hat{\beta}C_i]$. By replacing each y_i with its prediction, *given the vector of circumstances* (which is identical for all individuals of the same type), all intra-group inequality is eliminated, giving direct estimates of inequality of opportunity, $IOA = I(\{\hat{y}\})$ and $IOR = I(\{\hat{y}\})/I(\{y\})$, where $I(\cdot)$ is an appropriate index of inequality. Following standard practice, we choose mean log deviation GE(0) as our inequality index.[7]

The vector of observed circumstances will only be a subset of all relevant circumstances that impact on individual earnings. As long as some unobserved circumstances are correlated with the observed circumstances (for example, IQ, which is almost certainly correlated with one's father's education and one's own earnings, but is not observed in the data), the estimated $\hat{\beta}$ coefficients will be biased and cannot be interpreted as causal links between a given circumstance and the outcome. However, for the overall measure of inequality of opportunity, this is not important: adding more circumstance variables to the observed set would necessarily increase the estimates of IOA and IOR, implying that these are *lower-bound* estimates of the 'true' inequality of opportunity that would be measured if all circumstance variables could be observed (Ferreira and Gignoux 2011).

In addition to these overall measures, we are interested in the partial contributions of each of the circumstance variables. A number of papers have continued to use the method put forward by Bourguignon et al. (2007), despite their 2011 corrigendum in which they conceded the measure was flawed. We improve on this method by instead using a Shapley-value decomposition, which involves turning one variable (such as gender) 'on' or 'off' (for example, by setting at 'male' for all individuals) and assessing how the overall inequality measure varies accordingly. This method accounts for the well-known problem that inequality decompositions depend on the order in which inequality from a particular source is measured, and so uses a normalised average across all possible orderings for each source. That said, we recognise that these partial results should be treated with caution, given the biases already acknowledged above.

The above method suffices for calculating IOA and IOR, and for identifying a set of circumstances that contribute to these. While this has become the dominant focus in the literature, there is more to learn from including some observable efforts in

---

7   For details on why this is the best measure, see Ferreira and Gignoux (2011).

the modelling exercise, as done in the seminal paper by Bourguignon et al. (2007). Returning to the structural form presented in Equations 12.1 and 12.2, it is clear that an individual's labour earnings depend on his or her circumstances through two distinct channels: a *direct* channel (reflected in the coefficients on each circumstance in Equation 12.1); and an *indirect* channel, via the effect of his or her circumstances on his or her effort in Equation 12.2. Bourguignon et al. (2007) attempted to separately estimate these direct and indirect effects in their application to male earnings in Brazil, but subsequently conceded their results were not statistically sound. While this means that Equations 12.1 and 12.2 cannot be used in the way originally intended, they are still useful for illustrating the complex link between circumstances and some identifiable 'effort' variables—and for demonstrating that these complex links work in different ways for different genders.

Inequality of opportunity: Data and results

Data and baseline regressions

We use the third wave of the Survey of Chinese Women's Social Status (2010), which is organised by the Women's Studies Institute of China, with joint sponsorship from the All-China Women's Federation and the National Bureau of Statistics of China. The complete database includes 29,694 observations from all 31 of China's provinces, each of which contains information on a randomly selected adult and child within each household. We choose annual labour income (or earnings) as our outcome of interest, including in the sample all individuals aged between 26 and 55 years of age with non-zero income. This yields a nationwide sample of 15,974 individuals. Individuals are divided into six age cohorts (from 26–30-year-olds through to 51–55-year-olds) to enable a comparison across those age groups (albeit not across time), which is the best available option for a single-country cross-sectional dataset.[8]

Drawing on the inequality of opportunity literature and the China-specific inequality literature cited above, we use the following set of circumstance variables for each of the six age cohorts:

1. Gender: male or female (female excluded in regressions).
2. Father's education: illiterate, primary school, junior high school and above (illiterate excluded).

---

8 The first and second waves of the Survey of Chinese Women's Social Status were completed in 1990 and 2000, respectively. If we are able to obtain these at a later stage, we will complement this work with analysis across two decades of reform.

3. Father's occupation: agriculture (including forestry and fisheries), low-skilled non-agriculture, high-skilled non-agriculture (agriculture excluded).

4. *Hukou* (household registration) status at birth: rural or urban (rural excluded).[9]

5. Region: east, central and west (west excluded).[10]

In combination, this implies that for each age cohort we are dealing with 108 types, in the 'comfortable' range of 72–108 types, according to Ferreira and Peragine (2015). For example, one type (a relatively 'unlucky' one, as it turns out) comprises rural females born in western China with illiterate fathers who work in agriculture. In the nationwide regressions for the entire sample, age cohorts are included as the sixth 'circumstance'—as one clearly cannot choose the year in which they are born.

We draw on Bourguignon et al. (2007) and the data available in the survey, to propose the following five 'effort' variables:

1. Own education: a dummy variable for those who have attained junior high or below, or senior high school and above.

2. Own occupation: a dummy variable representing those who work in the agricultural or non-agricultural sector.

3. Migration: a dummy variable for those who have 'ever worked or ran a business in a town or city different from where your *hukou* is for more than half a year' or who have 'never migrated'.

4. Communist Party membership (dummy variable for yes or no).

5. Marital status (married or not married, with the latter including people who have never married, are divorced or whose spouse has died).

One's own education is included to reflect the fact that schooling above junior high has never been compulsory in China, and to some extent reflects an individual's choice (although, as it turns out, a substantial part of that choice, or 'effort', is explained by one's circumstances). Likewise, it is also a matter of choice, to some extent at least, to migrate and/or work in occupations outside the agricultural sector. Communist Party membership is included to reflect the effort required to gain such membership, which may relate to one's political connections (*guanxi*), alongside the reasons identified by Shu and Bian (2003) and Appleton et al. (2009). The inclusion of marital status is in recognition of the fact that couples have interdependent

---

9   The survey includes village, town, town–city and city; 'rural' is equated with 'village', while the others are all classified as 'non-rural'.

10 We use the standard regional classifications for this. Ideally, we would have region of birth as this variable, but this is not available in the survey, so we use region identified at the time of the survey. While this is problematic in the sense that some people will have migrated since birth (a matter of choice, not circumstance), this only accounts for 9 per cent of the surveyed individuals. We considered this a reasonable sacrifice given the significant regional variations in levels of development across China and the standard practice of including 'region' as a circumstance in the comparable literature.

preferences that affect their household income decisions, in ways that often imply different employment choices for men and women, as shown in Zhang et al. (2008b) in the case of China.[11]

Table 12.1 presents the summary statistics for the nationwide sample and the female and male subsamples. Nearly everything is consistent with expectations. In terms of circumstances, people born in urban areas in eastern China, who have more-educated fathers in non-agricultural occupations out-earn those in relevant categories 'below' them, and average earnings fall across the age range, consistent with higher average educational attainments among younger generations. One outlier is that average income in the western region is higher than in the centre—underpinned by higher female (but not male) income in the west. In terms of 'effort', higher levels of education, non-agricultural occupations, Communist Party membership and non-migration are associated with higher income (because almost all migrants are from rural areas, where earnings are lower). Notably, marriage is associated with higher average income for men, but lower income for women—a point we return to below.

Table 12.1 Preliminary statistics: Labour income by gender, circumstance and 'effort'

	Nationwide	Females	Males	Female/male ratio
Number of individuals	15,974	7,592	8,382	
Mean labour income (RMB)	19,696	15,241	23,730	0.64
CIRCUMSTANCE VARIABLES				
Father's education				
Illiterate	12,877	8,658	16,374	0.53
Primary school	18,785	12,922	23,975	0.54
Junior high and above	26,090	22,435	29,732	0.75
Father's occupation				
Agriculture, forestry and fishery	15,532	11,481	19,223	0.60
Low-skill non-agricultural	26,195	21,647	30,113	0.72
High-skill non-agricultural	30,760	23,864	37,407	0.64
Born in				
Rural	16,843	12,220	21,070	0.58
Urban	26,512	22,583	29,992	0.75
Birth region				
East	24,089	18,083	29,164	0.62
Central	15,149	11,056	18,994	0.58
West	16,432	14,550	18,277	0.80

11 We leave aside the (important) debate as to whether Becker's (1974, 1976, 1991) view of these choices is credible or not (as made clear in Bergmann 1995; and Woolley 1996). For our purposes, it suffices to say that marriage has notably different associations with the earnings of women and men, as seen below.

	Nationwide	Females	Males	Female/male ratio
Age cohorts				
26–30	27,477	23,660	31,162	0.76
31–35	22,128	16,557	27,984	0.59
36–40	18,949	15,456	22,358	0.69
41–45	18,589	14,301	22,777	0.63
46–50	17,703	12,547	22,108	0.57
51–55	15,714	9,477	19,572	0.48
EFFORT VARIABLES				
Own education				
Junior high or below	13,531	9,372	17,662	0.53
Senior high school and above	29,029	25,296	31,966	0.79
Own occupation				
Agriculture, forestry and fishery	8,566	6,327	11,055	0.57
Non-agricultural	26,011	21,210	29,879	0.71
Political party				
No Communist Party membership	18,126	14,107	22,117	0.64
Communist Party member	28,577	24,506	30,722	0.80
Migration status				
Ever migrated	18,387	10,779	24,161	0.45
Never migrated	19,818	15,618	23,686	0.66
Marital status				
Married	19,543	14,867	23,828	0.62
Not married	21,235	19,294	22,800	0.85

Notes: Sample includes all surveyed individuals with non-zero labour income. 'Non-agricultural low-skill occupations' include craft and related trade workers, service and sales workers and clerical support. 'Non-agricultural high-skill occupations' include professionals and managers. 'Rural' is equated with 'village' and 'urban' with all other classifications: town, town–city and city.

Sources: Survey of Chinese Women's Social Status (2010) and authors' calculations.

What is most striking in Table 12.1 is the gender difference, summarised by the female/male earnings ratios in the final column. Gender inequality exists for every circumstance and at both ends of the socioeconomic spectrum—although the ratios are noticeably lower at the lower end of the spectrum. Some of these disparities may reflect the fact that women work fewer hours, which, given different retirement ages, is certainly the case for the oldest cohort, which has the lowest female/ male earnings ratio of just 0.48. Another explanation is likely to be the different occupational structures for men and women—for example, 40 per cent of women work in agriculture, compared with 28 per cent of men (on which more below). But this is not the whole story. And even if it was, it would still point to inequality of opportunity in annual labour, which is an important story in its own right.

Table 12.2 presents the regression results for the nationwide sample, with Column 1 including only the circumstance variables, as in Equation 12.3, and Column 2 extending this to include the 'effort' variables as well, as in Equation 12.1. As seen in Column 1, being male is associated with labour earnings that are 0.54 log points higher than females.[12] All coefficients take on their expected signs and relative magnitudes—for example, they are increasing with father's education and occupation, with urban *hukou* status and from west to east. The age profile now exhibits the expected inverted-U shape (in contrast with the raw data).

Table 12.2 Determinants of labour earnings: Circumstance and effort

Independent variables	Equation 12.3	Equation 12.1	Equation 12.1	Equation 12.1
Circumstance variables			Females	Males
Male	0.54***	0.44***		
Father primary	0.22***	0.11***	0.11***	0.12***
Father junior high and above	0.34***	0.14***	0.15***	0.13***
Father low-skill non-agricultural	0.30***	0.035	0.057*	0.017
Father high-skill non-agricultural	0.41***	0.13***	0.13***	0.14***
Urban	0.35***	0.058**	0.10***	0.016
Central region	0.09***	0.02***	-0.07***	0.12***
Eastern region	0.42***	0.29***	0.18***	0.40***
Age dummies	YES	YES	YES	YES
Effort variables				
Non-agricultural occupation		0.76***	0.79***	0.72***
Senior high and above		0.38***	0.44***	0.31***
Communist Party membership		0.20***	0.22***	0.19***
Migration		0.092***	0.023	0.14***
Married		0.16***	0.065	0.26***
Constant	8.9***	8.34***	8.35***	8.81***
Observations	15,974	15,974	7,592	8,382
Adjusted R²	0.248	0.400	0.392	0.337

* p < 0.05 ** p < 0.01 *** p < 0.005

Sources: Survey of Chinese Women's Social Status (2010) and authors' calculations.

As seen in Column 2, adding in the effort variables yields a considerable increase in the adjusted R-squared values, with the bulk of this increase coming from own occupation and own education, and only minor increases for Communist Party

---

12 For the log-linear form, the difference between the excluded dummy, x (e.g. male), and the included one, y (e.g. female), is given by $\ln(x) - \ln(y) = \ln(x/y)$. If x differs from y by a factor of $1 + e$, then $\ln(x/y) = \ln(1 + e)$, which is approximately e, the percentage difference between x and y, but only when e is small. The exact percentage change is given by $\exp(e - 1)$, which for the example given here amounts to 75 per cent.

membership, migration and marriage.[13] Working in a non-agricultural occupation is associated with earnings that are 0.68 log points higher than working in agriculture, while having senior high school education or above is associated with a 0.35 log point income boost. The coefficients on Communist Party membership and migration are positive and significant, but small.

As expected, coefficients on many of the circumstances fall compared with those in Column 1—an indication of the correlations between these and the two key effort variables of own education and own occupation (although none is too high to suggest multicollinearity as a serious problem). For example, the coefficient on having a father with more than junior high education falls from 0.41 to 0.14 due to the correlation between this and one's own education. Being male continues to have the highest positive association with income for the nationwide sample.

Columns 3 and 4 present the results for the female and male subsamples, respectively. The substantial gender differences seen in Table 12.1 are confirmed even with all controls added. The adjusted R-squared for the female subsample is considerably higher than for men, and the same is true when only circumstances are included in the regression (not presented here for space reasons). This provides the first indication that women's earnings are affected (that is, constrained) more by their circumstances than men's. This is also suggested by the higher magnitudes of most coefficients in the female regressions—more than double that for men for being born 'urban' and with higher returns for having educated fathers working outside agriculture as well.

The rewards for women associated with putting in the 'effort' to leave agriculture, attain senior high education and gain Communist Party membership are all higher than for men, while migration and marriage offer no significant returns for women, but do for men. The key point is that all of these circumstance and effort variables matter, and they matter in different ways for the two genders.

To calculate the inequality of opportunity in labour income, we focus on Equation 12.3 using the method described above. We are also interested in how this varies across age cohorts, so we first present, in Table 12.3, the baseline results for each age cohort. This confirms the significance of being male for all cohorts, with higher coefficients for older cohorts. Given the cross-sectional nature of the data, it is impossible to say whether this is because of an improvement in gender biases in income for younger cohorts or a deterioration with age as the circumstance of being male culminates in higher rewards.

---

13 In regressions adding these effort variables separately to the nationwide sample, the adjusted R-squared increases from 0.248 (Column 1, Table 12.2) to 0.367 for one's own occupation; 0.310 for one's own education; 0.272 for Communist Party membership; 0.250 for marriage; and negligible for migration.

Table 12.3 'Circumstantial' determinants of labour income by age cohort

Cohort	26–30	31–35	36–40	41–45	46–50	51–55
Independent variables						
Male	0.42***	0.49***	0.51***	0.51***	0.61***	0.69***
Father primary	0.21**	0.28***	0.24***	0.24***	0.18***	0.22***
Father junior high and above	0.33***	0.45***	0.40***	0.40***	0.29***	0.21**
Father low-skill non-agricultural	0.46***	0.35***	0.28***	0.28***	0.16**	0.27***
Father high-skill non-agricultural	0.61***	0.44***	0.46***	0.46***	0.34***	0.34***
Urban	0.25***	0.30***	0.28***	0.28***	0.36***	0.58***
Central region	0.04***	0.11***	0.10***	0.10***	0.10***	0.09***
Eastern region	0.45***	0.48***	0.40***	0.40***	0.45***	0.37***
Constant	8.97***	8.96***	8.89***	8.89***	8.83***	8.43***
Observations	1,889	2,336	3,460	3,460	2,839	2,125
Adjusted R^2	0.249	0.261	0.231	0.231	0.232	0.279

* $p < 0.05$ ** $p < 0.01$ *** $p < 0.005$

Sources: Survey of Chinese Women's Social Status (2010) and authors' calculations.

We use the regression results in Column 1 of Table 12.2 and all of Table 12.3 to calculate the inequality of opportunity in China's labour income. These results are presented in Table 12.4. The top two rows provide scalar measures of inequality in labour income using GE(0) and the Gini coefficient, for the nationwide sample and for each cohort. Gini coefficients are included to stress the point that income inequality across this sample is undeniably high—above 0.5 in all but two of the age cohort subsamples.

Table 12.4 Inequality of opportunity in labour income and decomposition by circumstance

	All	By birth cohort					
		26–30	31–35	36–40	41–45	46–50	51–55
Total inequality							
Mean log deviation (GE(0))	0.55	0.70	0.50	0.46	0.52	0.51	0.62
Gini	0.53	0.59	0.51	0.55	0.52	0.51	0.56
Inequality of opportunity							
Absolute (IOA)	0.14	0.14	0.14	0.12	0.07	0.13	0.13
Relative (IOR)	0.25	0.20	0.28	0.26	0.14	0.25	0.21
	Shapley-value decomposition (contribution to IOA, %)						
Gender	28	30.0	34.2	22.6	38.0	37.9	32.4
Father education type	18	10.0	14.4	20.0	13.5	11.9	12.9
Father occupation type	18	31.3	22.7	22.8	17.7	13.1	16.0
Born rural or not	9	1.9	7.3	13.0	18.3	7.2	17.5

	All	By birth cohort					
		26–30	31–35	36–40	41–45	46–50	51–55
Region	18	24.9	21.5	21.7	12.5	29.9	21.2
Age cohort	10						

Sources: Survey of Chinese Women's Social Status (2010) and authors' calculations.

The *IOR* provides the best gauge in terms of international comparisons to assert the point that the share of inequality of opportunity in total inequality in China's individual labour income is unquestionably high—with an *IOR* value of 0.25 (or 25 per cent) for the nationwide sample, and with all cohort-level *IOR*s above 0.2, with just one exception. This in itself is a major concern. But what is even more worrying are the Shapley-value decompositions, which reflect the partial contributions from each of the circumstances to the overall *IOA* (or *IOR*). These reveal that gender is the circumstance with the single largest contribution to inequality of opportunity in individual labour income, accounting for 28 per cent of the nationwide *IOA* (Column 1). This is followed by one's region, father's occupation, father's education, birth cohort and being rural or urban, in that order. For four of the six birth cohorts, gender is the largest contributor to inequality of opportunity, peaking at 38 per cent for the 41–45-year-old cohort. It ranks second for the two remaining cohorts (ages 26–30 and 36–40)—below father's occupation in both cases. Even if these calculations are biased by omitted variables—as they undoubtedly are—and reflect to some extent women's 'choices' about labour market participation, occupations and hours worked, as well as other unobserved characteristics that make men and women different, we argue that this finding should be taken seriously and investigated further.

One way of pushing the importance of gender further is to consider the relationship between each 'effort' variable and circumstances and how these differ across the male and female subsamples. Table 12.5 presents the results of probit regressions for each of the binary effort variables conditioned on the set of circumstance variables, as in Equation 12.2. Nearly all coefficients take on their expected signs and relative magnitudes. For example, as seen in Columns 1 and 2 for all three panels, individuals with more educated fathers in non-agricultural occupations are likely to be more educated and work in non-agricultural occupations themselves. Columns 4 and 5 of Panel A reveal that men are more likely to migrate but less likely to be married than women (reflecting the unbalanced sex ratio). Critically, the pseudo R-squared values are highest for the own education and own occupation regressions in Columns 1 and 2, and both of these are higher for the female subsample (in Panel B) than the male subsample (in Panel C), underpinned by larger magnitudes on just about all coefficients in the female subsample regressions. This indicates that circumstances matter more for women, not only directly (in that they are essentially penalised for their gender), but also indirectly, through their effect on prominent and identifiable forms of 'effort'.

Table 12.5 Probit regressions of 'efforts' determined by circumstances

Circumstances	Own education	Own occupation	Communist Party membership	Migration	Marriage
Panel A: Nationwide					
Male	0.20***	0.28***	0.37***	0.14***	−0.063*
Father primary	0.33***	0.20***	0.24***	0.013	0.16***
Father junior high and above	0.75***	0.35***	0.48***	−0.11*	0.15***
Father low-skill non-agricultural	0.49***	1.15***	0.12***	−0.25***	−0.14***
Father high-skill non-agricultural	0.71***	0.78***	0.30***	−0.22***	−0.068
Urban	0.74***	1.25***	0.20***	−0.87***	−0.38***
Central region	0.11**	0.21***	0.11	0.05***	0.199
Eastern region	0.19***	0.49***	0.091**	−0.16***	0.13***
Observations	15,974	15,974	15,974	15,974	15,974
Pseudo R²	0.214	0.280	0.059	0.097	0.062
Panel B: Female					
Father primary	0.32***	0.28***	0.27***	0.071	0.082
Father junior high and above	0.77***	0.44***	0.52***	−0.064	0.026
Father low-skill non-agricultural	0.63***	1.07***	0.22***	−0.27***	−0.21***
Father high-skill non-agricultural	0.75***	0.76***	0.30***	−0.29**	−0.099
Urban	0.87***	1.30***	0.34***	−0.81***	−0.48***
Central region	0.05**	0.15***	0.027	0.13***	0.16**
Eastern region	0.16***	0.53***	0.082	−0.16**	−0.0046
Observations	7,592	7,592	7,592	7,592	7,592
Pseudo R²	0.269	0.303	0.072	0.099	0.071
Panel C: Male					
Father primary	0.35***	0.13***	0.24***	−0.030	0.21***
Father junior high and above	0.73***	0.27***	0.46***	−0.14*	0.25***
Father low-skill non-agricultural	0.38***	1.25***	0.052	−0.23***	−0.087
Father high-skill non-agricultural	0.68***	0.81***	0.31***	−0.17	−0.030
Urban	0.62***	1.20***	0.093*	−0.91***	−0.33***
Central region	0.15	0.27***	0.17	−0.03**	0.227
Eastern region	0.21***	0.46***	0.099*	−0.17***	0.24***
Observations	8,382	8,382	8,382	8,382	8,382
Pseudo R²	0.172	0.256	0.037	0.097	0.075

*** $p < 0.01$ ** $p < 0.05$ * $p < 0.1$

Sources: Survey of Chinese Women's Social Status (2010) and authors' calculations.

From inequality of opportunity to gender discrimination

To further analyse the underlying causes of gender income inequality, we apply an Oaxaca–Blinder decomposition to the estimate of Equation 12.1, which is essentially an extended Mincer-type equation in which the combined set of circumstance and 'effort' variables comprises the individual characteristics that determine one's own income.[14] This apportions differences between male and female labour incomes into two parts: first, the differences between the male and female coefficients in two separate regressions for the male and female subsamples (as seen in the last two columns of Table 12.2 for the nationwide sample),[15] which form the 'unexplained' portion, used as a proxy for gender discrimination; and second, differences between male and female characteristics (the 'explained' portion), such as different levels of educational attainment.

Specifically, the gender earnings gap is the difference between average male income and average female income (Equation 12.4).

Equation 12.4

$$G = \overline{lny}(x_m; \gamma_m) - \overline{lny}(x_f; \gamma_f) = D + E$$

In Equation 12.4, γ_m is the vector of coefficients in Equation 12.1 for the male-only sample and γ_f is that for the female-only sample,[16] $D = \overline{lny}(x_m; \gamma_m) - \overline{lny}(x_m; \gamma_f)$ and $E = \overline{lny}(x_m; \gamma_f) - \overline{lny}(x_f; \gamma_f)$.

This decomposition corresponds to an evaluation of what the observed male/female income gap would be under the following conditions:

1. If men and women share the same sociodemographic characteristics (that of men in Equation 12.1), D is the pure difference-in-coefficients (or discrimination) effect.

2. If men and women face the same remuneration structure (that of women in Equation 12.1), E is the pure difference-in-characteristics effect.

---

14 The approach taken here is similar to that in Démurger et al. (2007).
15 A slight difference is that the regressions used for this decomposition categorise an individual's occupation to be consistent with those for father's occupation. This is because there are too few urban people working in agriculture (the dummy chosen for own occupation in Table 12.2). The more refined set of categories here is thus required for the urban and rural analyses, which adds an important dimension to our story, as seen below.
16 γ_m and γ_f correspond to the coefficients a, b and c in Equation 12.1 for the male-only sample and the female-only sample, respectively.

We further decompose both the pure discrimination effect, D, and the pure difference-in-characteristics effect, E, into contributions from each of the variables included in the regressions for the nationwide sample (as seen in Table 12.2), as well as for the urban and rural subsamples.[17]

Table 12.6 presents the decomposition results. The first point to make is that discrimination—that is, income differences stemming from differences in coefficients rather than characteristics—explains the dominant proportion of the nationwide gender gap, accounting for 86.8 per cent of the (log) income differential, with the remaining 14.6 per cent attributed to differences in characteristics. For the latter, the shares attributable to individual variables reveal dominant contributions from men's higher average levels of education and greater likelihood of being employed in non-agricultural occupations. In terms of the discrimination, one's marital status is associated with significantly higher income for males than females (accounting for 37.8 per cent of the discrimination effect, respectively), while differences in the returns to education and non-agricultural employment actually work in women's favour (with shares of –8.1 and –11.9 per cent, respectively).

Table 12.6 Oaxaca–Blinder decomposition of gender labour income differential

	Nationwide	Urban	Rural
Observed Ln labour income			
Men	9.59	9.95	9.44
Women	9.06	9.66	8.82
Differential	0.53	0.29	0.62
Decomposition shares (%)			
Difference in characteristics	14.6	–13.6	19.1
Discrimination	86.8	109.3	84.6
Share in difference-in-characteristics effect (%)			
Age	–16.9***	25.2	–7.9***
Own education	25.0***	24.0	24.5***
Own occupation	70.3***	56.3**	69.2***
Migration	0.6	0.0	0.0
Married	–0.9	–3.5	–1.4
Communist Party membership	16.8***	–19.5***	11.4***
Region	8.4**	–9.8	5.7**
Father's education	–4.6**	22.1**	–2.4*
Father's occupation	0.04	4.4	–0.3
Born non-rural	0.7		

---

17 For space reasons, we don't report the urban and rural regression results used for these decompositions. They are available from the authors on request.

	Nationwide	Urban	Rural
Share in discrimination effect (%)			
Age	−0.8	−0.1	−1
Own education	−8.1**	−10.6	-5.6**
Own occupation	−11.9**	−31.3	−8.5***
Migration	2.2**	2.0*	2.3*
Married	37.8***	−13.7	58.5***
Communist Party membership	−0.6	0.5	−0.4
Region	−15.9***	−10.4	−17.4***
Father's education	0.3	−23.1	0.9
Father's occupation	−1.1	3.6	−0.6
Born non-rural	−4.3		
Constant	102.2***	183.3***	72.0***

Sources: Survey of Chinese Women's Social Status (2010) and authors' calculations.

The results in Columns 2 and 3 reveal significant variations between the sources of the gender income gap in the urban and rural subsamples. For example, for the urban sample discrimination in fact contributes over 100 per cent to the gender income gap, because the difference-in-characteristics effect is negative (at −11.9 per cent)—that is, it *reduces* the gap. This reduction stems from the fact that, unlike in the rural and nationwide samples, urban women are more likely to be employed in highly skilled work and are more likely to have fathers with higher levels of education, so both these factors *reduce* the gender income gap.[18] Meanwhile, unlike in rural China, the urban results indicate that one's own education makes an insignificant contribution to the gap, reflecting the much closer average education levels across genders in urban areas.

Turning to the discrimination effect, the most striking differences are in the contributions from one's own education and occupation, as well as marriage. In the urban subsample, none of these make a significant contribution, whereas in the rural subsample, one's marital status increases the gap (accounting for 58.5 per cent of the discrimination effect), while occupational and educational 'efforts' work in women's favour.

---

18 Note that because the difference-in-characterstics' share is *negative* in the urban sample, a *positive* share implies that the variable in question *reduces* the gap. All other positive shares in Table 12.6 imply the opposite: that the variable works in favour of men.

The finding that marriage makes a positive contribution to the gender income gap nationwide stems from the fact that it is significantly and positively associated with male income, but not with female income, as seen in Columns 3 and 4 of Table 12.2. It turns out that this is driven entirely by the rural subsample (as the marriage coefficient is insignificant in the urban subsample analysis).[19]

We can think of one reason why this might be the case. As our survey data reveals, 76 per cent of married males in rural China state that they never or rarely cook, 80 per cent never or rarely wash dishes, and 82 per cent never or rarely do washing or cleaning. This suggests a relatively weak position of rural women in intra-household bargaining relating to the time allocation for housework. We are not suggesting that urban Chinese women are 'taking it easy' at home either (for example, 65 per cent of married urban males never or rarely cook). But the results here indicate that the problem is more significant in rural China—a topic for further research.

Conclusions

This chapter has revealed that there is a serious lack of equal opportunity in the annual labour income of Chinese individuals. Unequal opportunities were shown to stem primarily from a substantial gender divide, but also from other circumstances that lie beyond an individual's control, including their region, father's occupation, father's education, birth cohort and rural or urban *hukou* status. We stress that we have *not* attributed causality to any of these circumstances, and we concede that biases possibly exist in all of them, due to omitted variables. While this means the decomposition results also need to be treated with caution, there seems no doubt that China faces a serious problem in terms of its gender income gap—with the contribution of gender to inequality of opportunity exceeding those of any other country for which comparable analysis exists.

We also investigated the role of five identifiable 'efforts'—one's own education and occupation, Communist Party membership, and migration and marital status—and demonstrated that an individual's 'efforts' are to a certain extent determined, or constrained, by their circumstances, in ways that differ significantly for men and women in the survey sample.

We took this analysis one step further by reinterpreting Equation 12.1 as an extended Mincer-type earnings equation and using Oaxaca–Blinder decompositions to understand the sources of the gender income gap at a more micro level. This revealed that discrimination—reflected in different coefficients on the male and female subsample regressions—dominated differences in characteristics, working

---

19 As per footnote 17, the urban and rural regression results are available from the authors on request.

most strikingly against women in the rural sample, in terms of their income 'returns' to marriage. However, it is also clear that our explanation is far from complete; the contribution of the constant term significantly exceeded that of our observed variables, suggesting numerous other sources of gender discrimination in China's labour markets that we have not captured here.

In the meantime, the results presented in this chapter suggest a number of equal opportunity policies that could level the gender playing field in China in the foreseeable future. The fact that women's income, as well as their education and occupational choices, is more closely associated with their father's education and occupational status than men's suggests that it would be eminently reasonable for educational policies to specifically target girls from poor, rural families as a starting point for expanding their earnings opportunities later in life. Measures to assist young women to exit the agricultural sector and find off-farm employment would also likely improve their earnings potential in the future. Ongoing reforms to the *hukou* system of household registration to ensure that rural migrants are not discriminated against in urban areas, in terms of their access to jobs and social welfare and the pay cheques they receive, would also go some way towards equalising the opportunities they face with those of their urban counterparts.

Finally, the importance of marriage in the decompositions, and its different impact on the annual incomes of rural men and women in particular, points to the fact that China's 'gender discrimination' begins in the home. The gender divide in household chores revealed in our survey (and elsewhere, as in Zhang et al. 2008b) is indicative of just one of the costs that Chinese married women bear disproportionately, and it is little wonder that their annual income suffers as a result. Efforts to improve childcare systems and grant paternity, as well as maternity, leave are two obvious equal opportunity policies that could make a small dent in this regard, especially in rural areas. Even more important would be a cultural shift towards equal contributions by men and women to chores within the household—a challenge that is far from unique to China, but rather a global fight worth fighting.

References

Appleton, S., Knight, J., Song, L. and Xia, Q. (2009), The economics of Communist Party membership: The curious case of rising numbers and wage premium during China's transition, *Journal of Development Studies* 45(2): 256–75. doi.org/10.1080/00220380802264739.

Arneson, R. (1989), Equality and equal opportunity for welfare, *Philosophy Studies* 56: 77–93. doi.org/10.1007/BF00646210.

Becker, G. (1974), A theory of social interactions, *Journal of Political Economy* 82(6): 1063–94. doi.org/10.1086/260265.

Becker, G. (1976), *The Economic Approach to Human Behavior*, Chicago: University of Chicago Press.

Becker, G.S. (1991), *Treatise on the Family*, Cambridge, MA: Harvard University Press.

Bergmann, B. (1995), Becker's theory of the family: Preposterous conclusions, *Feminist Economics* 1(1): 141–50. doi.org/10.1080/714042218.

Björkland, A, Jäntti, M. and Roemer, J. (2012), Equality of opportunity and the distribution of long-run income in Sweden, *Social Choice and Welfare* 39(2–3): 675–96. doi.org/10.1007/s00355-011-0609-3.

Blinder, A.S. (1973), Wage discrimination: Reduced form and structural estimates, *Journal of Human Resources* 8(4): 436–55. doi.org/10.2307/144855.

Bourguignon, F., Ferreira, F. and Menéndez, M. (2007), Inequality of opportunity in Brazil, *Review of Income and Wealth* 53(4): 585–618. doi.org/10.1111/j.1475-4991.2007.00247.x.

Bourguignon, F., Ferreira, F.H.G. and Menéndez, M. (2011), Inequality of opportunity in Brazil: A corrigendum, *Review of Income and Wealth* 59(3): 551–5. doi.org/10.1111/roiw.12045.

Brunori, P., Ferreira, F.H.G. and Peragine, V. (2013), *Inequality of opportunity, income inequality and economic mobility: Some international comparisons*, IZA Discussion Paper No. 7155, January, Frankfurt am Main: Institute of Labor Economics. doi.org/10.1057/9781137333117_5.

Checchi, D., Peragine, V. and Serlenga, L. (2010), *Fair and unfair income inequalities in Europe*, IZA Discussion Paper No. 5025, June, Frankfurt am Main: Institute of Labor Economics.

Chi, W. and Li, B. (2014), Trends in China's gender employment and pay gap: Estimating gender pay gaps with employment selection, *Journal of Comparative Economics* 42: 708–25. doi.org/10.1016/j.jce.2013.06.008.

Cohen, G. (1989), On the currency of egalitarian justice, *Ethics* 99: 906–44. doi.org/10.1086/293126.

Connelly, R., Dong, X.-Y., Jacobsen, J. and Zhao, Y. (2018), The care economy in post-reform China: Feminist research on unpaid work and paid work and well-being, *Feminist Economics* 24(2): 1–30. doi.org/10.1080/13545701.2018.1441534.

Cook, S. and Dong, X. (2011), Harsh choices: Chinese women's paid work and unpaid care responsibilities under economic reform, *Development and Change* 42(4): 947–65. doi.org/10.1111/j.1467-7660.2011.01721.x.

De Barros, R., Ferreira, F., Vega, J. and Chanduri, J. (2009), *Measuring Inequality of Opportunities in Latin America and the Caribbean*, Washington, DC: The World Bank.

Démurger, S., Fournier, M. and Chen, Y. (2007), The evolution of gender earnings gaps and discrimination in urban China, 1988–95, *The Developing Economies* 45(1): 97–121. doi.org/10.1111/j.1746-1049.2007.00031.x.

Ding, S., Dong, X.-Y. and Maurer-Fazio, M. (2018), Childcare, household composition, Muslim ethnicity and off-farm work in rural China, *Feminist Economics* 24(2): 77–99. doi.org/10.1080/13545701.2017.1407032.

Dworkin, R. (1981a), What is equality? Part 1: Equality of welfare, *Philosophy and Public Affairs* 10: 185–246.

Dworkin, R. (1981b), What is equality? Part 2: Equality of resources, *Philosophy and Public Affairs* 10: 283–345.

Ferreira, F. and Gignoux, J. (2011), The measurement of inequality of opportunity: Theory and an application to Latin America, *Review of Income and Wealth* 57(4): 622–57. doi.org/10.1111/j.1475-4991.2011.00467.x.

Ferreira, F. and Peragine, V. (2015), *Equality of opportunity*, IZA Discussion Paper No. 8994, April, Frankfurt am Main: Institute of Labor Economics.

Fincher, L.H. (2016), *Leftover Women: The resurgence of gender inequality in China*, 2nd edn, London: Zed Books.

Golley, J. (2007), *The Dynamics of Regional Development in China: Market nature, state nurture*, Cheltenham, UK: Edward Elgar Publishing.

Golley, J. and Kong, S.T. (2018), Inequality of opportunity in China's educational outcomes, *China Economic Review* 51(October): 116–28. doi.org/10.1016/j.chieco.2016.07.002.

Golley, J. and Tyers, R. (2012), Gender rebalancing in China, *Asian Population Studies* 10(2): 125–43. doi.org/10.1080/17441730.2014.902159.

Gustafsson, B., Li, S. and Sicular, T. (eds) (2008), *Inequality and Public Policy in China*, New York: Cambridge University Press. doi.org/10.1017/CBO9780511510922.

Hannum, E., Kong, P. and Zhang, Y. (2009), Family sources of educational gender inequality in rural China: A critical assessment, *International Journal of Educational Development* 29(5): 474–86. doi.org/10.1016/j.ijedudev.2009.04.007.

Hederos, K., Jäntti, M. and Lindahl, L. (2017), Gender and inequality of opportunity in Sweden, *Social Choice Welfare* 49(3–4): 605–35. doi.org/10.1007/s00355-017-1076-2.

Jusot, F., Tubeuf, S. and Trannoy, A. (2013), Circumstances and efforts: How important is their correlation for the measurement of inequality of opportunity in health?, *Health Economics* 22(12): 1470–95. doi.org/10.1002/hec.2896.

Kanbur, R. and Zhang, X. (2005), Fifty years of regional inequality in China: A journey through central planning, reform and openness, *Review of Development Economics* 9(1): 87–106. doi.org/10.1111/j.1467-9361.2005.00265.x.

Knight, J. (2014), Inequality in China: An overview, *World Bank Research Observer* 29(1): 1–19. doi.org/10.1093/wbro/lkt006.

Knight, J., Shi, L. and Wan, H. (2016), *The increasing inequality of wealth in China, 2002–2013*, Department of Economics Discussion Paper Series No. 816, Oxford: University of Oxford.

Li, C. (2010), Expansion of higher education and inequality of opportunity in education: A study of the effect of the expansion policy on equalisation of educational attainment, [in Chinese], *Sociological Studies* 3: 82–113.

Li, S., Satō, H. and Sicular, T. (2013), *Rising Inequality in China: Challenges to a harmonious society*, Cambridge: Cambridge University Press. doi.org/10.1017/CBO9781139035057.

Li, S., Song, J. and Liu, X. (2011), Evolution of the gender wage gap among China's urban employees, *Social Sciences in China* 32(3): 161–80. doi.org/10.1080/02529203.2011. 598307.

Liu, L., Dong, X.-Y. and Zheng, X. (2010), Parental care and married women's labour supply in urban China, *Feminist Economics* 16(3): 169–92. doi.org/10.1080/1354570 1.2010.493717.

Marrero, G. and Rodríguez, J.G. (2012), Inequality of opportunity in Europe, *Review of Income and Wealth* 58(4): 597–620. doi.org/10.1111/j.1475-4991.2012.00496.x.

Martinez, A., Rampino, T., Western, M., Tomaszewski, W. and Roque, J.D. (2017), Estimating the contribution of circumstances that reflect inequality of opportunity, *Economic Papers* 36(4): 380–400. doi.org/10.1111/1759-3441.12184.

Meng, X. (1998), Male–female wage discrimination and gender wage discrimination in China's rural industrial sector, *Labour Economics* 5: 67–89. doi.org/10.1016/S0927-5371(97)00028-6.

Ministry of Foreign Affairs (2015), Xi Jinping attends and addresses global leaders' meeting on gender equality and women's empowerment, stressing to promote women's all-round development and jointly construct and share wonderful world, Press release, 29 September, Beijing, available from: www.fmprc.gov.cn/mfa_eng/topics_665678/ xjpdmgjxgsfwbcxlhgcl70znxlfh/t1302736.shtml.

Oaxaca, R. (1973), Male–female wage differentials in urban labor markets, *International Economic Review* 14(13): 693–709. doi.org/10.2307/2525981.

Piketty, T., Yang, L. and Zucman, G. (2017), *Capital accumulation, private property and rising inequality in China, 1978–2015*, NBER Working Paper No. 23368, Cambridge, MA: National Bureau of Economic Research. doi.org/10.3386/w23368.

Pollak, R. (2003), Gary Becker's contribution to family and household economics, *Review of Economics of the Household* 1(1): 111–41. doi.org/10.1023/A:1021803615737.

Roemer, J. (1993), A pragmatic theory of responsibility for the egalitarian planner, *Philosophy and Public Affairs* 22: 146–66.

Roemer, J. (1998), *Equality of Opportunity*, Cambridge, MA: Harvard University Press.

Rozelle, S., Dong, X., Zhang, L. and Mason, A. (2002), Gender wage gaps in post-reform rural China, *Pacific Economic Review* 7(1): 157–79. doi.org/10.1111/1468-0106.00009.

Shu, X. and Bian, Y. (2003), Market transition and the gender gap in earnings in urban China, *Social Forces* 81(4): 1107–45. doi.org/10.1353/sof.2003.0070.

Shu, X., Zhu, Y. and Zhang, Z. (2007), Global economy and gender inequalities: The case of the urban Chinese labour market, *Social Science Quarterly* 88(5): 1307–32. doi.org/10.1111/j.1540-6237.2007.00504.x.

Sicular, T., Yue, X., Gustafsson, B. and Shi, L. (2007), The urban–rural income gap and inequality in China, *Review of Income and Wealth* 53(1): 93–126. doi.org/10.1111/j.1475-4991.2007.00219.x.

Singh, A. (2012), Inequality of opportunity in earnings and consumption expenditure: The case of Indian men, *Review of Income and Wealth* 58(1): 79–106. doi.org/10.1111/j.1475-4991.2011.00485.x.

Song, J., Sicular, T. and Gustafsson, B. (2017), *China's urban gender wage gap: A new direction*, CHCP Working Paper Series No. 2017-23, London, Ontario: Centre for Human Capital and Productivity.

Song, Y. and Dong, X.-Y. (2018), Childcare costs and migrant and local mothers' labor force participation in urban China, *Feminist Economics* 24(2): 122–46. doi.org/10.1080/13545701.2017.1398405.

Su, B. and Heshmati, A. (2011), *Analysis of gender wage differential in China's urban labor market*, IZA Discussion Paper Series No. 6252, Frankfurt am Main: Institute of Labor Economics.

Tang, Y. (2016), *Class and Gender: Social stratification of women in contemporary urban China*, Cambridge: Cambridge Scholars Publication.

Wang, M. and Cai, F. (2008), Gender earnings differential in urban China, *Review of Development Economics* 12(2): 442–54. doi.org/10.1111/j.1467-9361.2008.00450.x.

Woolley, F. (1996), Getting the better of Becker, *Feminist Economics* 2(1): 114–20. doi.org/10.1080/738552692.

Xie, K. (2017), Her China dream: The aspirations of China's privileged daughters, *Discover Society*, 9 September, [Online], available from: discoversociety.org/2017/09/05/her-china-dream-the-aspirations-of-chinas-privileged-daughters/?utm_source=SupChina&utm_campaign=e859050b63-20170907-372+TheDPRK'Students-cum-spies&utm_medium=email&utm_term=0_caef3ab334-e859050b63-164871129.

Zhang, J., Han, J., Liu, P.-W. and Zhao, Y. (2008a), Trends in the gender earnings differential in urban China, 1988–2004, *Industrial and Labor Relations Review* 61(2): 224–43. doi.org/10.1177/001979390806100205.

Zhang, J., Pang, X., Zhang, L., Medina, A. and Rozelle, S. (2012), *Gender inequality of education in China: A meta-regression analysis*, REAP Working Paper 239, May, Stockholm: Resources and Energy Analysis Programme.

Zhang, Q.F. (2013), Gender disparities in self-employment in urban China's market transition: Income inequality, occupational segregation and mobility processes, *China Quarterly* 215(September): 744–63. doi.org/10.1017/S030574101300074X.

Zhang, Y., Hannum, E. and Wang, M. (2008b), Gender-based employment and income differences in urban China: Considering the contributions of marriage and parenthood, *Social Forces* 86(4): 1529–60. doi.org/10.1353/sof.0.0035.

Zhang, Y., Kao, G. and Hannum, E. (2007), Do mothers in rural China practice gender equality in educational aspirations for their children?, *Comparative Education Review* 51(2): 131–57. doi.org/10.1086/512023.

Zhang, Z. and Chen, Q. (2014), The expansion of higher education admissions and the gender equalization of higher education opportunity: An empirical study based on Chinese General Social Survey (CGSS2008) data, *The Journal of Chinese Sociology* 1: 1–19. doi.org/10.1186/s40711-014-0001-7.

Zhou, Y. and Song, L. (2016), Income inequality in China: Causes and policy responses, *China Economic Journal* 9(2): 186–208. doi.org/10.1080/17538963.2016.1168203.

13. What types of Chinese ODI activities are most prone to political intervention?

Bijun Wang and Xiao He

China's outward direct investment (ODI) activities have increased rapidly. At the same time, Chinese enterprises are frequently encountering obstacles as they invest in overseas markets. Although investment liberalisation and promotion remain mainstream policies in overseas markets, more and more countries are strengthening their regulation of foreign investment.

This chapter studies Chinese ODI activities that encounter political obstacles in host countries. Above all, two concepts should be clarified. First, what does it mean to 'encounter obstacles'? In this study, it means Chinese enterprises that have failed to complete their ODI projects for various reasons and it does not cover those that have completed their investment projects (even if their investment has proved a failure or incurred losses). Second, what are the 'political factors' in host countries? These are factors related to the activities of the host country government that can influence foreign investors, including national security reviews, changes of government, policy changes, nationalisation and government default.

Chinese enterprises should draw lessons from their overseas investment activities so that the high price they have paid can be transformed into precious lessons for the future. This chapter conducts theoretical analysis of the political influence of foreign investment on host countries and reactions to it. Meanwhile, based on 22 cases of attempts by Chinese enterprises to invest overseas that encountered political obstacles in the host country and 432 cases of Chinese enterprises successfully completing their overseas investment projects during the period 2005–15, the chapter attempts to conduct empirical analysis to reveal the important factors affecting Chinese ODI before putting forward solutions to the challenge.

Political influence of foreign direct investment on host countries and counter reactions

Foreign direct investment (FDI) activities are often politicised because they can have multiple impacts on the domestic politics of host countries. First, whether intended or not, investing countries may acquire the capability to menace the national security of host countries through ODI; moreover, the more complicated the international environment of the host country, the more serious are the potential risks brought by ODI. Second, ODI can bring new rules and practices for corporate operation, which can trigger political debates regarding standards of 'market behaviour' in host countries. Third, ODI may also lead to structural changes in the incomes of various social groups in the host country, which impacts on their vested interests and reshapes their domestic political alliances (Kerner 2014). To sum up, since ODI can bring risks to national security and controversies about business standards and trigger changes in the incomes and political structures of host countries, the investing countries are likely to face political counterreactions to their investment activities.

ODI and national security

ODI can easily become intertwined with issues of national security, and may prompt direct political counterreactions through the host country's review of national security. Although the Organisation for Economic Co-operation and Development (OECD) has consistently tried to clearly define 'national security' and establish principles for its review—such as nondiscrimination, transparency and predictability, regulatory proportionality and accountability—the process of such reviews remains quite opaque (OECD 2009: 1–4). Although quite a few countries have set investment and industry thresholds to trigger national security reviews, the process involved remains covert and is subject almost entirely to the discretion of the relevant agencies in the host country (Kirchner 2012).

ODI can bring national security risks because of the differences in national policy goals between the investing and the host countries, and also because investing countries can take control of the strategic assets of host countries through direct investment in fields such as energy, telecommunications and infrastructure, and acquire the capability to prevent host countries from achieving their policy goals (Hemphill 2009). History shows such risks exist. In the 1970s, the oil-producing countries in the Middle East made use of the supply of oil to pressure Western countries to change their policies towards Israel. Such moves made the United States unprecedentedly cautious about the large amounts of FDI assets held by oil-producing countries. It therefore established the Committee on Foreign Investment in the United States (CFIUS) in 1975 with a view to examine investment by members of the Organization of the Petroleum Exporting Countries (OPEC) in the United States. After the 11 September 2001 terror attacks in the United States, Dubai Ports World made an attempt to purchase the Peninsular and Oriental Steam Navigation Company (P&O), prompting the US Government to strengthen its national security review mechanisms and clarify, on the appeal of the Congress, the definition of critical infrastructure; meanwhile, it also adopted the principle of reverse burden of proof in dealing with relevant matters. What is noteworthy is that there is not a positive correlation between national security reviews and national policy differences. Developed countries can still use national security as an excuse to restrict investment in some major infrastructure areas by their allies even though they do not have obvious policy differences. For instance, the US Reagan administration stopped the purchase of Fairchild Semiconductor by Fujitsu in 1988, and Japan also made use of a similar mechanism to stop British companies entering its telecommunications industry (Watai 2013).

Scholars and international organisations that support liberalisation of direct global investment have been pushing for a transparent national security review mechanism. For instance, they want a clear definition of the scope of 'sensitive industries' and formulation of unified international review procedures. However, many governments, including the US Government, would like to maintain the current flexible security review mechanism. From the perspective of countries and enterprises that make ODI, there are two issues with the current national security review mechanism, which is dominated by the administrative departments of host countries: given its power of discretion, a government can make use of the mechanism to resist pressure from domestic vested interests; and it can also make use of the mechanism's lack of transparency to serve those interest groups.

Conflict about market rules brought by ODI

Apart from the issue of national security, ODI flooding into host countries can also lead to the spread of the rules and conventions governing economic activity in the investing countries. If the host and parent countries are in different development phases or have divergent social structures and abide by different economic principles, there can be a conflict in the rules, which is especially evident between developing and developed countries.

Initially, developing countries are the ones most subject to the 'rule shocks' brought by ODI by foreign countries. Foreign enterprises operating in developing countries rely on their business prowess or their own governments to directly or indirectly exert pressure and demand changes to local systems. The laws, conventions and rules of the developing countries receiving ODI are often seen as a source of political risk to modern economic activities and those countries, therefore, are continually required to change their systems to the practices of Western countries or 'raise their political system quality' (Hayakawa et al. 2013). Despite such potential conflicts, developing countries remain attractive to ODI from developed countries; the developing countries, as recipients of ODI, in most cases will opt to accept 'new rules' to satisfy the demands of the capital-exporting countries (Blanton and Blanton 2007). In recent years, the rapid growth of two-way investment among developing countries seems to indicate there is no absolute standard or environment that is most attractive for ODI, but the narrower the institutional distance between two countries, the more favourable it is to carry out ODI (Bénassy-Quéré et al. 2007). The dominant position of the developed countries, however, means any rules they favour will be spread to the host country.

However, as FDI by the emerging-market economies increases remarkably, developed countries have also started to face reverse 'standard shocks'. On the one hand, in developing countries such as those in Africa, outward direct investors from emerging-market economies generally are more tolerant of local corruption or 'bad governance', which to an extent offsets the spread of standards favoured by the developed economies (Wood et al. 2014). On the other hand, multinationals from the emerging-market economies, led by China, have sought to acquire strategic resources all over the world (Lu et al. 2010), including in developed countries, which has aroused complaints about 'nonmarket behaviour'. In the eyes of the developed countries, due to their different operational logic, emerging economies' ODI has brought illegitimate competition pressures to enterprises in the host countries. A balance can be struck only by improving the existing rules for market competition and imposing restrictions on enterprises receiving state support.

Currently, to reduce the advantages of state support of some emerging-economy multinationals, developed countries have focused on achieving neutrality in the current stage of rules-based competition and have required the reduction or even elimination of the special treatment enjoyed by state-run and private enterprises (Capobianco and Christiansen 2011). In the eyes of the United States and European countries, the governments of the emerging economies, including the Chinese Government, not only provide multiple policy supports to their own businesses, they also give detailed directions for the overseas operations of those enterprises (Rosen and Hanemann 2013); therefore, rules must be made promptly to address such behaviour. In the negotiations relating to the Trans-Pacific Partnership (TPP) and the Transatlantic Trade and Investment Partnership (TTIP), the European Union has expressed strong opposition to countries:

> inducing or ordering State-owned enterprises (SOEs) and enterprises granted special or exclusive rights or privileges (SERs) to engage in anti-competitive behavior, by taking regulatory measures favoring these companies, or by granting subsidies (or measures which have similar effects) to them. (European Commission Directorate-General for Trade 2013)

The United States has also expressed its concern over the abnormal policy support given to, and the 'uneconomic' behaviour of, SOEs and private companies that obey state orders (US Chamber of Commerce and National Foreign Trade Council 2012).

Whether they receive or export ODI, developing countries must face the conflicts brought about by differing sets of rules, and they are often in a disadvantageous position. If, in the first phase of exporting ODI, developed countries aim to spread free-trade principles and shape countries to be competitive in the international system by stressing the efficiency of multinationals and state capability in attracting foreign investment (Fougner 2006), they have undoubtedly engaged in a type of gaming that tilts the international economic and trade rules towards cutting direct linkages between the state and enterprises, thus eliminating the emerging economies' advantage in exporting ODI and ensuring the continual spread of free-market principles.

Effects of ODI on distribution and domestic politics

Apart from conflicts over national security and rule-setting caused by differing economic models, the most direct effect of ODI is changing the income distribution of social groups in the host country. Such changes can also lead to a reshaping of domestic political unions in host countries. However, the academic circle is still divided over what political effects ODI can bring. Those with positive views of ODI believe it can significantly increase demand for labour in the host country and contribute to improvement in labour conditions. Local owners of capital, however, are likely to encounter rising costs and intensified market competition. Therefore, the more democratic a government is, the more positive will be that government's attitude towards ODI (Pandya 2014). In contrast, those with a negative view of ODI hold that both horizontal ODI, targeting the market, and vertical FDI, targeting efficiency, or the comprehensive knowledge–capital model of ODI, may widen labour income gaps and worsen conditions for low-income groups (Lankhuizen 2014). In some extreme cases, ODI will not lead to a rise in wages for any labour groups and only local capital owners will benefit from such investment (Waldkirch 2010). In real-world politics, the ruling group also treats ODI activities differently. For instance, a pro-labour government may encourage ODI inflows that contribute to improvements in workers' wellbeing, while a pro-capital government may encourage ODI inflows that will lower labour costs (Pinto and Pinto 2008). Therefore, the type of political obstacles ODI will encounter is closely related to redistribution in the host country.

Among the many ODI-related indicators, employment security is the one that has the biggest political appeal. However, existing studies are yet to prove whether ODI has a long-term and positive effect on employment security. Most researchers acknowledge that ODI enterprises generally have a competitive advantage and offer higher wages and more stable jobs, but they also stress that this does not necessarily mean there will be an increase in overall social wellbeing (Girma and Görg 2007), because the ODI inflows—especially those with an extensive margin—will have a negative effect on the employment of low-skilled workers in the recipient industry

(Bachmann et al. 2014). Moreover, not all foreign enterprises have a competitive edge. Some small-scale ODI that is made by private companies in non-export sectors can threaten employment security given the lack of local operational networks (Andrews et al. 2012). Research shows that vertical ODI that has acquired export enterprises is conducive to long-term employment security and overall employment rate growth (Bandick and Görg 2010).

Apart from employment security, income disparity is an equally important political factor. Horizontal comparisons show that the more advanced the technologies of the host country, the less significant will be the effect of ODI on domestic income disparity. This means ODI activities of the same nature will have different effects on income disparity in developed and developing countries. In developed countries, the effect of ODI on widening income disparity is often not very obvious, because in economically developed and technologically advanced countries, foreign enterprises generally play the role of technology receivers, not initiators; as a result, they will not significantly increase demand for skilled workers, nor will they cause income disparity (Bode and Nunnenkamp 2011). Such a characteristic is especially apparent in the United States. In the 1980s, Japan made large amounts of direct investment in the United States, but the investment did not promote industrial upgrading within the United States, nor did it help increase the incomes of highly skilled workers; on the contrary, it increased demand for low-skilled workers and widened income gaps (Blonigen and Slaughter 2001).

Therefore, the effect of ODI on income distribution among different social groups in a host country mainly hinges on the nature of the ODI and the development level of the host country. Groups that have or are likely to see their interests affected will use existing political mechanisms to block the entry and operation of ODI. What needs to be stressed is that, for the United States, its leading role in technology actually provides a more favourable domestic political environment for the entry of ODI. On the one hand, ODI does not mean being more competitive and generally does not lead to significantly intensified competition in the domestic market; on the other hand, foreign investment in the United States is generally not efficiency-driven and seldom involves reduction in numbers of jobs or wages, and therefore does not pose a significant threat to the wellbeing of the local labour force. Therefore, the 'political' challenges facing overseas direct investors in a developed economy such as the United States come mainly from their rivals in acquisitions and the federal government, not from local voters or state governments.

The above analysis points to the three main effects of ODI on the domestic politics of host countries and the subsequent backlash. In most cases, the business rivals of investors making ODI make use of the above factors and political environment to block the entry of competitive ODI. After sorting out the theoretical aspects of the issue, this chapter will carry out analysis using real cases.

Case studies of China's blocked ODI projects

The cases of blocked investment in this chapter are projects that have not been completed for political reasons in the host country. Few scholars and institutions have thoroughly investigated such projects carried out by Chinese investors and therefore this chapter collects a total of 22 cases from 2005 to 2015—including cases labelled 'withdraw' in the BVD-Zephyr database; data dubbed 'troubled transactions' in the China Global Investment Tracker system of the American Enterprise Institute and the Heritage Foundation; and cases revealed by media outlets within China and abroad, such as Caixin, Reuters, Bloomberg, the *Financial Times*, the *China Securities Journal*, as well as information disclosure on the websites of the companies concerned (see Table 13.1).

Table 13.1 Cases of blocked Chinese ODI projects

1	2005	China Minmetals Corporation's bid to buy Canadian metals company Noranda
2	2005	The bid by China National Offshore Oil Corporation to buy US energy company Unocal
3	2008	Huawei's bid to buy US-based 3COM
4	2009	Chinalco's increase in investment in Australia-based Rio Tinto
5	2009	Northwest Non-Ferrous International Investment Company's investment in US-based Firstgold Corp.
6	2009	PetroChina's bid to buy Canada-based Verenex Energy, Inc.
7	2010	Huawei's bid to buy the wireless equipment business of Motorola
8	2010	Huawei's bid to buy privately owned broadband internet software provider 2Wire
9	2010	Tangshan Caofeidian Investment Corporation's investment in US-based EMCORE Corporation
10	2011	Huawei's bid to buy 3Leaf Systems
11	2011	China Shenhua Energy Company Limited's investment in Mongolia's Tavan Tolgoi
12	2012	Chinalco's bid to buy interests in Canada-based SouthGobi Resources Limited
13	2012	Zhongkun Investment Group's tourism development project in Iceland
14	2013	China North Industries Group Corporation's investment in a copper mining project in Myanmar
15	2014	China National Arts & Crafts Group Corporation's bid to buy two platinum assets from South Africa's Aquarius Platinum
16	2014	China Railway Group Limited's investment in a railway connecting Kyaukpyu in Myanmar and Kunming in Yunnan Province
17	2015	Yantai Taihai Group Co. Ltd's bid to buy Sheffield Forgemasters International
18	2015	Bid by Chinese consortium formed by GSR Ventures and Oak Investment Partners to buy Royal Philips NV's LED business, Lumileds
19	2015	Tsinghua Unigroup Co. Ltd's bid to acquire US chip storage giant Micron Technology, Inc.
20	2015	China Communications Construction's Colombo Port City project in Sri Lanka
21	2015	Shanghai Pengxin Group Co. Ltd's bid to buy Australian beef producer S. Kidman & Co.
22	2015	Cancellation of a successful bid by China Railway Construction Corporation Limited to build a high-speed railway in Mexico

Source: Compiled by the authors.

Characteristics of blocked investment cases

Cases of blocked acquisitions have the following characteristics (see Table 13.2).

Table 13.2 Characteristics of the cases of China's blocked ODI

	No.	Ratio (%)	Value ($m)	Ratio (%)
Ownership				
Private	8	36.36	7,590.15	11.90
State-owned	14	63.64	56,196.81	88.10
Industry				
Agriculture, forestry, animal husbandry, fishery	1	4.55	250.00	0.39
Mining	9	40.91	47,979.01	75.22
Manufacturing	8	36.36	9,659.95	15.14
Among them: telecommunications equipment, computer and other electronic equipment manufacturing	5	22.73	6,324.50	9.92
Construction	3	13.64	5,890.00	9.23
Culture, sport and entertainment	1	4.55	8.00	0.01
Country				
Developing	8	36.36	10,497.00	16.46
Mongolia	2	9.09	3,800.00	5.96
Myanmar	2	9.09	1,070.00	1.68
Mexico	1	4.55	3,700.00	5.80
Sri Lanka	1	4.55	1,430.00	2.24
Libya	1	4.55	460.00	0.72
South Africa	1	4.55	37.00	0.06
Developed	14	63.64	53,289.96	83.54
US	9	40.91	28,178.30	44.18
Australia	2	9.09	19,750.00	30.96
Canada	1	4.55	5,346.01	8.38
Iceland	1	4.55	8.00	0.01
UK	1	4.55	7.65	0.01

Source: Compiled by the authors.

First, they mainly involve SOEs. In the 22 cases in Table 13.1, 14 are SOEs, accounting for 64 per cent of the total cases; and the value of the deals involved in those 14 cases accounts for 88 per cent of the total value. Among the 14 SOEs, 10 are centrally administered. There are eight private enterprises involved in the 22 cases and four of the cases involve Chinese technology company Huawei—all in the United States: the company's bid to buy 3COM in 2008; its bid to buy 2Wire, a private broadband internet software provider, in 2010; its bid to buy the wireless equipment business of Motorola in 2010; and its bid to buy 3Leaf in 2011.

Second, mining, telecommunications and construction are the main industries involved in the blocked investment cases. Of the total number of blocked investments, 41 per cent involve investment in mining, accounting for 75 per cent of the total value of the deals involved. They include two coalmining projects, two oil and gas projects and five projects in iron, aluminium, copper and goldmining. Telecommunications is the second most seriously affected industry, accounting for 23 per cent of the total number of the blocked investments and 10 per cent of their total value. Moreover, three cases involve the construction industry, accounting for 10 per cent of the total value of the 22 cases.

Third, most of the investment blocked (84 per cent) was in developed economies, especially the United States, where nine of the cases occurred, accounting for 64 per cent of the total cases in developed economies and 53 per cent of their value. Apart from the United States, investment was blocked in developed economies including Australia, Canada, Iceland and the United Kingdom. China has encountered relatively fewer hurdles in developing markets, where cases of its investment being blocked account for 36 per cent of the total 22 cases and 16 per cent of the total value. Among the cases of blocked investment in developing countries, two were in Mongolia and Myanmar, and one each in Mexico, Sri Lanka, Libya and South Africa.

Analysis of reasons for blocked investment

Analysis of the 22 cases involving Chinese ODI shows that national security, conflict over rules and distribution effects are the factors behind investment being blocked. Among these, national security is the most frequently cited factor and has been used to block investment in both developed and developing countries. Cases of blocked investment arising from conflicting market rules have occurred mainly in developed countries and are largely included in the scope of a national security review. In terms of distribution effects, Chinese investors encounter direct blocks arising from local political factors in developing countries, while in developed countries, the blocking often takes effect through a national security review.

National security

As mentioned earlier, national security is quite a blurred concept and different countries may have different explanations and apply the concept in different manners. For CFIUS, national security includes four key factors. The first is crucial infrastructure, including agriculture and food, national defence industries, energy, public health and health care, banking and finance, water, chemical products, business facilities, dams, information technology, telecommunications, postal services and transportation. Second are key technologies, mainly those closely related to national security. Third are key locations within the United States or areas close to key infrastructure. Fourth are enterprises and capital backed by foreign governments. The CFIUS categorisation is quite typical; in the cases of blocked Chinese investment, the second and the third factors can each constitute a reason for refusing the investment, while the first and fourth factors are often cited together.

Key technology

In Case No. 2 (Table 13.1), the China National Offshore Oil Corporation (CNOOC) proposed acquiring US-based oil company Unocal in 2005, which aroused strong opposition in US political circles. The US House of Representatives voted 398 to 15 to pass a resolution protesting against the deal and called on then president George W. Bush to review the bid under the CFIUS mechanism, citing threats to national security. The main concern was that Unocal's advanced submarine surveying and mapping technology could be acquired by CNOOC to assist China's submarine technology development. In Case No. 17, the Yantai Taihai Group Co. Ltd's bid to buy Sheffield Forgemasters International was blocked by British authorities. Sheffield Forgemasters International forges precision components for manufacturing of military aircraft engines in Europe; it is also a supplier of heavy forging parts for the construction of surface ships in Europe. As a result, the United Kingdom was concerned that the transfer of the controlling shares of the company to a Chinese enterprise would ultimately lead to the disguised transfer of key military technology to China.

Geological locations

In Case No. 5, after the Northwest Non-Ferrous International Investment Company, which belongs to the Northwest Non-Ferrous Geological Survey Bureau, announced its planned investment in the US-based Firstgold Corp. in 2009, the CFIUS suggested the Chinese company drop its plan, citing some of Firstgold's assets in the State of Nevada that are close to Naval Air Station Fallon, which is a 'key location'. Similarly, in Case No. 21, Shanghai Pengxin Group Co. Ltd's bid to acquire a cattle farm was blocked by Australia's Foreign Investment Review Board; an important reason for the blocking was that half of the property sits within the weapons testing range of the Woomera Prohibited Area in South Australia.

Sensitive industry and foreign government backing

In Case No. 2, the CNOOC sought to acquire US oil producer Unocal in 2005. On the one hand, Sino–US trade relations were soured by bilateral trade frictions and the United States had been pressuring China on issues such as renminbi appreciation and China's fulfilment of its World Trade Organization (WTO) commitments; on the other hand, the United States at that time attached utmost importance to energy security. As a result, CNOOC's purchase plan triggered an explosion of concern among US politicians and Congress even voted to demand that the government investigate the real motives of the Chinese side in the bid. In Case No. 8, Huawei offered to purchase 2Wire, a US private broadband internet software provider, at a time when the United States and the international community attached great importance to internet security; meanwhile, there had been a series of accusations that China-based hackers had attacked government and corporate websites in other countries to steal crucial information. Yu Chengdong, then chief marketing officer of Huawei, told the media that Huawei had failed to grasp the opportunities in the North American markets at a time when political factors played a relatively small role in influencing corporate decisions. If it had grasped the opportunities at that time, he said, Huawei may have become a major supplier to the North American markets and it would have been much easier to solve the problems it faced (Southern Metropolis Daily 2011). In Case No. 10, Huawei did not encounter major technological challenges in its bid to purchase 3Lead, but the CFIUS ultimately suggested it withdraw its bid due to the company's alleged links with the Chinese military. In Case No. 4, when Chinalco proposed increasing its investment in Rio Tinto, there were accusations that Chinalco was controlled by the Chinese Government and claims that 'China should not be allowed to own Australia'. The Australian Government bowed to pressure and repeatedly postponed the approval of the bid. In the end, Rio Tinto unilaterally cancelled its agreement with Chinalco and announced the formation of an iron ore joint venture with BHP Billiton Limited (now BHP). But the competition authorities in Australia turned this idea down, and Rio Tinto and BHP are fierce competitors in iron ore today.

All in all, national security is a political concept and therefore any review of it is bound to be discriminatory. For instance, in Case No. 5, also situated close to Naval Air Station Fallon are the operations of other foreign mining companies—such as Canada's Barrick Gold Corporation and Australia's Rio Tinto—some of which are even closer to the station than Firstgold. In practice, there are no unified criteria for conducting national security reviews targeted at foreign investment and it is still up to the discretion of the relevant administrative departments in the host countries.

Apart from developed countries such as the United States, Canada and Australia, Chinese enterprises have also encountered investment blocks citing national security concerns in developing countries. In Case No. 6, PetroChina offered to purchase Verenex, a Canada-based energy company, whose business is mainly in Libya, with 86.3 per cent of its oil output belonging to the Libyan Government. However, the Libyan Government refused to approve the acquisition offer, citing concerns about 'excessive control by China'. In Case No. 12, Chinalco planned to acquire some shares of the Canadian SouthGobi Resources, whose assets are mainly in Mongolia; the Mongolian authorities cancelled some of SouthGobi's exploration and mining certificates, citing national security threats, and Chinalco was forced to withdraw the offer.

Market rules

Currently, although developed countries have attached increasing importance to the 'market neutrality principle', there has also been an increase in criticism of Chinese enterprises for enjoying certain privileges, although there are yet to be any cases of investment being blocked solely due to 'competition advantage'. In contrast, suspicions that Chinese enterprises conduct 'noncommercial activities' are an important factor behind the blocking of the activities of Chinese enterprises abroad. For instance, in Case No. 2, in which the CNOOC offered to acquire Unocal, Case No. 4, in which Chinalco proposed increasing its investment in Rio Tinto, Case No. 8, in which Huawei offered to acquire 2Wire, and Case No. 10, in which Huawei offered to acquire 3Lead, national security was cited as the reason for the blocking of those deals. It is considered a national security issue because the governments and societies of those developed countries, such as the United States and Australia, suspect that Chinese enterprises carry out investment activities with noncommercial motives, such as influencing the foreign policy of host countries, making strategic arrangements and ensuring energy supply for China. Before the principle of competition neutrality—including the principle of restricting the activities of SOEs and other privileged enterprises—plays a larger role in ODI reviews, it can be said that market rules have become part of the national security factor.

Distribution effect and domestic politics

China's ODI, due to its huge scale, often has a major bearing on domestic industrial development and wealth distribution in developing countries, especially those small and mid-sized countries with problematic governance and serious social division, thus triggering fierce domestic political strife. In developed countries, China's technology, market and branding-oriented investment activities generally will not have a significant impact on overall social interest distribution and the political landscape. Chinese enterprises will face blocking from a small number of local rivals whose interests are damaged by Chinese investment; these groups may make use of, or even manipulate, a special political agenda to block investment from China.

In developing countries, China's ODI projects are often seen as offering political and economic support for the incumbent government and thus are prone to fierce backlash from opposition forces. China's investment in Myanmar is a case in point. In Cases No. 14 and No. 16, the investment agreements signed by Chinese investors with the country's military government were cancelled after the country initiated democratic reforms. In carrying out their investment activities, Chinese enterprises have prioritised winning support from host country governments and have failed to understand and attach importance to social changes and the appeals of ordinary citizens in the host country; as a result, there have been repeated protests organised by local people and political organisations against Chinese investment. In Case No. 20, China had a close relationship with the Mahinda Rajapaksa Government of

Sri Lanka, but after the country's power shift, the government of the new President, Maithripala Sirisena, immediately announced the cancellation of the Colombo Port City project involving China Communications Construction Group and subjected it to an investment review. During the election process, Sirisena and the opposition party had argued that the interest rates on loans for the project were too high and the environment would be damaged; they also claimed that only Rajapaksa and a small group of people would benefit from the project. In Case No. 22, an international consortium led by the China Railway Construction Corporation Limited successfully won the bid to build a high-speed railway connecting Mexico City and Querétaro state in Mexico. However, three days later, the project was cancelled; one important reason offered was that the four companies cooperating with the Chinese enterprise were 'overly close' to the ruling party, and the opposition party accused them of engaging in unfair deals. Conflicts arising from the distribution of benefits are not confined to developing countries. In Case No. 13, the Zhongkun Investment Group—at the invitation of the Government of Iceland—offered to acquire 300 square kilometres of land for tourism and ecological development. Due to partisan differences, however, the country's internal affairs ministry rejected the deal, citing procedural problems.

In developed countries, Chinese enterprises may face competition from their local rivals, who often make use of election politics to thwart investment and acquisitions—as in Australia. There are two main political forces in Australia—namely, the Australian Labor Party and the Liberal–National Party Coalition. The country holds general elections every three years. Such a tight election schedule means the ruling party must be especially mindful of public opinion, while dealing with criticisms from the opposition party. In Case No. 4, Chinalco's competitor BHP is the second-largest mining group in the world; it is also one of the largest enterprises in Australia, having a great influence on Australian society. One former Australian government official said BHP had strong connections in the Australian government (Garnaut 2009). BHP produced and made use of a public relations campaign against Chinalco to play up the alleged threat the Chinese company posed to Australia's national security, ultimately ensuring its deal to increase its investment in Rio Tinto was used by the opposition party to attack the government. The opposition party accused Chinalco of being backed by the Chinese Government, which it claimed had a close relationship with the ruling Labor Party. Under pressure, the Labor Party became very cautious in reviewing the deal to show that it had no inappropriate relationship with China. As a result, the approval of the Chinalco investment project was delayed and Rio Tinto turned to BHP to form a new joint venture.

Moreover, national security reviews in developed countries can easily be used by rivals of Chinese enterprises to set investment hurdles through politicising business competition. In Case No. 2, US congressman Richard Pombo put forward a resolution to suggest that approval of investment by Chinese enterprises in US oil companies should be postponed by at least 120 days. What is noteworthy is that Pombo represents the State of California, where CNOOC's competitor in the Unocal bid, Chevron, is headquartered. In addition, US telecommunications enterprises such as Cisco have played a role in blocking Huawei's investments in the US market through lobbying of government.

Empirical analysis of factors behind blocked investment

After theoretical analysis and case studies in previous sections, this section uses the probit model to estimate the major influential factors in deciding whether the ODI of Chinese enterprises is blocked.

Data and variables

Analysis of the blocking of China's ODI activities should include both 'blocked' (uncompleted investment) samples and 'successful' (completed investment) samples. The 'blocked' samples, as mentioned earlier, include 22 cases during the period 2005–15. Meanwhile, the 'successful' samples include 432 investment projects. For information on these investment projects, we first check the list of approved ODI projects of China's National Development and Reform Commission and retrieve basic information such as investment scale, the countries invested in and the targets of investment. Then, through corporate information disclosures and media reports, we sort out the projects with disclosed information on their investment scale and targets and which have Chinese investors holding more than 10 per cent of shares. We exclude a project if it involves a Chinese enterprise investing in another Chinese enterprise and is categorised as 'return investment'—that is, the ultimate destination of the proposed investment is the Chinese mainland.

The empirical analysis of this chapter includes the following variables that may influence the blocking of investment.

i. **State-owned enterprise.** This is a virtual variable: 1 represents SOE; 0 represents non-SOE. Enterprises and capital with government backing are prone to arousing the attention of authorities in the host country. For example, in its reviews, CFIUS targets whether: 1) a foreign government can substantially influence the enterprise concerned and order it to acquire US enterprises with key technologies; 2) a foreign government can provide targeted and overly generous incentives, such as grants, preferential loans and tax preferences. China's SOEs have access to government policy and resource support and are prone to accusations of threatening the host country's national security and jeopardising fair market competition; therefore, they are more likely to encounter hurdles to investing overseas.

ii. **Investment scale, with the unit being $1 million.** The larger the investment scale, the greater is the probability that the project will have a bearing on local affairs in the host country; therefore, it is more likely the project will receive attention from the regulators, society and media of the host country.

iii. **Political risk and institutional distance.** This chapter complies with the existing documents and adopts the International Country Risk Guide political risk index, released by the Political Risk Service Group, to measure the political risks in host countries. The index is a qualitative variable, covering 12 aspects, such as political stability, military intervention in politics, internal and external conflicts, corruption, law and administrative efficiency. The bigger the value, the smaller is the political risk. As mentioned in the literature review in the second part of this chapter, no consensus has been reached on measuring the influence of political risks in the host country on China's ODI. Apart from absolute institutional quality (here, this refers to political risks in the host country), the institutional distance between the parent and host countries may also play a role in whether the enterprise encounters hurdles in investing in the host country and therefore also becomes a variable, defined as the gap between the political risk index in the host country and that in China.

iv. **Bilateral political relations.** The indicator of bilateral political relations in the *Country-risk Rating of Overseas Investment from China report* (Zhang and Wang 2018), compiled by the Chinese Academy of Social Sciences, is adopted in this chapter. Good bilateral relations are conducive to the development of direct investment and serve as a lubricant for enterprises to invest and operate in host countries, thus lowering the negative impacts on international investment of the social and political risks in host countries. However, some studies also show that, given the existence of sunk costs, the worsening of international relations does not have a significant negative impact on the investment decision-making of multinationals (Davis and Meunier 2011).

v. **Natural resources.** This indicator is calculated based on the trade-in-goods matrix data of the UN Conference on Trade and Development and measured by the aggregate fuel and mineral exports to GDP ratio in the host country. As the world's factory and most populous country, China has a great demand for natural resources. One of the main driving forces of China's ODI is accessing stable sources of raw materials. Resources, including minerals, coal and oil, are nonrenewable. Meanwhile, resource exploitation can easily cause environmental problems and lead to corruption, thus triggering complaints from local people.

vi. **Patent.** This refers to the indicator of resident applications per million population in the database of the World Intellectual Property Organization.[1] Although it cannot fully reflect a country's technological level, it can, to an extent, reflect a country's technological research and development input–output level and its technological knowledge level. It is widely used in the literature as a measure of technological level. The acquisition of strategic assets, such as technology and brands, is conducive to improvement in the competitiveness of Chinese enterprises and helps them move higher in the value chain. ODI is an important way of achieving those goals. However, as Chinese enterprises increase their technology acquisition–oriented direct investment, host countries have become increasingly concerned about loss of key technologies.

vii. **Invested industry.** The blocking of ODI activities due to political factors may also be related to the nature of the invested industries. For instance, the French Monetary and Financial Code says that, in 11 specific industries, foreign investors in local enterprises should be subject to foreign investment review on the grounds of defending France's public order, public safety or national defence interests (US GAO 2008). The US *Foreign Investment and National Security Act* of 2007 also lists several economic sectors that are categorised as 'important infrastructure'. We mark industries based on the industrial classification and codes for national economic activities provided by the National Bureau of Statistics of China. According to Table 13.2, cases of blocked investment occur in agriculture, forestry, animal husbandry and fisheries, mining, telecommunications, construction, culture, sport and entertainment. We set those industries as virtual variables. If an industry is the invested industry, the variable is 1; otherwise, it is 0.

viii. **Other controlled variables.** These include economic growth in the host country, the distance between the capital cities of two countries and the year of investment.

Econometric model and regression results

Based on the above analysis, we estimate the influence of the above-mentioned factors on whether the ODI activities of Chinese enterprises are blocked. Since whether they are blocked is a discrete choice, the estimation equation can be expressed as the following probit model (Equation 13.1).

Equation 13.1

$$\Pr(Failure_{ODI_i} = 1 \mid X_i) = \Psi(X_i\beta)$$

1　Country ownership of patents is based on the nationality of patent applicants.

In Equation 13.1, the dependent variable denotes the possibility of the investment being blocked—that is, 1 if the investment is blocked and 0 if the investment is completed; *i* refers to the specific enterprise; *X* refers to the set of all explanatory variables; *ß* is the coefficient of the corresponding variable; and Ψ denotes the cumulative distribution function of standard normal distribution. Apart from the probit model, we also use the linear probability model (LPM) to conduct regression analysis. In the LPM, the ordinary least squares (OLS) method is used to estimate the binary choice model; since it has some problems, it is not as accurate as the probit model.[2] Here, the LPM regression is introduced to serve as the comparison of the probit model estimation.

Table 13.3 provides the regression results of probit and LPM. It is found that the ownership of an enterprise is not the main factor behind its investment being blocked; however, the larger the investment scale is, the more probable it is that the investment will be blocked. Table 13.2 shows that most cases of blocked investment involve SOEs; however, regression results indicate that the ownership of an enterprise does not have a major impact on whether its investment will be blocked. This is because, in the sample interval, China's ODI activities are carried out mainly by SOEs,[3] which signifies that many SOEs have already completed their ODI. As a result, the variable of 'SOE' is not significant in the statistics. However, the variable of 'investment scale' passing the 1 per cent significance test is the main factor behind the blocking of investment by Chinese enterprises; more specifically, the larger the investment scale, the more probable it is that an enterprise's ODI will be blocked. This may be because of the effect known as 'a tall tree catches the wind': projects of larger investment scale may attract more attention and become targets of attack.

The political risks in the host country and institutional distance are not significant factors influencing whether an investment project will be blocked. However, the better the bilateral political relations, the less probable it is the investment of a Chinese enterprise will be blocked in the host country. Neither the absolute institutional indicator (political risk in host countries) nor the relative institutional indicator (institutional distance) is significant in the statistics. But the significance of the variable of 'bilateral political relations' is negative and it passes the 1 per cent significance test. It is found that good bilateral relations are conducive to the entry of Chinese enterprises into local markets and to reducing resistance to Chinese investment.

---

2   For example: 1) there is a linear relationship between the assumptive independent variable of LPM and the probability of Y = 1, although such relationships are often nonlinear; 2) the fitted value may be < 0 or > 1, but the probability value must be within a closed interval between 0 and 1; and 3) the disturbance term is subject to binary distribution, not normal distribution.

3   From 2006 to 2014, ODI by nonfinancial central SOEs accounted for 77 per cent of China's total nonfinancial overseas investment stock.

Table 13.3 Regression results of factors behind blocked investment

	(1) Probit	(2) LMP	(3) Probit	(4) LPM	(5) Probit	(6) LPM
SOE	0.41	−0.00446	0.537	-0.00621	0.536	−0.00659
	(0.43200)	(0.02330)	(0.47700)	(0.02310)	(0.47800)	(0.02310)
Investment scale	0.000406***	5.33e-05***	0.000451***	5.25e-05***	0.000448***	5.24e-05***
	(0.00013)	(0.00001)	(0.00014)	(0.00001)	(0.00014)	(0.00001)
Political risk	0.00667	−0.000213	−0.0199	−0.00164		
	(0.01840)	(0.00105)	(0.02430)	(0.00129)		
Institutional distance					−0.0214	−0.00171
					(0.02430)	(0.00128)
Bilateral political relations	−6.681***	−0.275**	−6.597***	−0.307***	−6.621***	−0.306***
	(2.37100)	(0.11100)	(2.39000)	(0.11500)	(2.40100)	(0.11500)
Natural resources			0.0131	0.000235	0.0132	0.000218
			(0.03670)	(0.00175)	(0.03660)	(0.00174)
Patent			0.262*	0.0124*	0.269*	0.0128*
			(0.13800)	(0.00667)	(0.14000)	(0.00672)
Agriculture, forestry, animal husbandry and fisheries	2.080**	0.119*	2.745***	0.127**	2.750***	0.126**
	(0.89200)	(0.06060)	(0.97800)	(0.06030)	(0.97700)	(0.06030)
Mining	1.478***	0.0408	1.862***	0.0623**	1.870***	0.0618**
	(0.55900)	(0.02720)	(0.62900)	(0.02950)	(0.63300)	(0.02920)
Construction	1.991**	0.485***	2.085**	0.397***	2.099**	0.399***
	(0.79500)	(0.08980)	(0.98200)	(0.09860)	(0.98300)	(0.09850)
Telecommunications	2.615***	0.309***	2.601***	0.295***	2.604***	0.295***
	(0.66100)	(0.05270)	(0.68200)	(0.05250)	(0.68200)	(0.05250)
Economic growth	-0.00834	0.00112	0.0272	0.003	0.032	0.00302
	(0.06440)	(0.00368)	(0.07310)	(0.00394)	(0.07350)	(0.00393)
Distance between two countries	0.139	0.0165	0.0825	0.0161	0.0836	0.0161
	(0.30300)	(0.01940)	(0.31400)	(0.01940)	(0.31400)	(0.01940)
Year of investment	0.222***	0.00685**	0.207***	0.00619*	0.224***	0.00737**
	(0.07990)	(0.00325)	(0.07740)	(0.00326)	(0.07680)	(0.00327)
R^2	0.5222	0.3246	0.5465	0.3079	0.5473	0.3083

*** $p < 0.01$ ** $p < 0.05$ * $p < 0.1$

Notes: The standard errors of mean are in parentheses; R^2 in the probit regression is pseudo R^2; R^2 in the LPM regression is adjusted R^2.

Source: Authors' regression analysis of relevant data using Stata econometric software.

Whether a host country is rich in natural resources is not a significant factor behind blocked investment activities. But the higher the technological level of the host country, the more probable it is Chinese enterprises will have their investment blocked. The variable of 'natural resources' is positive, but not significant. The variable of 'patent' is also positive and passes the 10 per cent significance test.

This variable is an indicator of technological level; its result shows that the higher the technological level of the host country, the more probable it is that investment by Chinese enterprises in local markets will be blocked. This is a reflection of the fact that those host countries with a relatively high technological level are worried about Chinese enterprises 'stealing' their key technologies and weakening their economic competitive edge. As a result, these kinds of host countries have blocked the entry of more Chinese enterprises.

Some industries are more prone than others to encountering investment hurdles. The significance of the variable of 'telecommunications' is positive and it has passed the 1 per cent significance test in all regressions. The significance of the variables of 'agriculture, forestry, animal husbandry and fisheries', 'mining' and 'construction' is also positive, but their significance falls remarkably, and some regressions have passed the 5 per cent significance test. This indicates that investment by Chinese enterprises in overseas telecommunications, agriculture, forestry, animal husbandry and fisheries, mining and construction industries is more likely to be blocked.

The significance of the coefficient of 'year of investment' is positive, which indicates that the probability of Chinese ODI being blocked in overseas markets has been rising in recent years.

Countermeasures and suggestions for coping with blocked ODI

The empirical analysis in this chapter shows that the larger the investment scale and the higher the technological level of the host country, the more probable it is that the investment by Chinese enterprises in overseas markets will be blocked; the better the bilateral relations, the smaller is the probability of Chinese enterprises encountering hurdles to investing in local markets. Moreover, investment by Chinese enterprises in certain industries—such as telecommunications, agriculture, forestry, animal husbandry and fisheries, mining and construction— is more likely than others to be blocked. Based on the above analysis, we offer the following suggestions for reducing investment hurdles.

First, investors should break up large-scale investment into several smaller investment programs to avoid attracting the attention of the host country government, community and media. Chinese enterprises generally lack experience in investing abroad and most do not know how to deal properly with local communities and media; they also lack transparency and are weak in terms of information disclosure, making it very difficult for the host country society to determine their investment motives and development philosophy. Therefore, Chinese enterprises should avoid making large-scale ODI; if they really need to carry out large-scale investment programs, they should break these into smaller-scale programs and gradually increase investment in local enterprises; they should first become noncontrolling or minority-controlling shareholders of local enterprises or collaborate and share interests with local enterprises.

Second, Chinese enterprises should invest in industries with relatively easier review procedures and avoid directly entering sensitive industries—such as telecommunications, aerospace, energy and infrastructure—that raise concerns about national security, geopolitics and national competitiveness. Foreign enterprises may encounter intervention from the government of the host country when they enter these types of industries. Therefore, Chinese enterprises should try to avoid investing in crucial industries and sensitive sectors and should first enter industries with relatively easier review procedures; they should gradually increase their investment and establish a good reputation before they start acquiring local enterprises in sensitive industries so as to ease concerns among the government and public of the host country.

Third, Chinese enterprises should improve their protection of intellectual property rights and continually increase research and development (R&D) inputs in the host countries. In response to the concerns of host countries over the loss of key technologies, Chinese enterprises should attach importance to and enhance protection of the brands and intellectual property rights of the enterprises in which they invest and establish an insulation mechanism to ensure the security of business secrets and customer data. Meanwhile, Chinese enterprises should also provide support for the companies in which they invest so they can hire more R&D staff, improve their research facilities and increase R&D inputs and establish relevant mechanisms to maintain and strengthen the business's independence, management stability and technological edge.

Fourth, Chinese enterprises should enhance strategic mutual trust with host countries and use political means to resolve political risks. Making their investment projects more mutually beneficial is the key to reducing the concerns of host country governments and the public. The key to expanding mutual benefits from investment in sensitive industries is enhancing the mutual trust between China and the host countries. It is the trust gap that has led to the repeated success of some interest groups in politicising the commercial projects of Chinese enterprises. Currently, whether in terms of investment scale or industrial penetration, China's ODI has reached a stage of development at which better political relations are needed to clear the barriers to business investment; political relations should facilitate business cooperation and economic relations should no longer serve as the ballast for various types of bilateral relations. China should cooperate with other countries, especially developed countries, in traditional and nontraditional security areas to acknowledge and resolve the security concerns of those countries instead of relying on the spillover effects of their economic and trade relations to make up for their inadequate cooperation in strategic areas.

Apart from the above suggestions, China can adopt clearer strategies in response to the political backlash triggered by its ODI activities.

First, Chinese enterprises should make more thorough preparations for coping with national security reviews; they should hire professionals and intermediaries to carry out thorough research and investigations, understand and abide by the host country's legal system, regulatory framework and review procedures and prepare documents and emergency plans for going through the review procedure. Admittedly, the expansion of the national security concept and the increasing political factors in the process of national security reviews have become an entrenched trend and it is very difficult for enterprises to predict whether their investment will trigger a national security review in the host country. While host countries have increasingly used such tools to block investment by Chinese enterprises, the fact that the outcome of a national security review cannot be legally challenged means it is difficult for Chinese enterprises to respond to a review. However, since the Sani Group successfully brought a suit against a CFIUS decision, citing procedural injustice, Chinese enterprises may be able to use legal means to protect their interests if they fully understand the legal and political rules of the host countries.

Second, in coping with market rule conflicts, Chinese enterprises, especially SOEs, should improve their transparency in accordance with international standards, actively clarify their internal structure, their relationship with the Chinese Government, their investment goals and policies and their future development plans. Meanwhile, they should become more profit-oriented in making international investment decisions; while investing in sensitive and important industries, they should avoid offering unrealistically high prices or shouldering excessively high business risks regardless of their capital utilisation efficiency or the real costs of investment—behaviour that can easily arouse suspicion from the government and public of the host countries and doubts about whether Chinese enterprises are real market players or government affiliates. At the state level, China should actively contribute to the build-up of the system of international investment governance and actively participate in the establishment of international investment rules to create a favourable environment for Chinese enterprises investing abroad.

Last but not least, Chinese enterprises should build an image of being neutral and not politically oriented to better cope with the distribution effect and local politics of the host country and avoid being overly close to any one political force (especially the incumbent government). Meanwhile, before the launch of their investment projects, they should take into consideration the distribution effect in the host country and clarify it in project contracts to properly guarantee the interests of different local groups. They should ensure their investment projects can serve the interests of local communities and pay special attention to the relative changes in benefits to different groups, providing more benefits to those who could be adversely affected by their projects. Moreover, Chinese enterprises should also thoroughly assess the possible reactions of local competitors and related interest groups, and establish and strengthen communication with local media and non-governmental and community organisations; and they should also focus on highlighting the mutually beneficial aspects of their cooperation with the local community to build favourable public relations.

References

Andrews, M., Bellmann, L., Schank, T. and Upward, R. (2012), Foreign-owned plants and job security, *Review of World Economics* 148(1): 89–117. doi.org/10.1007/s10290-011-0110-1.

Bachmann, R., Baumgarten, D. and Stiebale, J. (2014), Foreign direct investment, heterogeneous workers and employment security: Evidence from Germany, *Canadian Journal of Economics* 47(3): 720–57. doi.org/10.1111/caje.12094.

Bandick, R. and Görg, H. (2010), Foreign acquisition, plant survival and employment growth, *Canadian Journal of Economics* 43(2): 547–73. doi.org/10.1111/j.1540-5982.2010.01583.x.

Bénassy-Quéré, A., Coupet, M. and Mayer, T. (2007), Institutional determinants of foreign direct investment, *The World Economy* 30(5): 764–82. doi.org/10.1111/j.1467-9701.2007.01022.x.

Blanton, S.L. and Blanton, R.G. (2007), What attracts foreign investors: An examination of human rights and foreign direct investment, *The Journal of Politics* 69(1): 143–55. doi.org/10.1111/j.1468-2508.2007.00500.x.

Blonigen, B.A. and Slaughter, M.J. (2001), Foreign-affiliate activity and US skill upgrading, *Review of Economics and Statistics* 83(2): 362–76. doi.org/10.1162/00346530151143888.

Bode, E. and Nunnenkamp, P. (2011), Does foreign direct investment promote regional development in developed countries? A Markov chain approach for US states, *Review of World Economics* 147(2): 351–83. doi.org/10.1007/s10290-010-0086-2.

Capobianco, A. and Christiansen, H. (2011), *Competitive neutrality and state-owned enterprises: Challenges and policy options*, OECD Corporate Governance Working Papers No.1, Paris: OECD Publishing.

Davis, C.L. and Meunier, S. (2011), Business as usual? Economic response to political tensions, *American Journal of Political Science* 55(3): 628–46. doi.org/10.1111/j.1540-5907.2010.00507.x.

European Commission Directorate-General for Trade (2013), Trade relations with the United States and Canada: TIPP Rules Group, anti-trust & mergers, government influence and subsidies, Initial Position Papers for 1st Round Negotiations, 19 June, Brussels.

Fougner, T. (2006), The state, international competitiveness and neoliberal globalization: Is there a future beyond the competition state?, *Review of International Studies* 32(1): 165–85. doi.org/10.1017/S0260210506006978.

Garnaut, J. (2009), Rudd policy on China 'set by BHP', *The Age*, [Melbourne], 15 October.

Girma, S. and Görg, H. (2007), Evaluating the foreign ownership wage premium using a difference-in-differences matching approach, *Journal of International Economics* 72(1): 97–112. doi.org/10.1016/j.jinteco.2006.07.006.

Hayakawa, K., Kimura, F. and Lee, H. (2013), How does country risk matter for foreign direct investment?, *The Developing Economies* 51(1): 60–78. doi.org/10.1111/deve.12002.

Hemphill, T.A. (2009), Sovereign wealth funds: National security risks in a global free trade environment, *Thunderbird International Business Review* 51(6): 551–66. doi.org/10.1002/tie.20299.

Kerner, A. (2014), What we talk about when we talk about foreign direct investment, *International Studies Quarterly* 58(4): 804–15. doi.org/10.1111/isqu.12147.

Kirchner, S. (2012), Foreign direct investment in Australia following the Australia–US Free Trade Agreement, *The Australian Economic Review* 45(4): 410–21. doi.org/10.1111/j.1467-8462.2012.00686.x.

Lankhuizen, M. (2014), The (im)possibility of distinguishing horizontal and vertical motivations for ODI, *Review of Development Economics* 18(1): 139–51. doi.org/10.1111/rode.12074.

Lu, J., Liu, X. and Wang, H. (2010), Motives for outward ODI of Chinese private firms: Firm resources, industry dynamics, and government policies, *Management and Organization Review* 7(2): 223–48. doi.org/10.1111/j.1740-8784.2010.00184.x.

Organisation for Economic Co-operation and Development (OECD) (2009), *Guidelines for Recipient Country Investment Policies Relating to National Security: Recommendation adopted by the OECD Council, 25 May 2009*, Paris: OECD Investment Division.

Pandya, S.S. (2014), Democratization and foreign direct investment liberalization, 1970–2000, *International Studies Quarterly* 58(3): 475–88. doi.org/10.1111/isqu.12125.

Pinto, P.M. and Pinto, S.M. (2008), The politics of investment partisanship and the sectoral allocation of foreign direct investment, *Economics & Politics* 20(2): 216–54. doi.org/10.1111/j.1468-0343.2008.00330.x.

Rosen, D. and Hanemann, T. (2013), China's direct investment in the advanced economies: The cases of Europe and the US, *International Economic Review* 1: 94–108.

Southern Metropolis Daily (2011), Huawei dropped bid to purchase 3Leaf again for 'security concerns', *Southern Metropolis Daily*, 22 February.

United States Chamber of Commerce and National Foreign Trade Council (2012), Establishing rules of the road: Commercial SOEs and private actors, SOE Presentation, 4 March, Melbourne.

United States Government Accountability Office (US GAO) (2008), *Laws and policies regulating foreign investment in 10 countries: Report to the Honorable Richard Shelby, Ranking Member, Committee on Banking, Housing, and Urban Affairs, US Senate*, GAO-08-320, February, Washington, DC: GAO.

Waldkirch, A. (2010), The effects of foreign direct investment in Mexico since NAFTA, *The World Economy* 33(5): 710–45. doi.org/10.1111/j.1467-9701.2009.01244.x.

Watai, R. (2013), US and Japanese national security regulation on foreign direct investment, *Asia Pacific Bulletin* (219)(2 July).

Wood, G., Mazouz, K., Yin, S. and Cheah, J. (2014), Foreign direct investment from emerging markets to Africa: The HRM context, *Human Resource Management* 53(1): 179–201. doi.org/10.1002/hrm.21550.

Zhang, M. and Wang, B. (2018), *Report of Country-risk Rating of Overseas Investment from China (CROIC-IWEP) (2018)*, Beijing: China Social Sciences Press.

14. The impact of Chinese state capital during the iron ore boom

Luke Hurst[1]

China's recent push into global markets has been supported by a large banking system, which is dominated by state-owned and state-shareholding banks, massive foreign exchange reserves[2] and a managed exchange rate (Laurenceson 2008: 92; Song 2015: 200). But increasing the ability of Chinese investors to access state capital, to which foreign competitors do not have direct access, can affect the ability of non-Chinese competitors to compete for market access on commercial terms.

To gain a better understanding of the impact of Chinese state capital and investment abroad on global markets, this chapter analyses the extent and impact of Chinese procurement activities in the global iron ore market during the iron ore boom from 2002 to 2012.

The Chinese Government perceived the initial price boom following China's demand shock as a signal that the 'big three' Asian market exporters—Rio Tinto, BHP Billiton and Vale—held, and were exploiting, market power. To break up the perceived dominance of the big three, the barriers to market entry for fringe iron ore producers needed to be reduced.

To reduce these perceived barriers, the Chinese Government looked to support the development of fringe production and increase iron ore imports from Chinese-invested resources. In 2011, Li Xinchuang, Deputy Secretary-General of China Iron and Steel Association, said: 'China currently owns less than 10 per cent of imported iron ore. We should seek 50 per cent of ore from Chinese-invested overseas resources in the next five to 10 years' (Zhang 2011).

To assess the impact of China's international procurement strategies on the competitiveness of the iron ore market during the iron ore boom (2002–12), this chapter applies investment theory to a unique dataset of Chinese iron ore investment abroad. This chapter is structured as follows: first, it draws out Chinese iron ore procurement trends based on a unique dataset of 30 Chinese iron ore investments and 20 long-term contract (LTC) transactions; second, it outlines the extent of Chinese government support for overseas iron ore investment during this period;

---

1   I am indebted to David Murphy, Shiro Armstrong, Peter Drysdale and Ligang Song for comments on drafts of this chapter.

2   In 2006, China surpassed Japan as the largest holder of foreign exchange reserves globally—of about US$1.3 trillion at the end of June 2007 (Zheng and Yi 2007: 18).

next, the data on Chinese international iron ore procurement are examined; after that, the chapter assesses the impact of Chinese state-backed procurement on iron ore market outcomes, specifically whether Chinese state support provides advantages for Chinese iron ore investors over the short and long runs, and how state support affected international competitors' access to iron ore investments and supply.

Overview of Chinese iron ore procurement

Before the collapse of the benchmarking system in 2009 (Humphries 2018), iron ore market access was generally secured through LTCs or vertical integration. The choice between LTCs and vertical integration was largely based on the ownership, location and internalisation advantages of investing, such as the buyer's preference for *ex ante* contracting costs and *ex post* monitoring and negotiation costs associated with LTCs (Caves 2007: 16).

Firms' preferences for LTCs or vertical integration and the locations in which these different types of transactions take place provide insight into the motivation of buyers and the barriers they perceive in securing supplies. To analyse Chinese iron ore procurement following the recent demand shock, data were collected on a sample of 30 Chinese overseas iron ore investments and 20 LTC-only deals between 2002 and 2012; this is not a complete list but provides a representative sample of the publicly available information on Chinese iron ore procurement. The sample includes iron ore LTCs and investments (but not failed transactions, such as the 2009 Rio Tinto–Chinalco tie-up) from publicly available sources and the Intierra database.[3]

Table 14.1 provides an overview of the 30 Chinese overseas iron ore investments undertaken between 2002 and 2012. The projects were worth a total of US$36.5 billion and were concentrated in the period after the Global Financial Crisis (GFC); US$26.4 billion of the investments took place between 2008 and 2010 (72.2 per cent of the total value over the period 2002–12).

The economies of scale required and the capital-intensive nature of iron ore projects mean there is often a long lag between investment and production. Figure 14.1 shows how the lag between investment and production may impact Chinese projects: less than 50 million tonnes per annum (Mt/a) was planned to reach production by 2012. By 2018, the reported planned output of the Chinese iron ore investment projects sampled was 315.2 Mt/a (planned output data were available for 16 of the 30 projects). For context, the Australian Bureau of Resources and Energy Economics (BREE 2019) reported that, in 2018, global iron ore exports were approximately 1.547 billion tonnes.

---

3   www.intierra.com/ (accessed 1 March 2013).

Table 14.1 Chinese overseas iron ore investment, 2002–12

Year	No. of investments	Total value (US$m)	Average value (US$m)
2002	1	34.8	34.8
2003	0	0	0
2004	0	0	0
2005	0	0	0
2006	1	7,455.7	7,455.7
2007	1	2,154.9	2,154.9
2008	6*	17,522.6	2,920.4
2009	10	5,824.1	582.4
2010	5	3,004.5	600.9
2011	2	228.4	114.2
2012	4	275.7	68.9
Total	30	36,500.7	1,216.7

* Includes the successful US$14 billion Chinalco acquisition of 9 per cent of equity in Rio Tinto.

Sources: Intierra database; Wilson (2011: 269–70); Tex Report (2013).

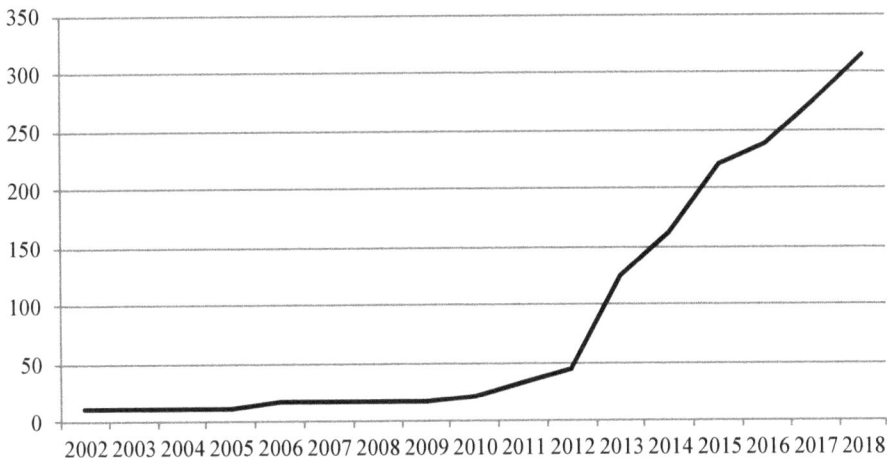

Figure 14.1 Potential supply increase from Chinese overseas iron ore investments, 2002–18 (Mt/a)

Sources: Intierra database; Wilson (2011: 269–70); Tex Report (2013).

Table 14.2 provides an overview of the 20 LTCs entered into by Chinese iron ore buyers in 2012. Chinese iron ore LTCs range from 0.5 to 20 Mt/a over three to 15 years. The available data on 20 LTCs entered into by Chinese importers (as at 2012) accounted for at least 64.9 to 95.1 Mt/a in 2012.[4]

---

4   The 20 LTCs recorded in the Tex Report (2013: 202) represent just 8.7 to 12.8 per cent of China's total iron ore imports in 2012 (743.4 Mt).

Table 14.2 Chinese iron ore LTCs, 2012

Chinese firm	Supplier	Country	Period	Volume (Mt/a)
Rizhao Steel	Mt Gibson	Australia	Lesser of life of mine or 15 years	1.5
Rizhao Steel	OneSteel	Australia	July 2008 – June 2018	> 6
Haixin Steel	OneSteel	Australia	July 2008 – June 2018	> 6
Tanshan Guafeng	OneSteel	Australia	October 2007 – 2016	> 6
Jinxi Steel	OneSteel	Australia	January 2008 – December 2017	> 5
Baosteel	FMG	Australia	10 years	5–20
Hebei Iron & Steel (Tanggang)	FMG	Australia	10 years	5–20
Xinxing Ductile Pipes	Vale	Brazil	5 years	0.5
Shanxi Zhongyang	Vale	Brazil	Long term (from December 2008)	N/A
Zongtian Iron & Steel	Vale	Brazil	Long term (from December 2008)	N/A
Hebei Iron & Steel	Aurox Resources	Australia	15 years	3
Rockcheck Steel	Aurox Resources	Australia	15 years	7
Baotou Steel	Centrex Metals	Australia	5 years	1
Shenyang Orient Steel	Centrex Metals	Australia	5 years	1
Hunan Valin Iron & Steel	GWR Group	Australia	15 years (from August 2008)	5
China Minmetals Corp.	SNIM	Mauritania	2008–12	1.5
Worldlin	CLM	Canada	7 years from 2007	7
Nanjing Iron & Steel	Grace Wise	Malaysia	June 2011 – May 2021	2
Tonghua Iron & Steel	IMX Resources	Australia	3 years	1.2–1.3
Sichuan Taifeng Group	IMX Resources	Australia	3 years	1.2–1.3

FMG = Fortescue Metals Group

SNIM = Société Nationale Industrielle et Minière (National Industrial and Mining Company)

N/A = not available

Source: Tex Report (2013: 102).

Table 14.3 shows that over the period 2002–12, Chinese overseas iron ore investments were concentrated in Australia, with 19 investments made, worth US$31.3 billion (the average size of each project was about US$1.65 billion); five smaller investments were made in Canada, worth a total of US$651.8 million (US$127.7 million each, on average); while the remaining six investments were spread across five countries, with an average value of US$903.1 million.

Table 14.3 Chinese overseas iron ore investment by country, 2002–12

Host country	No. of investments	Total value (US$m)	Average value (US$m)
Australia	19	31,333.3	1,649.1
Canada	5	651.8	127.7
Peru	2	1,330.4	665.2
Brazil	1	1,121.8	1,121.8
Liberia	1	426.2	426.2
Guinea	1	1,241.3	1,241.3
Russia	1	396.0	396.0
Total	30	36,500.8	1,216.9

Sources: Intierra database; Wilson (2011: 269–70); Tex Report (2013).

In 2009, the Chinese iron ore investors' preference for Australian projects appears to have changed. Just one Chinese overseas investment in iron ore was made outside Australia between 2002 and 2008, and none of the seven LTC-only deals was with any country other than Australia before 2007. From 2009 to 2012, 10 of 21 Chinese overseas investments in iron ore took place in countries other than Australia, and five of the 13 LTC-only deals were with countries other than Australia.

Chinese iron ore investors were initially drawn to Australian projects due to the relatively stable institutional environment, established infrastructure, technical mining knowledge and close geographic proximity. The freight-sharing mechanism, which provided Chinese importers with about 80 per cent[5] of the transport cost differential until 2010, made Australian production expansion particularly attractive for Chinese iron ore investors as the price of freight soared in the short run as the boom in international demand for iron ore developed (Hurst 2015).

Over the decade following the surge in China's international iron ore demand, Australia's operating environment became less attractive to iron ore investors. The cost of doing business in Australia rose due to the appreciation of the Australian

---

5   The 2008 freight-sharing mechanism.

dollar—from an average of US$0.54 in 2002 to US$0.85 in 2008 before peaking at US$1.10 in 2012—and there were growing labour shortages[6] in the mining sector. In 2011, Liu Han, former chairman of Hanlong Group,[7] said:

> Australia and Brazil both have great resources, but they don't provide many opportunities for Chinese investors due to rising cost pressures and policy barriers. Furthermore, most of their sources and the attached infrastructure are controlled by the largest mine companies. (Zhang 2011)

Large-scale investment failures in Australia seared Chinese investors and increased the relative attractiveness of pursuing projects in other locations (Laurenceson 2012). Two investments were particularly destructive to the perception of Australia as a stable and friendly investment location for Chinese iron ore investment: the CITIC Pacific Mining Sino Iron Ore project and the failed Rio Tinto–Chinalco tie-up.

The CITIC Pacific Mining Sino Iron Ore magnetite project in Western Australia, announced in 2006, experienced cost blowouts and delays. The budget for the project more than tripled by 2012—from an estimated US$2.5 billion to US$7.8 billion—because of poor due diligence, the rising Australian dollar and rising labour costs (Garvey 2012). In response to the CITIC Pacific Mining failures, China's State-owned Assets Supervision and Administration Commission (SASAC) suspended all investments in magnetite projects in Western Australia as of 2011 (Hurst et al. 2012: 21). By late 2018, CITIC had poured more than US$12 billion into the project amid multiple writedowns and continuing legal disputes with Australian leaseholder Mineralogy (Thompson 2018).

The failed 2009 Rio Tinto–Chinalco tie-up, worth US$19.5 billion (9.5 per cent equity), would have been the largest Chinese commercial investment abroad ever at that time. In its initial form, the deal would have reserved 30 per cent of Rio Tinto's iron ore production for a jointly run marketing company selling exclusively to China (Uren 2012: 106). The failed deal followed the successful 2008 investment by Chinalco, worth US$14 billion, for 9 per cent of Rio Tinto's equity.

The 2009 Rio Tinto–Chinalco deal fell apart due to failures by all those involved. The ad hoc foreign investment policy reforms undertaken by the Australian Government during the proposal screening process were perceived by many as signalling likely bias in Australia's investment review process against Chinese state-owned investors. For example, the then Foreign Investment Review Board (FIRB) general manager, Patrick Colmer, was quoted in a leaked US Embassy cable about the new foreign investment guidelines, which had been introduced during the 2009 Rio Tinto–Chinalco review process:

---

6 Chinese investors are unable to import labour into Australia.
7 Hanlong Group is a conglomerate with holdings in mineral exploration and other industries. Its subsidiary Hanlong Mining failed in a takeover bid for Sundance Resources, which owns mining rights to the Mbalam and Nabeba projects in Cameroon and Congo (Ker 2013).

The new guidelines reduce uncertainty for potential investors, but pose new disincentives for larger-scale Chinese investments.

… The new guidelines are mainly due to growing concerns about Chinese investments in the strategic resources sector. (Wikileaks 2009)

The failed Rio Tinto–Chinalco tie-up was eventually rejected when Rio Tinto's board withdrew support for the deal before the Australian Treasurer ruled on whether the investment was in the 'national interest'. But even without the government making the final call on the fate of the tie-up, the saga caused significant uncertainty and frustration for potential Chinese investors in the Australian investment process and heightened public anxiety about Chinese state-owned investors.

Chinese foreign investors, especially state-owned investors (discussed below), have often struggled to engage in Australia's investment environment and build local legitimacy.

The failed Rio Tinto–Chinalco deal also brought to bear the inexperience of many Chinese investors in foreign markets and their ignorance of the importance of establishing legitimacy with the host public. According to Pokarier (2004: 218), identity is a key part of nationalism and therefore fear of investment from culturally separate countries is to be expected; this is especially true for state-owned foreign investors, which may be seen as pursuing government strategies over profits. A report by the Chinese State Council's Development Research Centre revealed that Chinalco had not been able to match BHP Billiton in terms of its lobbying of the public and policymakers:

> BHP Billiton took advantage of its skilful mass media propaganda and lobbying capacity to arouse the public emotions so as to influence the judgment of the government policy makers. BHP Billiton tightly seized the point that Chinalco had the state-owned background. (Uren 2012: 109)

State support for Chinese iron ore investment abroad

State support for Chinese overseas iron ore investors was provided through the state-owned banking system, which provided preferential access to financing to increase imports from Chinese-owned iron ore projects. Financing was available from two state-owned policy banks—the China Export–Import Bank (China Exim Bank) and China Development Bank (CDB)—which provide 'policy finance', often on concessional terms; and four state-owned banks (SOBs), which are mandated to finance state-owned enterprise (SOE) activities and to support state industrial plans (Laurenceson and Chai 2010: 22; der Heiden and Taube 2011: 60–72; Wilson 2011: 270).

Information is scarce on the terms of financing for Chinese iron ore projects. Data collected by Wilson (2011: 269–70) on the source of financing for Chinese iron ore projects between 2002 and 2010 are used here as a proxy for the extent of Chinese state engagement in iron ore investment.

Table 14.4 presents the data for 32 international iron ore investments undertaken by Chinese investors. It shows that the average value of privately funded projects was lowest at US$27.2 million (across two projects), while SOB-funded projects were worth, on average, US$943.7 million (across 21 projects); sovereign wealth fund (SWF) financing averaged US$475.9 million (across two projects); policy bank–funded projects averaged $367.8 million (across six projects); and there was one provincial bank–financed project worth US$1.3 billion. The average equity taken by state-financed investors also appears to have been higher than that taken by privately financed investors, who took 16.5 per cent equity, on average. SOB-financed projects took, on average, 32.2 per cent equity, SWF projects averaged 57.5 per cent, policy bank–funded projects averaged 43.1 per cent equity and the provincial bank–financed project took 100 per cent equity.

Table 14.4 Source of iron ore investment funding, 2002–10

Source of finance	No. of investments	Value (US$m)	Average value (US$m)	Average equity (%)
Private bank	2	54.3	27.2	16.5
SOB	21	19,816.9	943.7	32.2
SWF	2	1,427.6	475.9	57.5
Policy bank	6	2,206.7	367.8	43.1
Provincial bank	1	1,300.1	1,300.1	100.0
Total	32	24,805.6	3,114.6	49.9

Note: Policy banks are the CDB and China Exim Bank.
Sources: Wilson (2011: 269–70); author's calculations.

The data in Table 14.5 show that the sources of financing provided to private Chinese overseas iron ore investors included a private bank (one project, worth US$46.4 million) and SOBs (three projects, worth an average of just US$14.6 million). Financing for centrally owned SOEs' international iron ore investments came from SOBs (nine projects, worth an average of US$1.8 billion) and policy banks (two projects, worth an average of US$603 million). Subcentral (provincial and prefectural) SOEs received financing from all sources; one project received US$7.9 million from a private bank, nine projects received financing from SOBs worth an average of US$365.7 million, two projects were funded by SWFs worth an average of US$713.8 million and one project received provincial bank funding of US$1.3 billion.

Table 14.5 Source of iron ore investment funding by firm ownership type, 2002–10

Source of finance	Central SOE			Sub-central SOE			Private enterprise		
	#	Total value (US$m)	Average value (US$m)	#	Total value (US$m)	Average value (US$m)	#	Total value (US$m)	Average value (US$m)
Private	0	0	0	1	7.9	7.9	1	46.4	46.4
SOB	9	16,481.3	1,831.2	9	3,291.6	365.7	3	43.9	14.6
SWF	0	0	0	2	1,427.6	713.8	0	0	0
Policy bank	2	1,206.1	603	4	1,000.5	250.1	0	0	0
Provincial bank	0	0	0	1	1,300.1	1,300.1	0	0	0

Sources: Wilson (2011: 269–70); author's calculations.

As suggested above, the GFC appears to have encouraged a large increase in Chinese overseas investment in iron ore. According to CDB head Chen Yuan, investing in energy and minerals in the aftermath of the GFC provided a hedge against the declining US dollar and rising commodity prices. In 2009, Chen stated:

> Everybody is saying that we should go to the international markets to buy up low-price assets. But I don't think we should go to Wall Street. We should think more about making acquisitions or partnerships in areas with natural resources. (Downs 2011: 73)

A report published by Ernst & Young estimated that the market value of mining and metal companies dropped about 40 to 60 per cent due to the global economic downturn (cited in Yang 2009). In 2009, China's Ministry of Industry and Information Technology released the 'Adjustment and Revitalization Program for the Iron and Steel Industry' (Downs 2011). The program instructed 'companies [to] seize opportunities and actively pursue the Going Global Strategy'—specifically, to make full use of three special funds: the Fund for Mining Rights to Overseas Mineral Resources, the Fund for Economic and Technical Co-operation Overseas and the Fund for Reducing Risk in Prospecting of Overseas Mineral Deposits. The Ministry of Commerce (MOFCOM) also signed agreements on the protection of investments, with many countries and the state-owned China Export and Credit Insurance Company to provide investment insurance services (der Heiden and Taube 2011).

China's iron ore investment push following the GFC is reflected in the data, with 27 of the 30 state-financed projects tracked in Table 14.5 occurring between 2008 and 2010. The international iron ore investments occurring between 2008 and 2010 accounted for 97.4 per cent of the value of state financing for iron ore projects from 2002 to 2010.

The increased push by Chinese investors into iron ore projects largely reflects the fact that Western banks were highly risk-averse following the GFC. Chinese state-owned lenders saw opportunities in investing in iron ore as projects struggled to attract financing (Hurst 2013: 528–9).

Impact of Chinese state procurement support on market outcomes

In 2011, Australian Senator Barnaby Joyce announced that Chinese state-owned foreign investors 'have a long-term view, they don't necessarily have to rely on the market principle' (Grattan 2011). The remarks by Senator Joyce relate to the distortions Chinese state support might have on 'competitive neutrality'. Competitive neutrality requires that government business activities should not enjoy net competitive advantages over their private sector competitors simply by virtue of public sector ownership.

The impact of Chinese state support on competitive neutrality has been cited widely in the academic literature.[8] Proponents of the argument—that preferential access to state financing distorts the competitive landscape—conclude that Chinese state-backed procurement negatively impacts the ability of private sector actors to compete on commercial terms, and that access to state financing can lead to moral hazard[9] as Chinese investors are able to overbid for procurement contracts without fear of reprisal if investments fail.

The Chinese Government offers several different kinds of loan finance, which have supported the majority of iron ore projects (Tables 14.3 and 14.4). Although information on the terms of individual iron ore loans is scarce, Bräutigam (2011) found that most loans made by China Exim Bank and the CDB (the two sources of official bank financing that are used as tools to support government policy) were made on commercial terms—London Interbank Offered Rate[10] (LIBOR) plus a margin—rather than on a concessional basis.[11]

China Exim Bank's main mandate in the iron ore industry is to facilitate exports and assist imports for Chinese companies with comparative advantages in their offshore project contracting and outbound investment, and to promote international economic cooperation and trade. To support its mission, China Exim Bank loans are given at LIBOR plus a margin,[12] usually with a maturity of 12 to 15 years and a grace period of two to five years. A small proportion of the export buyers' credits are offered at preferential rates, usually with a fixed interest rate of 2 or 3 per cent (Bräutigam 2009: 335).

---

8   See, for example, Buckley et al. (2007); Sauvant and Chen (2014).
9   This refers to a situation where the agent is encouraged to increase their appetite for risk knowing that the cost of failure will be incurred by another party.
10 LIBOR is the interest rate applied to comparatively short-term borrowing of funds in the London interbank market (loans between banks). LIBOR is a preferential rate for low-risk borrowers and is often used as a baseline for less-preferred borrowers who pay a rate of LIBOR plus a margin.
11 When a donor government provides a loan at a rate equivalent to the private capital market plus a margin, this is not concessional as there is no subsidy at all (Bräutigam 2011: 755).
12 The lowest rate of credit for which information is publicly available was issued at LIBOR plus 1 per cent (100 basis points).

The CDB was originally set up to provide finance for China's own development, but in recent years it has been providing very large lines of credit overseas.[13] The bank issues commercial loans based on LIBOR plus a margin—usually at least 200 basis points (Bräutigam 2011: 206). For example, the 12-year Karara Iron Ore project loan facility was provided on competitive commercial terms principally by the CDB and the Bank of China, based on the US six-month LIBOR with a competitive margin (the actual margin was not specified publicly) (Gindalbie Metals Ltd 2010).

While the terms of China Exim Bank and CDB loans are generally based on international benchmarks plus a margin, the margin appears to be lower than that available to international competitors who do not have direct access to Chinese state financing. For example, Chinalco's profits dropped by 99 per cent in 2008 owing to the collapse in demand for aluminium, and its original 2008 investment of US$14 billion for a 9 per cent stake in Rio Tinto lost 70 per cent of its market value—about US$10 billion by 2009 (Yao and Sutherland 2009: 829). Despite Chinalco's losses, four of the biggest Chinese state-owned banks—the China Development Bank, China Exim Bank, the Agricultural Bank of China and the Bank of China—offered to lend US$21 billion, which was more than the US$19.5 billion required for the additional 9 per cent equity to fund Chinalco's Rio Tinto tie-up (discussed above). Interest on the loan was just 94.5 basis points above the six-month LIBOR, and a repayment period was not set. In contrast, following Chinalco's bid, BHP Billiton offered Rio Tinto a 15-year bond, which charged interest at 345 basis points above the six-month LIBOR (White 2009; Yao and Sutherland 2009: 832).

The above analysis indicates that Chinese overseas iron ore investors did have access to cheap state financing that was not directly available to competitors. Song (2015: 200–1) notes that the Chinese banking system is dominated by state-owned and state-shareholding banks, which traditionally favour SOEs. The favouritism towards SOEs by Chinese state banks is due to the perception that SOEs pose a lower risk or are 'at least backed by the government in the event of loan forfeiture'.

In a paper analysing the impact of state financing on Chinese investment (across all sectors), Buckley et al. (2007: 514–15) concluded:

> More challenging is the unprecedented finding that Chinese ODI is attracted, rather than deterred, by political risk (as measured conventionally and with market returns controlled for by market size). This suggests that Chinese firms do not perceive or behave towards risk in the same way as do industrialised country firms. In accordance with our theory, we attribute this to the low cost of capital that Chinese firms

---

13 To complement the increased access to state capital, the CDB set up branch offices in 2006. The branch offices operate out of Chinese embassies and are mandated to gather information about the host countries and establish relationships with local officials and businesses to support Chinese energy and mining companies to find investment opportunities. By the end of 2009, the CDB had established work teams in 141 countries, including 45 in Africa (Downs 2011: 28).

(for the most part SOEs) enjoy as a consequence of home country capital market imperfections. Indeed, state ownership can be considered as a firm-specific advantage for many Chinese MNEs [multinational enterprises] in this context.

… State-sponsored soft budget constraints make acquisition by Chinese enterprises a 'normal' mode of entering and penetrating a host economy … Over-bidding by Chinese MNEs is attributed to the absence of private shareholders and sanguine views of the associated technical, commercial and political risks, to limited fear of failure, close government support and low cost of capital.

There are two important questions arising from Buckley et al.'s (2007) conclusion that need to be addressed:

1. Has Chinese state support through low-cost capital provided ownership advantages for Chinese iron ore investors over their foreign competitors?

2. Has the access to state support for Chinese investors reduced opportunities for non-Chinese iron ore investors and procurers to compete on commercial terms?

Implications for non-Chinese iron ore investors

In line with the Chinese state's objective of diversifying supply away from the big three, only three[14] of the 30 Chinese iron ore foreign investments analysed involved any of the big three (all Rio Tinto). The three projects were Baosteel's 2002 joint venture with Rio Tinto in the BaoHI Ranges, worth US$34.8 million, and Chinalco's initial investment of US$14 billion for a 9 per cent share of Rio Tinto shares in 2008 and a 47 per cent (US$1.5 billion) stake in Rio Tinto's Simandou development project in Guinea.

The desire to diversify supply away from the big three meant that Chinese investors were required to look to less well-established projects to acquire or develop, often entailing higher risk. These higher-risk projects frequently faced long financing lags with commercial banks (especially following the GFC), which created a new business opportunity for the CDB. According to the CDB's (2004) annual report:

A number of Chinese enterprises have been exploring opportunities overseas and some of the potential projects are relatively large. The high risk inherent in such projects and their relatively large borrowing requirements have made many commercial banks uncomfortable about participating in their funding. Many of the enterprises in search of financing for outbound investment have turned to us. In reality, these projects are typical of the development financing that we typically undertake and we are well positioned to be of service. We are known to have both the adequate resources to fund these projects and a demonstrated track record of achievement in effectively managing the credit risk.

---

14 Chinalco's failed tie-up for a further 9.5 per cent of Rio Tinto shares worth US$19.5 billion was not included in the dataset.

Ownership decisions for international investors are largely based on a firm possessing advantages over competitors in the host country, such as managerial skills or proprietary knowledge. But the favouritism of China's banking system towards SOEs and the involvement of the CDB and China Exim Bank have seen most of the financing for Chinese iron ore investments abroad provided to the largely state-owned iron and steel production (not mining) sector.

Of the 30 Chinese iron ore investments reviewed for this study, 21 were made by Chinese firms with an operating competency outside mining; only one is listed as a specialised iron ore miner. The lack of mining expertise by Chinese international iron ore investors suggests they have, on average, few long-run operational ownership advantages and instead rely on their access to cheap state capital to gain access to concessions. Access to cheap capital and support for Chinese investors abroad may have provided short-run ownership advantages over foreign competitors that do not have access to the Chinese state capital, as they are able to overcome financing lags and can potentially 'overbid' for projects due to the relatively cheap cost of capital (Buckley et al. 2007).

The short-run ownership advantages provided by Chinese iron ore investors' access to state capital create the potential for moral hazard. Downs (2011: 61), however, suggests that, on a straight commercial basis, it may be rational for the CDB to offer lower interest rates than Western banks because it is backed by the Chinese Government; borrowers who fail to fulfil their loan agreements with the CDB risk angering not only the bank, but also the Chinese Government, which could lower the risk of moral hazard.

The acknowledgement of the lack of long-run ownership advantages of Chinese iron ore investors is shown in the trend towards taking minority equity positions ('quasi-integration') in partnership with specialised non-Chinese fringe iron ore firms (discussed above). The Chinese iron ore procurement data presented above, although incomplete, indicate that Chinese procurers are entering both LTC-only deals and vertical integration through minority ownership. The sampled Chinese iron ore investments exhibited a preference for joint ventures and minority acquisitions (22 of 30 investments) taking, on average, 41.1 per cent equity. Eight investments were wholly owned acquisitions or development projects.

Chinese iron ore investors—mainly steel mills—generally lacked the long-run ownership advantages required to develop complex iron ore mine projects. The lack of long-run ownership advantages caused Chinese iron ore investors to engage in quasi-integration, whereby they would take minority ownership shares and partner with specialised mining firms, which would develop and operate the projects. This quasi-integration provided increased supply security compared with LTC-only procurement and the needed capital for large-scale projects to overcome the lag associated with finalising financing. The quasi-integration strategy also ensured project partners had specialised skills to develop complex mine projects while having more 'skin in the game' compared with contractors.

The preference to partner with non-Chinese fringe iron ore firms has meant that the provision of Chinese state capital has, in fact, increased access to partnership opportunities for non-Chinese iron ore investors, rather than reducing opportunities. The increased access to partnership opportunities is especially important in the context of the post-GFC business environment, which further reduced opportunities for non-Chinese fringe iron ore projects to secure financing.

Impact of Chinese state procurement on competitors' market access

Analysts have also raised the issue of whether Chinese iron ore investors could use their advantageous access to state capital to limit market access for foreign competitors. These concerns were highlighted by Brahma Chellaney in his 2012 testimony to the US–China Economic and Security Review Commission hearing on 'China's Global Quest for Resources and Implications for the United States'. During his testimony, Chellaney (2012) stated:

> China has pursued an aggressive strategy to secure (and even lock up) supplies of strategic resources like water, energy and mineral ores. Gaining access to or control of resources has been a key driver of its foreign and domestic policies. China, with the world's most resource-hungry economy, is pursuing the world's most-assertive policies to gain control of important resources.

> Much of the international attention on China's resource strategy has focused on its scramble to secure supplies of hydrocarbons and mineral ores. Such attention is justified by the fact that China is seeking to conserve its own mineral resources and rely on imports. For example, China, a major steel consumer, has substantial reserves of iron ore, yet it has banned exports of this commodity. It actually encourages its own steel producers to import iron ore. China, in fact, has emerged as the largest importer of iron ore, accounting for a third of all global imports. India, in contrast, remains a major exporter of iron ore to China, although the latter has iron-ore deposits more than two-and-half times that of India.

To assess Chellaney's claims about the ability of Chinese investors to reduce market access for competitors, this study applies Moran's (2010) scorecard approach, which attempts to operationalise a definition of 'tying up' resources. The scorecard identifies four fundamental natural resource procurement patterns a large buyer can take:

1. Special relationship with major producer.
2. Special relationship with competitive fringe.
3. Loan capital to major producer to be repaid in output.
4. Loan capital to competitive fringe to be repaid in output.

The first of Moran's (2010) procurement categories involves the investor taking an equity stake in a very large established producer to secure an equity share of production on terms comparable with other co-owners. This form of supply internalisation provides some degree of control to the investor over the long-run strategic decision-making of the project, and is zero-sum (tying up) as the acquired project is already in production; the investment does not expand production. The second procurement pattern describes when a buyer takes an equity position in a project that is yet to reach production on terms comparable with other co-owners; this strategy expands the overall supply base while providing the investor some degree of control over the long-run strategic direction of the project.

The third category of Moran's (2010) scorecard occurs when buyers and/or their government make a loan to an already established producer in return for a purchase agreement to service the loan, such as an LTC. The LTC in category three does not provide long-term control over the operations of the producer but does increase the buyer's legal claim to preexisting resource supply (zero-sum). This is seen as a strategy to tie up resources. The final procurement strategy in Moran's scorecard occurs when a buyer and/or their government makes a loan to finance an up-and-coming producer in return for a purchase agreement to service the loan; this can include infrastructure for resources and resource-contingent loans. This category supports the expansion of the supply base without conferring long-term strategic control to the investor (categories are summarised in Table 14.6) (Moran 2010).

Table 14.6 Summary of Moran's procurement scorecard

	Tying up (zero-sum)	Expansion (positive-sum)
Equity	Category 1: Special relationship with major producer Buyers and/or their home governments take an equity stake in a 'major' producer to procure an equity share of production on terms comparable with other co-owners.	Category 2: Special relationship with competitive fringe Buyers and/or their home governments take an equity stake in an 'independent' producer to procure an equity share of production on terms comparable with other co-owners.
Non-equity (LTC)	Category 3: Loan capital to major producer to be repaid in output Buyers and/or their home governments make a loan to a 'price maker' producer in return for a purchase agreement to service the loan.	Category 4: Loan capital to competitive fringe to be repaid in output Buyers and/or their home governments make a loan to a 'price taker' producer in return for a purchase agreement to service the loan.

Source: Kotschwar et al. (2012: 27).

The procurement scorecard provides a useful method to proxy whether there are zero-sum (tying up) implications from a country's procurement activities—that is, whether they consolidate their legal claim to resources, which is captured by the first and third categories. If the country's resource procurement activities result in an expansion and/or diversification of supply beyond the growth of their demand, all consumers will have access to a more competitive export market; this positive-sum result is captured by the second and fourth categories in the scorecard.

Of the sample of 50 iron ore procurement arrangements entered into by Chinese investors between 2002 and 2012 (see Figure 14.2), three were identified as a special relationship with a major producer (Category 1); 27 were special relationships with the competitive fringe (Category 2); seven saw capital loaned to major producers for output (Category 3); and 13 procurement arrangements saw capital loaned to the competitive fringe to be repaid in output (Category 4). The results of the scorecard suggest the majority of Chinese procurement arrangements were in development projects and served to expand the competitive supply base over the long run rather than reduce market access for competitors.[15]

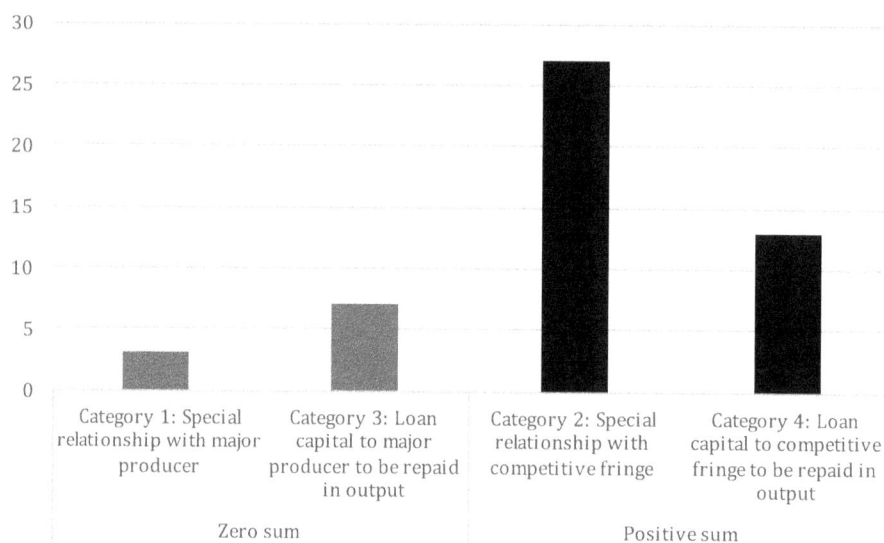

Figure 14.2 Chinese procurement arrangements by category, 2002–12 (by number)
Sources: Intierra database; Wilson (2011: 269–70); Tex Report (2013: 102).

The scorecard result is consistent with Moran's (2010) analysis of 16 Chinese oil and mining procurement arrangements, which found that, in 13 of 16 cases, Chinese investors took an equity stake and/or wrote long-term procurement contracts with producers on the competitive fringe. In that study, the authors concluded:

> Chinese investors will be more willing to take on new frontier—or even fringe— projects that the major established oil and mining companies might pass by ... Chinese efforts, like Japanese deployments of capital and purchase agreements in the late 1970s through the 1980s, predominantly help expand, diversify, and make the global energy-supply system more competitive. (Moran 2010: 2)

---

15 There were eight LTC-only transactions, but only eight of the 29 projects with publicly available information recorded having an LTC with the Chinese investor recipient.

The findings of the scorecard analysis are also supported by the data collected on 32 iron ore investments between 2002 and 2010 by Wilson (2011). The investment data show that, in nine of 32 iron ore investments, no LTC was entered into by the Chinese investors. In the remaining 23 cases where LTCs were entered into, only 63.8 per cent of projected iron ore output was reserved for the Chinese investor. This provides support for the conclusion that Chinese procurement has expanded, not tied up, the competitive supply base.

The results of the scorecard analysis on Chinese iron ore procurement outcomes contradict Chellaney's claim that China's supply security strategy has locked up iron ore supply. Chellaney's testimony is also flawed in its understanding of China's iron ore endowments, as it overlooks the high average cost of China's iron ore production and the fact that domestic producers would be unable to compete on the global market with the added cost of seaborne freight. Chellaney is also incorrect in his comparison between China's and India's iron ore protectionism. In fact, in 2011, Indian authorities adopted policies to ensure steel production would be served by its own iron ore supply—the same charge of nonmarket orientation that Chellaney levelled at China. On 2 January 2012—22 days before Chellaney's testimony—the Indian Government announced a further increase of export tariffs to iron ore lump and fines of up to 30 per cent.

Conclusion

The Chinese Government viewed the iron ore price boom as a signal of a coordinated effort by the big three to inflate prices. In response, it moved to reduce reliance on the big three and to secure long-run market access for its steel industry by supporting international investment in alternative (fringe) supplies.

To reduce reliance on the big three and secure supplies for the Chinese steel industry, the Chinese Government supported investment in international iron ore projects to reduce the barriers for fringe operators to enter the market. Chinese Government support was delivered mainly through its state financing institutions in the form of project financing, insurance and information.

Prior to 2008, the majority of Chinese investments and LTC-only transactions were undertaken in Australia. Since 2008, the decreasing attractiveness of Australia as an investment destination due to the increasing cost of doing business and large-scale Chinese project failures have seen Chinese investors diversify in terms of destination. There are similarities between China's movement away from Australia and Japan's push into the Brazilian market, providing an example of the long-run contestability of the iron ore market despite Australia's constrained bilateral monopoly with Asia (Hurst 2017: 48).

Analysis of Chinese iron ore procurement arrangements shows that state-owned financing institutions were involved in the majority of investments and most investments were undertaken by central and provincial SOEs in concert with non-Chinese partners. The link between the Chinese state and the firms procuring iron ore has led many commentators to raise concerns that the increased access to finance provides Chinese investors with advantages over other competitors and creates barriers for investors competing on commercial terms.

Chinese iron ore investors were most often operating outside their core competency and lack of long-run ownership advantages. The lack of iron ore development and operating competence meant they generally paired with a non-Chinese specialised iron ore fringe producer. The preference for quasi-integration through joint ventures with non-Chinese fringe iron ore producers means that Chinese state support effectively lowered barriers to market entry for non-Chinese fringe iron ore miners.

The second issue related to the strong link between the Chinese Government and firms responsible for the procurement of iron ore is the potential of Chinese iron ore procurers to tie up supply and reduce market access for foreign steel producers. Moran's (2010) procurement scorecard was applied to data on a sample of 50 iron ore procurement arrangements to assess the claim that '[g]aining access to or control of resources has been a key driver of [China's] foreign and domestic policies' (Chellaney 2012). The application of the procurement scorecard to the Chinese iron ore procurement dataset suggests that instead of tying up resources, China's aggregate iron ore procurement arrangements have led to a broadening of the competitive global supply base and increased access to iron ore for other buyers in the Asian market, as did Japanese procurement arrangements in the 1970s and 1980s.

References

Alston, L.J. (2008), The case for case studies in new institutional economics, in É. Brousseau and J.-M. Glachant (eds), *New Institutional Economics: A guidebook*, Cambridge: Cambridge University Press.

Bräutigam, D. (2009), *The Dragon's Gift: The real story of China in Africa*, Oxford: Oxford University Press.

Bräutigam, D. (2011), Aid 'with Chinese characteristics': Chinese foreign aid and development finance meet the OECD–DAC aid regime, *Journal of International Development* 23: 752–64. doi.org/10.1002/jid.1798.

Buckley, P.J., Clegg, L.J., Cross, A.R., Liu, X., Voss, H. and Zheng, P. (2007), The determinants of Chinese outward foreign direct investment, *Journal of International Business Studies* 38: 499–518. doi.org/10.1057/palgrave.jibs.8400277.

Bureau of Resources and Energy Economics (BREE) (2019), *Resources and Energy Quarterly*, Canberra: BREE.

Cai, P. (2012), China takes a tougher line, *The Age*, [Melbourne], 13 April.

Caves, R.E. (2007), *Multinational Enterprise and Economic Analysis*, Cambridge: Cambridge University Press. doi.org/10.1017/CBO9780511619113.

Chellaney, B. (2012), Testimony before the US–China Economic and Security Review Commission hearing: China's Global Quest for Resources and Implications for the United States, 26 January, Washington, DC.

China Development Bank (2004), *Annual Report*, Beijing: China Development Bank Corporation.

der Heiden, P. and Taube, M. (2011), China's iron and steel industry at the global markets interface: Structural developments and industrial policy interventions, *The Copenhagen Journal of Asian Studies* 29(2): 110–42. doi.org/10.22439/cjas.v29i2.4029.

Downs, E. (2011), *Inside China, Inc: China Development Bank's cross-border energy deals*, John L. Thornton China Center Monograph Series No. 3, Washington, DC: The Brookings Institution.

Drysdale, P. (2009), Australia needs to get its act together on China, and fast, *East Asia Forum*, 7 June.

Drysdale, P. (2011), A new look at Chinese FDI in Australia, *China & World Economy* 19(4): 54–73. doi.org/10.1111/j.1749-124X.2011.01250.x.

Garvey, P. (2012), Citic Pacific's Sino Iron project faces new delay, *The Australian*, 17 August.

Gindalbie Metals Limited (2010), First drawdown under US$1.2 billion project loan facility for Karara iron ore project, Securities Exchange announcement and media release, 16 August, Perth.

Grattan, M. (2011), Barnaby Joyce warns of threat to resource security, *The Age*, [Melbourne], 29 August.

Humphries, D. (2018), The mining industry after the boom, *Mineral Economics*, 13 March. doi.org/10.1007/s13563-018-0155-x.

Hurst, L. (2013), West and Central African iron ore development and its impact on world prices, *The Australian Journal of Agricultural and Resource Economics* 57(4): 521–38. doi.org/10.1111/1467-8489.12007.

Hurst, L. (2015), *A lesson in market contestability: Calculating the cost of Chinese state intervention in iron ore price negotiations*, EABER Working Paper 94, Canberra: East Asian Bureau of Economic Research, The Australian National University.

Hurst, L. (2017), *China's Iron Ore Boom*, London: Routledge. doi.org/10.4324/978131 5559315.

Hurst, L., Cai, P.Y. and Findlay, C. (2012), *Chinese direct investment in Australia: Public reaction, policy response, investor adaptation*, EABER Working Paper 81, Canberra: East Asian Bureau of Economic Research, The Australian National University.

Ker, P. (2013), Sundance slumps after Hanlong bid fails, *Sydney Morning Herald*, 9 April.

Kotschwar, B.K., Moran, T.H. and Muir, J. (2012), *Chinese investment in Latin American resources: The good, the bad, and the ugly*, Peterson Institute Working Paper Series 12-3, Washington, DC: Peterson Institute for International Economics.

Laurenceson, J. (2008), Chinese investment in Australia, *Economic Papers* 27(1): 87–94. doi.org/10.1111/j.1759-3441.2008.tb01028.x.

Laurenceson, J. (2012), Chinese investment is Australia's great untapped resource, *East Asia Forum*, 12 May.

Laurenceson, J. and Chai, J.C.H. (2010), The economic performance of China's state-owned industrial enterprises, *Journal of Contemporary China* 9(23): 21–39. doi.org/10.1080/106705600112038.

Moran, T.H. (2010), China's strategy to secure natural resources: Risks, dangers, and opportunities, *Policy Analysis in International Economics* 92(July).

Pokarier, C. (2004), The controversy over Japanese investment in Australia, 1987–1991, *Japanese Studies* 24(2): 215–31. doi.org/10.1080/1037139042000302519.

Sauvant, K.P. and Chen, V.Z. (2014), China's regulatory framework for outward foreign direct investment, *China Economic Journal* 7(1): 141–63. doi.org/10.1080/17538963.2013.874072.

Song, L. (2015), State and non-state enterprises in China's economic transition, in G.C. Chow and D.H. Perkins (eds), *Routledge Handbook of the Chinese Economy*, New York: Routledge.

Tex Report (2013), *Iron Ore Manual 2011–2012*, Tokyo: The Tex Report.

Thompson, B. (2018), Billion-dollar writedown for China's flagship Sino Iron project, *Australian Financial Review*, 12 March.

Uren, D. (2012), *The Kingdom and the Quarry*, Melbourne: Black Inc.

White, G. (2009), Chinalco confident on Rio Tinto deal approval, *The Telegraph*, [UK], 31 March.

Wikileaks (2009), New foreign investment guidelines target China, [Online], Cable: 09CANBERRA900_a-WikiLeaks, available from: wikileaks.org/plusd/cables/09CANBERRA900_a.html.

Wilson, J.D. (2011), Public and private sources of governance in global production networks: The case of the Asia-Pacific steel industry, PhD Dissertation, The Australian National University, Canberra.

Yang, Z. (2009), Easier loans lean to more mergers and acquisitions, *China Daily*, 20 April.

Yao, S. and Sutherland, D. (2009), Chinalco and Rio Tinto: A long march for China's national champions, *China Quarterly* 199: 829–36. doi.org/10.1017/S030574100999049X.

Zhang, Q. (2011), Ore target to break foreign grip, *China Daily*, 25 July.

Zheng, Y. and Yi, J. (2007), China's rapid accumulation of foreign exchange reserves and its policy implications, *China & World Economy* 15(1): 14–25.

Index

www.ingramcontent.com/pod-product-compliance
Lightning Source LLC
Chambersburg PA
CBHW050038220326
41599CB00041B/7205